3a7ª

Women Who Made the News
Female Journalists in Canada, 1880–1945

From the end of the nineteenth century to the middle of the twentieth century, the press was the pre-eminent source of information in Canadian society. While the dominant voice of the Fourth Estate was undoubtedly male, a diverse and dispersed group of Canadian women sought and won access to this powerful domain. They were able to do this because they were talented, ambitious, persistent, and, paradoxically, because they were women.

The first newspaperwomen were employed to attract female subscribers and advertising revenue. Once hired, they found themselves confined to a narrow range of specialties that catered to conventionally defined women's interests – homemaking, fashion, and high society – and most were patronized by their male peers. But these women journalists did more than simply deliver female consumers to advertisers. Some of them eventually made names for themselves as commercial reporters or political and even war correspondents. By making news about women for women, they created a distinctly female culture within the newspaper, chronicling the increasing participation of women in public affairs.

Women Who Made the News is the story of the women who helped raise Canadian women's collective awareness of each other and of their achievements in the period leading up to the Second World War.

MARJORY LANG teaches history at Langara College, Vancouver, British Columbia.

Women Who Made the News

Female Journalists in Canada, 1880–1945

MARJORY LANG

McGill-Queen's University Press
Montreal & Kingston · London · Ithaca

Legal deposit third quarter 1999
Bibliothèque nationale du Québec

Printed in Canada on acid-free paper

This book has been published with the help of a
grant from the Humanities and Social Sciences
Federation of Canada, using funds provided by the
Social Sciences and Humanities Research Council
of Canada.

McGill-Queen's University Press acknowledges the
support of the Government of Canada through the
Book Publishing Industry Development Program
for its activities. We also acknowledge the support
of the Canada Council for the Arts for our
publishing program.

Canadian Cataloguing in Publication Data

Marjory Lang
Women who made the news : female journalists
in Canada, 1880–1945

Includes bibliographical references and index.
ISBN 0-7735-1838-X

1. Women journalists – Canada – History. I. Title

PN4912.L35 1999   070'.082'0971   C99-900418-2

This book was typeset by Acappella
in 10/12 Baskerville

To David and the memory of my father, Arthur Lang

Contents

Illustrations

Tables and Figure

Acknowledgments

This project was inspired by the Women and Work program of the Social Sciences and Humanities Research Council of Canada. The mandate to study all categories of women as workers encouraged me to focus a diffused interest in women writers onto the problem of women writing as a paid work opportunity. It was at this point I discovered that very little work had been done on women journalists in Canada or, indeed, on women journalists anywhere. The opportunity to devote three years to the project and to travel to the widely dispersed archives that housed relevant documention was a privilege made possible by this program.

Linda Hale shared this project at its very beginning. Together we planned the research, scrounged through archives, constructed profiles of careers, and came to know the women of the press. She trudged around the prairie archives, and her skills as a librarian and bibliographer elicited the generous help we received from other librarians and archivists. In addition, she read early drafts of some of the chapters and contributed advice and suggestions. Barbara Freeman provided a lively exchange of insights, constant encouragement, and collaboration in a variety of conference panels over the years. Her own book on Kit Coleman has been an inspiration. As a professor of journalism, she has borne witness time and again to the need for more research on women's roles in the Canadian media. Carole Gerson, working on a closely allied project, traded biographical information about individual writers and read parts of early versions of the manuscript. Wendie Nelson's reading of the first draft challenged me to rethink the material in several places. Carmela Patrias was an unfailingly supportive and inventive adviser, whose counsel by phone, e-mail, and letter was invaluable. Frances Pine read the final draft and offered timely advice. Lorraine McMullen was also encouraging and included an early version of the second chapter in *Re(dis)covering Our Foremothers: Nineteenth-Century Canadian Women Writers* (Ottawa: University of Ottawa Press 1990). Alan Johnstone saved me from many a slip. My husband David offered essential editorial advice and patiently untangled the technological snarls that cropped up with unnerving frequency.

Two children, Ben and Pippa, born in the course of this project, made me appreciate even more poignantly the "dual struggle" many women journalists mastered. My burden was very much lightened by their grandparents, June and Alan Johnstone and Patricia and Arthur Lang.

A project whose sources are scattered all over the country incurs many debts to archivists and librarians. The help given by David Fraser of the National Archives of Canada was invaluable in compensating for the huge distances this study embraced. He sent microfilm, xeroxes and, in the later stages, e-mail messages with gratifying speed. Susan Bellingham of the Special Collections, University of Waterloo, took a special interest in the project and not only answered queries but directed attention to new sources as her library acquired them. Barry Hyman of the Provincial Archives of Manitoba was also cooperative in sending copies of archival material. Anne Yandel and the staff of the Special Collections at the University of British Columbia housed the project for many years. The continual help of University of British Columbia Interlibrary Loans staff also helped shrink the distances.

Joan Harcourt of McGill-Queen's University Press showed unflagging confidence in this project and revived my spirits with regular cheerful messages. Carlotta Lemieux's meticulous editing alerted me to countless mistakes and oversights. Her stylistic advice has made this a more polished manuscript. Any errors that remain are mine alone.

I am grateful too for the assistance and support of the women journalists who were willing to talk about their lives and careers. Edith McCook wrote marvellously informative letters that filled me in on the details of managing journalism and motherhood. Her ability to remember exact salary figures and the details of every department in the women's section was a great asset. Mamie Moloney Boggs wrote about her days on the *Sun* and how she had combined marriage and motherhood. Florence Taylor contributed memories of her days on the Victoria *Times-Colonist* and of her boss Bessie Forbes. Lois Reynolds Kerr graciously endured many questions and lent typescripts of her plays. Other contacts along the way included Kay Rex and Marlene Hancock, who reminisced about her aunt, Eileen Purkiss of the *Columbian*.

Most of all, I am indebted to the women journalists of the Canadian Women's Press Club, who loved their careers and their club enough to devote hours of their spare time to organizing their storehouse of memories. In particular, Kay Mathers masterminded the creation of the club archives and conducted the painstaking task of sorting truth from lore in order to recreate its history in 1954, the year of the club's bicentennial. Edna Brown Baker, who spent her retirement assembling a scrapbook of early records of the Vancouver branch of the club, summed up her own motives: "When you love a Club enough to belong to it all those years [42], it is no task to do a little service for it; in fact it is a joy."

Women Who Made the News

CHAPTER ONE

Introduction

The most transient visitor to this planet ... who picked up this paper could not fail to be aware ... that England is under the rule of a patriarchy.

Virginia Woolf, *A Room of One's Own*, 1929

Addressing the National Council of Women in 1923, Charlotte Whitton urged her listeners to pay close attention to the status of women journalists, particularly those who edited women's pages, because their freedom and autonomy had "a very definite bearing" on the progress of women in Canada: "For it is through the great disseminating power of the Press, more than through any other channel, that questions relating to women, women's part in the national life, and all the general mass of information, and knowledge that make possible fresh advance in the field of women's and children's interest, are brought into the radius of action of the women of Canada."[1] This book sets out to do Whitton's bidding, to explore the situation and experiences of the women who worked as journalists in the heyday of the Canadian press during the late nineteenth century and first half of the twentieth. Charlotte Whitton, herself an active clubwoman and professional social worker, was keenly aware of the importance of the work presswomen did, making news for women and about women. Without communication, without knowledge of what other women were achieving in all walks of life and throughout the nation, Canadian women could not hope to make progress. But it was as a writer that Charlotte Whitton made her plea. As a recently qualified member of the Canadian Women's Press Club, she was acutely sensitive to the aspirations and frustrations of the small but rapidly expanding number of journalists who made the news that other women read.

GENDER AND JOURNALISM HISTORY

By the time Charlotte Whitton remarked upon them, women journalists had become fixtures in the Canadian newspaper scene and
journalism had become established as a possible if not conventional
career choice for women.[2] For three decades women had been employed by Canadian periodicals, primarily as magnets to attract female
subscribers. The census of 1921 acknowledged 248 women "editors and
reporters."[3] This was not a large number compared with other fields in
which women laboured in the early twentieth century,[4] but their
proportional representation – around 13 per cent of the total number
of journalists – was roughly comparable to women's participation rate
of 15.45 per cent in the general labour force.[5] Moreover, the fact that
women had achieved a presence in the mouthpieces of the nation had
a symbolic significance beyond the numerical.[6] The aura of power and
influence that clung to the world of journalism in the late nineteenth
century and early twentieth rendered women's participation in the
print media something of a flagship for the advancing status of women.
They were earning a living in a male-dominated field, as were other
women in prestigious professions, and, even more important, their
presence was visible to every Canadian family that took a newspaper.

Not only did presswomen symbolize women's expanding participation in the paid workplace, but they publicized the situation and
achievements of other women. Their professional mandate was to
chronicle the many facets of Canadian women's lives, both private and
public. Thus, as Charlotte Whitton made plain, women journalists'
careers intertwined with the changing context of Canadian womanhood. As working women who were frequently wives and mothers as
well, they wrote for and about other working women, whose occupational setting might be the paid labour force or the home or both,
and all of whom struggled with new responsibilities and challenges.

As the nineteenth century turned into the twentieth, women journalists helped the female newspaper-reading public adapt to the
shifting expectations of women about the lives they would lead. It was a
period in which employed women were able to move away from a
narrow range of occupations – such as domestic service, the largest
single occupational category – to new opportunities in manufacturing
industries, and in which improving education qualified women to take
up positions in the expanding bureaucracy and service sectors, and
numerically to dominate professions such as teaching and nursing.
While women in general advanced in civil rights and participation in
the arena of public life, the working lives of individual women varied
according to class and region and fluctuated in times of national stress,

particularly during the two world wars and the Great Depression.[7] Women journalists heralded the breakthroughs women made in the paid workforce and drew attention to the frustrations and injustices women encountered in their work in the home, on the farm, and in the factory. Their columns also charted the migrations of women to Canada, across Canada, and from the country to the city.[8]

For all women, including women journalists, an older notion of "separate spheres" still governed their choices and chances in the first half of the twentieth century, even as the range of opportunities considered suitable for women widened. The majority of women in the paid labour force worked in sectors where they did not compete directly with men. Even more women continued to devote their lives to unpaid work in the home, thereby complementing the dominant ideology of "the family wage" earned by a male breadwinner. But even as the occupation of homemaker appeared traditional, the substance of that job altered dramatically as Canada evolved from a primarily resource-based to a more diverse industrial and urban society. The homemaking woman's responsibilities for production diminished, and the pool of domestic servants available to help her shrank, while consumer choices became more complex and standards of domestic competence escalated. Sections addressed to women in Canadian newspapers and magazines blueprinted the changing domestic scene as presswomen assumed the role of expert adviser.

It was in part because women journalists provided a necessary service for other Canadian women that they became so well established in newspapers and magazines. From the time of their official debut in the 1891 census, where they appeared as a lonely 35 out of a total of 786, women journalists progressed rapidly. Their proportionate representation in the Canadian press expanded most impressively during the decade of the First World War, even though that was a period of draconian consolidation to the extent that forty daily newspapers disappeared (see table 1.)[9] In the following years, the number of women employed on Canadian newspapers and magazines continued to escalate. But despite Charlotte Whitton's injunction to pay heed to women journalists, comparatively little attention has been paid to the women whose work it was to construct the public face of Canadian womanhood. Those who stormed into the newsrooms in the 1880s and 1890s made an impact as individual personalities, but although they were famous in their day, they have been largely forgotten. Only a few have been remembered in a small number of biographies.[10] However, since they were disproportionately prominent in the social and political struggles of their day, their role as individuals has received attention in treatments of particular problems in Canadian history.[11] It

Table 1
Census figures for journalists (male and female) and wage earners (male and female), 1891–1941

Census year	Journalists						Wage earners[3]					
	Total		Female		Male		Total		Female		Male	
	No.	Inc.*	No.	Inc.*	No.	Inc.*	No.	Inc.*	No.	Inc.*	No.	Inc.*
1891	786		35		751							
1901	1,306	66	52	49	1,254	67						
1911	1,008	-23	69	33	939	-25						
1921	1,914	90	248	259	1,666	77						
1931[1]	3,344	75	464	87	2,880	73	2,867		357		2,510	
1941[2]	4,147	24	713	54	3,434	19	3,439	20	528	48	2,911	16

Sources: Census of Canada, 1921, vol. 4, table 1; 1931, vol. 6, table 28, and vol. 7, table 41; 1941, vol. 6, table 6, and vol. 7, table 12
* Inc. = Increase in percentages
[1] Includes authors.
[2] Includes authors but does not include anyone on active service.
[3] Excludes employers and self-employed workers.

is ironic that as women's participation in journalism became more commonplace, the spotlight that focused on them dimmed even as the news and views they recorded, shaped, and publicized assumed enhanced social, intellectual, and, not least, commercial significance. There has been no overview of what it was like to be a woman journalist or about how uniquely female areas of specialization developed in the late-nineteenth and early-twentieth-century Canadian press.[12]

Why is it that so little is known about a group of women who occupied a conspicuously public niche in the labour force? The answer lies in the familiar context of a gender-segregated workforce.[13] Although women journalists seemed to have "broken into" a male-dominated occupation, most of them spent their working lives in a world of women. They worked with women to produce material for women readers. Their careers and their strategies to promote themselves did not fit the pattern of success recognizable to those who dominated the field of journalism. In the period under consideration here – the late nineteenth century and first half of the twentieth – women journalists occupied the borderlands of the press world, whose barons tolerated but barely acknowledged their presence. Their marginality in their own times is encoded in the annals of Canadian press history, in which women journalists win only passing mention.[14] In part their invisibility stemmed from the preoccupations of contemporary male journalists with individualism and competition. In a tradition of press history that centred on the fierce personal rivalries, murderous mergers, and competitive skyscraper building of big-business newspapers, the story of the women in the press, whose contribution seemed far removed from these titanic struggles, was easily overlooked.[15]

At the level of popular culture, the pervading image of the world-weary reporter – with his all-night vigils chasing ambulances, fire trucks, and police vans, warmed by the ever-present pocket flask – hardly encapsulated the usual female experience on the newspaper.[16] A few women, most notably E. Cora Hind of the *Manitoba Free Press*, entered the canon of journalistic fame. Alone she tramped through the wheat fields and challenged the pessimistic forecasts of the Chicago commodity brokers. When Cora Hind spoke on wheat, her words went round the world.[17] Hers was a stunning achievement – and one that conformed in many ways to the male tradition. As the American media historian Catherine Covert has observed, "Journalism history has classically celebrated independence and individual autonomy rather than subordination and dependence."[18] Most newspaperwomen did not have the authority or prestige to follow where Cora Hind led. Nor did most operate according to the solitary and combative principles that guided newspaper legends. Rather, they built professional networks among themselves and established cooperative liaisons with their communities. Significantly, Cora Hind herself passionately participated both in the network among presswomen and in community action.

Moreover, because women journalists' working lives often straddled the boundaries between public and private, they were difficult to pigeonhole into conventional categories. Their public role dealt with the private realm. They wrote for women as women about things that traditionally occupied women in the home. They coached and re-shaped the "private" role by the "public" advice they gave about consumption, child rearing, techniques of housewifery, domestic relationships, fashionable society, and a host of issues that connected private life to the wider community. As servants of the Canadian media, they were integrally involved in defining normative roles for Canadian women – and not only for anglophone middle-class women like themselves but also, as Jennifer Scanlon demonstrated with the *Ladies' Home Journal* in the United States, for working-class and immigrant women who looked to the media for cues as they too were swept into the mainstream of consumer culture.[19] Since what they produced was an essential element in the gender formation of Canadian womanhood, it is important to explore the situation and context of these presswomen who wrote primarily for other women.

Women's role in journalism intersected only tangentially with the standard themes of press history such as the freedom of the press from state censorship, liberation from the control of political parties, and the advance of technological innovation. The contribution most press-women made to the evolution of journalism is better understood in the context of a theoretical framework that focuses on the development of the newspaper as a market commodity and on the press as a feature of a mass-entertainment industry.[20] Throughout the English-speaking world, increasing literacy, urbanization, leisure time, and consumerism created market opportunities for mass-circulation newspapers.[21] Once organs of partisan opinion intended for a narrow elite, newspapers became highly profitable businesses delivering information and entertainment to a vast and diverse audience.

The cluster of social and economic forces that encouraged the popularization and commercialization of the British and American press developed in Canadian society somewhat later.[22] Canadian newspapers followed traditions already established in Britain and the United States, but while Canadians respected the British style at its most lofty and while this reverence tended to temper the exuberance of their popular periodicals, in general it was American innovations that had the most profound impact on the appearance, format and content of Canadian journalism. As Peter Desbarats has noted, "Historically, Canadian journalism has been closer to Main Street, U.S.A., than to Fleet Street."[23]

In terms of women's experience in journalism, the redefinition in modern periodicals of what was news and newsworthy profoundly influenced their opportunities. The greater concentration on local events, human interest, culture, and social affairs that distinguished the new popular journals from their predecessors meant that women writers, whose opinions on politics or finance might be discounted, were not disqualified for reasons of sex from commenting on their communities. But the primary reason women found opportunities in journalism was the changing structure of newspaper and magazine finance. As newspaper and magazine proprietors were liberated from political patronage, they became dependent on advertising revenue. Women journalists were hired as a result of the major advertisers' recognition that homemakers were the primary consumers. The businesses that bankrolled newspapers wanted women to be exposed to their advertisements and therefore wanted newspapers to be attractive to women readers. Women journalists were employed to create a specifically feminine form of news that would popularize a gender identity for women readers within the existing newspaper or magazine. As Paul Rutherford has observed, "The women's department ... might range over many subjects and much of the globe. But such surveillance was always predicated upon the assumption that there was a woman's sphere with a routine and a rhythm quite distinct from the concerns of society at large. Thus was perpetuated that Victorian myth of the separate natures of the sexes."[24]

The gendered nature of the news they "made" defined the gender-specific working lives women journalists experienced. The very changes that furnished women with opportunities to work as journalists also structured the career patterns women found possible. While bondage to the profit motive impinged on all journalists in the twentieth century, the fetters were plainly visible in the case of women writers, whose intended function on the paper was almost wholly commercial – to attract and instruct the female consumer.

Women journalists were to find a variety of ways of serving their readers and assembling their careers, but these strategies were likely to be very different from those of their male colleagues. From their entry-level jobs to their career mobility to their retirement, the profiles of women's contributions to journalism and their experiences as journalists distinguished their career patterns from those of men. For the most part, women competed with each other for the few positions in the women's section. When a small paper had its "lady journalist," it needed no other. Women were far more likely to move laterally into advertising and public relations work than to rise into the ranks of city editor or managing editor. This was partly because of entrenched obstacles to their promotion but also because their work as journalists in women's sections was often an admirable preparation for more overtly commercial opportunities.

Even that central pillar of the modern reporter's ethic, "objectivity," had a different meaning in the experience of most women journalists. Carolyn Heilbrun has written, "There is no 'objective' or universal tone in literature, for however long we have been told there is. There is only the white, middle-class male tone."[25] For the woman journalist, the problem of voice went beyond that shared by all women writers. Her basic news-gathering abilities were moulded by the facts of gender. The job of the archetypal reporter was ostensibly to witness events as they were happening, with no personal interpretation distorting the facts. The reporter was the "eyes of the public."[26] A woman could not even enter the pretence of being the "invisible eyes" of the public, for everywhere she went she was physically noticeable; a woman alone on a street corner, a woman taking notes at a political meeting, or a woman in a police court stood out from the crowd in a way that a male reporter did not. The presence of a woman distorted the event just by her being there, and it made obvious the fact that what was defined as the public world of "newsworthiness" was a world of men and that "objectivity" was a privileged perspective, not a universal one.

During the heyday of the "objectivity" ethos, the fourth estate established itself as the watchdog of democratic society – ever vigilant on behalf of the public. It was commonplace for reporters to maintain that they did not make the news, they merely recorded it.[27] The model reporter was the anonymous chronicler of the passing scene whose own identity was subsumed in the collective newspaper personality. Only in the editorial section did newspapermen overtly aim to lead community opinion, and this function was supposed to be clearly differentiated from the rest of the paper.[28] In the women's specialties, on the other hand the element of construction – of making news – was more obvious. Women usually wrote "soft news features" rather than the fast-breaking stories of the street. These stories were chosen, moulded, and packaged for the woman reader, where the "hard" news story might not be so malleable.

In this same period, the women's section exuded its own atmosphere, which was distinct from the terse and tense relation of current affairs that defined the rest of the paper. Cloistered discreetly within the corpus of the newspaper, the women's section revolved around domestic and community issues and exclusive society. It was to be wholesome and uplifting, the "good news" part of the paper, in contrast to the stories of conflict, power, vice, and crime that filled the main body of the paper. As Carl Ackerman, who was dean of the Columbia University School of Journalism in 1949, put it, "The inside of a newspaper should be like the inside of a home."[29]

In contrast to the tradition of newspaper anonymity, the editor of the women's page frequently created her own newspaper identity, often earmarked by a catchy pseudonym with which her readers could identify. Her editorial might take the form an "over-the-fence" chat, projecting the illusion of private communication into a public venue. For isolated rural readers, the editor was a surrogate friend and the women's page a kind of neighbourhood forum. In urban centres, where the communities had grown too large to be cemented by female ties, the women's page carried on the tradition of telling women things about other women whom they did not know but whom they came to recognize as mainstays of the society or clubs column. Thus, the editors of women's sections were not so much passive observers of the passing scene as active moulders of a culture of women in the newspaper. Although the woman journalist might never rise to the rank of city editor or editor in chief, she could nonetheless create a "newspaper within the newspaper" where women were the newsmakers.

Women's page editorials and columns gave women writers a mandate to put forward their ideas and opinions in a highly influential public platform. It could be a powerful position of authority over their constituency; not infrequently, newswomen used their stature in the community and their public platform to advance specific causes and reforms, as Susan Jackel has demonstrated with regard to the activist presswomen of the prairies.[30] Through the women's section, some journalists managed to educate and politicize, to give women readers a knowledge of and pride in the collective achievement of women in Canada. Women journalists had the potential to create a subculture which, although marginalized within the overtly patriarchal newspaper world, could nonetheless render service to their chosen community of women.[31] This outcome had probably not been anticipated by those who wanted merely to attract female subscribers for their advertising patrons.

The automatic assignation of women journalists to the women's department mirrored the traditional gender-specific division of labour in society at large. It was infuriating to some ambitious newswomen to be sidelined in this fashion. They chafed against the explicitly feminine content and low status accorded the "pink tea circuit." A minority of women journalists who made their careers on the so-called news side did so by escaping or side-stepping the women's section. Even so, many of those who took up male-dominated beats and whose stories appeared throughout the body of the paper still found themselves doing a "woman's angle" on contemporary events – for instance, how war affected women's lives in Europe.

When presswoman aspired to compete directly with newsmen they were obliged, as Maureen Beasley and Sheila Gibbons argue, to work within the news values developed by men and thus perpetuate male-dominated structures.[32] The most successful of these newswomen were usually discounted as anomalies. The way that Frank Oliver, founder of the Edmonton *Bulletin*, recommended his agricultural reporter, Miriam Green Ellis – "She's the best damn man I've got" – may have excited her professional pride, but it was hardly calculated to advance the careers of women who came after her.[33] When, as so often happened, the path closed up after the pathbreakers, they and their achievements were forgotten. Too often it has been assumed that women did not "break out" of the women's section until the 1960s and 1970s.[34]

THE NATURE OF THE EVIDENCE

Perhaps it is not surprising that the women who spent their careers making news for and about women or who "made it" to the newsroom should remain obscure. After all, almost by definition, journalists live in the fleeting moment, the current event. History is old news; yesterday's newspaper is discarded. Professionally preoccupied with the present, newspapers as institutions and businesses have tended to disregard their own past. Even in their own time it was difficult to ascertain the identities and positions of many of the women who were working as journalists in the cities and small towns across the nation. Marjory MacMurchy, who was among the most respected newswomen of her time in the early twentieth century, admitted the difficulty of tracing her sisters of the pen or determining what jobs they performed in Canadian journalism: "Many of the press women of the Dominion are engaged in work that is at least partially editorial, but the line of work taken up in particular cases is difficult to trace on account of the fact that the workers are scattered through so vast a country. Moreover, much editorial work is done by women who are in charge of very important departments of publications, which, in the main, are editored by men."[35]

The newspapers and magazines that employed women remain as the products of their labour; they are thus an important source of evidence about the working lives of women journalists. Magazines, in particular, held a unique position in the development of Canadian journalism, giving writers access to a national forum at a time when there were no national dailies.[36] They were especially useful to women, who tended to specialize in the kinds of feature that were staples in magazines. As well, magazines provided the potential for income during a woman writer's episodic forays into the paid labour force, and they were a godsend for women who were trying to make their way as fiction writers in the restricted Canadian marketplace. Many freelance journalists turned their talents to fiction as well as features in periodicals – but except for cases where newswomen used the newspaper scene as a setting to reflect their own experiences, women who specialized in magazine fiction will not be examined here.

While the focus of this study is the journalists as workers rather than the journalism they produced, it is often difficult to disentangle the two. A sample of the women's sections in Canadian newspapers and women's features in the family magazines on which significant numbers of women journalists worked over the years was surveyed to explore the characteristics of women's sections in different periods and regions.[37] Where there were significant changes, they reflected the sensitivity of the periodicals to the transformation of Canadian women's lives, but here the focus is on how innovations in the women's section indicated changes in the priorities and responsibilities of those who made up those sections.

Although their handiwork survives, the identities of the workers often remain a mystery. The journalistic traditions of anonymity and pseudonymity render newspapers an uncertain source of information about the people who produced them. Looking for entertainment or guidance, readers might turn to the editor of "Woman's World" or "My Lady's Realm" in their urban daily without realizing that a number of different women had occupied that identity for a time and then moved on. Even in the case of well-known newspaper personalities who used a daily or weekly platform to express their views or what they believed the public would appreciate as their views, the historian cannot necessarily reconstruct the person from the columns she left behind. Women journalists were skilled and self-conscious crafters of public personas, unusually adept at shielding their private selves behind their newspaper selves, which were carefully constructed to amuse, entertain, persuade, or even intimidate their audience.[38]

In Canada it has been relatively uncommon for women journalists to reflect publicly on their careers. In contrast to the numerous reminiscences of male journalists – who, almost ritually, ended their careers by writing about their "front-row" seat in the history of their times – only a handful of Canadian newswomen have written memoirs.[39] The few who did so employed a self-consciously light tone, perhaps with the intention of deflecting serious scrutiny. This tendency was most marked in journalists who wrote women's features. Lotta Dempsey, for instance, portrayed herself as a "madcap," as did Alixe Carson Carter, whose title aptly reflected the tone – *Stop the Press! I've Made a Little Error*. The inference was that women journalists' presentation of their careers paralleled an internalized estimation of their journalism as lightweight, an amusing sideshow rather than the main event. In their consciously crafted published lives they did not reveal pain, humiliation, and frustration. This part of the emotional spectrum, according to Carolyn Heilbrun, was not until recently available to the woman autobiographer: "What has been forbidden to women is anger, together with the open admission of the desire for power and control over one's life."[40] Anger seethed from Francis Beynon's *Aleta Dey*, but she wrote her story as a novel. For the most part, women journalists avoided the limelight which they so often shone on others.

The women who happened upon journalism as a career were a diverse lot, as were other women who carved out paths for themselves in male-dominated professions. Some women were attracted to the job precisely because it was untypical for women of their generation to work in the public press. Usually, there would be only one woman employed by a particular newspaper or by one department of a paper. There might be only one "lady journalist" in a small town. For some, this uniqueness was a source of pride. As Byrne Hope Sanders, the long-time editor of *Chatelaine*, put it, "Each of us is a prima donna."[41] With such variation, the search for a representative type of woman journalist is likely to be futile. Is Byrne Hope Sanders typical? – a woman whose career spanned more than three decades and encompassed every facet of journalism, including women's page editing in Toronto and Woodstock, advertising writing, magazine editing, and even public relations work for the government during the Second World War, and who all the while maintained a private life as a married woman. Or does one find the norm in Isabel Black, who worked for a few years in the early 1920s as society reporter for the *Vancouver Sun* and then the *Province* but left her job upon marriage and never resumed it? Or were most women journalists like Edna Kells? – an unmarried woman who spent her career in the teens and twenties advising women in Edmonton how to run their homes. The diversity of the journalists' working lives defies attempts to pigeonhole them into a group biography.[42]

Nevertheless, census material, drained as it is of personality, yields some generalizations about the population under consideration here, though even in the census, the definition of the group being counted is not consistent. Conventionally, a journalist was someone who contributed to a regularly issued periodical as an editor or writer. The census of 1921 (the first to designate them as an employment category) enumerated just such a group, defined them as journalists, editors, and reporters, and included a historical retrospective on their numbers in 1891, 1901, and 1911.[43] The 1921 category usefully isolated individuals who identified themselves primarily as journalists, rather than as novelists or poets, even if they happened to do both kinds of work, as many did.[44] In 1931, authors, who earlier had been tallied in with librarians, were added to the category of "editor and journalist." For the remaining censuses relevant to this study, "authors, editors and journalists," were counted together.

The apparently random shuffling of professionals associated with literature, whether as librarians, journalists, editors, or authors, is indicative of their uncertain status in the labour market – and perhaps also of their versatility. Presumably, the definer "gainfully employed" excluded those who did not regularly earn income, but there is no stipulation that an individual had to make a living wage from her work. Further, the census distinction between "wage earners," who were regularly paid by employers, and "gainfully employed" persons, who might be self-employed, allows us to sort the conventionally employed newspaperwomen from the novelists or poets, though the latter then blend inextricably with the large group of freelance journalists who worked from home.[45] Categories of analysis, whether of age groupings or urban size, changed from census to census, further bedevilling the historian's quest for consistent data. Worse still, the raw data are occasionally contradictory. The census of 1941 contains internal inconsistencies (resulting perhaps from the fact that many workers were on active service). Most tables in the census list 713 as the total number of female authors, editors, and journalist, but a few give 714 as the total. Moreover, the figures for ethnic origin in table 12 of this census do not add up to 713, though the table gives that figure as the total.

Historical statistics on women journalists are inevitably less than rigorous.[46] Nevertheless, they yield some commonalities among the sorority of presswomen that are not nullified by the inconsistencies and idiosyncrasies of the census takers. They also underline some differences and some similarities between women and men in the field. A demographic profile of the women who were counted as journalists or authors yields some useful generalizations about ethnicity, age, regional concentration, and salary differentials, among other factors. In the first place, the vast majority of women journalists were born in Canada. As table 2 indicates, just over 78 per cent of women in journalism were Canadian born in 1931, and this figure rose to 81 per cent by 1941. A strong majority of Canadian women journalists traced British ancestry: 87 per cent in 1931 and 81 per cent by 1941. The ethnically French proportion rose from 8 per cent in 1931 to 12 per cent in 1941, a progression that may suggest a growing acceptance of women in the francophone press by that time.

It would seem that women found it more difficult to establish themselves in the older communities of Quebec and the Maritimes than in Ontario and the West, where at least three-quarters of the women employed in the Canadian press found work. As table 3 demonstrates, approximately one-third of Canadian male journalists worked in Quebec and the Atlantic provinces, the contrast between the number of men and women employed being most marked with respect to the Quebec press. Table 4 discloses a significant concentration of women in the principal urban centres of each province, which is not unduly surprising. But less predictable is their relative lack of mobility. In 1941, 89 per cent had lived for more than ten years in the same province, indicating at the very least that during the Depression and early war years, women stayed put or moved short distances to find work (see table 5).

Some women journalists were less mobile because they were married, but the majority (75.6 per cent in 1941) were single, though not as large a majority as obtained in the female-dominated professions.[47] While nearly one-quarter of the women in the "authors, editors and journalists" category had been married at some time in their lives, only 13.2 per cent were married at census time in 1941; some 8.5 per cent were widowed and another 2.7 per cent were divorced. These figures

Table 2
Birthplace and ethnicity of female authors, editors, and
journalists, 1931 and 1941

	1931		1941	
	Number	%	Number	%
PLACE OF BIRTH				
Canada	363	78.2	577	81.0
British Isles	54	12.0	85	12.0
British possessions	9	2.0		
United States	34	7.0	28	4.0
Europe	3	0.6	17	2.3
Asia	1	0.2	6	0.7
Total	464	100.0	713	100.0
ETHNIC ORIGIN[1]				
British	402	87.0	575	81.0
French	37	8.0	88	12.0
Other European	15	3.0	26	3.6
Hebrew	9	2.0	14	2.0
Asian	–	–	3	0.4

Source: Census of Canada, 1931, vol. 7, tables 44 and 49; 1941, vol. 7, table 12
[1] The census data on ethnic origin do not add up to the total number of
journalists given in other census tables.

Table 3
Regional distribution of gainfully employed journalists and editors, 1921, 1931, and
1941

Year	M/F	Total	Maritime provinces	Quebec	Ontario	Prairies	British Columbia
1921	Female	248	19 (7.7%)	34 (13.7%)	116 (46.8%)	41 (16.5%)	38 (15.3%)
	Male	1,666	119 (7.1%)	334 (20.0%)	686 (41.2%)	298 (17.9%)	229 (13.8%)
1931[1]	Female	464	28 (6.0%)	63 (13.6%)	236 (50.9%)	82 (17.7%)	55 (11.8%)
	Male	2,880	175 (6.0%)	725 (25.2%)	1,229 (42.7%)	438 (15.2%)	313 (10.9%)
1941[1]	Female	713	38 (5.3%)	139 (19.5%)	320 (44.9%)	115 (16.1%)	101 (14.2%)
	Male	3,434	180 (5.2%)	1,076 (31.3%)	1,383 (40.3%)	445 (13.0%)	350 (10.2%)

Source: Census of Canada, 1921, vol. 4, table 2; 1931, vol. 7, table 40; 1941, vol. 7, table 13
[1] Includes authors

Table 4
Women journalists gainfully employed in major urban
centres, 1921, 1931, and 1941[1]

Year	Total	Total urban	%
1921	248	156	63
1931[2]	464	316	68
1941[2]	714[3]	377	53

Sources: Census of Canada, 1921, vol. 4, table 3; 1931, vol. 7, tables
41 and 43; 1941, vol. 6, table 7
[1] The population of urban centres varied considerably over the
course of the three censuses. For purposes of comparison, the
following cities were deemed to be significant centres of anglophone journalism: Calgary, Edmonton, Halifax, Hamilton,
London, Montreal, Ottawa, Regina, Saint John, Saskatoon,
Toronto, Vancouver, Victoria, Winnipeg.
[2] Includes authors.
[3] Most tables give 713 as the total.

Table 5
Geographical mobility of women authors, editors, and journalists,
1931–1941: Years of residence in province of present abode

Total	< 2	2–4	5–8	10+
713	26	27	26	634
Percentage	3.6	3.7	3.6	89

Source: Census of Canada, 1941, vol. 7, table 13

Table 6
Marital status of gainfully occupied authors, editors, and journalists, 1931 and 1941

	Female		Male	
	No.	%	No.	%
1931				
Single	335	72.2	984	34.2
Married	63	13.6	1,802	62.6
Widowed/divorced	66	14.2	92	3.2
Total	464	100.0	2,878	100.0
1941				
Single	539	75.6	983	28.6
Married	94	13.2	2,306	67.2
Widowed	61	8.5	83	2.4
Divorced	19	2.7	62	1.8
Total	713	100.0	3,434	100.0

Source: Census of Canada, 1931, vol. 7, table 53; 1941, vol. 7, table 5

stand in marked contrast to the male journalists, 67.2 per cent of whom were married, 2.4 per cent widowed, and 1.8 per cent divorced (see table 6).

No doubt some of the presswomen who were unmarried in 1941 did marry later. More than 16 per cent of the group were under twenty-five. Nevertheless, the really young "girl" reporter was very much in the minority: 6 per cent of the women enumerated in 1921 were under twenty; by 1931 this had fallen to 2.8 per cent and by 1941 to 1.9 per cent. Although newspaperwork might seem especially attractive to the young and energetic, the majority of women who were employed in the business were relatively mature, as table 7 outlines. The large increase in the number of women journalists in 1921 reflects an influx of fairly young women, many of whom found their opportunity during the First World War. At that time, 62 per cent of the women in journalism were under thirty-five, while only 45 per cent of the men were in that age group. The smaller number of older women working in the field in 1921 was most likely a legacy of the scarcity of jobs for women in journalism in earlier times. In later censuses the demographic profile of women in journalism approached that of the men; by 1931, 57.3 per cent were over thirty-five and this pattern persisted throughout the 1930s and the early years of the Second World War.

The overall maturity of women journalists was at odds with the general demographic patterns of women in the labour force. In 1941, 44.4 per cent of women workers were under twenty-five, compared with 16.5 per cent of women journalists. At the same time, 26.9 per cent of women workers were thirty-five and over, compared with 56.4 per cent of women journalists.[48] The presence of older women in the group may suggest that, once established in the business of journalism, women were aging in their jobs. While we cannot verify that the older women in journalism had been so employed for long periods, anecdotal evidence suggests that many women did enjoy very long careers and continued them into old age. There were also the mavericks who began their careers in journalism as mature women. Details of some of these women will be discussed more fully in chapter 4. In both 1931 and 1941, 5 per cent were over sixty-five years old, approximately the same proportion as the post retirement-aged males.[49] The evident maturity of women in journalism may have been due to their education. While journalism did not require a lengthy academic preparation – indeed, there was some prejudice against the college graduate – a significant 41.7 per cent of women journalists in 1941 had postsecondary education, slightly more than the men.[50]

The census material also demonstrates the familiar fact that women earned less than men. While there was enormous variation in pay in this

Table 7
Age distribution of gainfully employed journalists, 1921–1941[1]

	1921		1931[2]		1941[2]	
	Female	Male	Female	Male	Female	Male
Under 18	5	27	0	5	2	10
18–24	62	240	80	475	116	281
25–34	87	488	118	804	193	1,060
35–64	89	865	242	1,454	366	1,895
65+	5	46	24	142	36	188
Total	248	1,666	464	2,880	713	3,434

Sources: Census of Canada, 1921, vol. 4, table 4; *1931*, vol. 7, table 41; *1941*, vol. 7, table 5
[1] Includes employers, self-employed, and wage earners.
[2] Includes authors.

highly competitive and individualistic occupation, crude statistical averages indicate that in every census decade the women were well behind the men in earning power. Of the wage-earning group in 1931, the average female journalist worked fifty weeks and earned $25.43 per week. In that same period, the average male journalist worked 49.5 weeks and earned $43.76 per week.[51] By 1941 the female wage earner in journalism worked an average of 45.11 weeks and earned $22.30 per week, while her male equivalent worked 48.29 weeks and earned $39.59 per week.[52] The figures for both groups reflect the wage slashes of the Great Depression, which were beginning to recover in the early years of the Second World War.

In fact, many women journalists earned a great deal less than their regularly employed colleagues, male or female. The freelance component was proportionately larger among female journalists than among male journalists in both census periods where they can be distinguished from the salaried employee. Around one-quarter of the "gainfully employed" female authors, editors, and journalists of Canada were freelance writers, whereas the proportion of men in this category was about half as large (see table 8). While we cannot verify how many of the female freelance journalists or authors were married and/or mothers, it seems likely that freelance journalism was an attractive alternative for women who wanted to continue their career while they managed a home.

While historical statistics allow for a generalized overview and give rise to some reasoned inferences about the situation of women working in journalism in the first half of the twentieth century, they do not allow much insight into the working lives of the first generations of Canadian presswomen. To hear the voices of the women who worked in the Canadian media in its formative years, we must turn to more articulated

Table 8
Status of authors, editors, and journalists, 1931 and 1941

	Total	Employer	Own account	Wage earner	Not paid
1931					
Female	464	2	105	357	–
		(0.5%)	(22.6%)	(76.9%)	
Male	2,880	50	320	2,510	–
		(1.7%)	(11.2%)	(87.1%)	
1941					
Female	713	3	175	528	7
		(0.4%)	(24.5%)	(74.1%)	(1.0%)
Male	3,434	43	475	2,911	5
		(1.2%)	(13.8%)	(84.9%)	(0.1%)

Sources: Census of Canada, 1931, vol. 7, table 50; *1941*, vol. 7, table 5

sources. For some individuals, collections of papers have been preserved in public archives;[53] but for most presswomen, their public writing was their legacy, and it was often deliberately silent about their personal lives as women, especially as women journalists. Journalism, newspaperwork in particular, can be a paradoxical occupation to analyse. Its practitioners were in the public eye, yet they avoided scrutiny as workers.[54] There were no mandatory professional schools or professional associations to mould the aggregate. Much of the work was unsigned, and even when it was bylined, pseudonyms cloaked the woman behind the name. In most cases the only clue to the identities of rising numbers of women spending some part of their working lives in journalism was the membership rolls of the Canadian Women's Press Club (CWPC).

The foundation of the CWPC was a direct response to gender segregation: the first generation of women journalists had come to realize that they were ignored and excluded as individuals and that they needed their own professional association. Founded in 1904, the club has existed continuously ever since (though from 1971 to 1993 it was called the Media Club of Canada).[55] While the present study is not a history of the CWPC, the existence of this all-female organization was integral to the experience of a significant number of the women who worked in Canadian journalism in the early years of the twentieth century. Moreover, the large and varied collection of documents assembled by the CWPC over the years has been an essential resource for this study. The early women journalists had a strong sense of making history as well as news, and they recognized the importance of preserving a record both of their collective identity and of their achievements as individuals. From the outset, a club "historian," responsible for chronicling landmarks in the lives of the members, held an executive position. Records of the voluminous transactions of the CWPC were carefully kept, again demonstrating the members' sense of collective destiny. They also saved their letters to each other – which indicates how much the active members of the club valued one another as friends and colleagues.

Under the auspices of the CWPC, an impressive variety of documents was assembled, both by the national organization and the branches spread across the country. In addition to the conventional records of meetings, finances, executive, and activities related specifically to the club as a club, the collection is itself an archive of the women who worked as journalists in Canada. It includes the papers of individual members, scrapbooks of clippings, letters, papers they delivered to each other at conventions, published and unpublished novels, poems, and essays. Membership records sketch in the changing status of individual members as they marry, have children, move, are promoted (or demoted), retire, and die. The records of the Beneficiary Fund, which the club established in 1913 to help members through illness or adversity, hints at the vulnerability of women in this competitive and unforgiving business. The club newsletter, the "Newspacket," was a chatty forum of insider communication and information in which they displayed the grittier side of the job – their complaints, friction on the "beat," resentment of their colleagues, and even irritation with each other – and in which they shared gripes and jokes and celebration of their individual and collective achievements. While common professional interests were the glue that held this diverse group of women together, the contexts of their personal experiences emerge episodically but vividly as snapshots of their lives as women as well as journalists.

But like snapshots in a family photo album, they may be suspect as evidence of the whole life. Are the women whose letters have survived or who contributed to the club newsletter or were elected to office in the local or national executive "typical" of the group as a whole? Are we hearing from a cross-section of working women journalists or merely the more audible voices of those who could talk a good line? No doubt the way that presswomen expressed themselves to each other was contrived – a shared insider's culture of women who were excluded from much of the overtly male insider's culture of their profession. As Natalie Zemon Davies has cautioned, women's own stories are constrained by "cultural notions of believability."[56] The anecdotes they confess about their working and private lives were not intended to be rigorously "representative" – they reflect the diversity of experience that different women had at various points in their lives. Even so, in recounting their experiences to their peers in the sheltered relationship of friendship and club, they anticipated an empathetic audience. While their peers may not have had identical experiences, the contributors could expect that their observations would ring true. Some journalists were more willing than others to reflect consciously on their experiences as women working in the field. Whether or not their more reticent sisters agreed with the positions taken we can discover only when they responded to the invitation to debate proffered at conferences and in the "Newspacket." As Mary Kinnear, treating a similarly rich but problematic database, counselled, the historian must not underestimate the difficulties but must "resist paralysis" in order to cultivate the evidence of women whose "testimony would otherwise be lost."[57]

Through these glimpses of their relationships, we see these women principally as journalists, but we also see them as friends, daughters, wives, mothers, and sisters. We see how their personal concerns intertwined with their professional performance – their motivation for becoming journalists, their anxiety about money and underemployment, their families' position in relation to their careers, and other factors that are rarely explored in conventional journalism history. The mingling of personal details with professional accomplishments in no way undermines their achievements. Rather, it allows us, as media historian Susan Henry argues, to recreate a rounded picture of how individuals did their work and how they fared in the business.[58]

Few professions have preserved so multifaceted an archival collection as that which exists about Canadian women journalists. In the time period embraced by this study, more than a thousand women qualified as members of the Canadian Women's Press Club.[59] But for all its breadth of membership and its diversity of information, we cannot simply assume that the CWPC represented the attitudes of all women journalists in Canada. Did the varying expressions of its membership give a fair reflection of the experiences of women who worked as journalists but did not qualify for or care to join a club comprised exclusively of other women in their field or closely related fields? Why some might not belong to a club that offered fellowship and professional guidance is open to speculation. Some may have scorned a group defined by its "female" constituency and may have preferred to make their way as individuals in the adventurous and sometimes hostile terrain of the newspaper world. Some may have been simply too busy juggling various dimensions of their lives as working women to attend meetings and conventions. Others, living far from a local branch, may have seen no advantage to membership when they could not enjoy the fellowship of regular meetings – though the women who called themselves the Lone Scribes used the club to establish a community when they were living in remote regions of Canada.

While the CWPC may not have recruited every woman journalist at work in Canada it seems that most were members, Rosa Shaw, president of the club in 1942 and a newspaperwoman with wide experience working in Montreal, Quebec, London, and Ottawa, stated in her report to the club, "There are comparatively few regularly employed newspaperwomen who are not members of the CWPC."[60] Yet the disparity between the club's total active membership and the total number of women who identified themselves on the census as authors, editors, or journalists widened as more and more women entered the field.[61] No doubt, some of the women who were working as journalists at the time of a particular census and did not belong to the club had at one time passed through it but had found it uncongenial and had ceased to be members. Irritation – sometimes fury – with the CWPC was occasionally expressed by women who felt let down. Whatever their feelings about the club, we can sometimes hear the voices of those who cared to participate. Those who did not and whose private papers have not been preserved are difficult to come to know. Outside this forum, which was specifically organized to address the needs of women journalists, there was nowhere that a newswoman could express herself as a woman working in journalism.

The scope of the present project was in part defined by the richness of the CWPC records and the rough guide provided by the censuses, which indicated where the majority of women journalists were concentrated. For the purposes of this study, which focuses exclusively on women who were in journalism as a paid-work opportunity, the membership rules of the club have provided a useful screen, excluding the amateur and the has-been.[62] Only women who could demonstrate their status as paid journalists were eligible to join the CWPC, and every year they had to prove their continued activity. Thus, women who acted as journalists in special-interest publications – who may not have been paid and whose devotion stemmed from idealism rather than professional commitment – have not been included. Excluded from the club and the present study, for instance, were many interesting women who contributed voluntarily to reform periodicals or the labour press.[63]

There were francophone members of the CWPC, but not many. The majority of club members in Quebec worked for the anglophone press and belonged to the Montreal branch; there was no branch in Quebec City until after the Second World War. The character of francophone journalism in Canada and the particular experience of women in the francophone press is distinct enough to warrant separate treatment.[64] By the same token, the ethnic press in Canada was rich and lively. Women took part in producing periodicals addressed to specific ethnic groups,[65] but their experience is better understood in the context of the communities they served than in company with women who worked as paid journalists in the commercial newspapers and magazines of Canada.

This book falls into two sections. The first part examines the working lives of Canadian women journalists; the second looks at the particular work they did and how the specialties they developed evolved over time. Women's group entry into journalism in the 1880s defined one end of the time frame; the Second World War, which saw women journalists establish themselves in all facets of newspaper work, provides the other. Women's experience in journalism, however, did not proceed in an orderly chronological sequence. The general approach chosen to analyse it is thus a thematic rather than chronological one, but periodicity enters as external events – the two world wars and the Depression, for instance – dictate the opportunities women cultivated.

The first women journalists in Canada, who worked in the nineteenth century, were singular enough to warrant separate treatment. In most cases, each was the first woman ever to be employed on a particular paper. They had a licence for individual fame and self-expression that women journalists would rarely find in later generations. At the same time, their situation raised issues that resurfaced in the working lives of their successors. The circumstances of women's entry into journalism were not unique to Canada, and therefore the experiences of Canada's first presswomen have been placed in the wider context of American and British press history. The pioneering generation wrote the first women's pages in Canadian newspapers. Thus, in order to showcase changes that occurred as the women's section evolved and professionalized, the writings of the first women's page editors reappear in the chapters on female specialities.

As noted above, their experience as anomalies, segregated from the newspaper communities in a "women's world" within newspapers, led a group of early women journalists to try to overcome their isolation by forming an all-female press club. The third chapter analyses the way the Canadian Women's Press Club reflected presswomen's aspirations for a respectable professional opportunity for themselves in the print world. Notwithstanding structural barriers to their progress up the newspaper hierarchy, women journalists aimed to develop a distinct craft pride, which their separate press association did much to foster. Their occupation was one where, by convention, individualism and competitiveness were the rules of life. Those who qualified for membership in the CWPC created a sense of community among themselves in which many of them found solace and companionship.

The fourth chapter explores the experiences of women for whom journalism was an unusual but, by the twentieth century, not an outlandish occupation. Women entered journalism in ever-increasing numbers in the first four decades of the twentieth century, usually in the women's sections, which had now become indispensable features of newspapers. In this chapter, snapshots along the "life course" of a particular career are assembled from the fleeting glimpses which women journalists revealed of their life stories. From entry-level jobs to career progress, marriage and motherhood, old age and retirement, a collective view emerges of the diversity the life might offer.

Chapters 5 to 8 explore the various dimensions of women's segregated work in the Canadian press, from the responsibilities of editing the women's section to the specialized departments of advising women readers and doing society and club reporting. In each chapter, the specialities are contextualized to demonstrate the milieux in which they developed and the way they contributed to the career pattern of women journalists'. The chapter on expert advice features the expanding economic roles of female consumers and the relationship of women journalists to the growing advertising industry. The chapter on the society column highlights women's role in determining the criteria of elite social status. The context of the chapter on club reporting is the flowering of women's political and social activism through voluntary organizations during the reform era and after. This chapter illustrates the way women journalists contributed to and reflected upon the various dimensions of the women's movement and the first wave of feminism in Canadian society.

As a contrast to the experience of the majority of presswomen, who spent their working lives serving a gender-specific audience of women readers, chapter 9 examines the careers of women who made their way in journalistic departments dominated by men – political and financial reporting, war correspondence, and general reporting. This chapter also balances the more individualistic approach of the first chapter, since like the first generation of women journalists, the women on the "news side" were often isolated anomalies.

Ambiguity of status ran through every facet of their lives as working women journalists: the identification of the first generation as a distinct subset of journalists, always accompanied by the definer "lady" journalist; the unfulfilled aspirations for clear-cut professional status; the right and ability of women to earn at various stages of life; the uncertain authority of editors of the women's pages; the incongruity of women who worked for pay to advise women how to do unpaid domestic work; the contradiction of working women commenting on the conspicuously leisured activities of the status elites; the discomfiture of women working in "unfeminine" fields; and, above all, the ambivalence women journalists had about their own work in a field dominated by male-defined news values. All these elements define the tensions that the women struggled with in their working lives. Their struggle parallels the challenge of the historian to validate their contribution to journalism without assuming that their work was inferior to that of newsmen, while at the same time acknowledging the constraints that in part dictated their situation.

CHAPTER TWO

The Second Species:
Early Women Journalists

In Fleet Street, there are not two sexes but two species, journalists
and women journalists.

Arnold Bennett, *Journalism for Women*, 1898

A century ago, two young Canadian women set off on a journey around
the world. They had decided to conduct their travel "the wrong way
round," crossing the Pacific before the Atlantic, as an adventure to write
up for the newspapers. Both of them had already established some
reputation in Canadian journalism. One was known as Garth Grafton to
the readers of the Toronto *Globe* and the *Montreal Star*. Her real name,
Sara Jeannette Duncan, would be recognized by the serious readers of
the *Week*. Duncan's companion, Lily Lewis, also wrote for the *Montreal
Star* and the *Week*, signing herself Louis Lloyd. Although both these
young women had assumed masculine pseudonyms, they wore their
disguise lightly, more as a daring accessory than a veil, as if to mock the
bygone strictures that had once forced female talent to parade itself as
male. Louis Lloyd did not attempt to disguise her own or, for that
matter, her travelling companion's femininity. On one occasion, for
instance, she gently teased Garth Grafton for her "peculiarly feminine,
interrogatory manner."[1] Only the occasional reader failed to address
Garth Grafton as "Dear Madam."[2]

Indeed, the chief point of journalistic interest in this excursion was
the fact that two women were undertaking it. The voyage of Miss
Duncan and Miss Lewis was to be a prefabricated news event by which
the two journalists and their newspapers intended to create public interest. Nineteenth-century newspapers pandered to their readers' wanderlust in regularly featured travel articles,[3] but there was a special novelty to travelogues by women. How two young and unescorted women

Mrs Sara Jeannette Cotes (née Duncan), first women's editor, with the
Toronto *Globe*, then *Montreal Star* (Johnston and Hoffmann/National
Archives of Canada [NA], C-46447)

would encounter the newly opened West, the dangerously exotic
Orient, and the old civilizations of the Mediterranean would make
remarkable reading – and would sell newspapers. As one of the most
shrewdly entrepreneurial newspaper publishers of the day observed of
the intrepid woman journalist, "Once launched upon the sea of adventure, trifles such as would hardly be read if written by a man become
thrilling or picturesque as an episode in the life of a woman."[4]

For the next two years, Duncan regularly regaled readers of the
Montreal Star with her experiences: riding a cowcatcher through the
Rockies, visiting a geisha in Japan, and travelling through the Egyptian
night by camel in order to scale the Great Pyramid at sunrise. At the
same time, the *Week* gave prominence to Lily Lewis's contributions in a
series entitled "Louis Lloyd's Letters." Plainly, their patrons believed
that the reports of these two female adventurers would boost sales of
their respective journals. The precise return on their investment was
perhaps incalculable, but one indication of the popularity of such
features may be drawn from the success of the book Duncan constructed from her newspaper articles. *A Social Departure: How Orthodocia
and I Went Round the World by Ourselves* sold better than anything else

Duncan wrote, even though, from a purely literary standpoint, her later works were more deserving of acclaim.[5]

It would seem that women doing unusual things held an intrinsic fascination for the late-nineteenth-century public. The newspapers of that era both catered to and stimulated popular curiosity about the unconventional woman. There was also an increasing appetite for information about the more conventional affairs of womankind. Thus, if a few women managed to make a living in the late-nineteenth-century Canadian press, it was because they were able to attract public interest simply by being presswomen and writing what a large number of people wanted to read.

This chapter examines the entry of women into journalism as an employment opportunity that opened in the last two decades of the nineteenth century. Because the participation of women in the newspaper business was so new, expectations of what they would do and how they would fit in were amorphous. Their opportunities occurred because of changes in the newspaper business which the journalist community was still trying to absorb. The women, for their part, came to their work not as fledgling reporters but as nineteenth-century women whose lives for various reasons did not conform to the pattern they had been raised to expect. The clash of expectations determined the experiences that the first generation would find as they tried to make a place for themselves in a world that was not always ready to receive them.

THE WOMEN WHO CAME FIRST

The actual number of women who wrote for the nineteenth-century Canadian press remains obscure because of the imprecision of contemporary surveys and the tradition of anonymity in newspaper writing. The first census for which any estimates are available, 1891, records 35 women editors, reporters, and journalists when there were 751 men in these occupations.[6] Less than a decade later, the National Council of Women described the careers of fifty-five women who were active as contributors, correspondents, and editors.[7] Both estimates probably excluded many women who were writing from home or working for family-owned newspapers. The participation of women in journalism embraced a group that ranged from the enthusiastic contributor of small-town gossip to the owner and operator of a country weekly. The National Council of Women included some expatriates working in the big-city dailies of New York and Chicago. The recency of women's entry into professional journalism permitted – indeed, demanded – variety and experimentation.

The type of woman who would become a journalist when to do so was still highly unconventional was, almost by definition, unique. Consequently, the first generation of women journalists fits uneasily into anything resembling a group portrait. These women did, however, share a few traits. Predictably, in the social setting of late nineteenth-century Canada, they were white. They were well educated, some remarkably so, with postgraduate degrees. They came from the section of the middle class that could afford to educate its daughters, yet they were not wealthy enough to live as leisured ladies; most chose paid journalism because they needed to support themselves.

It is difficult and ultimately rather fruitless to attempt to designate Canada's first woman journalist. As with so many areas of female achievement, the history of women in journalism is strewn with firsts. Sara Jeannette Duncan, sometimes vaunted as the first, was remarkable for being Canadian born, employed full time, and established in the office of the *Globe* by 1886. She overcame the reluctance of the newspaper establishment to tolerate the presence of a woman in its midst, but she was not the first woman to practise journalism in Canada. E.E. Sheppard, founder of *Saturday Night*, made reference to his "unsuccessful" experiment with a female employee of the Toronto *News* as he gently scotched the very inexperienced young Duncan's journalistic aspirations in 1884.[8]

Agnes Maule Machar was already writing articles under the *nom de plume* of Fidelis in the 1870s. To be sure, Machar was more of a belletrist than a journalist as she constructed her long, thoughtful essays for the *Canadian Monthly* in the peace of her own home.[9] Duncan's experience was closer to that of the work-a-day reporter as she marched downtown to the *Globe* office and dashed off her pieces amidst the hubbub of a hectic daily newspaper. Yet another predecessor, Kate Massiah, claimed to be the first professional "interviewer" in Canada when she began with the Montreal *Herald* in 1871. In 1879 she covered the debates on the National Policy from the Speaker's Gallery in the House of Commons. By 1889, as editor and proprietor of the *Independent Lachute*, she became a full-fledged member of the Canadian Press Association.[10] Massiah had already worked as a journalist in England before she emigrated to Canada, so her credentials as a journalist were sound. But no doubt her brother, J.L. Norris, editor of the *Herald*, cleared her path in the backwoods of Canadian journalism.

In a family setting, it was not uncommon for women in nineteenth-century North America to practise journalism. The daughters, wives, and sisters of owner-editors took part in all aspects of the trade from writing to managing circulation and even typesetting. Margaret Ellis began writing reviews and editorials for her father's paper, the Saint

John *Globe*, in the 1880s and continued sporadic contributions to the paper during and after her two marriages until her death in 1942.[11] In a few cases a woman continued to own and operate the business after the death (or during the absence) of her husband or father. Alice Lemmon Keeler, for instance, contributed to her husband's paper in Brantford in the 1830s and, after he had to flee the country because of his participation in the Upper Canadian rebellion, edited it until she remarried in 1839.[12] The pattern of women participating in journalism as their husband's or father's helpmate persisted on country weeklies well into the twentieth century.

There were, then, a few precedents for the generation of women who entered journalism in the 1880s and 1890s. But the fact that women had written for newspapers earlier in no way diminished the novelty of what this generation was doing. The women who earned their living as journalists at the end of the nineteenth century made their way, not primarily because of family connections but because they were talented, ambitious, persistent – and, paradoxically, because they were women. They carved out new fields of journalism that were intended to serve a largely female audience. The most famous among these pioneers won their renown by creating literary personae who attracted enormous followings. Newspaper owners could not fail to be impressed by the volume of mail that arrived on the desks of their female columnists. For the first generation of women journalists, personality and personal popularity were the keynotes of success.

WOMEN AND THE RISE OF THE
MASS-CIRCULATION PRESS

Women's opportunities in journalism stemmed directly from the advent of popular newspapers that depended on mass sales. Strange as it may now seem, the press had not always been so solicitous of mass readership. Earlier Canadian newspapers had served as organs of special-interest groups, which most often were defined by political party, though also by religion and ethnicity, and were dependent on their specific constituency in a closed circle of concurring opinion. The newspaper was the product of the owner-editor, who wrote most of it himself, sometimes with the help of family members. Even on the largest papers, the staff was small and not likely to welcome nonfamilial female employees. These early papers catered chiefly to the interests of the national powerbrokers and captains of industry. They consisted mainly of verbatim reports of parliamentary debates and editorial infighting based on political differences between rival party papers. Indeed, journalism was often a political apprenticeship; from newspaper editor to the House of Commons or the civil service was a fairly typical career move.[13] Hector Charlesworth was unusual in his indifference to the overtures of a Conservative politician who offered him patronage in the future in return for a partisan "plug" in the present.[14]

When newspapers had comparatively little to say about anything outside the realm of national politics and commerce, the opinions of unenfranchised women were unlikely to impress. Even Sara Jeannette Duncan – who, as a political correspondent for the *Montreal Star,* had enjoyed more than ample opportunity to observe the political process at work – met a frigid response when she commented on the Canadian political scene in her novel, *The Imperialist.* "A woman attempting politics must be judged leniently," condescended the *Canadian Magazine* of 1904.[15] Kit Coleman, who became the most admired columnist of her day, trespassed warily in the political realm. As she thanked a correspondent who had appreciated her election commentary, she admitted, "I was afraid the chief would come down on women drifting into politics, as if we didn't know a lot more about them than the men!"[16]

Women journalists owed their presence in the newspaper world to the structural changes in the ownership and operation of the press that took place in Canada in the last decades of the nineteenth century.[17] In the 1880s the big-city dailies multiplied and began to take on a distinctly popular style in order to appeal to a mass readership. Unlike the earlier party papers, the urban dailies wanted to claim political independence, though their political tilt continued to be obvious. In lieu of party coffers, they turned for revenue to advertising and large circulations. Newspapers then competed murderously with each other to secure the largest share of both. In their contest for the loyalty of the customer, newspaper proprietors concentrated on securing a female readership as a crucial element of financial success. Not only would the female subscriber boost sales, but her allegiance would be especially attractive to advertisers. Women now purchased many of the commodities formerly produced in the home, and manufacturers acknowledged the increasing importance of housewives as consumers. The newspaper that could direct women's attention to the advertisements for household goods, fashions, or patent medicines by displaying them in a section "of interest to women" would certainly have an advantage in the battle for revenue. Department stores such as Eaton's and Simpsons took the lead in commanding half or even whole pages of a newspaper to trumpet their daily specials,[18] and they wanted these advertisements to appear opposite a section that housewives would be sure to peruse. In consequence, a few women found a place for themselves in the press ranks by compiling and editing a weekly or daily section addressed to the female subscriber. Thus, the emergence of the women's page was a direct result of commercial pressure on newspaper owners and editors. This innovation, in turn, made newspaper reading a more respectable and interesting outlet for women.

By the last decades of the century, the nature of journalism and what the press deemed to be suitably newsworthy began to alter in women's favour. The popular press of the late nineteenth century was more local than national and more personal than political. Its appeal was no longer exclusively to the elite who managed politics and commerce. On the contrary, the press tried to entice ordinary people who had little interest in events outside their immediate experience. Most of the late-nineteenth-century newspaper readers were interested in family and community. They wanted to learn about what was happening in their neighbourhood; they wanted stories about people like themselves and gossip about the rich and famous.[19] In short, they wanted their newspaper to entertain them – not merely to harangue them – and to reflect the interests of women and children as well as the male head of the household. Indeed, Faith Fenton (Alice Fenton Freeman) of the Toronto *Empire*, assumed that women's choice was decisive: "Most journals have come to recognize that the paper that gets into a house ... must be one that will in some department win the favour of women."[20]

As Canadian newspapers attempted to reach a family audience, they established the metier of the female reporter who could specialize in community affairs and human-interest stories. If the reporter's opinions on national politics, international relations, or commerce were not elicited at first, her thoughts about people and community life were, and these were the features most valued in the penny press. These papers, as one newspaper historian has argued, tended to enhance the importance of everyday life by focusing attention on matters close at hand.[21] Contemporary estimates of women writers supposed them to be better at seeing life through the microscope than the telescope, at detailing the minutiae of personality and relationship rather than enlarging on grand themes. The woman reporter could be expected to take a sympathetic view of her community, to heighten local colour, and to elevate the drama of ordinary events.

Because many of the newest features of late-nineteenth-century journalism could be construed as "feminine" specialities, the most enterprising of the newspaper entrepreneurs were usually the first to profit from female talent. Edmund Ernest Sheppard, one of the most flamboyant of this group, was proud to have launched a number of successful female journalists. Although chagrined at having missed the great Sara Jeannette Duncan, he boasted as early as 1890 that he had "had the pleasure of introducing more than one bright woman to newspaper work."[22] His *Saturday Night* had an unusually brilliant society page under the direction of Lady Gay (Grace Denison), which featured commentary on Ottawa social life by Amaryllis (Agnes Scott). Sheppard's protégées included Kate Westlake and Elmira Elliott. Kate Westlake began her career as subeditor of the St. Thomas *Evening Journal*, where she gained useful all-round experience in newspaper work. But the opportunity to edit Sheppard's family magazine, the *Canadian Fireside*, gave her more prominence in Canadian journalism.[23] Elmira Elliott was sending occasional contributions to Sheppard's paper from her farm home in Oakville when he lured her to Toronto to edit *Saturday Night*'s women's page. She became renowned as Madge Merton, though she also wrote as Clip Carew and Frances Burton Clare.[24] Elliott went on to make her mark in other prominent Canadian papers, including the *Globe,* where she first met the man who later became famous as Joseph E. Atkinson of the *Star.* When the two journalists were married in 1892, the newly established trade journal, the *Canadian Printer and Publisher,* celebrated their wedding as the first event of its kind in Canadian newspaper history.[25] Atkinson was not loath to feature his wife's abilities: Madge Merton's columns adorned both the Montreal *Herald,* when he was editor, and the *Toronto Star,* which he published.

The greatest of Sheppard's discoveries was Kathleen Blake Watkins (later Coleman). Although the newly arrived Irish immigrant had no experience of journalism, Sheppard published a couple of her essays.[26] These attracted the attention of Christopher Bunting of the Toronto *Mail,* who offered her a staff position editing the women's page. This was in 1890 at a time when the *Mail* was attempting to extricate itself from direct dependence on the Conservative Party. The inauguration of a women's page was no doubt part of the strategy to gain independence by establishing commercial viability. The *Mail* did not, in the end, succeed in its bid for freedom and had to merge with the *Empire,* the Conservative Party organ that John A. Macdonald had launched to replace the recalcitrant *Mail.* Even so, Bunting never had cause to regret hiring the woman who became famous as "Kit of the *Mail.*" Kit's weekly pages in the *Mail* became one of the most widely read features in the whole newspaper industry. Households where political loyalties would normally prohibit the purchase of a Conservative paper overcame their scruples on Saturday for the sake of Kit's "Woman's Kingdom."[27] Liberal fans of Kit included the prime minister, Sir Wilfrid Laurier, and Kit in turn expressed her admiration for Laurier, despite the editorial hostility of her paper towards all things Liberal.[28] Kit also won the heart of the woman whom the Liberal-leaning *Globe* hired to compete with her. Jean Blewett christened her the Queen of Hearts in recognition of her popularity and her unrivalled rule in the land of the lovelorn.[29]

The general trend towards entertainment and popular appeal thus created a climate in which a few women journalists could flourish. Meanwhile, a larger number of women journalists came to profit from the increasing visibility of women in the public life of the local community. The extension of women's moral housekeeping role into the wider arena of urban life justified women's presence on school boards and hospital committees, and as poor-law guardians.[30] Similar rationales permitted female reporters to cover the local scene, especially when women were among the actors. At this time the women's club movement, which was already well established in the United States, was beginning to develop in Canada. Some enthusiasts of reform began their own journals to promote specific causes, particularly temperance.[31] The daily press regularly reported the activities of such organizations as the Woman's Christian Temperance Union and various church auxiliaries.[32] The Toronto *Globe* had a daily column on temperance and social reform, which was placed beside the "Woman's World" column in the 1880s. Often called the Scotsman's Bible because of its upright moral tone, the *Globe* went so far as to set all type on Saturday night so as not to break the Sabbath.

While publicizing the activities of strong-minded women reformers provided a portal through which a number of women journalists entered their chosen profession, recording the more frivolous goings on in the homes of social leaders furnished a much wider point of entry for others. Society gossip columns were an innovation that proved to be enormously popular both with the select circles whose names were recorded and with the less exalted reading public, who liked their daily fare to be spiced with gossip. Thus, social reporters were in demand on almost all newspapers, from the country weekly to the urban daily. Many social reporters found, though, that the easier path into journalism was not necessarily the most direct route to success. Although society reporting allowed aspiring writers to earn their living in the newspaper world, the job could turn into a cell rather than an avenue to better things. Florence Randal (later Livesay), for example, spent five years with the *Ottawa Journal* chronicling the activities of the capital's debutantes and dowagers, even though she had proved her talent publishing articles and poems in *Massey's Magazine*. For the most part, her work consisted of mere recitations of invitation lists. In the end, she fled to a concentration camp in South Africa, where she became a teacher of Boer children. The *Evening Journal* was then very happy to print with bylines two- or three-column letters from Miss Randal, its formerly anonymous social editor.[33]

It is possible that the conservative attitude of her paper contributed to the close rein on Florence Randal's freedom. She was the first society editor the *Ottawa Journal* had condescended to employ and, considering itself a serious paper, it had kept such trivial matters to a minimum. The Toronto *Globe* had similar reservations about the inauguration of its first gossip column in 1893. Mrs Willoughby Cummings (Emily McCausland Cummings) gradually expanded her empire at the *Globe* from weekly personal notes culled from cities around Ontario to a daily column of society gossip by 1896. As Melville Hammond recalled, at first there were "wry faces against such 'horrid vulgar stuff,'" but eventually the society column became as much a staple on the *Globe* as on other papers.[34]

STUNTS AND SENSATIONS: THE AMERICAN INFLUENCE

Innovative features such as gossip columns and advice to the lovelorn led some critics to complain that the press was feeding a depraved public taste.[35] Old hands in the newspaper business tended to interpret the changing emphasis as debasement and to attribute the decline in standards to the influx of women writers and readers. W.C. Brann, the editor of a western American paper, the *Iconoclast*, went so far as to blame women for the current addiction to sensationalism. "As a rule," he fumed, "women are either dilettanti in journalism or professional panderers to an unhealthy literary appetite ... A careful examination of the 'great dailies' will demonstrate that at least half the intellectual slime that is befouling the land is fished out of the gutter by females."[36]

What set Brann off on his binge of hyperbole was a craze in American journalism for "stunts", publicity events staged by a newspaper to create a sensation. An oft-repeated formula involved a young attractive woman journalist in disguise, who underwent some unseemly adventure in order to record her experiences for the readers of whatever newspaper sponsored her. This fashion, which was at its height in the late 1880s and the 1890s, cast a spell of infamy over the image of the woman journalist which only years of sober professional accomplishment finally exorcized. In her advice to aspiring reporters, Cynthia Westover Alden, one of the most respected women journalists in the United States, distanced herself from any association with the fashion of "yellow journals" for "sending a woman to spend a night in the Morgue, or to interview a repulsive criminal, or to pry into some domestic scandal." As Alden pointed out, "They print the matter turned in over the woman's signature, gratifying her vanity, and thereby aiding her to forget that she has been used purely in the interest of sensationalism."[37]

In an era when women were just beginning to escape the Victorian "cult of domesticity" that confined women in order to "protect" them, the yellow journals exploited the image of vulnerable womanhood-at-risk to produce a semipornographic titillation. When professional women journalists in later years spoke scornfully of those who "used sex" to get ahead as journalists, they meant precisely those who "prostituted their womanhood for the sake of a good story."[38] Some of the stories were indeed good, and the ideas of these stunt journalists prefigured a later and highly respectable tradition of investigative journalism.[39] The more popular papers developed a tradition of crusading that was intended to arouse the righteous indignation of their readers. It was this aspect of American journalistic methods – the moral mission – that appealed more to Canadian newspaper proprietors than the mere stunt.[40]

The opportunity to increase public awareness of distress and to provoke social and moral reform would most certainly have been the motivation for Faith Fenton (Alice Freeman) of the Toronto *Empire* when she sought asylum in a woman's shelter in Toronto in 1894.[41] Elmira Elliott (later Atkinson) made a similar descent into poverty for her readers' benefit when she visited Toronto churches disguised as an old woman or sought work as a servant in wealthy Toronto homes.[42] Although Elliott undertook her series for the Toronto *Globe* in the late 1880s, when such escapades were still novel even in New York (thus showing her alertness to the newest trends in journalism), she despised sensational papers. Years later, her moral rectitude kept comic strips and pictures of scantily dressed women out of her husband's paper, the *Toronto Star*.[43] In 1896 she counselled virtuous women readers to shun sensational papers and scolded those who declared that newspapers were not fit to read yet hypocritically devoured accounts of crime, murder, breach of promise, and divorce. Reluctantly she admitted, "Sensational papers do pay. It is only a question of who will help them to be successful."[44]

Undeniably, women journalists helped make sensational papers successful, and the cult of prefabricated news events made the names of a few enterprising women household words. The American Nellie Bly (Elizabeth Cochrane), the most successful of the so-called acrobatic journalists, was possibly the most famous woman of her day. The culmination of her career was in 1890 when she crossed the United States in the last leg of her trip around the world to best the fictional record set in Jules Verne's *Around the World in Eighty Days*. For seventy-two days, six hours, and eleven minutes, the readers of Joseph Pulitzer's New York *World* read breathless accounts of Nellie Bly's race with time.[45] Pulitzer was eager to exploit the commercial potential of intrepid women journalists in Canada as well. A year earlier than Nellie Bly's dash around the globe, he had defrayed some of the expenses of Sara Jeannette Duncan's more leisurely excursion.[46] Moreover, it was the

Pulitzer-inspired Sir Hugh Graham who sponsored the trip under the auspices of his paper, the *Montreal Star*. Of all the Canadian newspaper entrepreneurs, Graham, later Lord Atholstan, was the Canadian most willing to borrow Pulitzer's enterprising methods.[47]

Duncan herself was keenly alive to the modes of American newspaperwomen, having served her apprenticeship in the United States. She had landed her first newspaper staff position in the privileged realms of literary criticism and that from the lofty reaches of the *Washington Post*. She did not choose to hustle through the hurly-burly of New York City newspaper reporting, where by 1886 there were already more than two hundred women competing for stories.[48] Any escapade that might lessen her dignity was not likely to appeal to the patrician Miss Duncan. As one of her contemporaries noted, she conducted her world travels with gentility even while she mocked orthodoxy. Hector Charlesworth mentioned no names when he observed, "Other women of this continent have made the same journey and earned only a reputation for lack of femininity."[49]

Like Charlesworth, Duncan was contemptuous of the Nellie Bly tradition: "These things do not come within what is considered the legitimate scope of women's work on newspapers, and are by no means of necessity a part of any woman's experience on the press."[50] She took her condemnation of vulgar sensationalism further in the novel she wrote in 1894 about an American woman journalist in England. *A Daughter of To-day* features the beautiful Elfrida, who tries to create copy by disguising herself as a chorus girl in a disreputable music hall, only to find that, in the wake of her escapade, her highbrow friends recoil in repugnance. As Elfrida's moral and artistic downfall leads to her suicide, Duncan underscored her own apprehensions about the too-eager woman writer's vulnerability in the commercial world of the press. Duncan's code of propriety notwithstanding, her round-the-world trip with Lily Lewis and her mildly unorthodox adventures while travelling were the closest Canada came to the stunt journalism that was so popular in the United States.

The reluctance of the Canadian press to borrow all the excesses of American journalism narrowed the scope of women aspiring to a career in journalism in Canada. Sara Jeannette Duncan had, within a year or two of her debut, exhausted some of the best chances newspaperdom afforded a woman. This perhaps accounts for the discouraged tone of the column she wrote about women in journalism for the *Montreal Star* of 25 January 1888: "Here in Canada nothing, comparatively speaking, has been accomplished by women in journalism, partly because the Canadian newspaper world is so small as to be easily occupied by some half dozen influential journals, partly because it is a very conservative world indeed, and we know what conservatism means in relation to the scope of women's work." She concluded by referring to difficulties "which look insuperable at first and can only be surmounted by the exercise of the divinest kind of patience."[51] However, if one traces Duncan's mobility during the four or so years she worked as a journalist – starting as a correspondent for the *Brantford Expositor*, becoming literary editor of the *Washington Post*, then a columnist on the Toronto *Globe*, and then parliamentary correspondent for the *Montreal Star*, before taking off round the world – it would seem that brilliance rather than patience characterized her progress. During those years she was feverishly productive, writing regular columns for the *Week* as Garth Grafton or S.J.D. in addition to her daily newspaper work. Then, before any savour of routine could dull the piquancy of her writing, she dropped out of Canadian journalism.

Duncan's career path of a successful apprenticeship in the United States, which enabled her to win a start in Canada, was fairly common among the first generation of Canadian journalists. Ambitious Canadian women writers found that they had to go abroad to enhance their reputation or find more attractive employment. Margaret Graham began her career in journalism in Halifax in 1889 doing the sort of marginal work available to women in Canada at that time. But after a few years as a freelance writer in New York, she won the plum assignment of covering Ottawa society for the *Halifax Herald*, and by 1904 she was selling her Ottawa commentary to the distant Vancouver *World*.[52] Lily Barry proved her abilities by acting as verse editor and reviewer, women's page editor, and Canadian edition editor for the well-known New York magazine *Collier's Weekly* from 1893 to 1896, before she took over the women's and children's departments of the *Montreal Star*. Ethelwyn Wetherald had already had a few years' experience on the *Globe* and the *London Advertiser*, when she sought to broaden her journalistic experience by working for the *Ladies' Home Journal* in Philadelphia. But although the American literati were willing to embrace her as one of their own, the pull of her Canadian roots brought her back.[53]

The comparatively huge American market and the more enterprising commercial environment afforded a greater volume and variety of opportunities for women writers than the Canadian scene. Despite these advantages, women journalists were often reluctant to leave Canada permanently. Mary McOuat was one of the temporary emigrées who found herself stranded in the United States. As a staff member of the New York *Recorder* and *Tribune*, she had earned a reputation for her "solid and wearing qualities" in journalism. But she was proud of her Canadian roots – and also of her father, the distinguished scientist and academic Walter McOuat. In a letter to another expatriate Canadian woman journalist, McOuat confided that she was "a stranger and a pilgrim in the land." She added, "Nothing but circumstances over which I have, at present, no control, would keep me away from my own country. I am always looking forward to going back, and hope at least to lay my bones in British soil."[54] Eventually her wishes came true. By the turn of the century she was back in Canada, working in the editorial department of Ottawa's *Evening Journal.*

One of the most successful of these emigrants was Eve Brodlique. Like Sara Jeannette Duncan, she had reached the apex of opportunity open to a newspaperwoman in Canada. She covered the House of Commons as the sole parliamentary correspondent for the *London Advertiser* and was the only woman in the press gallery until Duncan arrived in 1888. Brodlique gained a widespread reputation for accurate and unbiased "telegraphic political work," and her articles, signed Willice Wharton, attracted attention all across Canada. But Canada did not provide enough scope for her ambition.[55] So, although she claimed she would always be a loyal Canadian, she sought fame and fortune in the United States. By 1896 she was a staff writer on the Chicago *Times-Herald* and president of the Chicago Women's Press Club. Although Canadian newspaper work was changing, it had not done so fast enough to keep her: "The change in American journalism, which made a place for women, came rapidly, while in Canada, the taint of old-time conservatism clung persistently, and the change came slowly."[56]

Although Brodlique professed to being a "strict Sabbatarian," she held that the absence of Sunday papers in Canada was largely responsible for the dearth of opportunities for women journalists. The American magazinelike Sunday supplements had a huge appetite for the kind of entertaining features which women writers frequently made their specialty.[57] Moreover, the competition among rival American Sunday papers was especially fierce and involved their proprietors in upward spirals of extravagance and size, all to the benefit of those who wrote for them. In Canada the Saturday edition of the more enterprising papers such as the *Globe* served much the same purpose of weekend entertainment. Toronto's popular *Sunday World* was, like the *Globe,* entirely produced on Saturday to avoid infringing the Lord's Day Act. When the *Toronto Star* launched its weekend supplement in 1910, Elmira Elliott Atkinson's views about the Sabbath persuaded her husband to call it the *Star Weekly* instead of the *Sunday Star.*[58] These weekly editions carried book reviews and children's pages, music and drama, notices, and humorous personal essays. But Saturdays were not uniformly a day of rest in nineteenth-century Canada, and the Saturday newspapers did not have the same leisured quality as the American Sunday papers.

MAKING A NAME: PERSONALITY AND PERSONA

An interpreter of the Canadian literary scene at the turn of the century, Walter Blackburn Harte, charged that Canadian inhibitions deprived its journalism of the lively contributions that women were making in the United States. He blamed "the lingering English prejudice against the development of strong personalities, with its natural sequence of signed articles – a common feature of every Sunday paper in the United States to-day" – for turning ambitious women away from the profession and forcing others into "work of a character which offered little or no opportunity of making a reputation."[59] But Harte overestimated the force of this "lingering English prejudice" against parading personalities in the columns of Canadian newspapers. In this respect, Canadians were led more by American traditions than British. Where a British writer counselled her readers not to use their own names or striking pseudonyms in their women's newspaper writing if they had any intention of ever doing "better" work, Canadian women were happy to broadcast their names or their pen names.[60] Gone were the days when a genteel writer such as Agnes Maule Machar shielded her literary persona, Fidelis, even from her family.[61] Laura Durand, under the androgynous pseudonym Pharos, endowed herself with the powers of lighting the darkness. She used this name for her children's page in the Toronto *Globe*, but she expected that anyone who cared to would discover her real identity; correspondents who addressed her as if she were a man irritated her.[62] She was more than a little petulant when the critic Thomas O'Hagan omitted her from his article on Canadian women writers: "I could not but be contemptuous of one who carries his enquiries so short a way."[63] But although the lofty classical reference in her pseudonym may have indicated her sense of professional mission as a beacon of enlightenment in a benighted world, it hardly advertised her gender. No more revealing was the L.B.D. with which she signed "The Library Table." Yet she demanded personal recognition for her accomplishments.

For the most part, Canadian newspapers were more than willing to publicize their female personalities. Kit was a byword for readers of the *Mail*, just as "Madge Merton's Page" was a banner headline over the reconstituted women's section of the *Toronto Star* in 1900.[64] Similarly, Sara Jeannette Duncan had become such a celebrity by 1888 that her movements were reported by other journalists. The names of women journalists were commercial commodities which they and their newspapers marketed. With the notable exception of Garth Grafton and Louis Lloyd, few of the first rank of Canadian newspaperwomen chose male

names as their pseudonyms. Yet almost all of this generation of women
writers felt compelled to use a pseudonym of some sort. So did most
American women writers: Annie Laurie, the most famous of the "sob
sisters" was really Winifred Black Bonfils, just as Nellie Bly was Elizabeth
Cochrane. Pseudonyms were, of course, a deeply etched convention in
newspaper writing, one that had originally served to enhance freedom
of speech. For women, however, the motive for disguise was different. It
was a psychological necessity to create some barrier between the public
personality a woman writer projected for her readers and her private
identity. An alternate identity could also be an emblem of freedom.
Sandra Gilbert and Susan Gubar have observed how "the pseudonym
began to function more prominently as a name of power, the mark of a
private christening into a second self, a rebirth into linguistic
primacy."[65] A pen name became a pen-creation of self – a larger-than-
life archetype of whatever style of femininity a woman writer chose to
represent.

In the United States there was a tradition of rather silly pseudonyms
for women writers; Fannie Fern (Sara Willis Parton) and Jennie June
(Jane Cunningham Croly) were the most famous writers for mid-
nineteenth-century American women's papers. It was as if the writers
aimed to disarm with coyness those who might charge them with
boldness for venturing to express themselves. Thus, when the expatriate Canadian, Mary Bouchier Sanford, proposed to call herself Tabitha
Twitters for a series in the *Home-Maker*, editor Jennie June was enthusiastic, even though she had earlier suggested that Sanford devise a male
pseudonym: "View's of any kind, are accepted, or laughed at from a
woman that would be considered silly, or impertinent from a man and
you want to be able to say anything."[66]

Most Canadian women writers tended towards sobriety rather than
levity in their choice of pen names. Agnes Ethelwyn Wetherald took her
grandmother's name, Bel Thistlethwaite, for her newspaper writings;
Irene Currie Love also took a family name, Margaret Currie, to masthead her long-running column in the *Montreal Star*. Alice Fenton
Freeman not only made the name Faith Fenton, known to readers of
the Toronto *Empire*, but she made it famous when she reported from
the Klondike for the *Globe*. Kate Simpson Hayes, as Mary Markwell,
stood alone in the women's pages of western Canada's newspapers for
many years. Writers of society gossip may have had some reason to
disguise their real identity, since they circulated as social intimates
amongst the people they later turned into copy. But the masquerade
was hard to maintain for long. "The Marchioness" may have fooled
some of the Ottawa *Free Press*'s less-informed readers, but when in 1900
the National Council of Women identified women journalists in the

ranks of women working in Canada, Agnes Scott stood revealed.[67] By
the same stroke, Lady Gay was unmasked as Grace Denison, and Sama
as Emily McCausland Cummings.

Only on the periphery of the Canadian newspaper scene did the use
of male disguises linger on. Grace Campbell wrote for years for the
Saint John *Progress* under the name Geoffrey Cuthbert Strange. At the
other side of the nation, an immigrant Englishwoman, Julia Henshaw,
chose Julian Durham for her "serious" writing and G'wan for her
"women's work." As well, there may have been many "outside contributors" who successfully hid their female identity under a male pseudonym and thus will never be revealed. In any case, there were comparatively fewer male than female bylines in newspapers, and it was probably
easier to win fame as a female rather than male newspaper personality.
By the turn of the century, when there were strong incentives for
appearing as a woman, especially as a writer for female readers, most
Canadian women journalists were prepared to publicize their newspaper selves. Cora Hind, who became the most authoritative commercial
and agricultural journalist in Canada, had a specifically feminist motivation for promoting her identity as a woman. When she was beginning
her career as a freelancer in the 1890s, she was exasperated to discover
that the editors of the two trade journals she contributed to attempted
to shroud the female authorship of her material so as not to detract
from its credibility. "E.C. Hind" insisted that henceforth her articles
would appear under the name E. Cora Hind. "I felt I owed this to other
women writers," she told her friend and biographer Kennethe Haig.[68]

Despite the misgivings of Walter Blackburn Harte, then, it was
possible for a Canadian newspaperwoman to win fame, if not fortune,
through her professional personality. In any case, the sort of renown
newspaper personalities won through even daily exposure was fleeting.
Harte's surmise that only a few determined women would accept the
"drudgery of daily journalism for the excellent training it affords"
suggested that newspaper work was not a career in itself but merely a
stopping post en route to more laudable achievements in literature.
Sara Jeannette Duncan topped his list of prominent Canadian women
journalists, and by 1891 she had already left Canadian journalism and
launched her career as a novelist.

LITERARY LONGINGS

Journalism became an increasingly logical preparation for would-be
writers as the evolution of the ethos of reportorial "objectivity" combined with the literary genre of "realism".[69] Duncan consciously used
journalism as an apprenticeship for a more permanent contribution to

literature. Having found her literary feet writing about things that happened to her or that she observed first-hand, she decided to gather as much of that sort of experience as possible to draw upon in later years.[70] Newspaper work gave Duncan the opportunity to investigate all sorts and conditions of people in the course of her daily round, as well as the discipline of daily production and almost instantaneous audience response to what she wrote. Yet even the self-confident Sara Jeannette faltered occasionally in her grand design to become a novelist. In her autobiographical essay, "How an American Girl Became a Journalist," the heroine, Margery Blunt, traded her immature "secret purpose" to distinguish herself in literature for the more practical ambition of writing a political leader.[71] Ultimately, though, the real Sara Jeannette Duncan nurtured her own secret purpose and willingly relinquished the work-a-day life of journalism for marriage and a productive literary career.[72]

Duncan's attitude towards journalism was perhaps more calculated than most of her female colleagues. Even so, almost all the women who achieved some prominence in the nineteenth-century Canadian press not only entered journalism to make money but also aspired to literary success. Almost all wrote stories, poetry, or novels in addition to their regular newspaper or magazine work. Agnes Laut, after her 1895 debut on the *Manitoba Free Press*, used journalism as a licence to travel all over North America gathering material for what would be a literary career writing stories of the frontier. As she put it, "I was bumping up against reality; farmers, miners, pioneers, half-breeds, navvies – history was being made by these men before my eyes, and I simply described what I saw and felt."[73] Laut continued to write articles for Canadian magazines but found sufficient literary success for her novels to live and write on a country estate in upstate New York.

Ethelwyn Wetherald, who took over the "Woman's World" department of the *Globe* when Duncan left, subsequently became the principal editorial writer for the *London Advertiser* while she co-edited a women's magazine called *Wives and Daughters*. But for all this journalistic activity, she saw herself as a poet rather than a newspaperwoman. Even when she seemed headed for striking success as literary editor of the prestigious *Ladies' Home Journal* in Philadelphia, she sighed for the contemplative life. "I shall be rather glad to go back to Fenwick and the sweet realities of life away from the bubbles and baubles of journalism," she confessed to Wilfred Campbell.[74] Later she recalled why journalism frustrated her: "It was a lasting dissatisfaction to feel, at the end of each day, that I was too tired to do any creative work of my own."[75] Although Wetherald worked as a journalist sporadically from the late 1880s into the early years of the twentieth century, her primary commitment was to poetry. Thus she limited her forays into journalism and was able to achieve the kind of reputation her talents warranted. One critic pronounced her *House of Trees* the best collection of poetry ever written by a Canadian woman.[76]

In contrast, Grace Blackburn was not able to focus on poetry and left only hints of a fine literary sensibility. The professor who summed up her career warned readers that her literary reputation should rest not on "the efforts inspired by journalistic demands" but on a few poems that reflected her essentially lyrical nature.[77] The daughter of Josiah Blackburn, owner of the *London Free Press*, Grace Blackburn had once yearned to join Canada's nascent literary community; she had an acute critical sense, which writers such as Arthur Stringer appreciated.[78] In her newspaper persona of FanFan, she was responsible for many editorials as well as the literary and dramatic criticism in the *London Free Press*; as a member of the founding family, she served also as assistant managing editor.[79] Like so many Canadian women journalists, Blackburn must have found that the enormous appetite of the periodical press for articles, reports, and chit-chat devoured her creativity and channelled her output towards the easily digestible piece that would satisfy and soon be forgotten.[80]

Given the commercial aims of their proprietors, daily newspapers were the best possible forum for the talents of Jean Blewett. She was a poet and writer whose work was easily assimilated and was enormously popular with her audience. In her case, a literary reputation preceded her journalism, and it probably earned her her first newspaper opportunity when the Toronto *Globe* decided it needed a popular figure to compete with the irresistible allure of "Kit of the *Mail*." Blewett's colleague on the *Globe*, Laura Durand, was witheringly contemptuous of her abilities, commenting, "She writes poor prose and worse verse and is entirely mediocre in range and sentiment; yet there seems to be a conspiracy abroad to foist her into Canadian literature."[81] Blewett's fans evidently disagreed with Durand's estimation. Her homespun philosophy and maudlin little tales suited the newspaper-reading public and charmed even the literary critic Thomas O'Hagan.[82]

The fact that Blewett's cousin, Eve Brodlique, was so successful in newspaper work may have encouraged the young poet to veer towards journalism as a way of broadening her literary horizons. Brodlique was the more successful journalist of the two, but she in turn may have envied Blewett's literary reputation, for she confessed that she "would rather be a poet than anything else in the world." Despite being called by Walter Blackburn Harte "the most practical newspaper woman in Canada," Brodlique laid claim to an artistic spirit that "longed to get away from the noise and grime, and chatter of words."[83] For Elmira

Elliott Atkinson, marriage to the newspaper tycoon Joseph Atkinson afforded her the financial security she required to fulfil her literary ambitions. Although she continued to write for newspapers and magazines,
she cultivated her poetic aspirations. These culminated in 1915 when she
won the London *Bookman* prize for her poem "Green Gauntlet."[84]

It was not surprising that young women with poetic yearnings and a
passion for scribbling should want to enter journalism.[85] Novices saw it
as an exciting opportunity to practise their craft and be taken seriously
as writers. But experience soon disenchanted the idealists. A sense of
disappointment pervades the private confessions of those whose
literary longings could not be realized in the daily grind of newspaper
work. Florence Randal (later Livesay) was typical in her lament to her
diary in 1904: "It's so tiresome to have a little literary ability that will
never amount to anything and yet hounds one out of laissez faire. I
never had any pretension to ability above the usual one of people 'with'
a gift for that sort of thing and yet there comes so often the sense of
failure."[86] To avoid such a conflict, Mary McOuat abandoned the
literary ambition of her younger days. Writing to a fellow Canadian
woman journalist who was writing a novel, McOuat demurred, "I
attempt nothing outside of my work for the paper, for that takes all my
strength and if I tried to write things I want to write they would turn out
to be trash, and there is enough of that on the market now."[87]

The ephemeral nature of writing for the daily press – the knowledge
that however good one's piece, it would be thrown out with yesterday's
rubbish – haunted those who wished to make a permanent contribution to Canadian letters. What was true for literary women was, of
course, equally true for men. Joe Clark of *Saturday Night* charged that
the medical man scribbling at his leisure would have a better chance of
literary success than the journalist who had "exhausted in routine
labour the forces that are required for literary production."[88]

Kathleen Blake Coleman, whose literary ambition remained unre-
quited, struck a philosophical pose in a letter to Katherine Hale (Amelia Warnock Garvin) on "our ephemeral work," whose fate it was to be
"wrapped around the charwoman's chop ... to go into the poor home –
where the great authors never go – haply to be read, a line here, a line
there, as the chop is being eaten, and some little message of hope or
comfort to cheer a meagre heart, worn with worry and effort, then to
help light the fire." She concluded, "Ah, comrade, fancies may be, but I
love to think that the newspaper has its own great separate work to
do."[89] The *Edmonton Journal*'s obituary of "Kit of the *Mail*" regretted the
fleeting nature of her work: "It is one of the tragedies of newspaper
work that a great deal that deserves to live appears in the daily press,
makes a strong impression for a day or a week and then is forgotten ... It
isn't right that one who for more than a generation brightened and

stimulated so many lives and who provided such faithful pictures of so many different phases of the Canadian life of her time should pass out of the public memory."[90]

Kit's friends were unanimous in their faith in her apparently boundless talent, and they lamented the way that newspaper work, week in and week out, absorbed her creativity and all her mental and physical resources. One of her friends and admirers, a successful Canadian woman journalist and novelist residing in the United States, wrote to Kit urging her not "to waste herself in journalism but to write the novel that she could write which would bring her more permanent fame."[91] Perhaps unknown to her friends, Kit was in fact working on a novel, though she never published it.[92] As she congratulated Mary Bouchier Sanford, a Canadian journalist working in the United States, for writing a novel, she admitted, "I have struggled with a like enterprise for some time but owing to the press of work, and poor health, worry etc., have entirely shelved it. There seems to be so little time for anything outside the daily routine – that is the worst of journalism."[93] It is likely, too, that she harboured misgivings that her novel might not live up to the expectations her public had of the great Kit. With her sharp critical faculties, she had no great faith in her purely creative ability. For instance, in 1899 she wrote to John Willison begging him not to oust anyone from the *Globe* Christmas number on her behalf because her story "might not be acceptable." She explained, "I am a poor writer of stories – as no doubt you know, but I am anxious to get on."[94]

MAKING MONEY

Aspirations for the higher flight of literature notwithstanding, the first generations of women journalists needed money. Writing novels or poetry was not sufficiently lucrative to support them – and in many cases their children too. Jean Blewett, although she had established a considerable reputation as a poet, badly needed the income newspaper writing ensured. In 1905 she wrote to John Willison asking to be taken on salary at his new venture, the Toronto *News*: "If you felt fifteen dollars a week was too much you could make it less, the thing is that I may have a certain amount coming in regularly for a while."[95] She explained that her husband was sick. Because she had a well-known name, she may have felt entitled to ask for the same salary as a man. (In 1905 J.H. Cranston, with six years' experience and a university degree, earned fifteen dollars a week reporting for the *Toronto Star*.[96]

Women often had no idea what to ask for in payment. The retiring young poet Ethelwyn Wetherald was baffled when asked to name her price for the pieces published in the *Globe*. She later recalled her bemusement: "After considering the pleasure I had had in writing them, the honor of appearing in the *Globe* alongside L.C. and S. [Archibald Lampman, Wilfred Campbell, and Duncan Campbell Scott] and the dazzling possibility of an increase in salary later on if I didn't ask too much at first, I replied that a dollar a piece would be about right."[97] Wetherald would not intentionally have impaired the earning power of her female colleagues by asking too little. But even when John Cameron enticed her away from the *Globe* to become a principal editorial writer on his paper, the *London Advertiser*, in addition to the responsibility of editing *Wives and Daughters*, she was reluctant to press for a suitable salary. Her one-time colleague on the *Globe*, E.W. Thomson, scolded her for her meekness when she subsequently moved to the *Ladies' Home Journal:* "For goodness sake set a high value on yourself and your services. Don't let anyone imagine that you could stay in Philadelphia for $100 a month! You are sure to get a good chance – but if you do not act shrewdly in your bargaining those fellows will be like John Cameron was, living on the credit of your brains, and paying you a most wretched pittance, and working you out of all reason, and making a slave of you." Thomson urged her to hold out for $1,500 a year after her month of trial at the *Journal* and to expect $2,500 to $3,000 in the near future.[98]

Since Thomson was for a time editor of the *Youth's Companion* in Boston, he might have been expected to know the American salary range for journalists. Yet he and other Canadians often had an exaggerated notion of how much American papers paid.[99] Wetherald's employer, Edward Bok, tried to inject a note of realism into the discussion when he raised the issue in the *Ladies' Home Journal.* In response, one of his fellow editors observed, "We are supposed to pay our women better than any paper in New York: yet of the lot, the highest paid receives only 42 dollars a week. She is generally credited as getting 100 dollars a week but, actually, she gets what I say, since I pay her each Friday. And hers is an unusual success."[100] Had Wetherald pressed for the salary Thomson envisaged, she would have almost approached this summit. In any case, the gentle Wetherald was hardly likely to confront Mr Bok, a man she wryly described as looking perpetually "fresh from a bout with a punching bag and a cold shower."[101]

Journalists' salaries varied enormously, and neither men nor women could expect to get rich. An Ontario wage survey for 1884 estimated the average salary for a newspaper reporter to be $550 a year – less than $11 for an arduous and long week's work.[102] It is little wonder that Sara Jeannette Duncan took a sardonic tone when she answered a correspondent's inquiry about the salary a woman journalist might expect. She gestured with one hand towards the dizzying height of $6,000 that was reputedly reached by the American journalist Mary Mapes Dodge for editing *St Nicholas*. With the other hand, she pointed to the pittance paid by "local newspapers for amateur poetry." Advising her reader to use her "unassisted imagination" to negotiate the descent, she added somewhat ominously, "I am firmly convinced that that is the most comfortable way of accomplishing it."[103]

It was the need for an income, however small, that induced Mary Agnes Fitzgibbon to tap out her first literary efforts on a typewriter in order to support herself and her child. Niece of Lady Macdonald and stepdaughter of the Conservative MP D'Alton McCarthy, the young Mary Agnes Bernard was launched into the best circles of Ottawa and London society. When she married Clare Valentine Fitzgibbon, grandson of the Earl of Clare, she seemed destined to continue a charmed life. But her married life ended disastrously with her husband confined to a mental institution.[104] She moved back to Canada to live with her mother and stepfather, but calamity struck again. D'Alton McCarthy was mortally injured in a carriage accident and his estate was not sufficient to support his widow as well as his stepdaughter and her child. With no training beyond a good secondary education and a well-rounded general knowledge gleaned from conversations with Canada's cultural and political elite, Mary Agnes Fitzgibbon began to turn out articles on a variety of topics. Later she was able to admit how ill prepared she had been for the career she undertook: "I never thought of writing until within the last five years, and have none of the 'training' of which she [her correspondent] speaks."[105]

Despite her inexperience, the fact that Fitzgibbon had well-placed friends helped launch her career. One of them passed her early productions on to J.S. Willison, editor of the *Globe*. As an "outside contributor" of articles on Doukhobors and new settlements in western Canada, Fitzgibbon gained sufficient credibility as a journalist to earn a regular position as a columnist by 1901. Writing "Driftwood" for the *Globe* gave her some regularity of employment, but financial security eluded her for most of her life. Willison remained a loyal patron and hired her to conduct the "London Letter" for the Toronto *News* when he became that paper's editor in 1903, but three years later he raised the spectre of ending her column. Fitzgibbon was devastated: "It is such a blow that I can hardly think the matter out. I have been from the begining [sic] of my journalistic career identified with your editorship, and it was a source of really great pride and pleasure to me, not only a matter of steady earning power ... I am absolutely [sic] dependent now, on my own earning power, and it will mean a tremendous struggle to find some other means of making up the loss to my weekly 'wage' if my 'News' letter cease."[106] Evidently on very friendly terms with Willison, as the intimate tone of her correspondence indicates, Fitzgibbon gained a

Mary Agnes Fitzgibbon (Lally Bernard of the Toronto *Globe* and then the *News*), dressed as the Duchess of Kent for a fancy-dress ball given by Lord and Lady Aberdeen, December 1897 (F.W. Lyonde/NA, PA-138846)

reprieve for another year. When she returned to Canada, her fellow newspaperwomen in Toronto regarded her as the "glamorous career woman" because she wrote political news from Westminster.[107] But as the main support for an invalid mother and grown-up but chronically ill daughter, Fitzgibbon constantly teetered on the edge of insolvency as she moved across the country in search of health for her dependents and stability for herself.[108]

It would seem, then, that even the best social connections, talent, enterprise, and personal charm were not enough to ensure a woman journalist a secure income. Fitzgibbon's situation, that of a gentle-woman thrown back on her own resources by a reversal of circum-stances, was typical of many of this first generation of women journal-ists. Emily Cummings, for instance, was well connected, but it was not mere happenstance that she entered the society department of the Toronto *Globe* the year after her husband died. Although Willoughby Cummings had been a barrister, he had not left his widow in circum-stances that would allow her to maintain her social position without resort to her facile pen.[109]

Women who longed for literary recognition had to make do with what newspaper work offered if they were the breadwinners. Kate Simpson Hayes, separated from her husband with two young children to support, had to put aside her literary explorations in order to stave off the "hard, binding beastly poverty" she had tasted in her first years as a self-supporting woman in Regina. "Time is my master, not my servant," she told her would-be mentor, Lawrence Burpee.[110] A similar breadwinner was Kate Lawson, who wrote as Katherine Leslie for the Toronto *World*. She had been raised to earn her living as a wordsmith, following the example of her mother, Jessie Kerr Lawson, who had supported her husband and ten children by writing for the periodical press of mid-nineteenth-century Scotland and Canada.

In the late nineteenth century, when educated women with refined literary aspirations began to seek work in newspapers and magazines, the contradiction between their need to earn and their status as "gentlewomen" created tensions which they internalized. The career of Kathleen (Kit) Watkins Coleman poignantly illustrates this plight. With two unhappy marriages behind her and two young children to support, she did not have the leisure to develop her literary talents methodically. When Christopher Bunting offered her a salaried position as the women's editor on the *Mail*, she was relieved and grateful. The lofty posture of sophistication she assumed in her newspaper persona persuaded many of her friends that she stayed with the *Mail* year after year out of loyalty and that she was indifferent to mere money. Her colleague J.V. MacAree regretted her lack of ambition: "Many times when Kit was living and often since her death we thought that she was wasted on this paper. The most popular feature writer of her day in the Canadian newspaper world, she was paid about twenty dollars a week. We doubt if she ever received more than $25. Had it been her luck to have written in the United States she might have been taken up by a publisher like Hearst or Pulitzer and made as famous as Dorothy Dix or Ella Wheeler Wilcox, and as richly rewarded. We do not recall an American woman writer of her time who was in her class."[111]

While there is no evidence that Kit looked for opportunities in the United States, she certainly sought advancement in Canada. She wasted no time in asking for a job when John Willison left the *Globe* to start his own paper: "I have been debating for some time as to whether I shall send in my resignation to the *Mail and Empire* and try for work on some other paper, or retire altogether. I like journalist work too well, however, to give it up yet awhile; also I need the income I receive from it. The many changes in the *Mail and Empire* office have not tended to make the position so desirable that I would not be willing to resign it, but I would like to be sure of another appointment before I give it up."[112] Kit's value to the *Mail* was widely acknowledged, and she told

Willison that on the two occasions when she had offered her resignation the manager had asked her to withdraw it.[113] But although her
paper traded on her name and exploits, she was not treated as a star on
assignment. The big-name reporters who had covered the Spanish-
American War for the American papers had earned up to $200 a week
and been relatively pampered.[114] Kit had earned no more than her
regular salary for undergoing conditions of considerable hardship: she
claimed to have had to forage for berries and to share her small supply
of quinine and fresh water with the wounded soldiers.[115]

Ultimately, it was a struggle over money that caused her resignation.
Asked to write a daily column in addition to her weekly two pages and
with no additional payment, she left the *Mail and Empire* in 1911 after
twenty-one years of service, and began to syndicate her popular column.[116] That she refused to sell her material to her old paper attests to
the depth of her anger with her long-time employer. Commiserating
with Katherine Hale in 1913 about the shabby treatment dealt the
young writer by the *Mail and Empire*, Kit gave vent to her own grievances: "But what else did you expect of the d— family compact? My dear
the man D [W.J. Douglas, managing editor] is the meanest soul that
ever was put into a body. Oh, I could tell you tales! I was with them 21
years – think of it – and when I returned from Cuba absolutely coinless
– I met with a rebuff from D – and when, in 1898, I married Dr. C—
[Coleman] I got nothing in wish or gift or anything save 'We won't lose
you by this?' How could they lose one pinched as we were!"[117]

Clearly, even her third marriage did not rescue Kit from financial
pressure. Since Dr Theobald Coleman could not earn enough to
maintain his family, Kit continued to write, sending in her weekly
column from the desolate mining town of Copper Cliff, where her
husband practised and which she abhorred. She carried on her work
when the family moved to Hamilton, and she continued writing her
syndicated column right up to her death from pneumonia in 1915. Kit
Coleman wrote to make a living, yet in her literary disguise she implied
that her writing was debased by mercenary motives. In a reverie about
women in olden times, who were not "always so alive to dollars and
cents as now-a-days," she rebuked herself: "'Why are you writing for, my
friend,' quoth I to myself, 'if not for those same greasy, stained, ragged
but inexpressively powerful greenbacks?'"[118] Yet on another occasion
she scolded a correspondent who had inquired about a writer's earnings: "It is an honor to write for nothing, if you write well. One must be
very humble about one's own value in the literary world."[119] In practical
terms, Kit Coleman obviously felt that she deserved more income than
she received, but her "literary" self tried to transcend the pursuit of
mammon. Although she wanted to achieve a lasting contribution to
literature, her newspaper career got the best of her.

The first generation of Canadian women journalists tended to invest more idealism and talent in their work than could be fulfilled in the narrow branches of journalism usually assigned to them. The author of the guidebook, *Press Work for Women* (1904) cautioned her readers that the opportunities open to women were simply "not worthy of the powers, knowledge and training of the highly cultivated woman," and she predicted that a woman who was determined to do only the finer kind of work in journalism would be destined for a middle age of "hack work and poverty very close to destitution."[120] Laura Bradshaw Durand was one who should have heeded this warning. Although she did not attend university, she had been privately educated to an exceptionally high degree of literary refinement, and her abilities must have been obvious to John Willison, who in 1892 gave her the chance to inaugurate the book review department for the Saturday *Globe*. Durand was also responsible for starting the *Globe*'s children's page, "The Circle of Young Canada," which gave many promising young Canadian writers, including Marjorie Pickthall, their first thrill of publication. When Durand began on the *Globe*, she was in her early twenties and had only a couple of years' experience in journalism.[121] Despite her youth, she was able to bring credit to her department and win some respect for her work. Emily McCausland Cummings described her as a "remarkably clever writer," whose "reviews in particular are criticized most favourably by men and women of learning."[122] J.S. Willison called her "one of the very best all round journalists on the Canadian press."[123] In these early years, Willison would have had little cause to regret hiring Durand: she was singularly dedicated to her work. As another colleague noted, "Laura Durand works very hard, giving up all social pleasure and every kind of recreation. As her work is unsigned [it] gets little encouragement or praise. Tries to read the books conscientiously and review them justly ... Her work is considered clever. In fact one person said she is more widely read and cleverer than all the older journalists put together."[124]

Yet the praise of a few of her colleagues was not sufficient to satisfy the fierce pride of this remarkable woman. In fact, she seemed to resent as presumption any comments about herself. For instance, when she found that Emily Cummings, the only other woman on the *Globe* staff at the time, had been asked to describe her, she bristled with indignation: "I can only say that no mere acquaintance knows me less than Mrs Cummings or is more thoroughly incapable of doing so or, I should express, constituted by nature and training to do so."[125] Personal animosity obviously motivated the vehemence of Durand's protest, but there can be little doubt that she felt herself to be unappreciated. When Mary Bouchier Sanford contacted Durand, hoping to make her a subject in a projected series of articles on Canadian women journalists, she received a scolding for her pains. Durand believed that anyone who wanted to know about her should read her work and not ask others for their opinions. She advised Sanford to give up her project rather than crowd her subject's achievements into the insufficient space her editor would allow.[126]

Laura Durand was proud of her accomplishments. Although she called herself a "serious person not too sanguine of success," she boasted that her children's page was the most popular department at the *Globe*, drawing hundreds of submissions from children all across Canada.[127] Her pride was well founded, for "The Circle of Young Canada" tradition persisted for decades as a characteristic feature of the paper. Moreover, she enjoyed unusually liberal opportunities on the *Globe*, which enabled her to demonstrate her abilities. An editorial series she did on the massacre of Armenians in the 1890s stimulated Canadian action on behalf of the persecuted.[128] She excelled in literary criticism. In Britain, Ethel Arnold, the niece of Matthew Arnold, won a reputation for her book reviews in the *Manchester Guardian*, but this was rare.[129] An experienced woman journalist cautioned aspiring newspaperwomen "to abandon all thought of reviewing, which is the prize of the journalistic profession."[130] Nevertheless, Durand was trusted with the Saturday book department, a dense page of literary commentary that usually covered five or six volumes of every type, from poetry to history, and even science. Durand admitted that she "braced herself" to do the work and found it taxing.[131] For this effort, she demanded editorial autonomy. On one occasion, she took exception to a missionary tract which claimed that Christianity was the sole remedy to right the wrongs of women in India. When Willison "killed" the review, she immediately offered her resignation: "Will it not be best ... to partition my work, placing a man, very conservative in views and of not so rigid a literary conscience, as reviewer, giving him latitude as is done on the best journals, and let me retain only the editorship of the children's page at a greatly reduced remuneration of course? I can eke out a livelihood by space writing and outside contributions, having three fourths more time. I strongly advise you to have a man as reviewer; you will trust his judgment and so be saved what must be racking anxiety over my literary work."[132]

In his reply to Durand's long diatribe (in which she not only upbraided Willison for his views on women's legal disabilities but also poured out her grievances against her father and the general malaise of the world), Willison's tone was measured. He assured her that he would not interfere with her private opinions but pointed out that "a unity must be preserved throughout the paper and no one can make the opinions of a paper except its editor."[133] Willison had given Durand exceptional leeway, a year's leave of absence to nurse her sister, the poet Evelyn Durand, through the last stages of tuberculosis. Understanding her despair at her sister's death, Willison did not fire her, even though he seemed hurt by her outbursts "Your attitude towards me has become one of hostility and defiance."[134] It would seem that Laura continued her turbulent ways with editors less lenient than Willison. Yet another storm with an editor provoked her final severance with the *Globe* in 1910. E.W. Thomson, a former *Globe* editor, applauded Durand's fighting spirit and suggested that editors habitually bullied women.[135] Nevertheless, Laura Bradshaw Durand was henceforth cast adrift on the uncertain seas of freelance writing, where making money was a constant struggle.

A BOHEMIAN WORLD

Notwithstanding the specific details of individual personalities, which inevitably complicated professional relationships, the question of how women journalists should be treated was a perplexing one to newspaper editors. Women were still unfamiliar figures in public positions of any sort. Writing for the press might seem to be a "genteel" occupation, but newspaper offices were not gentle environments. On the contrary, there was a tradition of convention flouting that newspaper folk revelled in – a reputation for hard drinking, smoking, swearing, and other "low life" pursuits.[136] In attempting to promote a more "professional" visage for the journalist, Walter Blackburn Harte regretted that "in Canada something of the old Bohemianism lingers " but hoped that new methods and new personnel would import respectability.[137] But the legends of the "boomers," the quasi-hobo adventurers who moved from one city to the next tossing off brilliant articles in an alcoholic daze, were part of the lore of newspaperdom. These stories lent an ultramasculine aura to newspaper work which male journalists were reluctant to renounce.[138]

In an era when women were still treated with exaggerated formality, when to appear before a lady in shirt-sleeves verged on the risqué and the street language of the pressroom was positively crude, it was perhaps not surprising that newspaper editors were apprehensive at best and implacably hostile at worst towards the idea of a woman in the office. Women with the audacity to invade their sanctums were not always treated with common courtesy. Marie Joussaye, a young working-class woman who won some fame as a labour leader but failed to make her way in journalism in the Toronto of the 1890s, later complained to J.S. Willison of the treatment she had met in newspaper offices: "The worst was scandal. If I spoke to an editor or haunted a newspaper office, there was an evil construction put upon it. Nobody seemed to think it was the paper I was after, not the editor – so far as I was or am yet concerned, the editors are all alike to me – merely the gateway to work and success. Young men pushed themselves forward by sheer persistence and a little talent, but what was permitted to them, was resented in my case."[139]

The would-be woman journalist and the male editor approached each other with caution and some trepidation. E.E. Sheppard, who welcomed many newspaperwomen into their jobs, complained that the young ladies who applied for a position on his newspaper expected to be escorted when they went out and "waited upon when they come in."[140] Outrageous as such demands might seem to the city editor, from the point of view of a woman living in an age when to be unaccompanied at night was tantamount to street-walking, an escort would have been a great comfort. For reasons of respectability and expediency, women were encouraged to confine their newspaper careers to the column or feature written in decorous safety. The *Girls' Own Paper* advised its readers to avoid the reporting branch of journalism altogether: "As things are at present the girl reporter has to assume a bold mien when, with her notebooks, she takes her place at a table among perhaps a dozen men ... It is not an occupation which tends to the development of feminine graces."[141]

Almost as soon as women journalists entered the workforce, they entered the popular imagination. Literature and magazine articles portrayed them as brazen hussies toughened by exposure to the world and the company of men. Lily Dougall, herself a writer for her family newspaper, the Montreal *Witness*, contributed to the stereotype in her novel *A Madonna of a Day*.[142] Her heroine, Mary Howard, smoked cigarettes, drank wine, and gambled with her male colleagues. She thought nothing of walking about Fleet Street at night. "You are very much behind the times if you think English girls over twenty-one need anyone to take care of them," she told a rather horrified Canadian missionary who had inquired about her work. "Why, you know, we have been in all sorts of out-of-the-way places. Of course it was often dangerous, but that made something to write to the papers about.[143]

Dougall's anxiety about the coarsening effect journalism had on a young woman's character was shared by others who could not reconcile the Victorian ideal of femininity with the advance of women's opportunities in a variety of occupations in the late nineteenth century. Journalism was the most controversial of these new experiments simply because the worldliness and the publicity function of the newspaper diametrically opposed the private sphere of "true" womanhood. To be a nurse, teacher, stenographer, or even a doctor was to carry on in the public realm, for wages, some of the duties women performed in private life. But to be a reporter was to gather facts about the world and to broadcast them; it was to know far more about life than womanly modesty – or, rather, ignorant innocence – could accommodate.

Edward Bok, editor of the *Ladies' Home Journal*, discovered that many women journalists had misgivings about the propriety of their occupation. In 1901 he conducted a survey among newspaperwomen and male editors, asking them whether they would allow their daughters to enter a newspaper office. He had an overwhelmingly negative response. Of forty-two newspaperwomen who responded, thirty-nine, many of them mothers, said they would not allow their daughters to follow in their footsteps. While some of their objections were simply to the strenuousness and irregularity of the life and its ill effects on health, most of the women protested on moral grounds. They complained, among other things, that the "freedom " of the work, the lack of regular hours, and the foul language and behaviour of male journalists afflicted the character of the woman who worked with them. One protested, "No! no! a young girl gets too close to the Tree of Knowledge in our business." Of the men, thirty replied to Bok's questionnaire and all replied in the negative. "I would rather have my daughter starve than that she should have ever heard or seen what the women on my staff have been compelled to hear and see" was a typical response.[144] Without inquiring too deeply into Bok's motives or his veracity as a pollster, it is evident he judged that *Ladies' Home Journal* readers were intrigued by women journalists but somewhat censorious about them.[145] His survey confirmed their prejudices. Newspaperwomen were public figures; a magnetic-print personality was the chief asset a woman journalist possessed. But as with all celebrities, people's curiosity about the intermingling of private person and public persona was occasionally more prurient than wholly admiring.

WOMEN JOURNALISTS AS PUBLIC COMMODITIES

As women began to occupy a place in newspapers, the public became fascinated, not just with what they wrote but also with who they were. The woman journalist herself was part of the newsmaking formula. She was more than a carrier of news that was of interest to women. Her presentation of herself as a newswoman was sufficient to generate public curiosity. Some of this interest translated into a fascination with the physical appearance of presswomen. Often it was their business to write about fashion and beauty, and inevitably their own looks became part of their professional apparatus – much to the discomfiture of those who had no interest in style. Mary McOuat had to respond to some bogus information about herself that, on one hand, intimated that she would wear nothing but silk and, on the other, suggested that she feared to look feminine. She had to admit that she could not afford to wear silk, but protested, "The femininity of my appearance has always given me satisfaction. It covers a multitude of sins."[146] Constance Boulton, gossiping to Mary Bouchier Sanford, reported that the music critic Seranus (Susie Frances Harrison) was the "most untidy looking person imaginable" and lamented that artistic and literary people were often unkempt: "'Kit' [Coleman] is perhaps the only exception in that respect I know of here and she succeeds in making herself one of the most conspicuous and most talked of women in Toronto by her remarkable costumes, appearance and conduct." That Boulton was making a moral rather than purely aesthetic judgment is plain by her follow-up complaint that there was a "ring of insincerity and often vulgarity" in Coleman's writing.[147]

As the most famous newspaperwoman in Canada, Kit Coleman was bound to attract comment. But she had a penchant for personal drama and may have courted notoriety, though no one knew better than she how to keep one's private life mysterious. Her fans adored her red hair, cinnamon brown eyes (occasionally reported as sea grey), and glamorous costumes; her detractors coolly noted the shabbiness of her gown, her "dusty, old chip hat," and her "face like a mask, powdered heavily, impassive, hard, cruel."[148] On many occasions Kit betrayed a teasing indifference to the conventional appraisals expressed by her readers.[149] She had made her newspaper self the transcendent female oracle of infinite worldly wisdom, entirely above the opinions of the merely commonplace.

While Coleman parried with her readers to keep them at bay, some women journalists dealt with the problem of visibility in a male-dominated profession by de-emphasizing gender in their choice of clothing. Melville Hammond, an editor on the *Globe*, criticized the tendency of early women journalists to dress in a "mannish" fashion and said he was grateful that women journalists had abandonned the practice.[150] Hammond did not identify the women he had in mind. Certainly, his comments would not have applied to two of the pioneer women on his paper, Sara Jeannette Duncan and Mary Agnes Fitzgibbon. Duncan had found no incongruity between the "new woman" style of feminism she projected in her columns and her love of finery. In her *Globe* column of 17 June 1885 she had lectured her readers to "wear not one glove-button or yard of embroidery the less ... because of these latter-day privileges of ours." Yet she recognized that women in the public eye had to be prudent in their choice of apparel. In her novel *A Daughter of To-day,* her heroine, Elfrida Bell, tries to use her attractiveness to make headway as a journalist. Dressing in her most devastating costume to beguile the editor of the *Consul*, she retreats in wilting humiliation when her intentions are too crudely interpreted by a vulgar office boy.

A ladylike appearance was vital to Mary Agnes Fitzgibbon's sense of her professional identity. Fitzgibbon took care that the external image she projected fused with the well-educated, well-to-do gentlewoman persona she adopted in her newspaper work. As she admitted to J.S. Willison, "I frankly confess I lived well – dressed well – went everywhere and carried out your policy of doing things well as a *Globe* correspondent."[151] Although Fitzgibbon successfully cultivated her professional image under the pseudonym Lally Bernard, she was less comfortable when her public attempted to invade the private woman. In her "Driftwood" column for the *Globe* on 26 September 1903, she deflected the prying of a reader: "I cannot give more of 'myself' to the readers of 'Driftwood' than I have done in the past. I don't think that in private life I am a person very much interested in personalities, either concerning myself or others ... I am just a very ordinary woman, leading the same life as thousands of other women." On another occasion, she was even more explicit in her refusal to lift the veil: "My correspondent asks me to make known my personal identity, what my daily life is, what I do, and to give more to the world the joys, the sorrows and the personal note which they believe to be the strong point of feminine writing. This I believe to be wrong. The whole education of a woman from the time she can speak is mainly that of reticence and restraint as far as her personal likes or dislikes are concerned, or her intimate personal joys or sorrows."[152]

Lally Bernard's reluctance to write about Mary Agnes Fitzgibbon accorded with the Victorian ideal of private womanhood as well as with her own sense of her professional mission to communicate events and ideas. But her readers' estimate of the importance of the personal element in feminine writing was more accurate. For the most part, women journalists were not valued for their abilities as objective reporters or editorial commentators. It was precisely in the obsession with "personality," which Fitzgibbon claimed to disdain, that the opportunity and success of the first generation of women journalists lay. It was their job to communicate "the woman's point of view" and to create in print an archetypal Woman to respond to whatever topic or situation suggested itself.

Coleman was the most successful of this generation of newspaperwoman and the most consummate weaver of legends about Kit. Obscure as her private life may have been, she created for her public a charmingly opinionated woman of the world. She scattered hints through her columns of many lovers, many travels, and an idyllic aristocratic childhood in the misty isle. That she was not an aristocratic Blake but was the somewhat more plebeian Catherine Ferguson and was eight years older than her official biography averred, only underscored her talent for myth making.[153] She created the sort of "self" guaranteed to attract public popularity and increase the circulation of her newspaper. It was a worthwhile investment for the *Mail and Empire* to send Kit to Chicago, California, and England. Her employers even tolerated last-minute extensions to her itinerary, such as a spur-of-the-moment trip to Mexico. Her copy was always interesting and profitable.

At the height of her fame, when Kit became the world's first officially accredited woman war correspondent – covering the Spanish-American War in Cuba – the *Mail and Empire* capitalized on her personal fame rather than on her skills as a reporter, which in fact were considerable; her ingenuity and industry in Tampa and in Cuba won her unstinting praise from the world's best male reporters, despite their initial dismay at the presence of a woman in their midst.[154] But although the *Mail and Empire* insisted that it had gone to the expense of sending its own correspondent in order to get a Canadian perspective on the war, it was evident that Kit's status as a "female personality" was her chief qualification for the job.[155] While Kit was on the assignment, the *Mail and Empire* continued to subscribe to the services of the male correspondent it shared with the *New York Herald,* and his anonymous reports appeared daily on the front page with the "hard" news items, while Kit's usually adorned the Saturday edition, placed somewhere in the middle alongside the "soft" human-interest and entertainment features. Similarly, the official news of the war appeared under the standard objective headlines encapsulating the story, whereas the banners over Kit's columns paraded her name: "Kit's Experiences at Tampa amidst a Hail of Bullets" (11 June 1898) or "Kit's Description of the Embarkation of Troops at Santiago" (18 June 1989). She starred in her own stories. How she felt and how she came upon her information was an integral part of her "news." Indeed, simply by being there, Kit made herself into news, just as a decade earlier, in less heroic times, Sara Jeannette Duncan had made news by travelling round the world.

In this era, women's anomalous presence as news gatherers was in itself newsworthy. Even the usually decorous *Globe* did not scruple to emblazon its front page with Faith Fenton's heroic exploits en route to the Klondike.[156] But the fact that editors were eager to promote the female "personalities" on their staff did not necessarily mean that they took the women seriously as journalists. From his experience as the editor of a woman's magazine in London, Arnold Bennett berated the whole subclass of women's journalism.[157] He bewailed the way women journalists were allowed undisciplined licence in the practice of their craft –

Faith Fenton, Toronto *Globe* correspondent, on the Stikine route to the Klondike, 1898 (H.J. Woodside/NA, PA-17213)

that editors tolerated sloppiness, poor punctuation, and lax punctuality by women when similar failings in a man would end his career.

Bennett's notion of women in journalism as a "second species" chimed with the patronizing reception many women journalists encountered. It did little to raise their sense of self-esteem. Mary Agnes Fitzgibbon seems to have internalized a sense of inferiority when she explained her shortcomings by referring tó the upbringing of young ladies in her day: "We women are brought up in an atmosphere which compels us to suppress any original ideas ... There is so much repression, so much, 'don't dear,' when we are small, that we get little chance of thinking and giving utterance to those thoughts in a manner which would interest the public. No, as far as I can tell, it is a struggle for a woman to get upon broad enough lines to make a really good journalist."[158] Even the apparently self-confident Sara Jeannette Duncan did not believe that women had the necessary attributes for conventional newswriting: "Reporting, with its unhesitating word and rapid phrase, its necessity for vigilance and penetration and perseverance and the ability to condense is not so well suited to their rather limited and uncertain views of things and their diffusive inclinations in talking about them."[159]

On the whole, the press treated its female members as diversions, accessories to the main process. In 1890 the *Manitoba Free Press* – which only a decade later became a harbour for serious and talented women journalists such as Cora Hind, Lillian Beynon, and Kennethe Haig – dismissed the appearance of women newspaper writers as a mere New York fad: "Unlike men, these aspirants for journalistic laurels regard the task of composing available newspaper reading about as seriously as they would that of sewing on their buttons ... Journalism with them is not a profession but a pastime."[160] Nevertheless, if the public wanted "the woman's point of view" and advertisers wanted to reach the public, newspapers would encourage their female writers to market their "womanliness." There were different journalistic standards for newspaperwomen. While male newswriters were required to hone their facts and write crisp copy, women journalists could indulge in "fine writing," a term of abuse in the newsroom. As Stinson Jarvis put it, female subscribers wanted "what newspapermen call 'guff' – that is by turns worldly wise, aesthetic, practical, sentimental, humourous, pathetic," and he hinted that they cared far less than men that their newspapers should supply them with absolute fact. The newspaperwoman, he wrote, was "one whose imagination is her daily bread," a person who "must not be entirely a prohibitionist with regard to untruth."[161]

The occasional male columnist also had a byline and a popular following – The Flaneur (H.H. Wilshire) of the *Mail*, for example, and Caleb Jenkins of the *Globe*. But projection of personality was not the norm for the male journalist, except insofar as his editorial voice represented the collective personality of the enterprise. The journalistic ethos taught the individual reporter to subsume his character under the masthead of his paper, much to the regret of those who aimed to raise the stature of the ordinary journalist. Joe Clark regretted the tradition of anonymous journalism which denied the (male) journalist any public recognition for his contribution,[162] and it must have been galling to find the newspapers taking such pains to advertise the names or pseudonyms of their female contributors and revelling in their feminine individuality. This vaunting of personality apparently came as a surprise to the writer of "In Fair Woman's Sphere," a new feature of the Vancouver *World* in 1895: "I had expected [my column] to be run as a regular department of the paper, emanating presumably from the regular staff, but perhaps it was too much for me to expect the aforesaid regular staff to shoulder all my shortcomings."[163]

Within their "Woman's Kingdoms" or "Worlds" or "Spheres," the most successful of this generation reigned as queens, each one alone in her contained department. As long as they did not overstep their borders, they were given remarkable latitude. But they could not advance, nor could they branch out. They could do no more than exploit the personalities they created for the newspaper, whether it was the spirited "new woman," the "fine lady," or the oracle of worldly wisdom. Although there was a certain cachet attached to being among the first generation of women accepted into the ranks of newspaperdom, the gloss soon wore off for most of them. The disparity between their personal literary aspirations and the commercial motives of their employers, between their public personae and private selves, and between their sense of status and their perceived lack of recognition and respect was disappointing. The most successful were allowed opportunities for personal aggrandizement that newspaperwomen would not enjoy again for generations, yet they were less committed to newspaper work per se than those who followed. The smell of printer's ink was the addiction of a later generation. A similar malaise afflicted male journalists whose aspirations went beyond the confines of reportorial work, but the most talented and ambitious moved on to other fields – such as law, politics, the civil service, and finance – fields that were not open to women.[164]

Because the women journalists of the late nineteenth century were the first, they were isolated within their separate spheres, though some private friendships did spring up between women on rival newspapers. Kit befriended Jean Blewett; Jean and her cousin Eve Brodlique were fervent fans of the great Kit. Grace Denison of *Saturday Night* shared a sophisticated appreciation of the ways of the world with Coleman and was also friendly with Faith Fenton of the *Empire*. Meanwhile the gentle, attractive Ethelwyn Wetherald managed to maintain a friendship with the irritable Laura Durand. But these women had no forum for professional collegiality. The bar and club of male camaraderie were off-limits. Moreover, some of them did not even experience the company of office mates. Coleman wrote her copy in her Toronto boarding house and delivered it once a week to the *Mail*, and although Ethelwyn Wetherald spent some time in newspaper offices in Toronto and London, much of her writing issued from her farm home at Fenwick.

Ultimately, a number of the nineteenth-century pioneers in journalism took steps to overcome their isolation. The legacy they left their followers was the Canadian Women's Press Club – an organization that allowed newspaperwoman to socialize and cooperate for mutual advancement. The first generation also left legends that acted powerfully on the imaginations and aspirations of subsequent groups of women journalists. Theirs was a hard act to follow. The first women who followed in their wake canonized Madge Merton, Faith Fenton, Sara Jeannette Duncan, and, most of all, Kit of the *Mail*. Peggy Balmer Watt, when still a newspaper novitiate, met the great Kit, and in later years, after a career spanning the continent and half a century, she remembered the peerless Kit Coleman as the mother of them all: "At that time women journalists in Canada could be counted on the fingers of one hand. Kit made it possible that we were even recognized. Behind her skirts we crept gropingly forward ... What a fighter she was! What a leader! The romantic days of women in journalism is [*sic*] no more. Today we are a well-organized army. Let us never forget who blazed the trail for us."[165]

CHAPTER THREE

The Canadian Women's Press Club and the Quest for Professional Status

Journalism is not exactly a profession, not exactly a trade,
not always a means of livelihood.

J.S. Willison, *Reminiscences Personal and Political*, 1919

THE ORIGINS OF THE CLUB

When Margaret Graham discovered that the Canadian Pacific Railway Company issued press passes for promotional excursions to newspapermen but did not extend the courtesy to women journalists, she accosted its publicity director, George Ham, to demand equal treatment. Having spent the past fifteen years working for various newspapers in Canada and the United States, Graham felt she had earned her status as a journalist and wanted the perquisites that attached to the job. Her specific aim was to get to St Louis to cover the world's fair. The response to her sally was patronizingly jovial: George Ham challenged her to produce twelve women who were bona fide journalists. When Graham hastily assembled a group of sixteen who were employed on newspapers and could persuade their employers to assign them to cover the fair, Ham conceded the point.[1] More than that, he personally shepherded the coterie of women journalists to St Louis and laid on luxurious touches – fresh flowers adorned their carriages each day, and each afternoon they had a special tea.

During that trip to St Louis in 1904, the Canadian Women's Press Club (CWPC) was born. Until a significant number gathered in the Pullman car that was taking them home from the fair, newspaperwomen as a group had been invisible. Although women had been working as journalists for decades, their status was anomalous, and they were isolated from one another, scattered in newspaper offices across

Some of the founding members of the Canadian Women's Press Club en route to the world's fair in St Louis, June 1904. *Front row, seated left*: Margaret Graham (later Horton); *standing, centre front*: Irene Love (later Archibald), Kate Hayes; *back row*: Katherine Hughes, A.H. Notman, Mary Dawson (later Snider), three unidentified, Robertine Barry, unidentified, George Ham, Peggy Balmer Watt, and C.E.E. Ussher. Kit Coleman was not pictured with the group (NA, PA-138844)

the country. In order to validate their collective presence in the Canadian print world, women journalists needed a professional association. George Ham was present when this original group decided to organize a club for their mutual support and professional advancement. Indeed, the club's historians often credited him with the idea of forming the organization, and he became their mascot as the only male member.[2]

Until 1971, when the club altered its name and nature to become the Media Club of Canada and opened its doors to a variety of male and female applicants, the CWPC was dedicated exclusively to advancing the interests of women journalists. This specificity was to define the conundrum faced by the club and its members: they wanted to advance in a field where, in terms of status and numbers, women were peripheral. As was illustrated in the previous chapter, the category "woman journalist" was not universally admired. Indeed, it was their sense of beleaguered isolation that induced these women to seek comfort in one another's company. Yet by associating with one another in an organization restricted to women, the members tacitly acknowledged that they comprised a separate constituency and would be treated as such. Journalism would continue to be a gender-segregated profession for most women.

A history of the CWPC as an institution would be a worthy project for the light it would shed on women's organizations in Canada.[3] The focus here, however, is on the way women journalists conceived their profession – its ethics and practice, the appropriate education and training for it, and its suitability for women. To this end, the club is significant both as a repository of material relevant to the journalists' professional lives and as a forum wherein they expressed their feelings about their status, their relations with colleagues and the newspaper establishment, the kinds of opportunity open to them, and the ways in which they could expand their realm. It is in terms of these discussions that the evolution of the CWPC becomes integral to the history of women working as journalists in Canada. Not all newswomen chose to belong to it, and we cannot know why.[4] Were they indifferent to it? Had they not heard about it? Or were they perhaps contemptuous of an all-female press club? The women who qualified and chose to belong had a conviction that the club was significant in the practice of their craft. It was only through the CWPC that presswomen were able to construct a female network with its own criteria of qualification and merit.

In terms of the all-female membership, the founders of the club had the intention of expanding it, ideally to embrace all women working as journalists in Canada. The CWPC was the first nationally organized women's press club to remain in continuous existence in the world. Other groups of presswomen had organized before, but none on an explicitly national basis. In Britain, for instance, the Society of Women Journalists, formed in 1894, was mainly confined to London and made little effort to extend its scope to provincial writers. In the United States, regional groups were formed in the nineteenth century, the first being the New England Women's Press Association and the Washington-based Women's National Press Association, both founded in 1882, but they had dwindled away by the outbreak of the First World War.[5] In 1885 the Illinois Women's Press Club was formed, and it elected the expatriate Canadian journalist Eve Brodlique as one of its first presidents. Much later, in 1919, when American newspaperwomen based in Washington found themselves excluded from the prestigious National Press Club, they banded together in the Women's National Press Club; but it was not until 1937 that local clubs in the United States formed the National Federation of Press Women.[6] By contrast, the Canadian Women's Press Club, right from its inception, made a conscious and sometimes laborious effort to embrace members from coast to coast and to maintain a regional representation in the executive.

Not only was the CWPC the world's first women's press club with a national organization, but it was also the first national club of working journalists in Canada. The Canadian Press Association, which first met

in 1859, represented the interests of proprietors rather than journalists,[7] and the so-called National Press Club was formed of reporters
based in Ottawa. Other male clubs were city-based, and many had
episodic existences that ebbed and flowed with the tides of newspaper
activity in particular towns. In contrast, newspaperwomen, wherever
they worked, had access to their own national organization even if there
was no local branch. Indeed, it was an oft-emphasized point that when a
woman earned membership in the CWPC, she belonged to a national
organization; the local branches existed for informal fellowship and
had no power to admit or reject members. Throughout the club's
history, the executives made a sincere and often taxing effort to represent the interests of a widely dispersed membership, which included
those who lived in densely populated cities that had many newspapers
and others who worked in rural isolation.

Although they pledged themselves to a national association, the
hastily assembled group that founded the club on the trip home from
St Louis were hardly representative of the various regions of Canada.
Most of the originators were from Ontario, where women journalists
had made the most headway by the turn of the century. The Ontario
members ranged from the famous Kit of the *Mail* to young Irene Currie
Love, a high school contributor to the *London Advertiser* (who, as Margaret Currie of the *Montreal Star*, would one day be as well loved as Kit
was at the turn of the century). Only two of the women, Sara McLagan
and Sara Crowe Atkins, came to the fair from points west of Ontario,
both having travelled all the way from Vancouver. Mrs Sara McLagan of
the Vancouver *World* was something of an anomaly in the group. As the
only female owner of a daily newspaper in Canada, she did not require
a press pass as urgently as the others. She chose to travel a more comfortable route to St Louis, through the United States. By all accounts, Sara
Crowe Atkins, who covered the fair for the Vancouver *Province*, accompanied her.[8] Although the prairie branches were to figure prominently
in the history of the club, only Kate Simpson Hayes represented them
on the inaugural journey. Well known as Mary Markwell of the *Manitoba
Free Press*, Hayes was living in Montreal in 1904 and acting as George
Ham's secretary. Maritimers also were represented only sparsely. Even
though women had contributed to Maritime newspapers for decades,
the only representative was the former Haligonian, Margaret Graham,
and she was at that time working for the *Montreal Star*. In contrast, there
was a strong francophone presence at the first meeting – stronger than
would be seen again in the history of the CWPC. Six women who worked
for French-language papers formed a sizable minority on the trip,
though only a few became members of the club, most notably the
distinguished Robertine Barry, founder of her own paper, *Le Journal de*

The Canadian Women's Press Club at its second general meeting, Winnipeg,
8 or 9 June 1906. Kit Coleman sits seventh from the left in the front row,
beside George Ham. (NA, PA-138845)

Françoise. Barry became the first vice-president of the club when the
famous Kit was elected president. Thereafter, although there was always
a scattering of francophone members, English-language journalists
dominated the Quebec contingent.

It took determination and perseverance to organize so fragmented a
group as women journalists across Canada. Had the future of the club
rested with the commitment of its first president, it might well have
languished. Kit Coleman called herself "a mere sleeping partner who
ought to be deposed at once." She credited Kate Simpson Hayes, club
secretary, with the organizing drive that made possible the first Canadian meeting in Winnipeg in 1906.[9] Hayes contacted more than a hundred women, forty-four of whom attended the Winnipeg convention.
The national railways, counting on favourable publicity from so many
sisters of the pen, were lavish hosts. Both the Canadian Pacific Railway
and the Canadian Northern cooperated to provide private cars for a
round trip through the prairies all the way to Banff. The contrast
between these trips, where the women were the majority, cosseted and
deferred to, and their ordinary lives, where they were isolated and
patronized in a male-dominated atmosphere, was heady. For Florence
Randal (later Livesay), the convention of 1906 represented a spike of
happiness in a long stretch of frustration in Winnipeg. She found it
demoralizing when she returned to the doldrums of her routine on the
Winnipeg Telegram.[10]

The conventions and the railway excursions gave presswomen a sense of collective identity. Although some of them had enjoyed fame and influence as individuals, the formation of their own organization seemed to confirm, to themselves at least, their presence in the Canadian scene. The reports they wrote of their meeting gave voice to their gratification: "For the first time in the pen history of Canada, Canadian women writers have been given recognition and their existence acknowledged by the public. For the first time in Canada the social smile has been granted pen-women wage earners ... Not one woman of the little band worth more than her week's wages, and yet all determined to hold together, to work, to wait, to prove themselves true women of the pen." [11]

That dozens of women were closeted together for a week at a time perhaps accounts for the fund of silly jokes, gossip, and ultimately firm friendships that cemented the club. A mood of schoolgirlish hilarity suffused their write-ups of the week – excitement, hope, and ambition laid in store to provide sufficient momentum to sustain the club through more torpid years, when the difficulty of gathering together hard-working and widely dispersed women seemed at times almost insuperable. The early resolution to meet annually soon proved unworkable – at the Toronto meeting in 1910 only two members from west of Ontario and none from points farther east were able to attend. Subsequently, a triennial format became the rule for national meetings, but even this became difficult during wartime and the depression, when freelance markets froze and the railways tightened their criteria for issuing passes. The triennials of 1916 and 1941 were cancelled. And once, the president of the organization very nearly missed the great event; in order to make the journey from Vancouver to Ottawa, Elizabeth Bailey Price had to borrow money from her son, who was working his way through university.[12]

Despite such difficulties, the members of the CWPC persisted in their determination to maintain their network across the nation, because their club was the only place where they could identify the problems of being a woman in a male-dominated profession. As they moulded their organization, women journalists delineated the shape of their profession as they envisioned it and the space they occupied as working women. The communication lines the club opened among this writing sorority allowed the members to cultivate professional solidarity, though it also hinted at friction within the group itself. The triumphant progress of individual members all too often underscored the malaise afflicting the general category of "women journalists." Over the years, the constituency of the organization and its mandate were debated and refined, demonstrating the way the career paths of women journalists altered to meet changing opportunities and conditions (see table 9). The common thread that united them was their commitment to honourable paid work as writers.

TO MAINTAIN AND IMPROVE THE STATUS OF JOURNALISM

Canadian women journalists eloquently encapsulated the high-minded aspirations they held for their profession in the objectives they enshrined in their club's constitution. These goals were formulated – not at that first railway-car meeting in the United States, but two years later – by the forty or so women who attended the first general meeting in Winnipeg in 1906. The first article of their constitution was a complex and ambitious statement of purpose: "Mutual sympathy, counsel and helpfulness among press women for promoting and protecting the personal and professional interests of its members, and to maintain and improve the status of journalism as a profession for women." In addition, the members pledged themselves to strengthen Canadian national identity in everything they wrote and to raise literary standards in Canadian periodicals.[13]

The original goals remained at the masthead of the club's constitution throughout its existence, even as the membership changed to include a whole variety of women, some rather tangentially connected to the press. These objectives embraced a wide spectrum of concerns and aspirations which the original club members held for their vocation and their place in it. They typified the kind of optimism that heralded women's entry into new territory in the late nineteenth and early twentieth centuries – the confidence that they would make headway as individuals and that as a group they would make a difference in whatever field of endeavour they graced. The club's success rested on the degree to which it was able to fulfil its members' expectations. Hence, a close examination of the context in which the club's mandate was generated is a necessary prelude to judging how effective it was in realizing its fundamental goal of improving the individual and collective status of women in journalism.

The primary object, "to maintain and improve the status of journalism as a profession for women," had an ambiguous phraseology which hinted at the founders' uneasiness about their place in the world of journalism. Had they stated their purpose as simply to improve women's status in the profession of journalism, the aim would have been a straightforward articulation of collective self-interest. But they expressed it obliquely, implying that the profession of journalism itself would require a moral renovation if it were to satisfy the standards of its

Table 9
Career diversity of CWPC members, 1923–1935

	1923–26[1]	*1929–32[1]*	*1932–35[1]*
Newspaper staff	101	92	125
Magazine staff	20	27	33
Newspaper correspondents	50	20	21
Publicity and advertising	29	14	15
Freelance journalists, authors, and poets	119	94	111
Publishing-house writers and editors	11	–	–
Artists in black and white	5	5	6
Unspecified[2]	30	–	–
Total active members	365	252	311

Sources: CWPC Triennial Report 1923–26, "Report of the Corresponding Secretary," 18–19; CWPC
Triennial Report 1932–35, "Historian's Report," 61
[1] Statistical analyses of club membership exist for these triennial conventions. Advertising and
publicity writers who had previously been journalists were first allowed to apply for membership
following the 1920 convention.
[2] The corresponding secretary for 1923–26 reported that some members had not filled in the work
forms sent them.

female aspirants. This statement encapsulated the welter of misgivings
which their contemporaries felt about the suitability of journalism as a
respectable occupation for anyone, male or female. It signalled women
journalists' determination to purify the press for the benefit of both the
public and the women who laboured in it. Their overall goal was to
make journalism into a bona fide profession wherein women had a
place they could be proud to occupy.

The hunger for professional status was integral to that "widening
sphere" which historians of the women's movement locate in the last
decades of the nineteenth century and first years of the twentieth.[14] It is
in this context that the formation of the CWPC belongs. The professional ethos of disinterested service to the public, of qualifications
based on education, and of a form of work in which power and influence ostensibly derived from merit was an extremely attractive one to
women. Unlike business or politics, which emphasized specifically
masculine virtues and vices, the professional creed had nothing in it
specifically to disqualify women or to make the female practitioner
necessarily unfeminine. The ideal of professionalism promised to
create a place where educated men and women could meet in enlightened discourse, united in a common endeavour. It seemed to be an
abstractly neutral ground where expertise and talent defined status, for
as one early journalist put it, "There is no sex in brains."[15]

Both Nancy Cott and Mary Kinnear have described how the potentially gender-neutral qualities associated with professionalism came to

Executive of the Canadian Women's Press Club, Vancouver, 1923. *Front row, left to right:* Mrs A.G. Casswell, Mae Clendenan, Kennethe Haig, Lucy Doyle, Margaret Graham (Mrs Albert Horton); *back row:* Mme E.P. Benoit, Mary Houston, Margaret Lawrence (Mrs M.E. Lawrence), Elizabeth Bailey Price (Mrs J.F. Price) (NA, PA-123230)

be defined as overtly male territory in the late nineteenth and early twentieth centuries.[16] Reality dashed the optimism of women who struggled into the professional colleges and into the unwelcoming territory of the well-established learned professions of law, medicine, and theology.[17] Women trying to upgrade the status of the female-dominated professions of teaching, nursing, and social work had an equally uphill task.[18]

The women who founded the CWPC and their predecessors were intimately aware of the status ambiguities of female-dominated occupations. Almost to a woman, they were fugitives from teaching – the conventional resort of literate women who needed to support themselves. Even the ambitious and confident Sara Jeannette Duncan had taken a brief turn as a schoolmistress. In her *Globe* column of 22 January 1887, she described the plight of country schoolteachers as a kind of martyrdom which she for one was not willing to suffer. Similarly, Cora Hind could scarcely contain her relief when she learned that she had failed her mathematics examination and had thus sabotaged her chance of a teaching career.[19] When she later became famous for her wheat crop estimates as commercial editor of the *Manitoba Free Press,* she proved her ability to put two and two together in a context that was far more congenial to her talent than the classroom would have been. If the humdrum life of an elementary schoolteacher did not enthral, the situation of the private governess was even more distasteful to a woman of independent spirit. As Mary McOuat put it, "I went into newspaper work because writing was the only thing in the world that I could do. I was a governess for a short time, but like Carlyle I would rather die in a ditch than live by such a trade."[20]

For women who had done stints of varying duration in female-dominated professions, journalism beckoned as a fresh opportunity, where they could try their talents and take part in the public life of the nation. Yet unlike law or teaching, journalism's "bohemian" associations undermined its respectability. The challenge of elevating the status of journalism was formidable, particularly for women. Not only were women not a majority in the group, but they were marginal. Nevertheless, a career in journalism seemed to some ambitious and unconventional women to be an ideal way of satisfying their yearning for a respectable and even influential place in the public realm.

One Canadian woman journalist, Eve Brodlique, believed that the optimal conditions already prevailed in the United States, and for this reason she chose to leave a successful if limited career in Canada for the wide-open horizons of America. As she explained, "Although my work was being accepted by my home papers and I was reasonably sure of ultimate success, yet the fact that in the States journalism was everywhere recognized as a profession as dignified and worthy as that of a teacher of mathematics or of morals; as equally dignified and honorable for women as for men, and not jeopardizing to her womanliness, decided me to go into the Union and cross swords, or rather pens, with the women of the States."[21] No doubt a great many American women would have disagreed with Brodlique's rather inflated estimation of the female journalist's status in their country. Rheta Childe Dorr, for one (who was ostensibly an editor on New York's *Evening Post* at about the time Brodlique went to Chicago), was made acutely conscious of her marginal status, which was inferior even to the ordinary reporters on the paper. Dorr's pay cheque gave her concrete proof of this. So did the fact that she was not allowed into the city room and had to receive her assignments and write her copy in the office boy's dark cubbyhole.[22]

Nevertheless, although individuals had their trials, the number of women working on American papers and the positions of responsibility some achieved on them gave rise to Brodlique's optimism. Cynthia Westover Alden ran the women's department of the *New York Tribune* with undiluted authority. In terms that echoed the solemnity of marriage vows, Alden asserted that newspaper work offered "the greatest sense of absolute equality with man, to the woman who will take it for better or for worse, and will consent to find in its work the highest pleasure of life, a consciousness of duty well done, that must make compensation for the abandonment of many other pleasures."[23] To pay homage to her achievement, the CWPC invited Alden to address its first national convention, in Winnipeg in 1906.

As a haven for professional aspirations, the "new journalism" that emerged in the United States, Britain, and Canada in the late nineteenth and early twentieth centuries appeared to present a fresh field. When journalists were no longer serving a particular interest group but were angling for the allegiance of the population at large, the perception that they were performing a public service became more credible. At this time, the press wielded – or at least was believed to wield – a pervasive power to shape public opinion. The veteran Canadian newspaperman Joe Clark compared the editor to a clergyman with a vastly inflated flock: "The editor of a daily newspaper reaches a congregation, not of five hundred, fifty-two days in the year, but of five thousand, or fifty thousand, over three hundred days in the year."[24] The idealistic Clark did not believe that the journals he surveyed even approached their majestic moral mission. Yet less fastidious members of the press corps proudly assumed that they were the public's watchdog. The ideal of "objectivity" became a central pillar of an emerging code of ethics.[25] The more popular newspapers especially fancied themselves as the guardians of society, collectively omniscient and omnipresent, recording and publicizing the life and crimes of their community.

The notion of the newspaper as a public institution gave journalists a sense of responsibility towards their clients, the readers, with no motive other than to keep them well and truly informed.[26] Agnes Deans Cameron, when dismissed from her position as a school principal in British Columbia, echoed Clark's sentiments as she turned to journalism. As far as she was concerned, writing in the public press was a way of continuing her educational mission: "Journalism drew me as offering a wider field, a wider educational field than teaching."[27] Both male and female journalists groped for a professional identity that would assure them the status and security they believed they deserved.

But if journalists were to exercise the moral sway they had appropriated in the public realm, they had to be able to control themselves. Self-governance was the key to professional autonomy in journalism as in other professions. To join the ranks of the respected professions, journalists had to be able to define a professional code of ethics; and in order to enjoin the precepts of their professional code, they had to be able to determine who was inside and who outside the circle of professional inclusion. The effort to achieve even the most rudimentary criteria of professional status baffled journalists, male and female, throughout the English-speaking world.[28] A calling that shaded off at one extreme into literature and at the other into hack ballyhoo was almost impossible to wrestle into a coherent shape. Yet during those years at the end of the nineteenth and beginning of the twentieth centuries when the press was changing dramatically, idealists believed that if only the press could liberate itself from servitude to mammon, as it had from political partisanship, it could become a noble fourth estate. If journalists as a group could bind themselves to their own professional code of honour, then popular newspapers would be able to realize their enlightened destiny.

Some of the founders of the Canadian Press Association believed that it might become a truly professional organization and achieve the kind of regulatory function enforced by the Canadian Bar Association or the College of Physicians and Surgeons. Goldwyn Smith, sage of the Canadian literary scene, challenged the Canadian Press Association to "give to journalism the character and tone of a regular profession." He argued, "Membership of a body which affords such guarantees could not fail to be, like membership of other honourable professions, an additional title to social respect. The legal, medical and military professionals are thoroughly organized; they can make their rules, enforce them against offenders and in the last resort purge their order of anyone who has flagrantly disgraced it."[29] But Smith's idea was hardly practical. Whereas a defrocked minister cannot preach, and a disbarred barrister cannot defend, who would be able to prevent an unethical journalist from writing? Where the press was "free," indeed sacredly free, it would be impossible to enforce a code of ethics.

Even more undermining to the idealists was the reality of commercialism. When unethical journalism could make money, the journalists' employers were loath to rein them in. For this reason it was unlikely that the Canadian Press Association would become the professional college Goldwyn Smith hoped for. As an organization of publishers rather than working journalists, its members' interests were primarily financial. The publishers were interested in profit, not necessarily in public service, though many were quick to highlight their public service if it meant profit. C.F. Hamilton, writing in 1917 for the *University Magazine*, described newspapers as "our eyes and our tongue" and was aghast that "this really vital function" was "left in private hands" and "discharged exclusively as a matter of money making."[30] A few years later, the influential American journalist Walter Lippmann linked a commercialized press to a jeopardized democracy, wondering "whether government by consent can survive in a time when the manufacture of consent is an unregulated private enterprise."[31]

It was the commercial nature of the press that, at bottom, foiled the journalists' efforts to establish an independent professional creed. Journalists could not enforce their own code of ethics when they were employees of men interested mainly in what was good for business – whatever would sell papers and lure advertisers. Judith Robinson, the fiercely independent political writer who started her own weekly *News* in Toronto, aired the fundamental contradiction between public interest and profit in her summation of Joseph Atkinson's career: "A large daily produced at a profit is not necessarily corrupt, even though that paper has given much space to the condemnation of the profit motive in business. But the publisher who regards news as a product to be prepared, packaged and sold for profit, like any other product, is apt to be corrupt. For news is not lard or sausage meat."[32]

The righteous indignation Robinson articulated mirrored a widely held conviction that the press was a public institution entrusted with the sacred duty of informing the citizenry. It was from this ideal that journalists derived their professional mission. The reality in the twentieth century was that newspapers were very large influential businesses. The disparity between the ideal and the reality led to what Minko Sotiron identified as an "unresolved social contradiction between public expectation and private purpose (the publisher's pursuit of profit) ."[33] Powerful newspaper magnates such as Atkinson of the *Star* had, over the course of their careers, transformed the professional idealism of their youth as reporters into the profit-seeking capitalism of their maturity.[34] That a brilliant career should unfold in such a way was the dilemma that historian Paul Rutherford encapsulated when he described journalism as essentially a "headless profession" whose most successful and senior members were at odds with the rank and file.[35]

Male journalists were struggling fruitlessly with the paradox of their quasi-professionalism as women prepared to take up the torch. As newcomers to the newspaper business in the early years of the twentieth century, the women were inspired by the notion of public service as they sought to obtain professional recognition. The founding goals of the Canadian Women's Press Club (CWPC) endowed their quest with a belief that it could be achieved. The charter members entered the field bristling with a sense of mission to uplift both the press and the profession of journalism by the force of their own example.

Most newspaperwomen were not content with the newspapers of their day, though few would have seconded Sara Jeannette Duncan's dismissal of the Ontario press as "politics and vituperation, temperance and vituperation, religion and vituperation."[36] The servings of temperance and religion at least were very much to the taste of the sober majority of early press club members. The Regina *Daily Standard*'s

report of the CWPC's visit in 1906 set out the presswomen's aspirations
in extravagant terms:

The City of Regina is doing fitting honor to a little band of loyal workers whose
influence for good is altogether disproportionate to their numbers. They are
the leaven of the Canadian press, and it is largely due to their exertions, their
example and their precept that the general standard of Canadian journalism
has been maintained at its high level of conscientious endeavour. They
redeem newspaper work from its more material aspects and do much to keep it
alive to its higher functions and responsibilities. As the natural guardians of
the ideals of home life they war incessantly though often unconsciously against
the debasing and corrupting influences of relaxing standards of public and
business affairs.[37]

No clearer expression of women's moral housekeeping role could
have heralded the era of maternal feminist fervour. The reforming
crusade of women journalists spilled over into all aspects of Canadian
society – particularly, as we shall see, into promoting worthy causes
through their columns. When Jean Graham, editor of the *Canadian
Home Journal*, addressed the alumnae of McMaster University on the
achievements of women in journalism, she emphasized that, given the
influence of the press, it was a great advantage to "philanthropic work
and public morals in general to have women in newspaper work."[38]

This collective sense of duty to rehabilitate the press and to reform
society through the power of the press persisted well into the 1920s. If
anything, the shock of the First World War, combined with the triumph
of the suffrage movement, reinvigorated the founding generations'
determination to uplift their calling. Male journalists apparently
seconded this resolve, seeming to endorse the proposition that women
journalists operated on a different plane. In his address to the 1920
triennial of the CWPC, J.F.B. Livesay of the Canadian Press saluted the
idealistic spirit women had brought to the profession: "They have the
courage and ambition to tackle these things from their fresh, sane,
original point of view; they are not and cannot be content to trail in the
traditional paths blazed by their menkind." Livesay urged his audience
to aim for ever-widening circles of influence and authority in the field:
"It must often strike the sincere and ardent newspaper woman how
relatively small is the part played by Canadian women in the control
and direction of that greatest of educational forces, the daily press of
Canada. You cannot hope to exercise your proper influence on politics
unless you can exercise some real measure of influence in the daily
columns of the newspaper that are read by men as well as women."[39]

Miriam Green Ellis's lecture at that same convention echoed Livesay's assumption that women would change the press for the better, but her remarks took a practical turn. She referred to the query of a male acquaintance: "Now that so many good women are going into the newspaper game, it seems to have been elevated. But can you tell me why there are so many poor types of irresponsible boys in the business?" Ellis could only speculate that "the poor salaries may have something to do in allowing poor types to come in."[40] Roy Sayles of the Canadian Weekly Newspaper Association further embroidered the theme that women somehow took a more altruistic approach to newspaper work. Admitting that women often earned less for their work than their male equivalents, he commended women writers for catering to "higher things."[41]

Speakers continued to occupy the moral and feminist high ground in subsequent conventions. Kennethe Haig, editorial writer for the *Manitoba Free Press*, outlined her principles of journalistic ethics in womanly terms, emphasizing the responsibility of maintaining "decency and cleanliness of tone" and warning against that occupational hazard peculiar to journalists – "the drying up of sympathy." She warned, "We have experienced everything, seen everything, hoped everything – or strenuously pretend to the rest of the world that we have. But may our guardian angels preserve us in our varied life from the sin of cynicism, which knows the price of everything and the value of nothing." Meanwhile, her hopeful assurance that "murders and suicides are not the really important items of news now in Canada, where art, music, literature and the church are coming into their own" betrayed an overoptimism that the goals of the CWPC were inexorably being attained.[42]

As if to enforce Haig's wishful thinking, at the next triennial convention, in 1926, two members from Calgary put forward the resolution that the CWPC appoint an advisory committee, whose duty it would be to scan "questionable reading matter." They proposed that the committee forward to the dominion censor a list of newspapers and magazines deemed to be salacious.[43] There is little evidence, however, that the dominion censor or any other responsible body took heed of the CWPC's various offers of advice and assistance. The naive confidence that they could uplift Canadian journalism and Canadian society by their own upright example began to fade as individual members gained more experience. When Grattan O'Leary of the *Ottawa Journal* addressed the club, he explicitly advised his audience to abandon the evangelical mission and concentrate on delivering the facts. "The truth is that men are not evangelists and journalism is not a cure of souls," he cautioned.[44]

By the 1930s and 1940s those women journalists who had worked in a variety of different departments were less likely to espouse ideals about purifying the press and were apt to take an unsentimental view of their work. Indeed, one president, Margaret Lawrence, confessed to a degree of uneasiness about the club's primary goal of "improving" the status of journalism as a profession for women. To Lawrence, this ambition seemed to suggest disloyalty both to employers and to the newspaper-reading public. She preferred the phrase "to maintain the status of journalism" as being more realistic and respectful.[45] Others came to agree with Lawrence. When the CWPC newsletter, the "Newspacket," interviewed a sample of prominent women journalists about whether they believed it was their duty to raise public taste through their writing, most said it was not their business. Doris Milligan, a versatile general reporter who became assistant city editor on the *Vancouver Sun* during the Second World War, cogently expressed a generally held view: "The job of a reporter ... is to report the news whether it is a waterfront murder or a meeting of the district temperance league. It is no concern of the newswriter that murders are degrading and shouldn't be played up on Page One or that temperance is uplifting and should be given more prominence than an 18 Karnak head on page 17." The only ethical consideration Milligan willingly conceded was that perhaps the journalist should resist the temptation to inflate sensation in the hope that she might thereby land on page one with a byline.[46]

MONITORING THE PROFESSIONALISM OF PRESSWOMEN

The more women journalists became integrated into the mainstream of the newspaper business, the more they began to recognize the futility of imposing a code of ethics on the entire profession. Over that same span, they also began to acknowledge the difficulty of enforcing a code of ethics geared specifically to their own circle of women. Initially, in trying to stand as moral exemplars to the profession and the nation, they attempted to contain any hints of idiosyncrasy or flamboyance within their own club. Their honoured first president, Kit Coleman, ran afoul of some of her western colleagues at the 1906 convention when she expressed her rather worldly conviction that the inhabitants of the Philippines had been innocent of lying and stealing until missionaries came among them. When an archdeacon left the room during Kit's speech and other mission promoters present made their displeasure known, Winnipeg presswomen were embarrassed. The *Western Home Monthly* later chided Kit with Christian mildness: "It is always a mistake to sneer at missions, foreign or domestic, and in her heart 'Kit' honors the brave men and women who have given their lives freely for Christ."[47]

At a later convention, members of the club went on guard against the postwar relaxation of mores, particularly when tell-tale signs of it emerged among their own flock. The young journalists who took up newspaper work during the First World War did not necessarily embrace the sober feminist goals of their predecessors and may even have identified vicariously with the bohemianism attributed to the male journalist fraternity. At the Vancouver meeting in 1923 a light-hearted mood took hold in some quarters, but not in all. When a local journalist calling herself Violette suggested in a piece for the convention souvenir booklet that some women enjoyed the occasional tipple, the Alberta contingent was outraged: "Violette may have thought that her article was clever, but coming from a woman it was only vulgar and evidenced a diseased mentality."[48] On returning home, the Alberta presswomen redoubled their efforts to enact prohibition.

The moralizing tone that flavoured the early annals of the club loosened over the years, but the presswomen's sense of being on trial in the newspaper world remained. Few would deny that the impression that any one newspaperwoman left rippled through the male establishment and affected attitudes towards all other women. As Miriam Green Ellis explained, "When one woman elevates herself in her profession, she reflects a part of her glory on all of us ... Do you newspaper women not realize that every time another hits the bull's eye it make you stronger with your editors and in your communities? ... Sometimes one will slip and then we all stumble a bit ... For perfectly selfish reasons we cannot afford to let them."[49] Unfortunately, individual success was not nearly as likely as failure to reflect back onto the collective of women. It was particularly vexing when women made themselves notorious doing a kind of journalism which the ethical and ambitious among them disparaged. Most especially, women journalists longed to shed the "sob sister" stigma that deflated their collective progress as serious newswriters.

Accordingly, many of the ethical sermons that CWPC members directed at each other after the First World War were intended to make women journalists unexceptional rather than morally superior. There was increasingly little in the later ethical pronouncements to distinguish the woman journalist from the male, except perhaps that the woman was expressly enjoined to minimize her feminine identity as she approached the reportorial ideal. Miriam Green Ellis had long worked as an equal among her male colleagues, and she shuddered to contemplate the woman journalist who would exploit her sex appeal to get ahead: "There is no sex in newspaper work. It is a vicious thing and very humiliating."[50] Towards the end of her career, Ellis summed up her creed as that of the "competent reporter" whose duty was to gather straight facts without any descent into "yellow journalism."[51]

Yet even as women reached towards a neutral professional persona, they recognized that they would be judged as women and that their performance would colour attitudes towards other women. At a round table discussion of newspaper and editorial writing during the 1938 triennial, participants concurred that "each woman reporter was to a great degree responsible for the reactions of her men colleagues towards women in general. " Given a mentality that made each woman stand for all, it was, they urged, "highly important that women journalists should strive always to observe a high standard of professional ethics."[52] Reinforcing the point during the Second World War, the "Newspacket" quoted Mary Winspear's CBC broadcast as a cue to members: "Every time a woman takes a difficult job, accepts responsibility and carries it through, she is making it easier for every other woman in the country. And every time she refuses to tackle a job or falls down on one, she makes it harder."[53] Acceptance of this kind of monolithic judgment put the onus on the women themselves to behave as model representatives of their sex.

Moreover, their own club seemed to brandish a coercive power to ensure conformity. From the beginning, the constitution of the CWPC contained a provision for disciplining any member whose acts "would reflect adversely on the profession." The ultimate punishment, expulsion, would result if the general membership concurred with "charges preferred by another member" after the accused had stated her case.[54] Later, this procedure was refined with the provision that the executive would conduct an official investigation of any member whose actions were thought to "reflect adversely on the profession." But although the club created official channels for reporting and investigating transgressing members, it did not define explicitly what kind of behaviour constituted an infraction.[55]

Once fissures began to divide members of local branches, the vagueness of the ethical code and the provisions for expulsion became an issue. During the First World War, Genevieve Lipsett-Skinner proposed that the local branch exercise the "privilege of black-balling anyone whose general reputation made her *persona non grata* to the members but who was otherwise eligible."[56] In all likelihood, this proposal was directed at Francis Marion Beynon, whose antiwar stance had cost her her job and won her the enmity of such staunch patriots as her fellow Winnipegger, Cora Hind.[57] The fact that local branches had no power to accept or evict members temporarily quashed the motion, but momentum for some kind of ruling on the enforcement of ethics was building during the war years.

Just after the war, the Vancouver branch raised the issue of professional conduct when one of its members offended the others by her high-handed manner. Beatrice Green, editor of the society and clubs page for the Vancouver *Province*, failed to mention the names of CWPC members when she wrote up club meetings for her paper. She rarely bothered to attend local branch meetings, yet she sent telegrams in the name of the branch without consulting her fellows. Moreover, she was arrogant and threatening towards her assistants, both of whom were upstanding members of the club. The compounding of these picayune infractions so infuriated her colleagues that they passed a local vote of censure against her and resolved to have her expelled from the CWPC for unprofessional conduct.[58]

Mrs Green may have demonstrated her indifference to "the harmony of the club," but nothing in her reported behaviour was unethical with respect to the profession of journalism. Evidently the members of the Vancouver branch had to learn to distinguish between personally offensive behaviour and professional transgression. It may have been to correct this confusion that Annie Dunn, herself a Vancouver member, lectured her fellows on the question of women cooperating with women at the national convention of 1923: "If women educate themselves now for professional work and citizenship in no other way than by learning how to play the game according to the rules, attending solely to their own morals, past, present and future – coupled with the deep realization that the past life of any individual woman is not the property or business of any other individual woman – then all else will come."[59] Nothing daunted, it was at this convention that the Vancouver branch's effort to expel Beatrice Green reached the dominion level. There, the ethical morass and the impotence of the club became obvious. The executive expressed its unwillingness to define "unprofessional conduct" explicitly, reserving the option of ruling on each case separately. In concluding the matter, the executive maintained that it was "clearly beyond the contemplation of the Club" to present a code of ethics to members.[60]

There was little point in any case in imposing strictures and punitive action on individuals. Membership in the CWPC was voluntary and had little effect on an individual's job prospects. There were always newspaperwomen who saw no particular benefit in club membership and evaded the recruiting efforts of local branches. The widely admired women's editor of *Saturday Night*, Grace Denison, had been on the original trip to St Louis but declined to take part in the birth of the press club. Similarly, Julia Henshaw, the first literary and theatre critic on the Vancouver *Province*, remained outside the Vancouver branch. Most tantalizing of all was the aloofness of Judith Robinson, a political commentator with a nationwide reputation.

The exclusive "closed shop" which doctors, lawyers, and other learned professionals had achieved, and which gave them disciplinary power over their members and prestige in the community, eluded the would-be profession of journalism. As wage earners rather than fee chargers, journalists forfeited their independence and consigned themselves to servitude. In the final reckoning, what the proprietor deemed newsworthy would define what was fit to print. Moreover, the proprietor would decide who were journalists by those he chose to employ. The employee had only the power of persuasion; the employer, that of coercion.[61]

Clearly, women journalists had no power to control personnel in the newspaper business or to define the boundaries of their trade. Nevertheless, within the confines of their own club, they had control over self-selection, and they were intent on exercising it, even if it had little significance outside the group. From the outset, the founders of the CWPC signalled their determination to create a rigorously professional organization of women who wrote for their living. The qualifications for membership were clearly defined. The initial constitution stated that each candidate had to prove that she was regularly employed on a newspaper or periodical, and had been for the last six months, or that she had published and been paid at the regular rates for at least six articles in the past year. She had to be sponsored by two other women journalists who would vouch for her professional calibre. This was not to be an association of "lady writers" whose work, if it saw the light of day at all, appeared in the vanity press. Charlotte Whitton put it candidly: "No voluntary contributors or letter-writers 'to the editor' need apply."[62] Unlike the Canadian Authors' Association, which collected a motley assortment of aspiring and erstwhile writers, members of the Canadian Women's Press Club had to demonstrate every year they renewed their membership that they continued to be active as paid writers. Thus, Emily Murphy was able to boast, "This club is perhaps the most sophisticated club in the Dominion, each member being a professional newspaper scribe, a magazine writer ... [These people know] the 'twist and cross' of wordly matters."[63]

Over the years, new categories of acceptable members were added as women writers broadened their horizons and their career options. First, freelance writers were included, then illustrators of periodicals, then authors of books, stories, and poetry, advertising and public relations writers, radio and screenplay writers, owner-editors of periodicals, and others associated with writing and journalism. But the dictum remained: the applicant for continuing membership had to prove that her income derived from her writing.

The execution of the club's laws varied according to the zeal of the membership committee. But it was enforced, and members were constantly being dropped. If a woman writer had managed to maintain her professional status for ten years and then either retired or ceased to qualify, she had the option of continuing the fellowship of the club as an associate member. While some elderly retired members were glad to continue as associates, others considered it a "demotion." There was some bitterness when freelancers were unsuccessful or when newspaper staffers were laid off and had their personal misfortune compounded by the actions of their professional women's club. Valance Patriarche, a freelance writer, refused to file a work form to show her year's work in 1935, yet she objected strenuously to the suggestion of associate status, she tendered her resignation instead.[64] Florence Randal Livesay also neglected to send in her work form, and after years of special writing not connected to newspaper work, she admitted that her resignation was long overdue. But she objected when threatened with exclusion: "I do think that a friendly jog to my memory might have been given before the ultimatum came."[65]

Firm as the successive executives tried to be in enforcing membership qualifications, there were always those who felt they were not strict enough. The Calgary branch, dominated as it was by newspaper staffers, took exception to a "press club" having so many members who were authors or poets. They wanted to limit membership to women who wrote for newspapers and magazines "dealing with news from day to day."[66] The Vancouver branch, although its early history had been studded with famous poets and writers, came round to the same view by the end of the Second World War – that the CWPC was useless as a press club unless it restricted membership to the salaried writer and jettisoned the poet, artist, and freelance.[67]

The rising generation of women journalists were often impatient with the motives of the older club members, who were inclined to stretch the membership rules in order to accommodate loyal oldtimers and writers for worthy causes. While Elizabeth Bailey Price (who was herself a professional scribe for good causes) was president of the club, she had to hear out the complaints of disgruntled youth that "we are not a real Press Club." One iconoclast went so far as to dismiss her sisters of the pen as "a bunch of old fogies who do very little active work." Meanwhile, the older generation deplored the "flippant attitude of the younger members of the profession," claiming that "they never accomplish anything of real value to the organization or to the community." Sympathetic as Price was with the idealism that still animated the moralistic oldsters, she had to remind them that the press club's mandate was not all-embracing: "We are primarily a selfish organization – banded together to save ourselves first."[68]

The tacit assumption behind the drive to limit membership was that a concisely defined Canadian Women's Press Club could become a professional organization that individuals would have to join if they were to practise as women journalists. The Vancouver branch led the way in probing the power of the club to protect and promote members' interests. In 1921 it expressed indignation that the local dailies were hiring as substitutes and space writers "women who have no journalistic training and who are, therefore, encroaching on the profession." They resolved to supply the managing editors of newspapers and magazines in the vicinity with a list of all those members who were available for piecework, urging them to give preference to club members.[69] But not much came of this or subsequent efforts to persuade newspapers to employ only press club members, for although the club believed that it embraced only thoroughly qualified practitioners, most employers gave membership in the CWPC short shrift as a credential. An exception was the St Catharines *Standard*, where the women's editor, Marjorie MacKay, was amused to discover that the proprietor liked to see her CWPC membership card displayed prominently on her desk.[70] Perhaps such badges of respectability were revered on a small-town paper even though they might be lampooned on a big-city daily.

All told, the CWPC floundered in a circular argument when it aspired to define practitioners of journalism. Its own criteria of membership was not an internal judgment of training and aptitude. Rather, to qualify for membership, the individual somehow had to persuade an employer somewhere to give her a chance. Unless she had a job or had sold sufficient articles, the newcomer would not be admitted. Independently, the club was unable or unwilling to mark the boundaries of the fluid territory of journalism. When it came to specifying what attributes made someone a "professional journalist," the CWPC was no more precise than any other body. For instance, in 1938, when the incoming president Rosa Shaw outlined her program, she affirmed, "We definitely do not wish to see unsuitable people, whether women or men, usurping functions in the service of the press which call for particular abilities and other personal qualifications."[71] But she was mute about what those abilities and qualifications were.

THE DEBATE ABOUT QUALIFICATIONS

Women journalists were not alone in fumbling with the definition of their craft. Male journalists were no more adept at wrestling the calling into a professional mould. The absence of strict qualifications for entry was one of the most serious impediments in the way of full-fledged professional status. No profession could hope to define sound practice if it could not regulate the influx of would-be practitioners. Yet, for women, the permeability of journalism was initially an advantage, since there was no male-controlled college to bar their way. No one, male or female, had to present to the city editor a certificate or university degree, or even to have finished high school.

Even so, the first generation of women journalists were remarkably well educated; on average they were better educated than the male journalists of the day. A number had earned advanced university degrees when women graduates were still a rarity. Helen Gregory (later MacGill), who reported for the *Globe*, had been the first woman to graduate in music from Trinity College, Toronto (in 1886), and in 1890 she had been the first woman to earn an MA from Trinity College. Madge Robertson (later Watt), who wrote a column for the *Globe* in the 1890s before continuing her newspaper work in the West, had been the first woman to earn an MA degree from the University of Toronto (also in 1890). She eventually became a member of the senate of the University of British Columbia. Lily Barry of the *Montreal Star* had graduated in arts from McGill in 1892, while Antoinette Forbes, proprietor of the Windsor *Tribune,* had a BA degree from Dalhousie. Mary McOuat was the daughter of a distinguished academic and held a BA from the University of Toronto, having graduated in 1891. Lily Laverock, whose journalistic career took place in Vancouver, had been the first woman to major in moral philosophy at McGill and had graduated with honours.[72] Although Laverock was offered a teaching position in the philosophy department at Smith College, she chose to remain in Canada.

At this time it was not usual for male journalists to be university educated. John Willison stressed the need for a liberally educated press corps if the Canadian press was ever to become "a sane, well-balanced, progressive force in public affairs."[73] But as Arthur Colquhoun admitted in an article advocating the utility of a general university education for improving the status of journalists and uplifting the overall quality of newspaper writing, "The scale of pecuniary reward for a Canadian newspaper writer is not tempting to a man conscious of talent and anxious to secure a substantial return. Obviously the expense of his education becomes a consideration. In Canada there are few prizes in journalism, so that the inducements to submit to an elaborate system of training are not strong."[74]

The opportunities in commerce, manufacturing, and finance, which, according to Colquhoun, drew off the university men who might otherwise have taken to journalism, were not options for university women. This may account for the comparatively high proportion of cultivated female intellects engaged in the Canadian periodical press. Moreover, the sort of work some of these women did for newspapers and magazines demanded a fair breadth of general knowledge as well as specific expertise. No doubt, the unusual academic accomplishments of Helen Gregory were partly responsible for her being entrusted by *Cosmopolitan Magazine* to cover the opening of the Japanese diet in 1890. Katherine Hale (Amelia Warnock Garvin), who was studying voice in New York when she began to send articles on Wagnerian opera to the *Globe*, had precise expertise in this one field before she branched out into more general criticism. The linguistic skills of two newspaperwomen from Montreal, Lily Barry of the *Montreal Star* and Robertine Barry of *La Presse*, were no doubt useful when they covered the Paris Exhibition in 1900. Similarly, the linguistic virtuosity of Kit of the *Mail* was invaluable when she covered the Spanish-American War and overwhelmed the high-powered American male reporters with her ability to converse in Spanish and thus get both sides of the story.[75]

But an advanced education was not essential, nor was it particularly appreciated; and the fact that anyone with a bent for scribbling could compete in the field precluded the exclusiveness essential to professional status. Some reformers clung to the notion that professional schools of journalism would do for their vocation what the recently accredited law and medical schools had done for those learned professions. Yet the task of defining a syllabus to train would-be journalists – and, more challenging still, to persuade newspaper proprietors to hire only certified graduates – continued to defy those who aimed to control entry into their fold.[76]

Despite the difficulties, schools of journalism began to spring up in the United States and, later, in Britain. By 1916 the United States had fifty-five such schools. Almost as soon as these professional schools were founded, female students enrolled, and by 1914 they comprised around 20 per cent of the student body, thus demonstrating their enthusiasm for anything that might validate their entry into their chosen field.[77] When the University of London established a diploma course in journalism as part of the program to help veterans of the First World War re-enter the workforce, the authorities were rather embarrassed at the swift numerical domination of women. In both the United States and Britain, journalism schools restricted the number of women allowed to register, pleading that opportunities for women in journalism were so narrow that few of the female graduates would find work.[78]

Plainly, women journalists in Britain and the United States wanted the professional cachet of formal education in their chosen field. To have a university accreditation was perhaps of greater advantage to a woman than to a man trying to enter the field. Jean James, who was vice-president of the Ohio Newspaper Women's Association in 1932, spelled out the benefits that formal training in journalism offered to a woman.

It was an opportunity, she said, that women could seldom get otherwise: "It is comparatively easy for a youth with no experience to drift into newspaper work and make a place for himself as reporter, department editor or desk man by the rather simple expedient of garnering a place as office boy and learning the ropes from the ground up. For the young woman this is practically impossible, save in a very few cases."[79]

James had a good point. Women's eagerness to obtain college training in journalism was partly predicated on a realistic assessment of their chances of learning the craft in any other setting. The mentoring process whereby a senior newspaperman nurtured the skills of a junior could be a way of excluding women. In the gender-segregated newspaper setting, newswomen rarely experienced the day-to-day workings of the newspaper as a whole. In 1913 Isabel MacLean explained why the "highest prizes of the profession" went to men; it was because "years of training have given the male journalist the equipment required." Women journalists, said MacLean, were hampered by lack of opportunity: Unless [a woman] had the good fortune to work under an editor of unusual light and leading, she has not been encouraged to extend her activities to a wider field."[80]

In Canada there was no school of journalism until after the Second World War.[81] Canadian women who wanted professional credentials had to go to the United States, where by 1930 more than two hundred and fifty colleges offered courses in journalism.[82] Many of the women who trained abroad never returned to Canada, and some returned only briefly. Flora Davis worked for four or five years on the Vancouver *World* after she graduated from the University of California School of Journalism in 1917, but California beckoned her back in the early 1920s.[83] Jo-Ann Price was another who left Canada after going south for professional training. Her mother, Elizabeth Bailey Price, although a staunch cultural nationalist, was so dedicated to her daughter's advancement in the field that she sold her house to help pay Jo-Ann's fees.[84] In the following years, Elizabeth's friends in the CWPC celebrated Jo-Ann's mounting triumphs as religious reporter for the *New York Herald-Tribune.*

Newswomen already in the field who wanted to enhance their skills could attend the summer writing courses offered at Columbia University in New York. It took an effort of extraordinary commitment to forgo one's summer salary for the sake of professional development, yet some were prepared to do so. Among them was Myrtle Patterson (later Gregory), a rising star on the Port Arthur *News-Chronicle* who yearned for a larger ambit. After taking the summer course at Columbia, Patterson landed a job on the *Vancouver Sun*, and by the mid-1920s she was reputedly the highest-paid female reporter in Canada.

On the whole, however, there was not much enthusiasm in the Canadian newspaper community for an academic approach to journalism. This attitude was still prevalent after the Second World War.[85] A 1940s guidebook, while advocating a general university education, concluded that learning was useless if one did not also have the instincts of a newswriter: "Writing is a craft. The sooner the beginner realizes this and starts to learn his job, the better. The only way to learn how to write is by writing."[86] Seasoned newspapermen were especially hostile to the notion of academic preparation. The Victoria *Times* editor B.P. Nichol ridiculed the very concept of a school of journalism, snorting, "How could you be taught to be a newspaper man, it was preposterous."[87] Lotta Dempsey had faced this sort of reception in the late 1920s when she had requested a six-week leave of absence to attend the Columbia University journalism course. Her boss arranged instead to send her to meet a number of American newspaper editors for a practical course in how the business really worked.[88]

Isabel Turnbull Dingman initially shared the general scepticism about the formal teaching of journalism. A well-educated woman with a master's degree from the University of Manitoba, she had had a strictly "hands-on" apprenticeship in the newspaper business. Over the course of her long career, Dingman had tried her hand at most departments of the field: general reporter, women's section editor, music and art critic, and syndicated columnist. Thus, she was well qualified to become one of the organizers of the new school of journalism at the University of Western Ontario, which opened in 1948. Her belated enthusiasm for professional education was wholehearted, if not without a tinge of self-interest.[89]

Until the period following the Second World War, academic training in journalism had not been an issue that preoccupied Canadian journalists. Women who had been integrated into the business were just as inclined as men to spout the adages of their craft – that a "flair for the work" or a "nose for news" was a more important qualification than a certificate from a school of journalism.[90] Indeed, when it was proposed that a scholarship, named for Kathleen Blake Coleman, be established to assist a female student of journalism at McMaster University, opponents of the scheme chafed against the notion that their gallant heroine should be associated with academic journalism. As Charlotte Whitton protested, "'Kit' was a real 'natural'... she would neigh and champ like a war-horse at the thought of some callous intellectual 'teaching' the flair of a story, the snap of a head-line."[91]

On the whole, the Canadian press continued to subscribe to the legend of the reporter who had learned on the job and could write up everything from a kindergarten graduation to an assassination. Women writers, especially those who had entered the work after the First World War, embraced the "can-do" bravado of all-purpose expertise which the male journalists affected. Evelyn Caldwell boasted about being a high school dropout who had sold her first stories when she was only fourteen and had gone on to become famous as Penny Wise of the *Vancouver Sun*, the first full-time consumer advocate writing for a Canadian newspaper.[92] Harriet Parsons, who initiated a series of extrasessional writing courses through the University of Toronto, prepared a practical handbook for working women journalists. She assumed that most of her readers would have had no professional schooling: "Chances are that you cut your journalistic teeth in a newspaper office on an editor's blue pencil and never read a book on journalism in your life."[93] Experience in the world, not the ivory tower, was the essential qualification of a journalist.

But despite the prejudice against academe, men and women with general university degrees continued to be attracted to journalism. Around 42 per cent had some postsecondary education in 1941. Many of these had had their first taste of printer's ink on a college newspaper.[94] For a young woman without experience who was anxious to enter the newspaper world, a sheaf of clippings from the college rag could make all the difference. This was how newly graduated Edith MacInnes (later McCook) landed her job on the Regina *Post* in 1927. Although she had no experience in paid journalism, the *Post* was impressed by her work for her university paper and hired her sight unseen.[95]

Few women acknowledged that their university background was resented by their colleagues on the paper. University men, however, frequently attested to the contempt and jealousy of their fellows, who assumed that "college men" were pretentious eggheads with little knowledge of the "real" world and that their privileged past vaulted them unfairly above their peers. To a degree this was true; university graduates rarely started at the bottom. Even in the nineteenth century, when a university education was not the norm in the newspaper business, those who had it were exceptionally successful.[96] This may have given rise to the stigmatization of the college graduate on the shop floor. Stuart Keate, when starting out at the Vancouver *Province*, smarted under the vituperation of a fellow reporter who sneered that the privileged elite were out of place on a daily paper.[97] No doubt the jibe hurt all the more because Keate had been attracted to the press precisely because of its "somewhat raffish, below-the-salt" character and because it "did not glorify itself as 'a profession'" and there was no formal training associated with it.[98]

It is doubtful that a university woman would have provoked the same resentment from the average male employee. The work most newspaperwomen did was distant enough from that of the "leg man" or "desk man" to render comparisons irrelevant. In the women's department, however, the university graduate may have caused some friction if she was thought to be receiving preferential treatment. There was a tinge of envy lurking behind Francis Beynon's observation that the woman of the world was "the strong woman rather than the college woman, who had little practical knowledge."[99] Moreover, although college graduates who had joined the "right" sororities did have a decided advantage on the society page, it was their social connections the paper courted and not their degrees.

In aggregate terms, university women were not flooding into journalism.[100] In 1920 the sociologist Elsinore MacPherson did a careful analysis of the careers of female graduates from Canadian universities; of the 3,751 women who had graduated before 1918 and were still living, she was able to account for only 17 journalists.[101] In her explanation of the press's low recruitment of apparently highly suitable female candidates, MacPherson referred to "a particular prejudice against college women and university education in journalism." Perhaps the stigma was warranted, she speculated, on the grounds that years of essay writing could extinguish the desire to write and that, in any case, academic writing would suffocate journalistic flair.[102]

It is equally possible that university-educated women simply could not find sufficiently attractive opportunities in journalism. When Harriet Parsons sent a questionnaire to the female graduating classes of 1938 from McMaster, Queen's, and the University of Toronto, she discovered that journalism was the third most popular choice of career among the job hunters. But Parsons had discouraging news for those who hoped to follow her vocation: "I'm afraid there are going to be some disappointments here – there just aren't fourteen openings for girl journalists this year, or any year."[103] Even as late as 1938, when women had proved themselves in a variety of journalistic specialties, the assumption remained that women, however well qualified and well informed, still competed with one another in the narrow corral of "women's journalism."

The persistence of the "separate sphere" for women in journalism remained the most recalcitrant barrier to women's professional advancement. It outraged Annie Hollis, a former militant suffragette who had worked by the side of Sylvia Pankhurst in the East End of London. A long-time contributor to the *Saskatchewan Farmer*, the Regina *Leader-Post*, and the *Free Press Prairie Farmer*, Hollis was exasperated that women still accepted the limitations that tradition had placed on their abilities. Too many were content to cover only things that were supposedly of interest to women. "Brains have no sex," insisted Hollis. "Training is what is needed, as women engineers, mechanics, doctors, etc are now showing."[104]

RAISING THE PROFILE OF WOMEN AND THE CWPC

As time passed, the original impetus for the all-female club remained; it was the fact that women journalists were usually relegated to a lonely separate sphere. "There is no more isolated creature on the face of the earth than the newspaper woman," lamented Florence Sherk, the women's editor of the Fort William *Times-Journal.* "One gets so hungry for communion with kindred spirits."[105] Miriam Green Ellis, looking back over the history of the club, recalled that women journalists were "considered rather outlaws" and that they needed "each other for strength and comfort."[106] Branch meetings, conventions, and the stream of letters they wrote to one another did something to foster a sense of community among them. The CWPC's dedication to "sympathy and mutual helpfulness" remained a vital prop for the women of the newspaper business, whose egos were so often undermined by the slights and snickers of their male colleagues. Esteem building was part of the hidden agenda of the club. Conventions, in addition to handling the business of the club, were exercises in self-congratulation in which the members advertised the triumphs of individuals as a measure of the group's progress. Raising the profile of women in the field was a more tangible goal than raising the status of the whole profession, and it was one that visibly tested the power of the club to benefit its members.

Predictably, as the CWPC explored methods of enhancing the options of Canadian women journalists, there were setbacks and roadblocks. Newspaper organizations did not always respect the seriousness of this collectivity of writing women. Thus, the club took steps to establish itself in a wider network of associations. One of the first affiliations it made was with a sister organization, the Society of Women Journalists in Britain. But a colonial insecurity came to characterize this liaison, one that veered between obsequiousness and resentment, especially at the absence of reciprocity. The Canadian club had to pay more than 5 per cent of its membership dues so that members posted overseas could make use of the London club's facilities. Yet British women journalists were eagerly welcomed and feted when they came to Canada, even though no levy was placed on their membership. The staunch Canadian nationalist Emily Murphy noted this unequal relationship in her presidential address of 1920 when she announced that the affiliation was about to be dropped. Even so, the Canadians did not forget the slight. Years later, when Kennethe Haig reported on her visit to Britain as the CWPC delegate to the Empire Press Union conference, she gloated that Canadian women were further ahead than their British sisters "both in comparative numbers and in the positions which we hold."[107]

Canadian women were willing to muffle their resentment far longer in their pursuit of recognition from the Empire Press Union. No women had ever attended as delegates until the conference held in Ottawa in 1920, when Marjory MacMurchy of the CWPC and Theresa Billington of the London *Telegraph* became the first women to participate. The presswomen were ecstatic about this connection. Meanwhile, the reception from the imperial pressmen was condescending. Noting blandly that women were now contributing to the press, the author of the conference proceedings lumped his remarks about presswomen into a chapter largely concerned with the wives of prominent newsmen.[108] Nevertheless, the women continued their association with the Empire Press Union. In 1930 the CWPC was again allowed to take part, and it sent Kennethe Haig to London as its official representative. In other years the crux of the matter was money. The women's organization was not as well off as the male institutions and could not afford to send a representative to distant places. When the conference of 1935 was held in South Africa, the CWPC was delighted to piggyback on the Canadian Newspaper Association, which selected Charles Barber as its delegate. The club then chose his wife Mary, co-editor of the Chilliwack, BC, *Progress*, as its delegate: "Where would a newspaper woman in Canada get $1500 and time off for such a trip in times like these?"[109]

Although the prestige of the Empire Press Union seemed unassailable, some CWPC members questioned the practical value of maintaining the liaison when women were so sporadically represented. In 1936, however, a newly launched program of intra-Empire exchanges ignited the ambition of Canadian presswomen. The intended purpose of the initiative was to broaden the experience of young (under thirty-five) journalists by giving them international working experience, but the architects of the plan did not initially contemplate including women in the scheme. The CWPC had to badger the Empire Press Union's executive to ensure that women were considered eligible, and in 1937 CWPC president Isabel Armstrong was elated to receive official permission for women to apply for exchanges – only to have the privilege wither in her hand. Pleading that the Empire Press Union had been flooded by applications from male journalists who wanted to come to London, the secretary said that if Canadian women further complicated the job of placing all these applicants, he would have very little chance of success. Would it not be more practical, he suggested, for the Canadian Women's Press Club to work through some similar organizations in Britain that could more successfully canvass employers for openings for women? (He seemed not to have been aware of the Society of Women Journalists in Britain.) But he did concede that such a manoeuvre would sidestep the Empire Press Union altogether.[110] Ironically, women not connected with the CWPC, may have had an advantage. Elizabeth Ruggles worked on the London *Daily Herald* as an Empire Press Union exchange in 1938, though she had only just started out on the Victoria *Times* and was not a member of the CWPC.[111] It is not surprising then that members of the club later instructed the executive to review the advantages of affiliation with the Empire Press Union.[112]

As the CWPC executive sorted out a new strategy for ensuring its members' opportunities for overseas experience, all such orderly exchanges were abruptly curtailed by the outbreak of the Second World War. But war, in turn, was to furnish a host of new opportunities for journalists. Once again, the club had to fight to ensure that women were identified as journalists and were considered for various postings as the government began to induct newspaper personnel into its propaganda machinery. It was an uphill struggle. In 1940 the president of the club, Rosa Shaw, objected to the fact that not one newspaperwoman had been appointed to any of the many publicity departments – "unless you like to count one who had been put in as a stenographer." In an address to her constituency, Shaw deplored the prejudices that continued to trammel women's career progress: "There is a quaint fixation among some of the boys in Ottawa that women, as a biological fact, are incapable of seeing and writing about the war in the same way as men ... If they talk about newspaper women at all, it is from that mysterious point of view called 'women's work,' probably something to do with knitting or making jam."[113]

By way of action on this matter, Shaw arranged a meeting in October 1941 between a group of newswomen and Canadian government officials. This meeting significantly raised the profile of the club; previously, Canadian officialdom seemed to have been unaware that women journalists had any collective identity whatsoever. Prime Minister Mackenzie King wrote pointedly to Shaw's successor, Dora Dibney, "I would like you to know that we all feel that the recent newspaper women's conference in Ottawa has meant a real contribution to a fuller appreciation of the war effort of our country."[114] Soon afterwards, the meeting began to bear fruit. Maud Ferguson, formerly women's editor of the *Calgary Herald*, was appointed women's editor of the news and features section of Public Information at Ottawa. Eventually a number of specialized and highly experienced women journalists, including Rosa Shaw herself, were seconded to Ottawa. True to form, it was the "women's work" angle that absorbed most of the recruits. The Wartime Prices and Trade Board had the greatest concentration of women journalists because their expertise in advising women in household matters was ideally suited to the war effort campaign to conserve raw materials and food ordinarily sold as consumer commodities. Presswomen operated as promoters of governmental initiative, explaining war effort policy to homemakers and advising them on the best ways to work with the restrictions. The fact that women were included at all was a small victory, but the club took satisfaction in the contribution members were making as prominent civil servants in wartime.

The CWPC executive was also anxious that women journalists gain experience as war correspondents. They were keenly aware of the fact that tour after tour of men left Canada's shores with no women along. When they pursued the idea of a special tour for Canadian women writers, they received no reply whatsoever from chief of the Wartime Information Branch, J.W.G. Clark. The practice of sending women journalists to the front was not without precedent. Towards the end of the First World War, four Canadian newswomen had participated in an all-female tour of the battlefields of France to report the work of women on active service.[115] But as the Second World War broke, the psychological barricades went up again as elaborate restrictions obstructed the would-be woman in the field. For instance, the rule that for every woman on board a ship, there must be a male companion in case of a torpedo attack, discouraged newspapers from sending female personnel overseas. Margaret Aitken of the Toronto *Telegram* was the only woman to cover the London conference of British Empire prime ministers in 1944. She was made to travel in a convoy that took sixteen days while the men in the party made the trip in six days. If Aitken herself made no protest, her colleagues in the CWPC were incensed. Ann Donnelly (secretary of Ottawa branch) asked the national executive whether they should request Aitken to do a piece on the discrimination for the next "Newspacket": "I don't know whether the national exec. could do anything, but it might be worthwhile having Dora [Dibney] ask her if she would make a report to place before the national executive as well." Referring to the recent furore over the salary of Claire Wallace, a radio journalist,[116] she asked, "Why are women picked on? We should be on our toes about these things. So far as I can find out Margaret Aitken didn't write anything for her paper about the discrimination or whatever it was in her case."

Male war correspondents did nothing to encourage their female colleagues to join them overseas. War correspondence was the most unyielding bastion of masculinity in the newspaper business. As the CWPC executive pursued the bureaucracy, members listened to lectures by war correspondents, most of whom discouraged women from front line journalism. Lionel Shapiro, for instance, peppered his talk with humorous anecdotes about the "difficulties arising in the informal life of the soldiers when a woman war correspondent makes her way to the front line."[117] Given the frustrating prohibitions that hedged round women's opportunities, their unbridled pride in those women who hurdled the barriers was understandable. The club newsletter regularly headlined the exploits of Gladys Arnold, Mollie McGee, and, most of all, Margaret Ecker Francis, Canadian Press's star female war correspondent. When Francis became the sole woman to witness the German defeat, her colleagues basked in reflected glory.

The press club could take quiet satisfaction from progress on the home front as well. Despite the fact that newsprint shortages involved cuts to many specialized departments where women had sheltered over the years, the war eventually increased mainstream opportunities for women, though not as quickly as presswomen had hoped. The Vancouver branch jubilantly reported that more women had landed jobs as general reporters than ever before: three newcomers had joined long-time staffers Mae Garnett and Doris Milligan in general work on the *Vancouver Sun*; the hidebound *Province* had finally surrendered the convention that had cloistered women workers in a separate department; and the *News-Herald* had placed eight women on its editorial staff. It was during this period, when so many male journalists enlisted, that a few women finally bridged the status chasm and became city editors or assistant editors. Helen Alexander MacMillan became the only woman editor of a Canadian news service, running the Central Press Canadian for her long-time employer, the Toronto Star Publishing Company.

Not only did women advance into jobs previously filled by men, but the war itself furnished stories that some women handled. Winnifred Stokes, for instance, was the first woman to bring out a "war extra" (for the Niagara Falls *Review*). She later advanced to the position of managing editor, an unprecedented promotion for women in journalism.[118] The *Halifax Mail* had two women writing columns on military affairs during the war; Jesse Coade's "Messdeck News" covered naval news, while Margaret Clarkson Dill wrote "In the Air" on RCAF activities. Margaret Aitken of the Toronto *Telegram* and Rica Farquharson of the *Canadian Home Journal* were the only women reporters covering the wartime conference between Churchill and Roosevelt held in Quebec City in 1943.[119]

According to CWPC president Dora Dibney (one of those who succeeded in a formerly male department), many more women could have taken on "men's work" if their bosses had not been so short-sighted and bigoted before the war. She reproached the male establishment for habitually overlooking qualified women reporters when it came to promotion. Now that there was a labour shortage, she griped, "news editors would like to find all round trained women who could fill ANY job that's going – or coming. And they could IF women had been given a chance to learn all the tricks of the trade, instead of being shunted off to one side."[120]

During the Second World War the CWPC became more assertive and was able to accomplish more for its members, both individually and collectively, than at any time in its history. Moreover, it grappled with the slights and oversights that stalled women's career progress in wartime, while its sister organization in the United States, the Women's National Press Club, was silent in the face of discrimination against women journalists.[121] But even as some members rejoiced in new opportunities, there were those who felt that the CWPC was not doing nearly enough. The "Gripe Column" featured in the "Newspacket" allowed the malcontents to air their grievances. Bitterness pervaded the imaginary scenario written by an unsuccessful journalist about what 1943 might have meant for Canadian women writers: "Back in 1943 our club, which was largely social, suddenly snapped out of it and became aware that only we could help ourselves, that it was sheer waste of time waiting for male editors to discover us and push us ahead. So certain moving spirits of that day proceeded to round up all the idle talent and put it to work. We had a slogan: each member with a job to find one other member whose talent was rusting and get her a job ... Masculine editors, seeing our determination, our sportsmanship, learned a new respect for the once sneered-at sob sisters ... Cautiously at first they began to find places for us that had nothing to do with pink teas, society chit-chat, weddings."[122] Snapping back to reality, the author identified herself only as "one of the forgotten members" who was unable to find work that would put her talents to use.

Clearly, the CWPC as an organization could do little to ensure success for the vast majority of its members. Informally, however, the social side of the club, so disparaged by the disgruntled griper above, furnished a network of connections that did help individuals in their career progress. Lois Reynolds (later Kerr) landed her first job as social reporter on the *Globe* because she attended one of the Toronto press club's social teas, where she met the *Globe's* women's editor, Margaret McCrimmon.[123] Isabel Armstrong shepherded young Beatrice Taylor – even though she worked for a rival paper – through her first days on the Ottawa news scene.[124] Club solidarity among newswomen often transcended the competitiveness which Peter Desbarats describes as a routine part of male journalism.[125] Nevertheless, although the club could lobby for more expansive opportunities for members, it could only persuade; it had no official status.

Moreover, the calling they longed to master had not yet achieved the position their foremothers had envisioned for it back in 1906. The persistently low status of journalism had not yielded to the continuing efforts of both male and female newswriters to raise it to the dignity of a profession. Thus, the gloom of disappointed expectations often gave rise to the craft archetype – the cynical journalist whose ideals were corroded by years of labouring to serve a public that didn't care.[126] A Winnipeg newsman struck this pose in a tribute to women journalists which praised their accomplishments yet wondered why they wanted to take on the "disconcertingly, dull, discouraging and difficult task of trying to mind everybody's business but their own, of telling one half the world how the other half lives, of struggling day in and day out and through the weary hours of the night as well with those five elusive w's of journalese – who, what, when, where and why."[127] The world-weary loner was, of course, a mask. Committed journalists were able to stay in the field only if they were buoyed up by a sense of self-referencing superiority to sustain them even when the outside world did not bolster their self-esteem.

But solid professional status remained elusive. An entirely different way of affirming their position in the workplace would be to unionize, but among female as well as male journalists the subject was controversial.[128] Those who aspired to learned professional status or literary gentility took a highly individualistic attitude towards their experience in the press. They attributed their own success to sheer talent and hard work, while considering that the failure of others was due to lack of resourcefulness and gumption. At the very least they assumed that income was a private matter. Cora Hind, for one, took exception to a questionnaire on women's salaries that asked her to reveal her earnings. She considered it "impertinent" to inquire "into the personal side of press women's life."[129]

At the same time, it was galling to labour for unrestricted hours exploiting one's talent and ingenuity in the service of a newspaper that paid for this devotion with less security and money than the unionized compositors received. A few women journalists had rallied to collective principles as early as the First World War. Mrs Claude Bowker had raised the issue in the CWPC report for 1913-20 when she gave a paper entitled "Trade Unionism and the Woman Journalist." She made it clear in her address that as far as she was concerned, trade unionism should mean for women "equal pay for equal work."[130] But others were hostile to the whole notion. The opinions registered at the regional conference of presswomen of Alberta and Saskatchewan in 1920 were negative. Mrs Byrtha Stavert of the *Calgary Herald* feared that unions would "destroy the initiative and creative ability of the worker" and that regular conferences between writers and editors would suffice to ensure "humane treatment from publishers."[131] Interestingly, at that same conference, Roy Sayles, the manager of the Canadian Weekly Newspaper Association, tried to explain why women were sometimes paid less than men. He regretfully pointed out that women had to compete with those "who are so anxious to have their writings in print that they will write for nothing."[132]

The fact that women journalists were still seen as a separate species, competing with each other, continued to plague their progress. When Irene Parlby wrote to Violet McNaughton on a range of questions relating to women and work, McNaughton responded vehemently to the query "Is there a tendency to keep women out of the higher paid jobs?" "Definitely yes, " McNaughton wrote, "But I wouldn't like to be quoted. The Canadian Women's Press Club feels quite strongly on this."[133] As noted above, the CWPC could do little to promote the practical interests of its members.

PROFESSIONALISM VS UNIONISM

In lieu of an assertive stance from their own press club, some women sought membership in organizations where male and female journalists worked together for their collective interest. One such organization was the British Columbia Institute of Journalists, which was formed at the end of 1919. Edna Brown was an early member. In explaining the group to her fellow presswomen, she outlined its lofty professional aspirations rather than its practical goals. Assuaging any fears that this was a trade union, she acknowledged that journalists "find it impossible and undesirable to conform to the rules and regulations obtaining in international labor unions," and she emphasized the educational impulse of the institute, its intention to launch courses and university degree programs.[134]

Although women were welcome in the British Columbia Institute of Journalists, only three of them went to its first meeting, largely because of employer opposition to anything remotely resembling a trade union: "One afternoon paper made no bones about it and frankly told its staff that the management would discharge any reporter, male or female, who took any part in the formation of a labour union."[135] In later years, Brown (by then Mrs Perrin Baker) admitted that the early members had hoped that the institute could help them protect their wages but that the aggressively negative response from proprietors had quashed any notion of a labour collective. "Shorn of its economic claws," the institute survived only because the employers accepted that it was merely a social and educational organization.[136]

The nature of journalism – individualistic, competitive, apparently based on talent and ingenuity rather than cooperation – seemed to preclude collective principles. But as it became harder to earn a living during the Depression and as employers took advantage of the desperation of their employees to slash wages and pile up workloads, the American Newspaper Guild began to make inroads in Canada.[137] In August 1936 a branch of the guild began to organize in Toronto, and the union was also making headway in Montreal. In Vancouver, journalists attending a clandestine meeting hoping to organize a unit were dismayed by the figure of a "strange little man" writing down all the names of those who entered the hotel. Later, the organizers of what was to be an abortive effort discovered that there was a "mole" in the group who reported everything back to management.[138] It took courage to defy the newspaper establishment at a time when jobs were scarce and journalists all too plentiful. The executive of the CWPC approached the subject of unionization hesitantly, reporting back to members that it was "considered by many editorial and news writers to be the probable solution to the question of long hours and inadequate remuneration, which for generations had hung over the editorial departments of many Canadian publications." The executive expressed no collective opinion on the explicit advantages a guild might have for women journalists.[139]

Conservative voices in the Canadian newspaper world reacted far more vehemently to the encroaching tide of organization. In an editorial of 1937, the Toronto *Globe and Mail* applauded the American newspaper publishers' rejection of the closed shop for journalists. Shrewdly, the editorial took the high ground of professionalism and ethics, dispelling any odour of capitalist self-interest: the question was one of principle not mere wages and hours. The *Globe and Mail* had no objection to organization by its mechanical staff, and indeed collective bargaining on that front ensured harmonious relations. But the situation of those who prepared and edited news was quite different. They had a duty to the public to ensure the unbiased collection and presentation of facts. Could they do this if they were members of an organization that had clear-cut positions on a number of issues, such as labour trouble or the Spanish war? For the Canadian reading public, the fact that these views issued from the United States further impinged on the right of the public to receive pure and unbiased information. The editorial concluded by saying that in rejecting the guild, the *Globe and Mail* was protecting the public, the freedom of the press, and even the freedom of its employees "individually to hold whatever political views they prefer ... A closed editorial shop equals a closed editorial mind."[140]

Behind such high-minded assertions of public spirit, the other major Toronto newspaper owners closed ranks to protect their interests. Even though the *Toronto Star* was supposed to be a "friend of the working man" and was derided in some circles as the "Toronto Daily Pravda,"[141] J.E. Atkinson was as committed as any of his peers to excluding the Toronto unit of the American Newspaper Guild.[142] Atkinson attempted to avoid a showdown by offering to satisfy the demands of *Star* employees without actually negotiating with the union. This was the strategy he suggested to Jessie MacTaggart, president of the *Star* unit in 1940.[143] Meanwhile, the *Globe and Mail* found a pretext to fire the chair of its local unit. Judith Robinson was ostensibly discharged because her editorials were too critical of the government's handling of the war effort: "The editor and I differed about the need of tanks in modern war."[144] But her first action on leaving the *Globe and Mail* was to found the *New Lead*, the house organ of the Toronto Guild.[145]

Women were in the front ranks of the early recruiting drive, and not always because they felt the most vulnerable and exploited. A social conscience activated by experiences during the Depression motivated women as well as men in promoting collective justice. Jessie MacTaggart, daughter of a railway worker, was one of the most active organizers for the Toronto unit. Because she advocated such radical notions as old age pensions and unemployment insurance she was known among her fellow workers as "the Communist." One of them, John W.H. Bassett, who even as a cub reporter had silver-spoon politics, provoked a showdown with the fiery MacTaggart. For three hours she harangued him until, exhausted, he retreated.[146]

Mamie Moloney Boggs was an activist whose union principles stemmed from the sights she saw as a reporter for the *Vancouver Sun*: the work camps and truncheon-wielding policemen had radicalized her.[147] As one of the early members of the Vancouver union, Boggs rejected the idea of an elitist "craft" union that would benefit only people like herself "in the more secure, higher paid echelons in editorial." She aimed at an inclusiveness that would extend from the "janitorial staff to the highest paid reporters."[148] Boggs became the first shop steward in the editorial department while her colleague on the *Sun*, Doris Milligan, was guild secretary of the Vancouver local.[149] One of the first actions taken by the union was on behalf of Ann Merrett and Norma Thorne, both of whom were working full time for the *Sun* but were paid at space rates. With the union behind them, they were able to get paid somewhat higher than the minimum according to their classification.[150] The *Vancouver Sun* was one of the first newspapers in Canada to be totally unionized from top to bottom. However, the proletarian tilt of this "vertically" organized union did not suit everyone. Being mixed up with janitors and elevator operators stung the pride of the reporter who believed he was a professional and did not want to "behave the way the maintenance man does."[151]

While individual members entered the fray, the Canadian Women's Press Club steered clear of the union battles that were being waged in the various regions of Canada. But by 1945 many women were in a more confident and confrontational mood. The Ottawa branch issued a proposed resolution that protested the low pay and abysmal working conditions in many newspapers and the wild fluctuations in rates of pay, which had no bearing on circulation or place. Noting that Canada lagged far behind Britain and Australia in organizing newspaper unions and that even the United States was establishing regulations for wages, hours, and holidays, the proposal urged male press clubs to join the CWPC in an organizational effort. Even so, the women maintained their loyalty to their first goal, professional status. Their proposed resolution urged the union to "defend and promote the professional status and interests of its members" with regard not only to pay and conditions but also to "professional usages and customs"; and by this time women journalists were shrewd enough to want it on record that the club endorsed the principle of "equal pay for equal work between men and women."[152]

There was little question that the expansion of the guild across Canada did much to counter the marked unevenness of conditions of work and salary among journalists. There was some doubt, however, whether an organization that embraced both male and female members was as sensitive to the particular needs and rhythms of a working woman's life as the CWPC had originally set out to be. Ishbel Ross, reporting to CWPC members on the progress of the newspaper guild in the United States and the gains it had won for journalists, applauded the reduction of exploitation – the endless hours, fluctuating wage rates, and perfunctory dismissals. She noted that American women were among the most active organizers and that several of them had lost their jobs as a result. But she remained sceptical that these changes were portentous in the annals of women in journalism. Women still failed to get the kind of opportunity and recognition accorded to male journalists: "Certainly no city editor has ever been known to remark: We need some good reporters. Why don't we hire some women. The prejudice against us seems to be quite considerable."[153]

The CWPC had been formed as a shelter against prejudice – a place where presswomen could find fellowship in a world that ignored or disparaged their status. Lily Laverock, one of the founders of the Vancouver branch in 1910, had hoped that the CWPC would deliver concrete economic advantages to women journalists once they had proved themselves capable of collective cooperation: "Among our male confreres there has been noticed also, a marked appreciation of a breadth of outlook that has enabled us to cast off individual professional prejudice and petty antagonism and merge our nobler sympathies and intellectual powers in an harmonious unity."[154] Despite these uplifting sentiments, the isolation and loneliness that had driven newspaperwomen to band together continued to be the major feature of their professional lives. It was as individuals that women waded through the personal and professional currents of their lives. The way that each responded to the rewards and shortcomings of her calling was embedded in her private situation as a woman as much as in her professional status.

CHAPTER FOUR

Making Their Way and Making It Pay: The Working Life Cycles of Canadian Women Journalists

I suppose the story of every woman worker in the world is the same, we never are able to get away from the intimate anxieties of family life, which the average man worker has been taught to throw aside from the begining [*sic*] of his career. The more I have to do with women the more I realize the dual struggle which wears them out. I have the chance of stepping into a very interesting world here, and getting at the very root of really great movements, social and political, if only it were not for the constant care and anxiety.

Mary Agnes Fitzgibbon, c. 1902

The episodic pattern of working women's lives was a facet of women journalists' experience that frequently surfaced in discussions among members of the Canadian Women's Press Club (CWPC). The Vancouver branch in 1935 tried to address the problem in a resolution to amend the constitution, stating that "since frequently women writers marry young and have an interruption in their work because of raising a family," membership rules should be relaxed somewhat to allow women who had worked for at least five years as journalists to retain associate status in the club.[1] The bid was rejected. Wary that their club might descend into a mere social gathering of would-be writers, the CWPC maintained the stricter rule of ten years in the field to earn the right to associate status.

Yet the club's aspiration for vigilant professionalism ran counter to its function as a specifically women's association dedicated to accommodating the rhythms of working women's life cycles. These two elements did not always synchronize, for the press club embraced a diverse membership that included single self-supporting full-timers, women with young children trying to keep their skills and contacts alive, older women returning to work after a hiatus of child rearing, and an assortment of individuals whose domestic lives did not follow conventional patterns. All members believed in the importance of protecting and improving the status and income of women journalists, but the difference of their various situations – plights, in some cases – gave rise to a variety of perspectives on their lives as working women writers.

Sometimes their differences pulled them in opposing directions. Because women journalists usually competed not with male journalists but with one another, some attributed the obstacles impeding their personal progress to other women trying to make their way at a different stage of their career and life cycle. Others remained steadfastly attuned to the necessity of advancing as a united front of women in a male-dominated career, and they tried to ensure that whatever they achieved as individuals would smooth the path for women following. In varying degrees, gender governed women's opportunities and experiences in journalism; and, conversely, their vocation flavoured the kind of lives they had as women.

This chapter looks at various points along the private life courses of individual women journalists, from their first breakthrough into print to their retirement. The intent is to capture something of the essence of their experiences as women trying to make their way in an exciting but not always accommodating career in the first half of the twentieth century. The individuals and their situations are so different that it would be impossible to claim a composite picture. Rather, it is a patchwork of their lives as women interlocking with their attempts to make a living as journalists.[2] Wherever possible, they tell their own stories and interpret their own experiences. How they expressed themselves at one point in their lives might not necessarily reflect their experience at an earlier or later stage. As Gillian Creese and Veronica Strong-Boag have pointed out, "the meaning attached to gender ... changes over an individual's life course, and age and family status interact with gender."[3] As women, they engaged with parents, siblings, friends, husbands, and children in ways that supported or undermined their ability to function as journalists.

Their ability to earn is a thread that runs throughout the patchwork. The fact of earning money was both a necessity and a symbol of "making it" in their chosen field. It was also a potentially divisive issue as their identities as women and as workers intersected with questions of earning power – who has the right to earn, how much, and at what stage of her life cycle. These were issues that affected all women in the paid labour force. But in a career where income levels varied considerably and where the size of the pay packet was a symbol of status and success, individuals could become resentful of the earnings of others. Since some were prosperous while others barely scraped by, this was not a small issue.

GETTING STARTED

Whether or not they went on to brilliant careers and/or marriage and motherhood, all of them experienced the breakthrough into the career of their dreams. Journalism as a career for women was sufficiently glamorous and its qualifications sufficiently ill-defined to render stories about how each got her foot in the door extremely varied. "No one path led to the newsroom," observed the prairie journalist Edith MacInnes McCook, especially as there were few openings compared with the more conventional female careers of nursing, teaching, and office work.[4] The legendary journey from printer's devil to proprietor had no female archetype, and indeed it was increasingly rare even in male experience. John Cameron of the *London Advertiser* was among the last to advance in this classical Ben Franklin style.[5] By the twentieth century few male journalists climbed all the rungs; the most successful had often begun in an editorial department, while the news gatherer or "leg man" might never rise higher.

Even when journalism became a more conventional career choice for women, it remained difficult to break into. An advice manual of the 1940s warned, "The chief disadvantage in journalistic work is the difficulty of getting a start. The number of newspapers in Canada is diminishing through amalgamation, and there has always been strong competition for the available positions. However, the potential journalist who has real ability and is not just attracted by the glamour of the profession can always get in, even if he has to start as a copy boy and work his way up."[6] Whatever the future might hold for him in the long run, a young man could get into a newspaper as an office boy. For a woman, the equivalent entry-level opportunity came to be filing in "the morgue" or typing letters for the publisher, neither of which exposed her to the daily life of the newspaper. She had to seize her chance to show that she could write. Florence Taylor landed one of these jobs on the Victoria *Times* and spent nearly a year persuading the managing editor that she was willing to "sweep floors, fetch coffee, or almost anything else to be in the news room." What writing she did get to do was after her regular hours as the managing editor's secretary.[7] Edna Kells "drifted" into newspaper work. Without any premeditation on her part, she found herself "on the staff of the *Edmonton Journal* as a sort of handy woman secretary to the late Mr. Jennings, managing director and stenographer to everybody else." After eighteen months she earned a transfer to the newsroom and then to the women's department, where she remained. It was much later that she recalled the advice that an old family friend had given her in 1907: "When he suggested that I take up newspaper work, the idea was so startling I never thought of it again until years later when my ears were full of the din of telephones and typewriters."[8]

In earlier days, when it was practically unheard-of for a woman to enter a newspaper office in any capacity, the would-be woman writer had to try some other career first. The first generation of newspaperwomen had, almost to a woman, been fugitives from teaching. What they achieved in establishing a permanent place for women in newspaper offices made it somewhat easier for later generations to begin their careers fresh from high school or university. In the twentieth century, women journalists frequently maintained that they had known since childhood that they would write for their living. Like newsmen, newswomen cast their experiences in the mould of journalistic folklore; theirs was a "calling," not just a job. Their lifelong passion for the newspaper world had gripped them when they were barely conscious and never subsided, not even when cynicism replaced naive idealism. Some began to contribute to the press while they were still children, writing for the children's section of their local newspaper (such as "Farmer Smith's Rainbow Page" in the *Edmonton Journal*, which published the young Lotta Dempsey's pieces).[9]

Others knew no other life. Judith Robinson, daughter of the redoubtable "Black Jack" Robinson, editor of the Toronto *Telegram*, was virtually born to the job. She expressed her career choice in a typically off-handed quip: "I started to write because it seemed to me it would be more difficult to make a living scrubbing. I have sometimes felt I was mistaken in that, but on the whole, perhaps not. Writing is a little easier, though the hours are worse."[10] But while Robinson could be disarmingly glib in print and warm in her personal letters, she was intensely shy and led a rather solitary life. She had been so delicate as a child that she was educated mainly at home; and she was never able to overcome a stutter which she felt disqualified her from any kind of public-speaking engagement.[11] Although she proved to be an exceptionally able journalist in the difficult terrain of political commentary, it is unlikely that she could have talked her way into her first job. In the event, she landed her first job on the Toronto *Globe* because the editor knew her father.

Not every aspiring newswoman had such impeccable connections. Having formed the conviction that "a newspaper job was the only heaven I wanted in this world," Ishbel Ross recalled approaching the editor of the *Toronto Star* during the First World War. She had clutched a little bundle of clippings from the *Globe*'s children's page, but editor John Bone had not been impressed. "Can you type?" he asked her. "Can you get from here to Bloor Street without asking your way?" When she hesitated, he barked, "Then what in the world makes you think you can be a reporter?" She set out straight away to learn typing, but even then the *Star* didn't hire her. Ishbel Ross had her start on the Toronto *News*, working as secretary to the business manager and then filing stories in the morgue, until she got her chance – the challenge to finesse an interview with the notorious militant suffragette, Emmeline Pankhurst. Ross blushed to relate how she negotiated her first breakthrough – by exploiting the feminist sympathies of Pankhurst. Pankhurst had laryngitis and at first rebuffed the young novice. Ross, knowing she would never get a chance at reporting again if she came back empty-handed, implored her not "to let down a fellow woman." Pankhurst gave her a peerless interview and ensured that Ross's first story was signed and on the front page.[12]

Another of the mythologies of newspaper lore that both male and female journalists adopted was that journalists were "born" not "made." If that special quality, a "nose for news," was missing, no amount of slogging would compensate; but if you had it, you would be found. Thus, many newspaperwomen's stories revolved around that moment of discovery when their big chance came and they were not found wanting. Elizabeth Parker, for instance, stormed the editor's office one day in order to complain about the lacklustre write-up of a performance she had seen. When the editor, John W. Dafoe, challenged her to do better, she did and won the coveted position of literary critic for the *Manitoba Free Press*.[13] Mamie Moloney's opportunity came when a well-known male columnist disappeared on a drinking binge. She was on the rewrite desk of the *Vancouver Sun* and had never written a column before, but her first effort translated into a forty-four-year career.[14]

Once an individual succumbed to the lure, a lifelong addiction to printer's ink was supposed to compensate for all the deprivations a working journalist might suffer. Clare Battle's rhapsody about her first job resonates with the nostalgia of an old woman looking back on her youth, but most of her contemporaries would have felt the same. "I joined the staff of the Vancouver *World* in the autumn of 1905," she recalled. "That is 54 years ago, but I still have a vivid remembrance of those golden days. How I loved my dear, dingy old office! The sound of the presses was more to me than any symphony. They were indeed the music to which the joyful current of my life was set. Can you wonder at my enthusiasm? I was eighteen. I had always wanted to write, and now I had been given the chance. I was so happy that as I walked down Hastings Street it was as though I walked on air."[15] Battle's attitude was typical of a great many aspiring writers, who were so grateful to get the chance to show what they could do that they were glad to get any salary at all. As both the women's editor and the religious editor, Battle earned four dollars a week – and she recalled eating a great deal of oatmeal, fish paste, and bread in her first year.[16]

For a very youthful Valance Berryman (later Patriarche) the two dollars a week she earned as a schoolgirl writing articles on a freelance basis for *Saturday Night* made her "an emancipated women" whose efforts at "experiencing like anything" in order to find material for her articles were interrupted by "annoying periods spent at school." The school in question was the highly regarded Harbord Collegiate. While Berryman made light of her adolescent conflicts with her parents over the suitability of the "experiences" she sought, her "life largely consisted of the things *Saturday Night* might see fit to publish."[17] From the time her fledgling efforts appeared in print she was smitten; writing was to be her life.

This sort of ethereal enthusiasm was precisely what many established writers of both sexes most disparaged in the apprentice "girl" journalist. They feared that her vanity might lead her to accept too little or even nothing in exchange for the thrill of seeing her work in print. E.E. Sheppard, editor of *Saturday Night*, berated women for undercutting one another in the literary marketplace. He deplored the plight of the professional woman journalist who, by dint of hard work and experience, had earned a situation on a newspaper yet still had to "shake herself loose from the competition of her sex who, living at home, [were] continually bidding against her for the trifle she [earned] both in money and reputation."[18] Sheppard took it for granted that such women did not imperil men's wages but only those of other women.

More often than thoughtless frivolity, it was uncertainty that caused women writers to undervalue their work. Jean Graham, women's editor of *Saturday Night*, implied that feminine diffidence encouraged the exploitation of young newspaperwomen. In an article about women's salaries in 1913, Graham quoted an experienced colleague's comments on a talented ingenue: "I could shake her when she assumes that apologetic tone about her work and refers to it as 'hack' journalism. She actually toils so she does – and, do you know, she was getting only eight dollars a week until a short while ago. It was shameful, and that editor ought to blush whenever he thinks of the amount and quality of that girl's work in comparison with the contents of her weekly envelope." According to Graham, the older woman had "an excellent financial estimate of her own handiwork" and had helped "several distrustful workers to more confidence in the worth of their own achievements." Graham finished her scenario on a happy note: the mentor had stiffened the spine of her junior, who had then demanded thirteen dollars a week, and the parsimonious editor had agreed because he recognized the youngster's worth as a newspaperwoman.[19]

Journalism was notoriously ill-paid work for newspapermen as well as women. While recommending that women might do better financially in business or teaching, Jean Graham believed that journalism was one field in which women had achieved a rough equality with men. In an article explaining why working women often earned less than men, she noted that "in journalism the salaries of women compare reasonably with those of men."[20] The veteran newspaperman Joe Clark made a doleful assessment of the wages which young male journalists, fresh from university, could expect. His figures indicate that wages had not risen significantly by the end of the century from where they stood in the 1880s: $4–8 per week to start, $10–12 per week after a year, rising to $12–14 per week, where they remained unless the reporter became an editor.[21] By this reckoning, the salary of $43 per month that Florence Randal (later Livesay) earned on the *Winnipeg Telegram* was within the range of acceptability for the early twentieth century.[22] For this wage she did two jobs: she was secretary to the editor, Sanford Evans, and she edited the women's page. Randal's previous experience as a writer for the *Ottawa Journal* may or may not have determined her salary. There was a great deal of variation in the business as a whole, but most women settled out at the low end of the pay scale.

While men and women might start out at fairly similar salaries, the speed at which men advanced often left the women far behind. Edith MacInnes (later McCook) began on the Regina *Post* in 1927 a week after she graduated from the University of Toronto; Wilfrid Eggleston began on the *Toronto Star* a few months earlier, in 1926, after leaving Queen's University just short of his BA. Both began at $25 a week, but while she was called "women's editor," he was a cub reporter. Within a year Eggleston was earning $55 a week as assistant city editor, and by 1929 he was the *Star*'s representative in the press gallery, where he stayed until 1933, earning $75 a week.[23] MacInnes by 1929 had reached the pinnacle of her earning power – $35 a week – as women's editor of the Calgary *Albertan;* and even though she retained the same job, her salary withered to $17.50 a week during the Depression.[24] As figure 1 illustrates, the contrasting career patterns of MacInnes and Eggleston match the larger statistical relationship between male and female career paths.

Journalists, male or female, did not enter the profession to get rich. As the Halifax journalist Margaret Lawrence put it in her presidential address of 1931, "Newspaper work in the hands of the real honest-to-

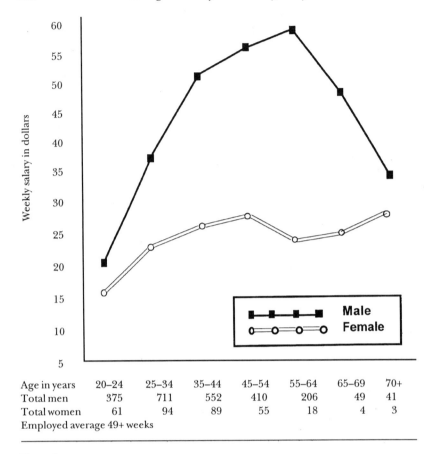

Age in years	20–24	25–34	35–44	45–54	55–64	65–69	70+
Total men	375	711	552	410	206	49	41
Total women	61	94	89	55	18	4	3

Employed average 49+ weeks

Figure 1
Average earnings in 1931 of male and female journalists, editors, and authors, by age
Source: Census of Canada, 1931, vol. 6, tables 19 and 31

goodness press woman is never just a job ... One needs to be a devotee rather than a mere wage earner."[25] Lawrence proved her devotion by writing for newspapers from youth to old age, through two marriages, and while moving from east to west and back again. She was still writing book reviews when she died in 1942.

MARRIED OR SINGLE: CAREER PROGRESS

Dedication to career was all very well, thought Anne Anderson Perry, but were women appreciated, in terms that counted, for what they achieved in their calling? "Are we satisfied with our accomplishments, standing, emoluments?" she asked fellow presswomen in 1933. "Despite all that has been said regarding our past and present achievements I do not know of one woman journalist in Canada today who is earning as editor, reporter, free lance journalist, or syndicator, a salary or other financial return of five thousand dollars a year."[26] Even Cora Hind, the most successful and presumably one of the best-paid women journalists, did not reach this summit. Hind was rather secretive about her earnings, but the census of 1931 disclosed one woman in Manitoba between the ages sixty-five and sixty-nine who earned $3,100 a year. This figure was so far above the average that it could be none other than the great Cora.[27]

The most often proffered excuse for paying women less was that they didn't need the money since they lived at home with their parents and would inevitably go off and marry just when they were becoming useful. This was less true of journalists than other categories of working women. In a period when relatively few married women maintained a career, a remarkable number of working women journalists married and continued to practise their craft.[28] Even among the first generation of the late nineteenth century, married women journalists were a significant presence; nineteen of the fifty journalists listed by the National Council of Women in 1900 were married.[29] The practice of women writers continuing to earn by the pen after marriage persisted through subsequent decades. It was the relative novelty of this expectation that gave rise to the coy tone of the marriage announcements at the meeting of the Winnipeg branch of the CWPC in 1911: "There appear to be two cases of bigamy to report, for we had every evidence that Miss Genevieve Lipsett and Miss Lillian Beynon were wedded to their profession ... Yet our records show them today as Mrs Skinner and Mrs Thomas. At the same time both profess their unabated devotion to their first and lawful loves."[30]

Both women worked as journalists and writers for the rest of their lives. But those lives and those marriages were very different. Beynon married a fellow newswriter, A.V. Thomas, whose lifestyle and views dovetailed with her own; and as she moved from newspaper work into creative writing, he encouraged her. Lipsett married a young businessman who was apprehensive about her ambition. At her marriage, Lipsett-Skinner was about to enter law school, and she became the first married woman in Manitoba to qualify. She deflected her husband's anxiety by assuring him that her law studies were more philanthropic than economic in intention. She believed that "many of the handicaps of women and children could be removed if more public-spirited women understood the laws as they are, and could constructively work for suitable amendments."[31] To appease her husband's pride in his earning power, she disparaged her own: "As to the financial side of [law], or of my journalistic work I shall always be poor because the Scotch part of me is always fighting with the Irish and the tendency to save is always combatted by my impulsive generosity ... So, although I earn a good deal with my pen it seldom stays with me or is used for my own direct benefit."[32]

Although in the early days of her marriage (which eventually failed), Genevieve Lipsett-Skinner called her husband her most "ardent supporter," it was her mother who gave her consistent backing: "Anything I may have accomplished ... is due in large part to my mother who put the ambition into both of us and kept it more or less on fire. To this day she is always setting new goals for us. She herself was born a generation too soon for her own advantage. I think she has, to a limited extent, realized her own thwarted ambition in us."[33] Genevieve's brother, Robert Lipsett, also became a journalist, but he had a much more meteoric rise. He began as a cub reporter on the *Winnipeg Telegram* at seventeen; by twenty-one he was city editor of the *Winnipeg Tribune* and by twenty-seven managing editor. Although some people assumed that Robert had smoothed the path for his sister, it was quite the reverse. Genevieve had been on the *Telegram* for two years when M.E. Nichols took Robert on as a cub because he "thought my brother might be a chip off the same block."[34]

For Genevieve Lipsett-Skinner marriage and an exceptionally dynamic career did not harmonize as much as she had hoped, but other women found it possible to continue journalism on a part-time basis. A highly motivated presswoman could continue to write while she kept house and raised children. She might then return to work after a sojourn in the suburbs. Married women appreciated this dimension of their careers, and so did the more broad-minded of their colleagues; but some single full-time journalists resented those of their married colleagues who worked part time or who freelanced from their homes. Their complaints made audible the rancour of self-supporting women towards those they believed enjoyed comfortable security and were merely playing at earning a living. Grace Denison of *Saturday Night* took to editing when her marriage broke down. She was entirely self-supporting and apparently so distant from her husband that she was not aware that he was ill until he had died.[35] Her scorn for the effluence of the homemaker's pen was perhaps as much personal as professional. For failed women journalists, she insinuated, "there are frequently homes and husbands, to break her fall and let her down easily with dignity." Unfortunately, she went on, once infected with "cacoethes scribendi," the would-be journalist could not resist the urge to "degenerate into rhymes about the offspring heaven sends her: one has known many to thus incense a long-suffering public."[36]

The newspapers and magazines of the early twentieth century printed volumes of sentimental poetry, personal essays, and short stories, and probably rejected twice as many manuscripts that had been hopefully submitted by bungalow scribes. But to be dismissed as mere dilettantes was galling to women whose economic need was desperate, especially when aggravated by having mouths other than their own to fill. Emily Murphy, for instance, wrote frantically for the *National Monthly* when her husband Arthur was ill with typhoid and unable to earn; her income was absolutely crucial to support their four children.[37]

Ruth Cohen underwent the transformation from pampered wife writing for fun to hard-pressed breadwinner in a critically short span. A genteelly raised Englishwoman, Cohen had come to Winnipeg as a young bride. In 1914, when her son was three, she began writing pieces as Sheila Rand for local papers, and continued to do so until 1918: "A local paper [the *Winnipeg Tribune*] paid me a weekly sum [five dollars], princely it seemed to me then, for supplying it with a woman's page, book reviews, an original page story usually humorous, and two other features which I called 'Rhymes of the Times' and 'Mother Goose's Sermons.'" She bought her husband presents with her earnings. Then her husband died very suddenly, and Ruth Cohen's need to earn was acute. Maintaining her home and keeping her young son at private school "was a continuous struggle and thundering hard work," she later recalled, "my days averaging fifteen hours steady brain work. However, being suddenly dependent upon myself, turned me from an inconsequential female to an independent woman."

Her first work was writing advertising for Eaton's, but she also began to write the little verses that would make her famous and well-to-do in later life. Writing as Wilhelmina Stitch, she composed her "daily stitch, short verse about the every day human and homely incidents and feelings of life," which the American Metropolitan Syndicate took up. Eventually Ruth Cohen (remarried as Ruth Collie) returned to Britain, took up a contract with the London *Daily Graphic* and then with the *Daily Herald*, where she reached two million readers every day. Wilhelmina Stitch had become a popular cultural institution that was so well established that the Cambridge theatrical productions parodied her. Ruth Cohen Collie continued to put her son through school and through his M SC, which though he achieved brilliant honours, did not help him find a job. "So mother is once again helping," she wrote to her friend Florence Randal Livesay, "and what a privilege [*sic*] to be able to do so!"[38] When she died in 1936, her legacy to that much-loved son was $35,000, a considerable bequest in the Depression.

Not many married women who turned to freelance work were so fortunate. The personal complications that obliged married women workers to accept low pay for part-time employment affected women journalists too.[39] The freelance writer was easily exploited or even defrauded, as Elizabeth Bailey Price discovered. Just starting her freelance career in 1918, she asked advice of the very successful writer Madge Macbeth: "*Canada Weekly* hasn't paid me one cent for my whole year's contributions – Can you suggest how to get the filthy lucre now that the season of new hats is upon us?"[40] Price at least had her work published and credited; as she observed to Macbeth, "This writing business seems to be a business of names."[41] (A few years later she turned Macbeth herself into copy).[42] Another freelancer, Margaret Bell Saunders, complained that editors frequently rejected her "new ideas" and then passed them on to regular staffers to "dress up." "No there is no law against the stealing of ideas. They are, perhaps, the easiest of all the professional kleptomaniac's duties."[43] It was a mark of Saunders's versatility that she was able to turn even setbacks into copy.

As a writer of occasional pieces, freelancers were competing in a field overstocked with applicants. Jean Graham, like many another analyst of women's achievements in the newspaper world, was inclined to attribute the low salaries and failure to advance to the fact that supply outstripped demand. She urged women to take their work as seriously as men did by making themselves into specialists. But there were lines that only a very few women could cross, she said. "It is only the exceptional woman who can report a railway wreck, attend a police court, or become a war correspondent. Personally I should prefer a housemaid's position to any such exploits. But a man reporter can be sent anywhere."[44]

Even before the First World War, women had already covered many of these beats and within a few years many more would follow.[45] But the fact that "exceptional" women advanced into unconventional territory did not necessarily carry the majority with them. Gwen Cash, while promoting herself as Canada's first female general reporter, admitted that her editor had felt obliged to send a male reporter to accompany her through the waterfront area of Vancouver in 1917 after late-night assignments.[46] Sally McAffrey's editor on the Woodstock *Sentinel Review* used the fact that she could not cover late-night council meetings, which might go on till midnight, as his excuse for marooning her in the society department.[47] Yet in large cities, society reporters spent most of their working lives covering evening events; for what was indisputably "female" work, city editors managed to find suitable arrangements for their employees. Lois Reynolds (later Kerr), after her duties as Toronto *Globe* society editor, regularly walked along Bloor Street after midnight carrying a police whistle "to ward off molesters," who never appeared.[48]

The complaint that women journalists could not "be sent anywhere" the way men could was not sufficient to explain why women failed to advance. Male newsgatherers, or "legmen," were neither highly respected nor highly paid. The really significant difference between the biography of a successful newspaperman and newspaperwoman was that the former might move on to the powerful positions of city editor, managing editor, editor-in-chief, and even publisher, while the woman's career path in the newspaper world would rise no higher than the columnist's fame. It was not until the Second World War that a small number of women ascended to the majesty of city editor.

May O'Regan was a signal example of arrested career progress even though she was "sent anywhere" and succeeded in getting the news. She started on the Halifax *Chronicle* in 1917, doing the "Sunshine Club Mailbag" as Cousin Peggy. Soon she added some general reporting to her ambit, including the police beat. As Howard Good has observed in his study of the autobiographies of journalists, many of the women were inclined to downplay their abilities and attribute all to their kind sources. This was true of O'Regan. The police, she intimated, felt sorry for her and gave her extra help. Their tips paid off, and soon her city editor was sending her out on some rather big crime stories. She also became known for unusual newsmaking strategies – riding a circus elephant, for instance, instead of covering the circus story from the sidewalk. She was the only woman reporter ever to visit the "graveyard of the Atlantic," Sable Island, where nearly two hundred and fifty ships had been wrecked. To crown her career, she gained an interview with British Prime Minister Ramsay MacDonald, who was summering with his daughter in Digby, Nova Scotia. All other reporters had been rebuffed, but O'Regan used the telephone and a style of somewhat contrived harmlessness to get through. Assuming she was talking to MacDonald's secretary, she claimed she just wanted to welcome him to Nova Scotia and dissembled: "I probably wouldn't know how to talk to the prime minister of Great Britain anyway." MacDonald then revealed himself and granted her the interview no one else was allowed.[50] With such scoops behind her, it might have been predicted that May O'Regan would advance to the city desk or to some sort of editorial position. Instead, thirty years into a career that was not distracted by marriage or children, O'Regan was still doing her entry-level job, conducting the "Sunshine Club Mailbag." The reason for her apparently stalled career remains a mystery. However, many of her greatest successes derived from the rather quirky style she adopted, which worked in the circumstances but may have encouraged editors to dismiss her as a "madcap."

It was just as likely that O'Regan was simply not taken seriously as a dedicated professional. Even single women, as Mary Kinnear has observed, "were not immune to the dominant notions of gender."[51]

The suspicion that any single woman might marry and have children, and thus waste years of training, dissuaded newspaper executives from mentoring a rising female talent. Lois Reynolds made light of this professional truism in her comedy *Among Those Present*, which appeared at the Hart House Theatre in 1933 when she was in the women's department of the Toronto *Globe*. Reynolds's heroine, a women's page editor, takes especial pains not to behave like a woman and not to respond to the flirtation of a co-worker. He sighs at her rebuff: "Alas! A woman in business associated with men must forget she is a woman ... The moment she forgets herself in the indulgence of even the most trivial feminine vanity, she severs every rung in the ladder whereby she might have scaled the highest peaks."[52]

While she was still at the beginning of what promised to be a brilliant career, Lois Reynolds could parody the constraints that shadowed most women's working lives. But her own experience proved to follow the familiar pattern, as she put it, "of a summer sky crossed by a glowing star of hope which faded into the clouds of autumn."[53] Reynolds was on the *Globe* for more than seven years, always in the women's department. In 1936, when the *Globe* merged with the *Mail and Empire*, publisher George McCullagh wanted an enlarged and splashier social section. Reynolds then ran an independent society department with an assistant to help her gather the social news.[54] Her salary did not rise with her status; she earned up to twenty-eight dollars a week, but this sank to seventeen dollars as pay packets shrank during the Depression. But since her room was in walking distance of the *Globe* and cost only five dollars a week with breakfast, she got by comfortably.[55] As society editor, her day started in the afternoon; in the mornings she worked at her playwriting, which drew heavily on her paid job for subject matter.

Reynolds's life changed in 1937 when she married a doctor and moved to Britain, where he did postdoctoral studies and she carried on freelance writing. For two years, Lois Reynolds Kerr wrote a column, "Canada in London," covering the social events connected with the Canadian community in Britain. When her first son was born in 1940 and her husband went overseas for war, she found maintaining her career more difficult. Her son was often sick at those times when she was assigned to cover one or another special event for the *Globe and Mail*. She had two more sons, yet she continued to write plays and features. But she never again achieved the plaudits her earlier career had amassed. In later life she felt that her career had not fulfilled its early promise: "Did I fail because, in the middle years, I put husband and family, friends and community before my writing?"[56] It was a question many married women might ask.

Lois Reynolds Kerr, society editor, *Globe and Mail*, c. 1939
(courtesy of Lois Reynolds Kerr)

MARRIED OR SINGLE: THE RIGHT TO EARN

The right of women per se to support themselves by paid employment was well established by the twentieth century, but how much they should be paid was still related to how much they were perceived to need. It was a question of the "living wage" versus "family wage" model of earning power.[57] Did women who would never support a family and perhaps lived with parents or husband need as much as men who did support a family? Did a mother have any business working for pay and perhaps neglecting her children? The conventional assumption that only single, unencumbered women should and could succeed in newspaper work thoroughly incensed Madge Macbeth. A widow, left alone after her husband's sudden death and with two very young sons to support, Macbeth took to writing as her only recourse. As she recalled in her memoir, "It required no financial outlay other than pen and ink and I could dash off material at home between cooking up baby food, changing wet clothes and performing the other jobs contingent upon a nurse."[58] Macbeth made a success of her doubly burdened career by prodigious productivity and versatility. In addition to newspaper and magazine features, she wrote advertising copy, novels, and plays, including the drama *Superwoman*, which was likely the first Canadian play written specifically for radio.[59]

Despite her achievements, Macbeth retained a jaundiced view of single working women who, she felt, failed to assume the financial responsibilities their salaries should entail. In an article entitled "Do Women Pay?" she took to task the unmarried working woman's addiction to selfishness: "In order that we may spend money, we are condemning ourselves to a half-baked life – spinsterhood. To do without *crepe de chine* underwear has become more terrifying than to do without a fully rounded existence, love, children. Our demand for money, which we spend mostly upon ourselves, forces men, who have to spend theirs upon us, into striking for higher wages. Men, under present conditions, need more money than we do."[60] This was a curious perspective from a hard-pressed single parent, but it underlined the situation in which women competed with each other for positions handed out by more powerful men. Macbeth's ire lodged with other women, who were perhaps better able than she to take up every opportunity that chance offered.

Predictably, unmarried women journalists had advantages when it came to advancing up the male-dominated hierarchy of command. Nevertheless, marriage was not necessarily an impediment for a journalist anxious to advance in her career. Mrs Eldred Archibald (who was born Irene Currie Love and wrote as Margaret Currie for the *Montreal Star*) and Mrs J.M. Sherk (Gay Page of the Fort William *Times-Journal*) both had careers that spanned three or four decades without interruption. Florence Sherk's long career may have been as much a necessity as a choice, as she hinted darkly in a letter to Madge Macbeth. Praising Macbeth's *Shackles*, a novel about marriage, as "a brief for the woman who wants a chance to cultivate her other gifts as well as those of domesticity," Sherk went on to say, "I've learned by experience that the one who marries a poor man, expecting him to improve his financial standing by the use of his talents and education, is as bad as one who marries a drunkard, expecting him to improve."[61] This may have been a lesson that Valance Patriarche learned as well. Comments she made to her friend Florence Randal Livesay indicate that she and not her husband, Hugh Racey Patriarche, was the financial pillar of the family. She told Livesay of an altercation with an "investigator" from the Pensions Department who seemed to believe she was concealing sources of income: "He spent nearly two hours taking a dossier, biography and (nearly) an obituary and got lost in the mazes of my divorce case which I try to forget and of which I am frequently reminded. He had a sinister and, to me, somewhat bitter interest in possible alimony! It is difficult to explain that the reverse is the case."[62]

Newspaperwomen, like other married professional women, had to deflect the criticism that by working, they were neglecting homes and family. The perceived need to accentuate femininity and domesticity escalated with career progress. Gertrude Pringle took pains to present Mary Barker, a journalist turned advertising whiz, as a very "womanly woman": "Were you to meet her, not knowing of her vocation, her gentle, even shy air, quiet low voice and calm expression would probably make you exclaim, 'Now, there's a real home woman.'"[63] This "home woman" was the mainstay of her family during the Depression, when her husband's once thriving business shrank to a mere remnant. In 1931 she had to leave her husband in Toronto while she took a job in Montreal in order to have any income at all. As she prepared to abandon her home in order to save it, Mrs Barker confessed to her friend Madge Macbeth, "Things are so unsettled here and business is so poor I simply could not turn it down."[64]

A number of well-educated prairie women wrote to supplement farm incomes during hard times. Their labours were not always appreciated. A.E.M. Hewlett took a sardonic approach to her husband's quibbles: "When I write every evening, Richard complains I write too much. When the paper comes out without one of my articles he is aggrieved. Masculine logic!"[65] It was Harry Cook, editor of the *Saskatchewan Farmer,* whom she credited for "'letting me loose' to write what and how I liked that gave me the confidence."[66] She was able to transform into copy her daily rituals with her children, her cleaning and cooking, and her appreciation of the beauty of the prairie. On the *Farmer's Advocate and Home Journal* she had a regular column signed Mater in the 1910s, and she alwo wrote regularly for the *Saskatchewan Farmer* – her column "Down on the Farm" ran through the 1930s and 1940s. Hewlett was energetic and enterprising. She wrote articles on international relations, children's stories, Bible stories, and critiques of agricultural policy. She sent her features all over Canada and farther afield to the London *Times* and *Daily Mail.* She even tried syndicates, but "found the pay such chicken feed" she did not pursue them further.[67] All this brought in enough to pay for extras on the farm, but there was not much left over for herself. Hewlett felt that going to conferences with fellow presswomen was too extravagant for her – "especially in the clothing line, my usual disability."[68]

May Hewlett's situation paralleled that of Annie Hollis. Both were well-educated Englishwomen who came to Canada to teach school and both became intimate friends with another English emigrant, Violet

McNaughton. Both married and found themselves isolated on prairie farms in the early decades of the twentieth century. In the press club they and other women in remote locations were known as the Lone Scribes. Writing was both an outlet and a source of income. Hollis had been one of the most ardent supporters of women's suffrage and continued to lobby for recognition of women's economic contribution to the farm economy: "I have been dubbed a feminist because I have always insisted on recognition of the rights and responsibilities of women citizens. However I strongly object to the term. No one is called a masculinist because he constantly speaks of men, as so many speakers and preachers do. So why not humanist?"[69]

Dealing with hail and drought on an isolated Saskatchewan farm, Hollis did not have time to write full time, but she freelanced for as many prairie papers as would accept her articles. As she explained to Violet McNaughton, "Ready cash is very acceptable these days." She was rarely able to attend press club conferences because, as a freelance, she did not qualify for railway passes; yet, isolated as she was, she needed the boost of supportive company more than most. One of her most reliable mainstays was a regular women's column in the *Saskatchewan Farmer*. Understandably, she was not able to share McNaughton's enthusiasm when Dora Dibney became editor of the *Saskatchewan Farmer* intending to turn into a trade journal this all-purpose rural weekly with a full-fledged women's section. Hollis found her income much reduced.[70] Within a few months of her disappointment with the *Saskatchewan Farmer*, she had a stroke and died. Nothing more poignantly illustrates the point she dedicated her life to prove than her husband's pathetic struggles to manage the house and farm without her.[71]

In some ways it was a shame that Hollis's setback came at the hands of the dynamic Dora Dibney, for in many ways Dibney's triumph in editing two agricultural papers represented the unfolding of what Hollis, Hewlett, and McNaughton had spent their lives struggling for – to make visible women's contribution to the agricultural economy of the West. As J.W. Dodd of the British Ministry of Information wrote to Dibney, "What sound policy to have a woman editing a farmer's paper! I never saw the point until I went through your paper. What is the ratio of women to men in the farming communities? It must be pretty high in any country."[72]

Married women, who were closely integrated with the working life of a farm, wrote in whatever spare time they could muster. Their husbands' support for this money-making pastime naturally varied according to temperament and circumstance. In an urban setting, where husband and wife were both in the newspaper business, combining career and family could be a little easier.[73] Edith MacInnes

McCook recommended that one choose a journalist for a husband because he would be more likely than others to understand one's irregular hours, challenging assignments, and the sheer stressfulness of the job.[74] She married a colleague on the Calgary *Albertan* in the early 1930s and carried on working: "My husband was my city editor. Had he wanted to fire me he would have had to support me, I always told him." McCook took a couple of years off when she had her first son, but she was back at work as editor of the women's department by 1934.[75]

Elizabeth and Joe Price had a mutually supportive relationship that included running the *Peace River Standard* together in the years before and during the First World War and collaborating on numerous projects. "It's the greatest thing in the world to have your family back you," Elizabeth told her daughter in later years. Family backing enabled Price to sustain a lively and demanding freelance career that included crossing the country fifty-two times. When she ghost-wrote MP Martha Black's memoirs, she had to be away from her two children for months at a time. Her husband Joe bolstered her in her multifaceted career, just as her furiously produced articles and potboilers shored up the family income when "depression days ... meant madeover clothes and moving vans for the Price household."[76] Price's friend in the press club, Evelyn Gowan Murphy, took care to emphasize that "Bailey" did not neglect her family despite her active career: "Joe's socks were always carefully darned, and buttons on where buttons belonged."[77] Price's daughter Jo-Ann knew from the inside how the family had cooperated to make possible her mother's work. Having become a newswoman herself, though never marrying, Jo-Ann Price marvelled at what her mother had accomplished: "She turned out a tremendous volume of material, much of it dealing with 'causes' – from press freedom to peace on the Pacific and illustrated with homey examples ... I am again and again amazed at HOW she managed to do it all, and yet keep the home fires burning. It became quite regular thing for my father, brother and me to 'batch' at home, while mother was out 'saving the world'."[78] Joe's death in 1942 knocked out her emotional foundation; Elizabeth Bailey Price died the next year, at the age of fifty-seven.

The West seemed to be a particularly congenial setting for intertwined careers such as those of the newspapering Murrays. Ma (Margaret) Murray became famous in her own right as a curmudgeon in Lillooet, British Columbia, but that was after years of family newspaper work with her husband George.[79] The Balmer Watts of Edmonton celebrated sixty years of marriage and newspaper work in 1963. Gertrude (Peggy) Balmer Watt was one of the founders of the Canadian Women's Press Club. While her editor husband was supportive of her career, her maid was somewhat dubious. In one column, Balmer Watt reconstructed a conversation with her maid who had asked her "what I meant I had to do by writing for a paper, when there were cushions to make, and heaps of other things to do. 'Was it important work, and did it have to be done just at a certain time?'"[80] While Balmer Watt related the incident as a source of amusement, the question of what was legitimate work for a married woman lay behind the exchange.

Despite the predictability of men and women journalists marrying each other, some newspapers refused to allow wives on the payroll if their husbands were on staff. An old Toronto *Globe* rule impelled Iris Naish to keep her marriage in 1937 to Jack Fleming secret. When the managing editor found out, Naish was fired, even though she had established her credentials as a first-rate reporter. Fortunately, the publisher, George McCullagh, had more modern attitudes and insisted that Naish be reinstated. When the managing editor tried to defend the old tradition, McCullagh retorted, "If she'd been living in sin, you wouldn't have fired her."[81]

During the Depression, when male as well as female incomes were precarious, every woman who dared to earn was made to feel like a usurper. Journalists were no exception. The assumption that women should be supported by men intensified and applied even to single women. Alixe Carson found this attitude dogging her career as long as she stayed in her hometown of Calgary. Even though she was self-supporting and lived in a bed-sitter on her own, the fact that her father was a prominent lawyer licensed George Bell, publisher of the Calgary *Albertan*, to underpay her: "I'm not going to give Percy Carson's little girl a raise. He can support her."[82] When Elizabeth Ruggles, much to the distress of her parents, took a job on the Victoria *Times*, her father received "poison pen letters from people saying, 'what are bankers' daughters doing taking the bread from the mouths of starving people?'"[83]

For married women, maintaining a job in an atmosphere of social disapproval came with a high psychological cost. One, who remained anonymous, commented on her situation to her colleagues in the press club: "I am freelancing it being considered quite immoral for a married woman to have a job in this town. Every businessman has done his best to convince me that a married woman's place is in the sink. I'm almost beginning to believe it."[84] Mamie Moloney was yet another news-paperwoman who kept her marriage secret for fear of losing her right to a pay cheque. Much to her surprise, Robert Cromie, publisher of the *Vancouver Sun*, was refreshingly supportive: "I think it's good for a woman reporter to be married," he told her. "I think it gives her a broader perspective and it'll make a better reporter of her. As far as I'm concerned that's fine and I'll keep your secret for as long as you want me to."[85]

Cromie's confidence was well founded. Mamie Moloney Boggs was a dedicated and versatile journalist who maintained her career regardless of whatever else was happening in her life. She wrote her *Sun* column, "In One Ear," from the maternity ward of the Vancouver General Hospital a few hours after the birth of her second son.[86] Less than two months later, she was off to San Francisco to cover the organizational sessions of the United Nations.[87] At home she managed to juggle both her domestic and professional roles by working out her columns in her head and then typing them up while her babies were napping.[88] But Boggs had worked hard and made some difficult decisions in her personal life to achieve the plateau where she could have her family and her career as well. Depression wage rates would not support a family, and, in any case, she was ambitious to make headway in the newspaper world.[89] In the eight years following her marriage, she had four abortions.[90] By the time her first son was born, she was well established with a personal following.

A columnist such as Boggs was better placed than almost any other category of working women to combine her career with marriage and motherhood. Because a column could be written at home and on whatever subject struck the writer's fancy, an inventive and energetic journalist could profitably integrate the two dimensions of her life. Hughena McCorquodale put a wickedly humorous slant on the domestic journalist's proclivity when giving a lecture to her colleagues in the Calgary branch: "Have you ever wondered if you were capable of one honest private emotion without slyly weighing it from the standpoint of good copy? While you smooth the fevered brow, ride down town in the street car, assure your lover of your undying affection, engage in your current argument with your husband, you are mentally reaching for a pencil."[91] The long-suffering families of at-home newspaperwomen had to endure, with good grace, their scrapes and foibles artfully packaged and broadcast to the wider world. For instance, the baby talk of the future poet Dorothy Livesay and her sister Sophie starred in the column their mother, Florence Randal Livesay, wrote for the *Manitoba Free Press.*

By such strategies, a woman journalist could maintain her reputation, provided she had established one. Lotta Dempsey was a star personality by the time she took on child rearing in the late 1930s.[92] Her well-known byline drew readers as she moved from the Toronto *Globe* to the *Star* and finally to *Chatelaine.* But in her early years as a journalist in the mid-1920s in Edmonton, she was not so adept at juggling her domestic life with her career; she attributed the failure of her first marriage to the fact that she loved newspaper work more than married life.[93]

The exceptional few, then, managed to pursue an active career even during the most challenging episodes of motherhood. But the majority of women who tried to keep up a career while they were raising children found freelancing too strenuous and had to surrender their membership in the press club, at least temporarily. Quite a number of newly married journalists entered their freelance phase determined to keep up their quota, only to fizzle out in discouragement when they could not manage to write with little children underfoot. Myrtle Patterson received many apologetic letters while she acted as corresponding secretary of the Vancouver branch. "My assignments have, I'm afraid been very weak," confessed Marie Lapsley Anderson, formerly of the *Province*, but chasing a toddler in 1928, she said, "I assigned myself to married life and I guess I have to stay put."[94] A more striking example of a writer with talent but without time was Kathleen Strange. She eventually became a prize-winning novelist, but during her child-rearing years she was grateful to C.O. Smith of the *Calgary Herald*, who believed in her and thought she would make a fine newspaperwoman. He kept offering her jobs, none of which she could take because she "had either just had a baby or was just about to have one." Despite her refusals, the *Herald* accepted her occasional pieces and supplemented a precariously stretched family income.[95]

Myrtle Patterson Gregory, once a star reporter of the *Vancouver Sun*, was a shining example of a woman who created opportunities that dovetailed with her changing life cycle. Although she "retired" from newspaper work when she had her first child, she ran a small advertising gossip sheet, "The West End Breeze," and made a profit even during the Depression. She sold it in 1934 when she found that the demands of two children plus her own publication overwhelmed her, but she managed to place enough articles to maintain her press club membership as a freelancer. In 1937, now with three children, she was writing advertising copy for the Price-Gourley agency and running a direct-mail advertising outfit. By the early 1940s she was back at newspaper work full time, running the *Vancouver Sun*'s "Edith Adams Cottage" feature.

For these women journalists, who were trying to maintain a career while they stayed at home with children, membership in the Canadian Women's Press Club was a vital link with their craft and their colleagues. Over one-third of the membership of the CWPC was in this category in 1935, compared with around one-quarter of women in the profession overall.[96] Freelancers, it would seem, were especially anxious to participate in the press club. The freelance category demanded that members publish five major articles or three short stories a year to qualify for renewal. It was intended to be a lenient measure of continuing activity, but even this was difficult for the homebound woman. When markets shrank during the 1930s, the challenge became insuperable for all but the most determined and productive writers. The president of the CWPC during the Depression, Elizabeth Bailey Price, urged members to turn the vicissitudes of the economy into some kind of advantage for the entrepreneurial freelance journalist: "Admittedly times are hard – but there are still markets for the persistent and serious writer. Have you noticed the many and varied bits of signed writing in the newspapers – more than ever before? Have you noticed the brevity of this copy? Have you noted that the erstwhile long article is now continued week by week, until concluded? More and more the big daily papers are taking on 'space writers' for special departments – rather than putting a department in charge of a member of the staff. 'Tis true it means one more regular job gone – but then it permits a competitor."[97] From the freelance writer's perspective, this pep talk was encouraging. But from the viewpoint of staff journalists facing layoffs because the paper could buy freelance copy cheaply, it was tantamount to treason that their own president was cheering on the "diluters" – women whose eagerness to publish might undercut the value of an article on the literary marketplace.

In times of economic and national stress, friction between various categories of members in the press club intensified. Married women journalists may have cherished the club as a network of mutual support, but that network did not universally welcome them. When jobs were scarce or when individuals were disappointed in their ambitions, schisms between the married and single, the part-timer and staffer, yawned once more. An anonymous malcontent who signed herself Re Guard sent a diatribe to the "Newspacket" in 1942, which eloquently if profusely articulated the grievances dividing married from unmarried journalists:

Hard working women editors and reporters who slave all hours with no hours off duty – are asking why every girl who ever took a pen in hand thinks she owes it to the world and to herself to keep on writing even after she has given up that career in favor of romance or other more alluring fields.

Journalism seems to be the one occupation to which one can always turn or return when weary of the common round, the daily task. It is nice for these "comebackers" but is it fair to the women who live by the pen, who have long tedious hours, are cut off from their friends because of their work and give all their time to their employer's publications? Is it fair to the young women who would, given a chance, become worthy scribes? What about the monetary side of the question? Has it ever struck these part-timers that they are holding down the salaries of the full-timers and the youngsters going in to learn the craft?[98]

This item elicited a flood of protest letters, some measured, some poignantly angry. Mary Alexander's rejoinder revealed a bitterness born out of desperation. Beginning by disparaging the "old wheeze, married women shouldn't work," she observed defiantly that "editors employ married women; prefer them in fact," and she went on to vindicate the married woman worker: "Marriage doesn't always solve the problem of making a living for oneself or for one or more dependents. Incomes sometimes vanish inadvertently. Are married women to starve?"[99] Alexander kept private the fact that her husband was blind and that she had been the sole support of the family for years, trying her hand at everything from music criticism to public relations to beauty articles. Given her predicament, her indictment of the whole press club was understandable: "Never in all my years of membership, has any member of the club ever lifted a finger to give any member out of a job at any time, a leg-up, when the earning of a living has been paramount, when the wolf was howling down the street. I wonder why I belong, in the face of this fact!"[100]

Myrtle Patterson Gregory's rebuttal of the "Re Guard" piece was less emotional but nonetheless to the point. Her plea was for variety and inclusiveness:

Marriage simply gives one a wider field of life to study. When I joined the Press Club in Port Arthur–Fort William more than 20 years ago, most of the local members were older women and their experience gave a color and richness to Club meetings that youngsters could never have done. I've always admired the older woman who keeps on writing to the day she dies. As for the older writers hanging back so that young scribes can be brought along, the youngsters have so much in their favour in dealing with editors that they ought to be able to make a place for themselves if they show any real promise. "Comebackers" get little enough encouragement. If they manage to survive, it's on sheer merit.[101]

Writers who saw above the putative competition and squabbles that persisted between the married and unmarried, the mothers and childless, framed the issue of justice for women in journalism in feminist terms. It was during the Second World War that the question of women's right to work emerged most dramatically. The war gave some women the opportunity to demonstrate their abilities in male-dominated specialties. But as Ruth Roach Pierson has demonstrated in other fields where women made strides, wartime employment of women in journalism raised the question of "staying on" after the soldiers returned.[102]

Dora Dibney was president of the CWPC during the war. Officially, she was Mrs Grant Wright, but marriage had represented merely a career hiatus in the mid-1920s when she had lived with her husband in remote coastal outposts of British Columbia; throughout her career she was known as Miss Dora Dibney. Without question, Dibney was a self-made woman. She had come to Winnipeg from Britain in 1904 at the age of ten, but when her father died the next year, her stepmother more or less abandoned her and returned to England. At the age of eleven, Dora was supporting herself working at Eaton's. At thirteen, she was a general servant, errand runner, and "junior bartender" for a Winnipeg callgirl. She put herself through high school and in 1912 landed a job on the *Manitoba Free Press*.[103] She went on to work in the mainstream department of telegraph editing on the *Free Press*, became night editor of the Regina *Leader*, and night telegraph editor of the Saskatoon *Star Phoenix*. By the time of the Second World War, she was editor of the *Saskatchewan Farmer* and editor and publisher of the *Canadian Hereford Digest*. She was the only Canadian newspaperwomen to be invited by the British Ministry of Information to tour the wreckage sites of the war.

In spite of Dibney's singular achievements, the Moose Jaw *Times Herald* of 24 November 1945 emphasized her unpretentiousness: "She does not have the feeling of a career woman, just that of a woman with a job. Her interest is with women, all women, remembering that they are citizens, people with as much responsibility in seeing that women have the right kind of civic, municipal and national government as men have." Never one to rest on her own accomplishments, Dibney fiercely defended all women's right to work, married or single. In an editorial for the "Newspacket," she bridled at the suggestion that women should return to their homes after the war and concentrate on rearing the rising generation. If these "greybeards" wanted to raise the birth rate, they should "remove economic fears," she retorted. In Dibney's analysis, decent maternity leave with full pay, modern nurseries, and free prenatal and postnatal care would encourage women to reproduce in a positive environment. "Other wise, a general strike by all women for about twenty or thirty years would seem a good line," Dibney concluded.[104]

Dibney's essay challenged a sample of women journalists across the country to respond to the question "Should married women in business resign after the war if they have other means of support?" There was no consensus. At one extreme, Marie-Rose Turcot, unmarried and employed writing French-language radio scripts, believed that the married woman worker was the epitome of selfishness: "The woman who makes pretext of her sense of business or her personal initiative and commercial ability, to remain in her own position, independently of her family, having nothing in mind but her own liberty away from the burden of housework and her functions of mother and housekeeper, will not wish to reconcile herself to normal conditions."[105] At the other extreme was Claire Wallace, an astronomically (for Canada) successful journalist and broadcaster, who for much of her career was a single parent. Her view was that "no one should be denied the right to work, irrespective of circumstances." She took the case of a married man whose wife had independent means – Would anyone suggest that he be prevented from working or painting pictures or writing books? Wallace muted her bid for equality with the light-hearted suggestion that few married women would want to "dig out of her home, be it ever so humble, morning after morning and spend the rest of the day in the business world, being bossed around by someone else. She'd much rather be home where she can do some first class bossing herself."[106]

Wallace had her reasons for caution in commenting even to fellow women journalists about the pitfalls of a married woman earning a living. When she wrote her opinion on the question in the autumn of 1944, she was just emerging, bruised and battered, from the most distressing episode in her career. Her story encapsulated in dramatic form the public's reaction to a highly visible married working woman. By the beginning of the Second World War, Wallace had advanced from the stables of the *Toronto Star*, where she had been a strikingly lively and enterprising reporter, to the air waves, where she was possibly the most popular broadcaster of her era. Because of her large following, the National War Finance Committee approached her with an offer to do five daily programs each week to advertise the sale of war stamps and bonds. The "They Tell Me" series seemed to be giving a healthy boost to the trade in bonds, and Wallace was worked off her feet finding ever-fresh material for her programs.[107] When her assistant quit from exhaustion, Wallace's workload was correspondingly increased. Because of her escalating duties, the National Radio Committee, on her behalf and without her requesting it, asked that her salary be raised from $170 per week to $200.

At this point, the "Affaire Financial" (as Wallace called it) hit the papers. Day in and day out the newspapers across Canada from the Toronto *Telegram* to the *Lethbridge Herald* excoriated Wallace for daring to earn so munificent a salary. Headlines blared scorn at the "radio gossiper" or "chitchatter."[108] Editorials took the opportunity to disparage her style and content: "The lady has the excruciating practice of tittering at her own bon mots"[109] ... "The paying of so much public money to any female artist of the airways suggests 'pull' and favoritism ... Many newspapermen who are paid only $40 or $50 per week, write more and better stuff than Claire Wallace does."[110] Another editor, after announcing that everyone in his household lunged to turn off the radio when Wallace's program began, archly disclaimed his ability to judge at all: "It is a women's program, and who are we to judge what is, and what is not, worth $200 a week?"[111]

The most eager baiters sharpened their rapiers on the fact that Wallace was married, the assumption being that she did not need any salary at all, let alone $200 a week. This last jab was unfair to all working married women, but it was extremely unjust to Claire Wallace, who had only recently become Mrs James Stutt after years on her own, raising a young son.[112] Wallace never did receive the controversial raise. The public protest was sufficient to cause the timorous National War Finance Committee to close down the broadcasts as of 23 June 1944. Throughout the furore, Wallace preserved a dignified silence, but inevitably she was hurt by the blast of anger against her.[113]

As a prominent public personality, Wallace was a lightning rod for the diffuse uneasiness and resentment that accompanied married and even single women's increasing presence in the paid labour force during the war. The title of Ruth Roach Pierson's analysis of women's paid work during the war, *They're Still Women After All*, aptly encapsulates the official efforts to defuse anxieties that surrounded the highly visible participation of women in the public realm. That these efforts were not uniformly successful is clear from one of the earlier editorials in the "Wallace Affair," which criticized her programs for glorifying the contribution that Canadian mothers were making to the war effort. The editor of the Rossburn *Review* fumed that inducting mothers into the labour force was nothing to be proud of and that a rising juvenile delinquency rate was the price Canadians would pay for this perversion of the natural order.[114]

Women may have been flooding into entry-level jobs in the factories and offices, but in journalism, opportunities for women increased rather more slowly. As Valance Patriarche commented to Florence Livesay, "This war must be a great disappointment to the women who expected to swarm into jobs and office as was done in 1914. This time we are distinctly *de trop*."[115] As we have seen, the CWPC had to launch a series of spirited protests to ensure that women journalists were included when the government recruited newspaper personnel to assist in public relations and promotional work. One of the few to benefit from the wartime public relations boom was Byrne Hope Sanders, editor of *Chatelaine*. As director of the Consumer Branch, Sanders occupied a highly visible and authoritative position – which, as with Claire Wallace, sparked public rancour. The press had a field day with figures about Sanders's living and travelling expenses. One paper fulminated about the iniquity of the fact that "Miss" Sanders, who ought to be living "like a maiden lady," received more than a soldier's wife with two children.[116] In private life, Miss Sanders was Mrs Frank Sperry, a fact that would hardly have decreased the animosity.

All told, the advances a few women journalists made into positions of prestige and authority during the Second World War were not unmixed blessings. There was still considerable resistance to women in high places even after demonstrated competence in their field of expertise.

FACING OLD AGE

The working life cycle of the fortunate few successful women journalists rarely matched the smooth curve of upward progress of the male success story. Every step had its peculiar challenges, and the end of a career could be as fraught with difficulties as its beginning. Journalism was a hard occupation to give up, especially since retirement could present the unappetizing prospect of poverty. Married or single, journalists' lives were as likely to be unconventional as not; a life of adventure did not usually lead to comfortable security. The constant scramble after stories, the fevered pursuit of one lead after another, too often petered out into destitution as health and strength ebbed away.

The Canadian Women's Press Club was acutely aware of the precariousness of the profession and how easily one could tumble down the ladder. At the first triennial meeting in 1913, the press club established the "Beneficiary Fund," which was intended to help out "any infirm, ailing or needy member who is in temporarily straightened circumstances financially."[117] The cases of journalists who applied to the fund discloses the plight of older women who were too frail or ill to carry on an arduous occupation and who had no other resources. Genevieve Lipsett-Skinner, at the height of her powers and confidence in her twenties, had proposed the motion to establish the fund; twenty years later she was a petitioner when illness had reduced her to helplessness.[118] She died a few months after her appeal to the Beneficiary Fund, leaving only enough in her estate to host her fellow Montreal branch members to a memorial dinner.[119] Another supplicant, Mary Pease, was a widow who began her career on the *Montreal Star* in 1913 and then edited the IODE house organ, *Echoes,* for twenty-five years. In her eighties, she was nearly blind but was still writing a column. Though very poor, she was too proud to apply on her own behalf, so the Toronto club used the fund to help this fifty-year member and past branch president through her last days.[120]

However appreciated, the Beneficiary Fund was no more than a palliative measure for emergencies. It was never intended to (nor could it) contend with long-term disability. Among newspaper folk there had been something of a heroic tradition of writing until death, and a few hard-working women journalists shared the all-too-common male fate of premature death, slumped over their typewriters. Blanche Robbins, who for eighteen years had written all the routine obituaries of the *Globe and Mail,* died at the age of forty-nine on her way home from work.[121] Mabel Clark was found at her desk on the Clinton, Ontario, *Record.*[122] It was the death of Florence Lediard Clutton of the Winnipeg *Farmer's Advocate,* only a few months after her marriage, that had inspired the formation of a Beneficiary Fund.

Almost every guide to a career in journalism emphasized good health as the most essential prerequisite. The women strong enough to brave the rigours of their calling were surprisingly durable. Lillian Foster was with the Toronto *Telegram* for forty-seven years and was still working when she died. Bessie Gowan Ferguson also had a long career, beginning with the Hamilton *Spectator* in 1919, then working as women's editor of the Toronto *Mail and Empire,* then with the *Globe and Mail.* She was continuously employed throughout her long career but felt for those who were not so fortunate. When she died in 1962, she left a bequest to the Beneficiary Fund.[123]

Cora Hind was another who lived a good span, and her work was the central fact of that life. She once confessed to Ethel Lindsay Osborne, "I have had no time for social contacts. Apart from my work, I have nothing."[124] Hind "detested the idea of retirement and she became angry with people who sought to surround her with comforts." The cub she raised to reporter status, Grant Dexter, recalled that she was actively engaged in her work right up to a week before she died.[125] Both Hind and her fellow agricultural reporter, Miriam Green Ellis, avoided the fate of poverty that befell so many of their friends and colleagues. They both left good estates, with substantial bequests to the CWPC Beneficiary Fund.[126]

Even at the age of seventy, Annie Mathewson expressed no interest in retirement after fifty years of newspaper work. As city editor of the Fredericton *Daily Gleaner,* she was hardly coasting on a comfortable sinecure. She had survived hard times as a widow with a family to support, and despite the pace and responsibilities of her job, she was not about to relinquish her moderately prosperous independence.[127] In similar fashion, Maria Lawson did not give up the job she had begun in 1907 for the Victoria *Colonist,* even when she turned eighty-two, winning the distinction in the CWPC as "Canada's oldest working woman journalist."[128] It may not have been commitment to her career that kept Lawson at work. The census of 1921 listed one female journalist over sixty-five living in Victoria who earned $9.23 a week working full time – when the average woman journalist was earning around $25 a week. If this was Maria Lawson, perhaps she could not afford to retire.

Quite apart from the insecurity and the prospect of poverty that was the lot of perhaps the majority of self-supporting women when they contemplated retirement, mature women often found their career in journalism too exhilarating to relinquish. Jean Graham reflected sadly in 1911, when ill health slowed her down, "It is quite time for me to recognize the melancholy fact that I am a 'retiring' journalist ... Down town scenes of toil shall know me no longer."[129] In fact she continued to edit the *Canadian Home Journal* for nearly two more decades and lived on until 1936. For Amy Roe, retirement meant a "wrenching loose of roots that are deep in the field of agricultural writing." For forty years she had dedicated her life to her career as home editor of the *Country Guide.* She bowed to the company retirement ruling but continued the voluntary work that had also marked her life.[130] Similarly, Rita Willard Myers thought she had come to the end of the line when she gave up her job as women's editor of the Vancouver *Province* in 1944. "I'm just tired of getting up at 6:30 am every day to be at my desk at 8:00," she sighed. "I have been doing it for 18 years. My job has become a grind. It's no longer fun to try to think up something new and original."[131] But she slept in for only a few months before leaping at a new opportunity in publicity for the Canadian Red Cross, which opened after Elizabeth Bailey Price's sudden death.

The pace of urban journalism was admittedly exhausting, and it required enormous stamina for men as well as women to maintain a long career span. But many mature women found their metier on rural papers, where they were free from the jibes and irritations that afflicted a woman journalist at all stages of her career – and not least towards the end, when her experience gave her wisdom which her younger colleagues did not always appreciate. In a rural context, the fact that she was a woman was rarely an impediment and frequently a positive asset to a senior journalist's work. Such was the experience of a successful city journalist who chose country journalism when her husband was killed at the Somme and left her a newspaper and a daughter. "I am often asked why I stay contentedly in this 'neck of the woods' in Alberta, when I might be a highly paid newspaper or literary lady of consequence on some big city daily," she observed. But she had a clear explanation: "In cities the way was sometimes made very rough for a woman with initiative ... for one woman who succeeds on a big city daily, there are ten who fall by the wayside in the stress and strain of daily work ... The human touch is more remote in a big city ... people are so carelessly cold, even unkind sometimes." In her rural setting, she was in control: "I have run my paper for years and have been owner, managing editor, advertising solicitor, accountant, city editor and society reporter all rolled into one. Doubtless the work of running a country newspaper is hard, but it gives one independence – freedom from taking orders or working under the eye of some tobacco-soaked, grouchy man."[132]

In the country, the function of a newspaper was part social service, part gossip network – the glue that held a community together. Some of the features which male journalists encountered as drawbacks to country journalism – the obligation of living in the locale, attending all the local meetings, and trying not to offend the town councillors (who might also be the biggest advertisers)[133] – were familiar experiences to any woman's page editor. Good reporters were hard to keep, as Rutherford points out, because rural weeklies were used as a training ground for newsmen, who moved on as soon as possible.[134] Women journalists, especially if they were married, were less mobile. These factors may have facilitated women's presence in country journalism even while they complicated the work experienced there.

Middle-aged women who knew their neighbours, who had quick wits and ready pens, could find no more congenial setting for the display of their talents. On the weekly newspaper they became the nerve centres of their region. As Margaret Murray, owner of the *Bridge River–Lillooet News,* put it, "Homely news items of local happenings in a weekly newspaper are of greater importance to country folk than world news, international propaganda or radio broadcasts and neighbourhood toleration cements community good will."[135] Hughena McCorquodale was another example of a woman whose potential ripened fruitfully at the helm of a country newspaper. Observing her beauty, culture, and "acid wit" as she sat at her editorial desk on the High River, Alberta, *Times,* Bruce Hutchison of the *Vancouver Sun* thought at first that she was wasted on the "little cow town." On reflection, he corrected himself: "She had been placed exactly where she belonged to preserve the muniments of her region ... Better than anyone else [she] expressed in print the foothill mores and commanded, like a queen, the worship of the High River Valley folk."[136]

McCorquodale turned to full-time newspaper work after eighteen years of motherhood raising three sons. During that time, she had written freelance features and acted as correspondent for the *Calgary Herald* and *Lethbridge Herald* so that, when the "empty nest" freed her energy for a new direction, her skills were honed for the job. Her extensive knowledge of the community gave her the background to cover the various dimensions of country life: "municipal affairs, ranching conditions, grain farming, soil drifting, oil development, political trends, legislation affecting the area, sport, church, school and social life."[137] Most of all, McCorquodale understood that a newspaper's function in the country was altogether different from its role in the city – "a matter of the heart rather than the head." Her woman's heart directed her towards material that would "weave together the strong sure threads of community life," even if this meant leaving out the "choicest stories from a news viewpoint."[138] Items that would divide neighbour from neighbour or blight the spirits of already depressed farmers were not the stuff of the country weekly. The formula McCorquodale knew to be right for her High River folk had a certain global applicability to rural settings in the Depression. During the years McCorquodale wrote for the High River *Times,* it was the only Canadian example chosen by Oklahoma University as one of the "All Star Eleven" weekly papers.[139]

The dream of owning one's own rural weekly beguiled many a hard-bitten city editor, and quite a few succumbed to the lure.[140] What is surprising is the number of women who managed to acquire and successfully run their own newspaper.[141] The majority of female newspaper owners carried on the tradition of family enterprise that had enfolded women in the business since the nineteenth century. Mrs A.S. Moore took over the Strathmore, Saskatchewan, *Standard* when her husband died in 1933, and she reaped so much satisfaction from being at the heart of her town that she had no intention of ever retiring, even after she became a great-grandmother. Women who run a country newspaper might "wear out," she observed, "but they won't rust out."[142] In fact, they often took a fair time to wear out. The first woman to edit and publish a newspaper in Saskatchewan, Mrs John Hawkes, died in 1944 at the age of ninety-three.[143]

Margaret Lapp was another who took over a family rural weekly, since neither of her brothers wanted to. Lapp commented that the running of newspapers by women ws a common practice in her family; her mother had run the *Ensign* of Brighton, Ontario, when her father went overseas in the First World War, and she assumed that she "was one of the few daughters to succeed her mother in this line of business."[144] There were frustrations, she acknowledged, in running a paper in a small town, where locals might take their important business elsewhere but expect instant service for spare-change printing jobs. Recounting once such incident, she noted dryly, "There are times when we long to be a man, occasions such as these when we feel quite confident only a man's language could possibly do justice to the situation." On the whole, she felt that publishing a newspaper did not "seem much different for a woman than for a man." She admitted that she took a "lot of ribbing" about how clean and tidy her establishment was, but to her, that was simply a mark of good business practice, not necessarily "a feminine touch." Writing in a column for the Canadian Weekly Newspapers Association reserved for "the feminine angle," Lapp prevaricated: "Being a woman, how am I to appreciate the differences between mine and a man's viewpoint? ... My viewpoint wasn't so much the woman's as it was a firm conviction that publishing and printing was what I most wanted to do."[145]

Lapp was born to the business, but for women without the prospect of inheriting a family business, the goal of running their own newspaper could seem utopian; few had the kind of capital or backing that a man could command. Yet a handful of women did amass sufficient capital on their own initiative to take over a newspaper and run their own show. The ownership of a country paper was an ideal career move for a woman with surplus energy and a certain amount of capital, who wanted a measure of power and security as she entered middle age. This was the attraction for Anne Anderson Perry. After a busy and successful career, which took her all across Canada and included a stint as editor of *Canadian Comment*, Perry returned to her hometown of Elora, Ontario, to run the local weekly: "I bought the *Express* to attain personal freedom; also that I might serve the community constructively by providing in public print a channel for independent thinking and writing in an environment far more promising for good results than in any great city ... I regard the weekly newspaper as one of the most useful and powerful tools in our Canadian democracy."[146]

Perry's considerable and varied experience transformed this rural paper by importing some big-city style. She restored the editorial and removed advertisements from the front page, where they still lingered even in the 1930s in some small-town papers.[147] Small merchants thought her action high handed, but the biggest advertisers wanted to be carried in a thriving paper so they went along with her. Perry flourished and so did the *Express*. Fellow CWPC members glowed with pride as the Elora *Express* carried across its masthead the logo of the Canadian Women's Press Club. Perry was also an active member of the Canadian Weekly Newspaper Association.

When Perry had had enough in 1941, she sold the paper to another woman, Katherine Marston, a widow with four young children to support. Although Marston had had no previous newspaper experience, she drove the *Express* to the pinnacle of excellence, winning the Canadian Weekly Newspaper Association award six times between 1944 and 1951, as well as the Joseph Clark Memorial Trophy in 1951.[148] Like her predecessor, Marston was an opinionated editor who passionately defended the editorial prerogative, even though she had to write the editorial after midnight on Sunday because that was the only free time she had.[149] To her mind, the weeklies were "the last outpost of independent voice and thought in an era of an amalgamated and controlled press."[150]

Perry and Marston were not the only journalists to solve their problems of independence and security by buying a newspaper. Earlier, at the turn of the century, a very successful teacher, Antoinette Forbes, who was vice-principal of Windsor Academy in Nova Scotia, became a newspaper proprietor when she discovered the paltry pension she could expect upon retirement from the academy. Forbes teamed up with the widow Jean Fielding to buy the Windsor *Tribune* on 27 March 1905. Not only had neither woman ever worked on a newspaper, but there were other strikes against them too: they lived in a conventional community, which viewed the prospect of women running a paper as preposterous; their paper had a Conservative orientation during a Liberal ascendancy; and they took up the cause of prohibition when the movement was just getting started and was meeting entrenched opposition. In spite of these drawbacks, they ran the *Tribune* for more than a quarter of a century.[151] At a convention of the Canadian Press Association in Toronto in the early 1920s, Mrs Fielding was asked if she was one of those women who ran a paper "just like men." On the contrary, she objected, "not like men, but exactly like women."[152] The pair retained their independence of style in all facets of their business, including scrapping the plans of the architect they hired to design them a building in 1914 and designing their own space.

While Perry and Marston, like Fielding and Forbes, acquired their papers from personal assets, Mrs Paul Smet (née Françoise Gaudet) came up with a novel approach to capital formation: she asked women for donations. In launching *La Paysana*, Smet set out specifically to serve rural women. For years she had been running the women's department of the *Farmer's Magazine*, but she wanted to do more for her chosen constituency. When she asked her father for money to start the project, he just laughed and so did his wealthy friends. Undaunted, she sent out a thousand pamphlets to women asking what they thought about her idea. Her respondents were enthusiastic and, more to the point, generous: they sent in donations totalling $800 for start-up capital. Their faith was warranted. By 1942, *La Paysana* circulated to thirty thousand readers.[153]

This was the pinnacle of a working woman journalist's success. While exceedingly few women achieved structural authority in urban journalism, in rural journalism a woman might possibly achieve the power to serve her community as she saw fit. As Ishbel Ross remarked at an address to the CWPC in 1938, "The only women who can claim full estate in journalism are those who run or own papers by inheritance, marriage or purchase."[154] It was in this arena that the senior woman journalist's career path might parallel that of the successful male journalist who had advanced to the uppermost ranks of an urban daily.

But such women were the fortunate exceptions. For most women journalists with lofty goals of public service, the arena was more narrowly circumscribed. Even among those with long years of experience in newspaper work, it was rare for an individual woman to take part in collective decision making or to influence the direction of policy. In lieu of having an acknowledged position of prestige and power, many of them resolved the conflict between their aspirations and the reality of their situation by delving into the woman's realm and serving their female constituency with the same dedication that a newspaper owner might devote to her flock. It was this sense of an especially womanly mission that Margaret Lawrence encapsulated as she mused on the attractions of her calling:

Of course there is no profession that offers quite the same opportunity to women as is to be found in newspaper work. The element of change, the opportunity for the last word; the sense of definite accomplishment when warm and clean the papers come off the press into one's hand is only equalled in the satisfaction with which the successful bathing of the first baby was regarded. The joy with which we read of the putting across of a pet scheme, some bit of reform, some contribution to the permanent life of the community, even the lurking suspicion that City Hall may have relented through sheer fatigue, cannot dim our ardour. The wee bit of sentiment, the little poem, all are inexpressibly dear to the heart of the newspaper woman who, despite her desire to appear to be indifferent, to take it all in the daily stride, is nevertheless, all radiant within.[155]

CHAPTER FIVE

In Woman's Realm:
The Evolution of the
Women's Section

The press woman today becomes not only the recorder of her sister woman, her efforts and aspirations, her achievements or failures, her strengths or feminine frailties, in her public and private life, but she may, if she will but realize her high vocation, become the interpreter of public affairs and social developments to the hundreds of thousands of Canadian women, who rely on the printed word for their primary contact with life and affairs.

Charlotte Whitton, 1924

In 1929, just after the British Privy Council declared that women were indeed "persons," one of the chief agitators, Nellie McClung, expressed the fervent wish that "we may yet live to see the day when women will be no longer news!"[1] What McClung envisaged was a society in which women were so thoroughly integrated into the mainstream of public life that it would not be remarkable for one woman to be a scientist, another an engineer, and yet another prime minister, and that none would have to "stop to explain, defend or apologize" for her sex.[2] As the most prominent feminist of her era, McClung had spent much of her public life defending and explaining her sex. Moreover, for nearly two decades every angle of her personal newsworthiness had been exploited by her friends and supporters – the newswomen of Canada. At the end of this struggle, her wish to be left alone, "a peaceful, happy, normal human being, pursuing my unimpeded way through life,"[3] was understandable; but as a much-valued member of a club whose members were largely dependent for their livelihood on women's news and women as news, her remarks may have seemed disloyal. It was precisely the sort of woman – the professional, entrepreneur, or adventurer – whose main claim to public attention was that she was female, that presswomen featured in interviews or celebrity sketches. A great many

Cartoon of women journalists from the souvenir booklet for the 1923 triennial meeting, Vancouver, B.C. The cartoon lampoons stereotypes associated with various "women's" specialties in journalism (City of Vancouver Archives, CVA 396, vol. 1, file 8)

newspaperwomen built their career by emphasizing the newsworthiness of women, in segregated sections designed to carry "news of interest to women."

McClung's logic would extend quite naturally to the newspaperwomen themselves. In her projected utopia, women journalists would not require women's news for their profession. Newswriting women would contribute to all sections of the newspaper – front page, editorial, business, politics, international relations, sports, culture, and entertainment – just as the exploits of newsmaking women would permeate the whole paper. But in the real world, the women's page remained the principal and, in some centres or some newspapers, the only opportunity open to the woman journalist, from the late nineteenth century through the first half of the twentieth. In 1949, even after the heady successes that some newswomen achieved during wartime, Marjorie Oliver of the *London Free Press* admitted, "We might as well face the fact ... that the majority of girls entering the world of ink and print will have to find positions in women's departments." She tempered her tidings by adding that if women's pages extended their scope, they could provide the rising generation with "work as satisfying as any on the paper."[4] By implication, Oliver conceded that women journalists could not expect a fair chance in other branches of newspaper work and that relegation to the women's section might deflate the ambition of young women aspiring to brilliant careers. The women's page lacked the aura of prestige and authority that sustained junior reporters through the drudgery of routine assignments.

After more than fifty years in Canadian newspapers, the status of the women's page and of those who made it was still ambiguous. It was a public venue where women could address other women, where they could, at least in part, define what was newsworthy for women and create a kind of woman-centred newspaper inside the newspaper. Many women journalists were proud of what they accomplished as women's page editors – "the girls," as Mabel Burkholder described them, "who take the daily grind and, as a reward, mould a great body of public opinion and give shape and cohesion to Canada's thought."[5] Yet though women's page editors might celebrate the achievements of their peers, their collective pride was hard to sustain in a profession that mocked their creation. This chapter examines the evolution of the women's section in newspapers and looks at how this separate department for women both furnished and limited career possibilities for newswomen.

THE STATUS OF THE WOMEN'S PAGE

In the last two decades of the nineteenth century, a motley assemblage of "things of interest to women" began to coalesce in British, American, and Canadian newspapers. The very innocence and innocuousness of the first "cut and paste" miscellanies made the page controversial. Both men and women were among its detractors. Well-educated and well-informed women were mortified at the suggestion that an ordinary newspaper was beyond their comprehension, that they could master nothing more taxing than a few fashion illustrations and recipes, and that the rest of the newspaper was above their reach. Insulting, too, was the assumption that events in which women featured as major players were not deemed to be of interest to the general reading public. An English woman writer argued vigorously that because newspaper owners did not recognize the importance of their female readership, items of vital importance to women were either ignored or were the "subject of a school-boy like jibe."[6] Sara Jeannette Duncan, in her own newspaper column for women, took exception to the announcement of a new women's journal produced and printed by women. She complained that such a division was unnatural, that men and women had common interests and complementary qualities that should not be severed.[7]

It was particularly vexing to serious women who laboured to extend women's horizons and rights in the public realm to discover that the current "ladies' papers" pandered solely to the most trivial, indeed baleful, tastes that ever were attributed to womankind. Flora Annie Steele, a regular contributor to the *Saturday Review of London*, made a survey of these papers, examining the cheapest to the dearest, to discern whether the "separate life of a woman" really warranted distinct recognition in newspapers and magazines. She found, to her dismay, that the "burning questions in the lives of those for whom the ladies' papers cater" arose solely from whatever calamity they faced in their looking glasses.[8]

That such banal productions became the semi-official exhibition of feminine lives and interests laid women open to the hilarity or rancour of male opponents of women's right to a public voice. The *Saturday Review* condemned a popular women's paper, the *Ladies' Mirror*, as "A Mirror for Fools," adding that women who were addle-brained enough to tolerate such drivel should forever be disqualified from the vote.[9] More seriously, Harry Quilter, in the *Fortnightly Review*, used his perusal of contemporary women's magazines to upbraid the entire sex for their addiction to vanity and for their want of "moral courage." He concluded that the multiplication of society journals in recent years had marked a retrogression rather than an advance in women's intellectual progress.[10]

Given the low estimation of women's page content, newspaperwomen trying to make their way in the potentially expansive field of journalism were frustrated to discover that whatever their tastes, talents, and inclinations, if they were fortunate enough to find a staff position it would invariably be in the women's department. Mary McOuat, a highly educated woman and the daughter of one of Canada's distinguished academics, Walter McOuat, railed against this confinement: "I have 'chopped copy,' conducted a cooking column, book reviews, interviews, answered in correspondence columns, and reported everything from an afternoon tea to a political meeting. This has all been done for the Women's Page, however, and as a consequence I am unspeakably weary of everything connected with the sex. The one thing I most wish is that I had had the good fortune to be born a man for then I would not have been obliged to write about women."[11] Although she averred that "nothing but dire necessity would induce her" to do either sewing or cooking, she spent much of her career instructing her readers on these matters. Florence Sherk, who began her career on the Fort William *Times-Journal* in the late nineteenth century and remained in the women's section for nearly four decades, was not as captious about her fate as McOuat. But as she congratulated those who had escaped it, she tacitly acknowledged the obscurity, in newspaper status, of the women's page. "Newspaper women are more and more extending the borders of their empire," she exulted in 1914. "The 'Woman's Page' is merely the vestibule into the more stately departments of the journalistic realm."[12]

The note of apology that often tinged the remarks that women writers made about their contribution to the newspaper derived from the conventional canons of journalism, which were inevitably based on the male point of view on what was news and what was mere drivel. It was an attitude that made ardent feminist Anne Anderson Perry explode with frustration: "The plain truth seems to be that we women still have an inferiority complex ... Most of us accept men's appraisals of our work. In this society we ought to be alive to the fact that just so long as we are thus acquiescent, just so long will we disbar ourselves from the far finer vision which might be ours."[13]

The ostensibly male and female departments of the newspaper seemed to separate serious affairs that made the world turn from those that were mainly recreational or ornamental. But this judgment rested on a double standard of newsworthiness. Women's pages usually contained far more sober matter on public affairs, as well as the kind of information that oiled the wheels of daily life, than sports pages did. Yet few sports writers cringed at the triviality of their subject; nor did their early speciality hobble their progress towards more august appointments.[14] The amount of money newspaper owners were willing to spend on sports reporting was eloquent testimony of its importance in their eyes. The Ottawa *Free Press*, for instance, staged an extravagant caper that involved setting up relays of reporters, typists, and telegraphers in the local hockey rink merely to get the report on the streets the moment the game ended.[15]

Sports columns or pages were a daily offering in virtually every newspaper, whatever the season, by the turn of the century. In contrast, women's pages were episodic, starting up and then disappearing in some papers for months or even years. The Toronto *Globe*, one of the pioneers of the women's page in Canada, had a daily column through the late 1880s. By the 1890s, women had only a weekend offering, but this was a solid two pages with a number of famous columnists - Lally Bernard (Mary Agnes Fitzgibbon), Madge Merton (Elmira Elliott Atkinson), and Madge Robertson (Watt). There was fashion, cookery, interior decorating, child-rearing advice, and other home and community features. But by the turn of the century, this had dwindled to a daily society column and a children's page; there was no women's column or page *per se*.

The unequal treatment of ostensibly male and female departments persisted even when the women's section became an expected fixture of the daily newspaper. That a "so-called women's editor" of a big-city daily was paid on space rates while the newspaper establishment pandered to the sports editor and even the sports reporters exasperated Anne Anderson Perry in the 1930s.[16] Ethelwyn Hobbes, a newspaperwoman who had graduated into broadcasting, echoed this charge in the 1940s when she complained that newspapers devoted far too much space to sports and not nearly enough to women's interests. Her forecast was that improvement in the status of the women's pages would not likely occur until their editors were paid as well as sports page editors and until newspaper management was prepared to spend as much money on the women's section as it spent on sports coverage.[17]

The prejudice against the women's section reflected the established status divisions between "hard" and "soft" news. Gathering "hard" news as it was happening carried more prestige than the often more thoughtful "soft" news features, even if the "hard" news was as trivial as sports statistics or a story about an anthropomorphized captive of the local zoo.[18] Moreover, the slow-breaking stories about health, education, or welfare that filled the women's section moved lives more potently than much of the more ephemeral "hard" news that would be little more than "old" news tomorrow. Yet writers in the women's section were made to feel that they were creating mere window dressing while the real work of newsmaking occurred outside the women's department. It may have been small comfort to those who resented being sidelined that Arnold Bennett, in his guidebook addressed to women journalists, assured them that women were not utterly disqualified from attempting "male" subjects: "To argue that, because the male journalist does not usually touch women's affairs without being ridiculous, therefore the converse is true, is illogical. I lay stress on this."[19]

Among the male journalists who deigned to address the subject, there was a sense that any self-respecting man was demeaned by association with the women's section. The cartoon image of the grizzled old newspaperman hammering out a lovelorn column or a children's page never failed to raise a snigger. It was in this spirit that Gordon Sinclair used his stint on the *Toronto Star* women's page as a foil to set off the ultramasculinity of his other journalistic exploits. Sinclair was parachuted onto the women's page when the proprietor's wife, Mrs Atkinson (formerly Elmira Elliott and famous as Madge Merton) intervened in the running of the women's department. Apparently, she believed that the women currently conducting it were "a menace."[20] Clifford

Wallace was the first to win the invidious distinction of being the *Star's* male women's editor. Nicknamed Nellie for his trouble, he begged to be relieved of the post. Ironically, his sister, Claire, began her dazzling career on precisely that same page some years later, despite her brother's opposition to her joining the *Star*. But at this point, in 1922, the managing editor assigned the position to Sinclair, who treated his responsibilities with cavalier contempt: "From the beginning I never took the job seriously, expecting I would either be fired or soon moved to other work. As a consequence I used to come in at eight in the morning and, except on Saturdays, quit for the day about eleven. I shamelessly clipped most of my material from other newspapers, and stuck to the job for about fourteen months until young Joe Atkinson, who was at that time a proof reader, noticed that all my stuff had previously been published in some other paper."[21] So ended Sinclair's career on the women's page; he was transferred back to the newsroom. Few female women's page editors were so privileged that they could display such incompetence in their department and still retain their position, let alone advance.

On the whole, male journalists shrank from direct involvement with the women's department. There was a sense among the journalist fraternity that the whole newspaper enterprise was in danger of being suffused by "feminine subjects." E.E. Sheppard, who knew well that his bread was buttered by the efforts of the editors of his women's section, when asked why he tolerated so much society chit-chat in *Saturday Night* replied sardonically, "Well you'll notice that if pink teas are popular on the inside, they don't cut much of a figure on the front page."[22] The women's departments were rigorously contained on the "inside" lest they emasculate the other "serious" sections. As a result, news or items that had bearing on women's lives rarely had a male audience. Kit Coleman, for one, took exception to this: "Why do men look ashamed if they are caught reading the woman's page in a newspaper? Are women utter idiots? Do men believe that there is not a word to be written for our sex beyond frills and fopperies?"[23]

Coleman made a pitch for the male reader, promising that she would confine herself to topics interesting to the mind of man, in so far as a pedlar with a sackful of femininities can confine himself,"[24] and she often succeeded in luring masculine browsers, as her letters indicate.[25] Possibly it was more common for male readers to stray into women's sections in the early days when they were a novelty and when women's writers discussed literary, social, and intellectual issues that were not well represented in other parts of the newspaper. Emily Cummings was flattered when Trinity College Professor William Clark confessed to reading her column on a regular basis,[26] and Sara Jeannette Duncan responded in arch humility when a male correspondent solicited advice: "It affords me a satisfaction which I am loath to disguise, dear 'Homo,' to know that while my column is intended chiefly for the encouragement of my own sex in their various departments of usefulness, an occasional man is induced to avail himself of the admonishment vouchsafed to him herein."[27]On the whole, editors of the women's page seem to have been proud when they attracted male readers, as if masculine attention conferred legitimacy on them as journalists. Annie Merrill's column title, "For the Average Woman and the Occasional Man" in the Toronto *Mail and Empire,* was undoubtedly intended to invite male patronage – though quite likely it had the opposite effect, even on "occasional men."

As a physical symptom of the sentiment that separated women's news from "general" news, the women's page workers were sequestered from the rest of the newspaper staff. Alixe Carson of the *Calgary Herald* remembered a young reporter who blushed every time he had to come near the women's page office.[28] Initially, female staffers were not welcome at the newspaper office and were obliged to prepare their copy at home and deliver it by the deadline. The newsroom did not accommodate itself readily to the presence of women. When Lotta Dempsey began on the *Edmonton Journal* in the late 1920s, there were no women's washrooms in the newsrooms; nor did she find any in the Edmonton *Bulletin* or in the Toronto *Globe* or *Star.* It was assumed that the only newspaperwoman employed would be the social editor and that she would be away at teas all day.[29] When women did enter the newspaper building, they usually occupied a distant cubbyhole, a corner, or a separate office. The *Calgary Herald* newsroom in 1933 was a horseshoe-shaped arrangement of reporters and editors, with the women's section tucked away in a glassed-in cubicle.[30] Claire Wallace, hired as a reporter for the *Toronto Star* in the early 1930s, was similarly quarantined and had to walk down a long hallway to deliver her copy to the city editor.[31] Edith MacInnes (later McCook) shared a small office with Irene Moore, even though their papers, respectively the Regina *Post* and *Leader,* were competitors, with a single owner.[32] In the same period, all the Toronto *Globe* staff in any way connected with the women's department were crowded into one tiny dusty room that had opaque windows and was crammed with four desks. The women inhabited the room in successive shifts. In the morning, the "Home-Maker" (Mona Purser) shared the room with the church editor (Jane Scott), who was lodged there because she was female, even though her duties were not officially assigned to the women's department. At three o'clock, the society editor (Lois Reynolds) and club editor (Mary James) would arrive for their round of afternoon and nocturnal duties.

Margaret McCrimmon, overall editor of the women's page, spanned the shifts.[33]

The detachment of the women's page editor from the rest of the newspaper had some rationale. Edith MacInnes (McCook), women's editor of the Regina *Post* and then the Calgary *Albertan*, defended the cloistering on the grounds that privacy was very important to club-women and society matrons who might hesitate to tell their secrets and news items to the hurly-burly world outside the women's enclave.[34] Whatever its utility to the women journalists and their confidantes, it was evident that their confinement appeased the ambivalence which the regular newsroom personnel felt towards their female colleagues. Jim Dyer, starting out in 1933 on the Vancouver *Herald*, a shoestring operation run by a collective of journalists, was dismayed to find himself billeted with Bea Green and Evelyn Caldwell. "Tiring of the eternal clack of female tongues," he demanded and got his own office.[35] As late as 1942 at the *Toronto Star*, J.E. Atkinson believed that the presence of a woman in the city department would demoralize the male reporters. Thus, when Marjorie Earl joined the general reporting staff, her desk was in the women's section with a long telephone wire connecting her to the newsroom.[36]

The apartheid of male and female journalists in the newspaper office was evidence that the male press world resented the women *per se,* not just the sentimental and trivial "guff" that so many of them were obliged to produce. Furthermore, the reluctance of the press establishment to apportion any of the more expensive facilities to the women's department was indicative of its antipathy towards it. For years the Canadian Women's Press Club had bemoaned the indifference with which the Canadian Press Service treated "women's news" and the difficulty that women's page editors faced when trying to gather news of women's activities in the national scene. Pointedly they attributed this neglect to the fact that "Canadian Press correspondents are men who, as a rule place no importance on women's news or news of special import to women."[37]

In the newsroom the women's page had few male defenders. It was the advertising department that harboured champions of the women's section. When the Vancouver *Province* first began offering "women's news," the advertising manager heralded the experiment: "If the great publications, from the leading magazines down to the simple local country weeklies, are spending every energy along the lines of feminine desire, it is certainly necessary that the advertisers should not forget that there are as many women as men and that ... Woman is the pivot of trade turning."[38] A standard textbook on journalism, Harrington and Frankenburg's *Essentials in Journalism,* underlined this insight. While the authors dismissed as nonexistent the "intrinsic news value" of women's subjects, they conceded that they were "without peer" as circulation builders.[39] Thus, although newspaper publishers were eager to court women readers, it was not out of respect for women or women's interests. As one historian of the press put it, "For the newspaper industry, a woman's charm was purely financial."[40]

In the years following the First World War, the advertising industry propelled an increasingly consumer-driven economy, and the women's section acquired a market value that no newspaper could do without. Hugh McKanday, as advertising manager of the Toronto *Globe* during the 1920s and 1930s, was well placed to observe the commercial success directly attributable to the "Home-Maker" section under Mona Cleever's direction.[41] In the early 1930s a then relatively unknown Professor Gallup proved the profitability of women's pages scientifically when he conducted a rigorously documented survey of newspaper readers' habits. Among his conclusions, he observed that "editors don't appreciate the fact that the women's page is read more thoroughly than the front page."[42]

It was thus on grounds of hard-nosed commercialism that Canadian presswomen lobbied the Canadian Press to demand that the service hire an editor to distribute women's news items across Canada. In 1940 they argued that newspaper advertising revenue would most likely decrease during the war and that "the power of women's pages to increase both circulation and advertising should be more generally recognized."[43] Ultimately, it was the behind-the-scenes influence of Edna Kells, long-time women's editor of the *Edmonton Journal*, that secured a women's department in the Canadian Press.[44]

Armed with the irrefutable logic of dollars and cents, some women's editors were prepared to defend their handiwork. In the United States, women's pages were so well established even at the turn of the century that women editors would come forward assertively to argue the merits of their sections. Florence Jackman, who had years of experience in American newspapers, blew a fanfare for herself and her sisters on the women's page: "Few understand that the parading of women's doings, even in trivial things, is hourly making for a development of mental and political status that will bring about a juster estimate of the value of women's work, and create a demand for a higher grade of it intellectually as well as materially."[45]

Thus, she and others promised, newspaperwomen might make their debut in a modest sort of way in the women's page, but they could eventually hope that their section would grow as they did in wisdom, sophistication, and public esteem. It was this hope that sustained the most ambitious women's editors through the tedium of social trivia and commercial puffery that pre-empted much of their space. They believed that the women's page was a chronicle of women's advancing status and participation in the local community, the nation, and the world. Even Mary McOuat, who was almost past waiting for the redemption of the women's page as she knew it, glowed in admiration for a woman editor who commanded authority in the newspaper world. Cynthia Westover Alden was a heroine to women journalists in North America because she had gained the kind of unassailable success that silenced opposition. She ran her page on the *New York Tribune* according to her own lights, in full confidence that her public's interests extended beyond cooking and needlepoint. Although male editors occasionally complained that her page was too "solid," Alden's section "carried the paper" and "vastly increased the circulation." McOuat also appreciated that Alden would have none but women on her staff, which numbered up to ten at a time.[46]

THE STATUS OF THE WOMEN'S EDITOR

In Canada, the women's page editor usually occupied an ill-defined position in the newspaper hierarchy. Although many of these women described their post as "on the editorial staff" of their newspaper, the reality of that position when a woman occupied it varied from paper to paper. In the *Toronto Star* staff directory for 1927, for instance, the editorial staff was listed in the first section and included the editorial writers, the city and managing editors and their assistants, the night editors and deskmen, the sports editor, and the "special departments" people such as the music, drama, and literature critics. The two journalists in the women's department appeared in a separate listing in the directory, coming after the reporters and secretaries.[47] Newspaperwomen might call themselves women's editor or society editor but they were unlikely to enjoy the structural authority that usually fell to the editorial chair. As Anne Anderson Perry charged, "It is still only the exceptional paper and the exceptional editor which permit women as much freedom as is given male commentators in doing real editorial work."[48]

Even their autonomy within their segregated section was uncertain. By rights, as editors, they should have had complete charge of their page or section, with the authority to decide what items the page would carry that day, to distribute various assignments, and to send the made-up page directly to the composing room. In such a legitimate editorial position, only the managing editor would intervene between the section editor and the editor-in-chief. But women's page editors were frequently under the jurisdiction of the city editor, and unlike other editors, their work passed through the copy desk en route to the composing room. According to the city editor's interests and temperament, he might meddle with the running of the page, removing "live" news stories from the women's editor if they struck his fancy, borrowing her staff if city news required extra hands, and presiding over the hiring and firing. Even when, in the rare instance, a man was women's editor, he was denied total autonomy. When Richard Needham was woman's editor of the Toronto *Star* in 1934, he had to spell out to his assistants that they must let him see their copy before it went to the main desk for the actual editing. Because he was not a woman, Needham was not cloistered with his female staff in the women's section; a copy boy ran their pieces to his desk in the editorial room. Even so, the city editor, J.R. Heron, determined administrative details such as holiday schedules for the staff of the women's department, and Needham had only recently negotiated the right to assign stories to the women under his direction.[49]

The reality of their structural impotence was not always apparent to women's section editors. As long as they kept within conventional limits, they often were left to run their page as they saw fit without interference from above. But the meddling editorial pencil could strike at any moment. Anne Anderson Perry described the surprise of a women's page editor who had believed she wielded considerable authority in her own department until she took the initiative of running a series on public affairs. Although the material proved to be enormously popular, the series was stopped because it had an editorial aspect. According to Perry, independent opinion was not allowed on the women's page, especially comment on matters of national and international import. The head of the women's department might be called editor, Perry implied, but she was certainly not allowed to editorialize.[50] It was this kind of restraint that in 1910 prompted Lily Laverock to leave the Vancouver *News-Advertiser* and begin her own women's weekly, the *Chronicle*.[51] Decades later, in the 1940s, Bessie Forbes of the Victoria *Times* was cruelly snubbed by the male hierarchy of the paper. When she tried to exert editorial authority to protect her department and staff, her male colleagues sniggered that she was being difficult because it was "that time of her life."[52]

On some newspapers, the women's page editor was left alone by the writing and editorial staff but was subject to pressure from the business department. Advertisers who demanded space on her page would take precedence over her features and news. However much copy she had to trim, it was axiomatic that she make room for the advertisements.[53] Advertisers exercised pressure on the whole paper, to be sure, but in no other branch of the newspaper world did commentators so casually dispense with the distinction between news and advertising copy.[54]

The junior status of women's page editors was further evident in their participation in the reportorial functions. Bona fide editors did not collect the news they edited, yet newsgathering was frequently conducted by the editor of a women's page. On small newspapers, the editor was the whole department – she had to organize her assignments, collect the news, write up the stories, and make up the page. Edith MacInnes (later McCook), women's editor for the Regina *Post*, while noting that "no two days were alike," reconstructed a typical day in her early working life in 1927. In her office by 8:30 AM, her 11:30 deadline loomed. She would scan the rival *Leader* to ensure that she was not parroting old news, and then re-edit copy composed the day before – interviews, speeches, meetings, and social events. Her daily record book would indicate leads to follow that day: "By nine o'clock I was beginning to see a kind of pattern forming for the run to deadline." By phone, she would assemble the rest of the news for that day, calling her contacts among society women who would tell her about the parties they were giving or attending, and would pass on news of who was travelling or returning: "Phone calls had to be brief but profitable, time being of the essence." MacInnes found her contacts among clubwomen more interesting because of their civic, educational, or national context: "All had at least a core of news to be mined, again much by phone calls." After meeting her 11:30 deadline, she read proofs. The afternoon allowed more flexibility, for she could pursue a particularly interesting event or interview and write it up in comparative leisure for the next day's page.[55]

On a larger urban daily, the women's page editor usually had assistants. When MacInnes moved to the Calgary *Albertan*, for instance, a designated society reporter took over the personal column and most of the routine social events. This allowed MacInnes to "dig up stories with more depth"; and since the *Albertan* was a morning paper, the evening deadline of 7 PM made for a more leisurely pace than she had experienced on the Regina *Post*. But even when a metropolitan women's editor had a whole team of assistants, she still did far more legwork than was common for other editors. Margaret McCrimmon, women's editor of the Toronto *Globe*, regularly accompanied the social reporter Lois Reynolds (Kerr) on important functions.[56] On one hand, this could be an advantage to the journalist who enjoyed contact with the public; she could assign routine events to her assistants and retain the most interesting for herself – an important interview, a prestigious party, or a politically strategic club meeting. As one guidebook writer noted: "special editors" had the advantage of authority without the "crushing responsibility" and constant time pressure that burdened the city or managing editor.[57] On the other hand, the fragmentation of her energy and attention often undermined the ability of the women's page editor to achieve excellence. Elizabeth Long, veteran women's page editor of the *Winnipeg Free Press,* noted that the lack of assistance and the necessity of "constantly interviewing the public" sapped the editor's creativity. It was especially important that the women's page feature distinctive stories if it was to escape inanity, but the endless round of duties incumbent upon the women's page editor usually edged out originality.[58]

Paradoxically, the low status of the women's section and the low esteem in which male editors held it could mean autonomy by default for women's page editors. If the public seemed happy and advertisers were satisfied, a phlegmatic city editor might allow an enterprising and competent women's page editor to run her own department with little or no interference. The first society editor on the Toronto *Globe,* Emily Cummings, enjoyed a degree of autonomy, at least insofar as setting her own schedule. The *Globe* assignment books for 1901 chronicles the daily travels of the male reporters who scoured the city for stories, but it makes no mention of the female reporters, most likely because Mrs Cummings had her own assignment book and full charge of her staff.[59]

Female editorial autonomy was not at all unusual on prairie papers, where there was a tradition of assertive women's journalism.[60] Kennethe Haig, writing as Alison Craig for the Manitoba *Free Press,* ran an editorial column on the women's page for years until she graduated to the editorial page proper. Similarly, Edith MacInnes McCook perceived very little intervention from city editors on either the Regina *Post* or the Calgary *Albertan.* Although the city editor did read her copy in advance, this was mostly to ensure that there was no duplication with newsroom stories. In other respects, she maintained, the women's editor was "wholly responsible for what appeared on her page or pages." Shortly after joining the *Albertan,* Edith MacInnes had married her city editor, James McCook, and this likely conditioned her attitude towards her autonomy.[61]

Even on papers where the women's editor ruled her realm, she was excluded from group policy decisions.[62] Her authority extended no farther than the glass cubicle or cubbyhole that she and her staff occupied. By the same token, the rules that governed the "news side" of the paper did not necessarily apply to the women's section. The curious liberality which the *Western Producer* extended to Violet McNaughton illustrates the special status of the women's editor. Editor A.P. Waldron explained to her that while "the Editorial Section of the paper and ... its general outlook ... should be entirely impersonal" these restrictions did not apply to her: "To conduct a page such as yours I think the personal note is essential ... the more you lend your personality to the page the

Mrs Willoughby Cummings (Emily McCausland Cummings), first society editor
for the Toronto *Globe* (NA, PA-57336)

more I will like it."[63] At the same time, articles she had destined for the
women's section might appear elsewhere if the editor deemed them
important.[64] In her early years with the *Western Producer*, McNaughton
was conducting her page from her remote Saskatchewan farm home.
Clearly, there was no question of participating in policy decision
making with other editors.

The women's department was most often its own world. And although women's editors did not enjoy the power and camaraderie
associated with the editorial capacity of urban newspapers, they did
gain useful skills. On papers where women were allowed to run their
own department, the women's page editor gained invaluable supervi-
sory and executive experience with which to advance her career.
Elizabeth Long, for instance, went from women's editor of the Winnipeg *Tribune*, to the same position on the *Free Press*, and then to subeditor
of the *Free Press Prairie Farmer*. In 1938 she became the first woman hired
in an executive capacity by the Canadian Broadcasting Corporation to
direct the women's programs. Her expertise earned her a mandate to
run her department on her own authority.[65]

Long acquired an unusually strategic opportunity in the still flexible
hierarchy of radio. Her experience demonstrated that a woman editor
really could serve her constituency, the readers, rather than the adver-

tisers if she had the leeway to evaluate their needs. Because most "soft" news was associated with the women's department, interesting features such as welfare and social reform issues could find a berth in the centre of the paper, where the women's editor could play them up to adorn her page. Domestic architecture, with descriptions of plans and illustrations of innovative houses, became a women's page feature in Saturday editions across the nation. Similarly, horticulture and articles on education, health, social work, and urban planning frequently made their way to the women's section. The first book, music, and theatre reviews often lodged there as well. What Ishbel Ross called the "stepchild" of the profession could thus become "cerebral as well as decorative" if an experienced and enterprising journalist took charge.[66]

Most important for journalists and readers alike was the fact that the women's page could, in times of feminist activity and controversy, become a forum for women's news and views that were ignored in other sections of the paper. Nellie McClung gratefully saluted women's page editors for the vital role they performed in disseminating news of feminist activity and opinion.[67] Feminist newspaperwomen were self-conscious and confident about the power they wielded among their female constituency. Even in the earliest days of women's participation in press work, Sara Jeannette Duncan had jousted with her readers about feminist issues such as the municipal suffrage for married women.[68] And even though Faith Fenton (Alice Freeman) wrote for the politically conservative Toronto *Empire*, she had made her feminist and suffragist views plain, even as she acknowledged that her editor opposed women's rights.[69] Margaret Graham had introduced her column on Ottawa affairs with the promise that, as well as social affairs, she would focus on the political activities of Ottawa women.

Predictably, the pen-and-ink battles grew fiercer as suffrage activity escalated and as the committed sallied forth, well armed to meet opponents. On some women's pages, particularly in western Canada, there was scope for editorial comment as long as the opinions were confined to appropriately female subjects. As we shall see, it was under the auspices of "club reporting" that women journalists broadcast their vision of a just society. In addition, according to their own lights, ardent reformers, suffragists, pacifists, and patriots could use the editor's corner to patronize their favourite causes and inveigh against injustice.

It was unlikely, however, that radical views would find tolerance from the editor-in-chief if they differed profoundly from the collective personality of the newspaper. Francis Beynon's feminism matched the agrarian radicalism of her paper, the *Grain Growers' Guide*, but when her pacifism did not suit the temper of the times during the first World War, Beynon lost her job.[70] Florence Sherk, long-time women's editor

of the Fort William *Times-Journal,* believed that staff journalists who
were free to express themselves honestly, especially with respect to
women's issues, were a rare breed: "The women on the newspapers are
usually to [*sic*] much afraid of losing their jobs to give an opinion of
their own. I know this and feel I was privileged more than most newspaper women in being given liberty to say what I thought." Sherk was
trying to comfort Madge Macbeth when her novel, *Shackles,* a vivisection
of modern marriage, was being pilloried in the press. She recommended that Macbeth send the novel for review to specific individuals
whom she knew had editorial freedom: "Cornelia [Lucy Doyle of the
Toronto *Telegram*], she's allowed to say things ... and so are one or two
women in Vancouver and in Calgary." Irene Gardiner, society editor of
the Calgary *Albertan,* was another who Sherk believed, had sufficient
independence to be trustworthy.[71]

RELATING TO THE READERS

In lieu of interjecting their own opinions, women's editors on many
papers extended the editorial privilege to their readers. Readers'
forums, "wherein women may express their views on any subject on
their own page," as Irene Kent introduced her version on the Vancouver *News-Herald,* were a female alternative to the "letters to the editor"
page, which generally gave short shrift to women's opinions and
women's issues.[72] Mona Purser made explicit her version of freedom of
the press for readers who might shy away from frank expression of
opinion, encouraging them to use pen names when writing to the
Home-Maker's page of the *Globe.* "Their chief object ... is that of permit-
ting a correspondent to write freely, as she could not do if she felt that
people ... knew who she was and were judging what she wrote on the
basis of their previous knowledge of her."[73] Sometimes these forums
were as mundane as cooperative "helpful hints" exchanges – "The
Found Out" feature run in the Edmonton *Journal* in 1913, for instance.
More often, they enabled readers to communicate with each other on a
more substantial plane, where professional women, homemakers,
servants, sales clerks, newly married women, and older matrons could
show one another what the world looked like from their vantage point.

   One of the more lively exchanges erupted when the *Toronto Star's*
women's page ran a series on working women. In April 1910 women in
the labour force sparred with homemakers and society matrons and
gave vent to their frustration over exploitation and patronizing contempt. On 11 April 1910 one woman aired her indignation about the
"helpful hints" which well-to-do subscribers volunteered to show the
working poor how to make do with less. These interfering busybodies,

she exploded, were merely shifting the responsibility from employers and husbands, who gave too little to the already overburdened women. On the next day's page, a teacher argued for equal pay based on what a woman was worth to her employer rather than what she needed to live on. It was no no one's business, she said, whether a woman lived with her parents, supported others, or how much her boots cost her. Another reader called the working girl a "modern heroine" whose contribution to the good of the world was far in excess of that of the society woman, "who flits from tea to tea" and pays others to do work she should be doing herself. Editor Margaret Fairbairn's summary of the controversy was tame in comparison with the passion exhibited by her readers. Admitting the injustice of paying women too little to live on, she lamely concluded that employers had a dilemma too, in trying to make the best use of women while conserving the "great natural resource of wives and mothers."[74]

During times of national stress, the open forum allowed the exchange of viewpoints across regional and economic barriers. Just before the First World War, Eva Langley Jacobs used her women's page in the *Farm and Ranch Review and Nor'West Farmer* to connect destitute homeless women with farm wives who needed help and company.[75] Similarly, a reader of Violet McNaughton's welfare page in the *Saturday Press and Prairie Farm* catalogued the exhausting labours of a farm wife, which made her previously single life as an office worker seem like a holiday. She signed herself "No Occupation" to reinforce McNaughton's crusade to establish official recognition of women's work on prairie farms.[76] During the Depression a reader on a dairy farm used the Toronto *Globe*'s "Home-Maker" page to explain to urban readers why the price of butter had to rise.[77] The cumulative effect could not fail to help women understand one another and empathize with those in vastly different circumstances.

The circumstances of the women who read women's sections of Canadian newspapers differed profoundly, as their letters to the section disclosed. The women's pages themselves were not as diverse, and the differences were based on region more than on class. In urban centres where three or more papers might compete, proprietors tended to slant their product towards particular sectors of the market or certain political views; but the women's pages, as Paul Rutherford has noted, were "designed to appeal to any female whatever her class" and assumed that most women were "average" housewives and mothers.[78] A comparison of the "highbrow" morning paper, the Vancouver *Province*, with the popular afternoon *Vancouver Sun* bears out Rutherford's hunch. On Friday, 1 April 1932, the *Province* and *Sun* both featured social and club notes on pages with similar banner headlines in elegant

italicized script. Both featured a central photograph of a prominent society matron and club leader. Both identified the principal social events
and listed the guests in more or less identical order. And while the *Province* headlined the Royal Vancouver Yacht Club fete, the *Sun* described
the Vancouver Lawn Tennis Club dance first and then the yacht club
affair – a difference that likely had little to do with social tone, since
both were elitist events. Although the *Province* called its page "Society
and Women's Clubs," there was more attention given to women's clubs
that day on the *Sun's* page, called simply "Society." The *Sun* carried a
fashion illustration, a dress pattern, and a short recipe, while the
Province featured "Our Ottawa Letter" of social notes from the capital.
The advertisements covered approximately one-third of each page, for
very similar consumer goods (indeed, exactly the same piano company
and fur coat advertisements appear in both), and there were also full-
page department store advertisements placed close to the pages
directed at women. In neither paper was there any hint of the economic
disaster which many families were grappling with at that time.

While the women's page itself targeted a broad and largely undiffer-
entiated urban female audience, individual journalists may have felt
obliged to respond to the sensitivities of their readership. Lotta Dempsey discovered the caprices of public taste when she imported to the
popular *Toronto Star* her signature character, a cleaning woman whose
faulty grammar and quaint views amused the middle-class readers of the
Globe and Mail. "Down market," her column was not so well received. A
readership that included recent immigrants and domestic and factory
workers felt more patronized than charmed by Dempsey's humour.[79]

In rural areas, the newspaper might be the only source of information about new fashions for the farming wife; unlike her urban contemporary, she could not see the changes in every shop window. By the
same token, she had less need to be absolutely up to date, and she
probably had more use for direction towards the inexpensive and
conservative end of the fashion spectrum. More important, the rural
reader needed her daily or weekly women's page to divert and inform
her, but not to appall her. The women's page editor had to reflect a
world view that her readers would recognize. Thus, Katherine Irving,
women's editor on the Charlottetown *Guardian,* explained to her
largely urban colleagues the strictures that guided her in running a
women's page in Prince Edward Island. She defended her readers as
well-educated and critical women who projected a strong presence in
the community. At the same time, her audience of farming and fishing
wives formed a more homogeneous community than the more varied
urban audience, and she had to be careful to purge all material of any
offensive tinge. Off-colour or risqué humour that might be thought

"merely piquant" by an urban reader would alienate the upright wives and daughters of Charlottetown and its surrounds.[80]

On the prairies, the isolation of women from one another, their hard work, and their challenging lives made the women's page a more important factor than perhaps in any other Canadian setting. Kate Simpson Hayes was the prairie pioneer in women's page editing. For years she ran one of the only women's pages in western Canada. She began her career on the Regina *Leader* in the mid-1880s, but it was on the *Manitoba Free Press* that she made her mark. By the early twentieth century, her wisdom had spread as far west as Vancouver, where her "Mary Markwell" pieces appeared from time to time in the *World*. Her summation of her experiences as Mary Markwell, women's page editor, reflected the centrality of that role in the lives of prairie women: "The *Manitoba Free Press* was the first newspaper in Western Canada to provide the readers with a Women's Page. That the Women's Page filled a crying need was evidenced by the numerous letters received, some praising, some criticizing its columns, but at no time was any indifference shown. The Women's Page pleased and perhaps helped many farm women in these scattered homesteads of the west."[81] Hayes recalled the spate of questions she received, which ranged from the predictable fashion and recipe queries to scholarly items on books and quotations "written on Crane's best linen with crested envelopes – always from Alberta."[82] The poignant letters sent to her – from a newly-wed asking how to answer a mother-in-law's first letter, from a lone bachelor on how to find a wife, or from a new mother on what to name the expected baby – nearly flummoxed her: "This time the page fell down and admitted incompetence." But when Nellie McClung told her that a desperate young farm wife, on the point of suicide, had found new hope from a quotation on Mary Markwell's page, Hayes knew that her work was serving its purpose.[83] In such a setting the women's page had to be all things for all women – and men too, it would seem.

The needs of readers for information, advice, and expertise called for the utmost flexibility and empathy from the editor. Edna Kells, who was women's editor of the Edmonton *Bulletin* during the teens and twenties, described the challenge of "making a newspaper in the frontier city of a new country." Her readers came from "every corner of the earth," and her job – "reaching out into distant homes on lonely homesteads, trying to make strangers feel that 'they' as individuals belonged, and that their joys and sorrows and struggles were appreciated – was a hard, happy task."[84]

The breadth of interest demonstrated by the readers of women's pages was abundantly evident. But while the women's page editors aspired to nourish this diversity, their masters in the newspaper establishment were slow to respond. Again and again, presswomen stressed that women were not all the same and that even if most of them were wives and mothers, they required something more than recipes and baby lore to lift their horizons – and that women journalists were perfectly capable of serving an enlarged mission. Marjory MacMurchy felt obliged to spell out to the collected potentates of the Canadian Press Association in 1910 that "the conduct of a social page, a beauty department or a section on home adornment did not exhaust the possibilities of a newspaper woman."[85] Anne Anderson Perry in 1933, while acknowledging that "cooking, children, and domesticity" had "a big place in women's lives and departments on papers," asked, "But are they whole works?" She added, "The field for really strong stuff on women's pages is deep, wide, high. It is barely scratched," and she urged her fellow presswomen to make "desperate efforts ... to impress on men editors that segregated women's pages – if we must have them – ought to all have editorial comment, ought to have real stuff on economics; ought to have specialized information on legal, health, civic and political matters; ought to offer to the big army of business and professional women something worthy of their intellectual steel."[86] Less than a decade later, Ethelwyn Hobbes was sounding the same refrain, that women's pages should not be mere gossip collections but should include analyses of how national issues rebounded on women.[87]

As women contemplated their collective future during the Second World War, journalists put forward their ideas about the shape women's pages ought to assume if they were to serve the postwar woman. Gladys Arnold, just back from her adventures as Canadian Press foreign correspondent during the Nazi invasion of Paris, made a plea for the critical importance of an authentically national newspaper in Canada. The woman's page on such a paper would carry "national news of women written not from a woman's point of view, but on its straight news value."[88] Yet only a few years later, the Canadian Managing Editors' Conference sponsored a study of newspaper reading habits that identified a narrow range of interests for the female subscriber: "emotional, personal, practical and quite unpredictable."[89] Perhaps the patronizing "unpredictable" category offered the most scope for the enterprising women's page editor.

At its worst, the women's page was a hodgepodge of "canned copy" – syndicates and wire-service material, with little reflection of the local community. In such cases, the usual relationship between advertising and news gathering was reversed. Rather than advertising subsidizing the legitimate business of the newspaper to inform its readers, the "news" on these women's pages merely decorated the advertisements. At its best, with a strong and free editorial presence, the women's page directed and reflected the life of the community better than any other section of the newspaper. In a lively women's section, advertisements did not crowd out the editorials, advice, or news reports, nor were the contents of these items interchangeable with advertising copy. The women's page could be a "newspaper within the newspaper," including articles on politics, economics and finance, urban and social reform, religious news, family relations, literature, music, arts and society, and even international relations written from a woman's point of view.

The Peace River *Standard* fulfilled such a mission when Elizabeth Bailey Price ran the women's section. On a day in 1915 the page included an explanation of the newly passed Alberta dower law, an article on the dangers of the typhoid fly, a description of a hospital for soldiers in France, an analysis of Alberta's educational system, and an editorial essay contrasting the long peaceful Alberta nights with the war raging in Europe.[90] Whatever the section's depth and tone, the perennial fixtures that no women's page editor could neglect were society news, reports of women's philanthropic, cultural, and political activity in clubs, and the endless dispensation of practical advice on running a woman's life. In the hands of a skilful women's editor, these pieces all came together, as Marjorie Oliver of the Galt *Reporter* put it, like "a patchwork quilt."[91]

CHAPTER SIX

Fashions, Rations, and Passions: Information and Advice on the Women's Page

She told how to cut and fit a dress
And how to stew many a savoury mess
But she never had done it herself I guess
(Which none of her readers knew)
She wrote about children
Of course she had none
She wrote and was paid to fill space.

Isabel Armstrong, Regina *Leader*, 1911

"'That person in "Woman's World,"' remarked an aggrieved young lady in a Sherbourne street car, 'ought to be remonstrated with. Here I am just dying to know what I ought to wear this fall, trusting to her department for information, and what do I find? An onslaught upon the street railway company or a sermon on slang!'"[1] Thus chastened, the Toronto *Globe's* "Woman's World" columnist, Sara Jeannette Duncan, bowed to the clamour of her readers for fashion insights and proceeded to detail "what's in the shops." But while doing so, she indulged her literary penchants rather than her journalistic duty; she attended more closely to the shoppers, their poses and attitudes, than to the millinery, gloves, and boots they purchased. It was not that the stylish Miss Duncan had anything against sartorial affairs. It was merely that her intellectual mission, as she saw it, did not include such pedestrian assignments as peddling merchandise. Nor did other specifically feminine and domestic pursuits engage her interest. Needlework exhibitions aroused her peevish despair.[2] Most certainly she did not stoop to supplying recipes or child-rearing advice, and while she might dilate on the servant question – who could avoid it? – it would not enter her head to enlarge upon the techniques of rug-beating or window washing.

Such lofty indifference to the work most women did and the information most women required did not persist for long. "Service" was the watchword of the women's page, and in the name of serving their readers, women's page editors furnished everything from the price of carrots to marriage counselling. The editorial on the women's page might try to lift readers' thoughts above the plagues and plaints of their daily household chores – to remind them that "the life is more than meat and the body more than raiment"[3] – but in varying degrees, according to the character of the newspaper and its clientele, catalogues of practical information made the women's page (or home page, as it came to be called) into a kind of trade paper for the homemaker.

Much of the practical information had to do with the increasingly complex business of household consumption. Because women were the principal consumers and because most advertising directly targeted women, the women's section became the fulcrum around which revolved the interdependent elements of mass-consumer society. Mass production required mass sales, which mass-circulation newspapers could deliver if the manufacturers financed their newspapers by advertising.[4] Newspapers thus had to have special sections to attract female subscribers so that the advertisers could reach their target audience. All this was axiomatic. The function of attracting female readers to pages carrying advertisements applied to any "news of interest to women." But women writing in women's sections did more than just act as honey pots to lure readers towards advertisements. They engaged directly with changing roles of women, taking on the authoritative guise of professional experts in the many phases of modern women's lives. On the home page, they dispensed the information and advice that women required to conduct their daily routine as homemakers, wives, and mothers.

THE NEWSPAPER ADVISER AND THE CHANGING WORLD OF WOMEN

The transformation of the household economy from a production-based to primarily consumption-based unit was well underway before women's pages became established features. Nevertheless, the process was never entirely complete,[5] and women's pages continued to chart a shift that was still at work in women's roles. Where once a successful homemaker might have prided herself on her homemade bread, clothes, and even cosmetics, she increasingly judged her efficiency on how well she performed in the marketplace of consumption. As this marketplace expanded and became more elaborate, in the process transforming the nature of her work, she turned to the home page for guidance. As Jennifer Scanlon has observed, women's pages and magazines "helped naturalize women's link to the marketplace through consumption."[6] Women journalists and their readers were jointly creating a particularly feminine consumer culture.

The gendered nature of mass-consumer culture, particularly with respect to the department store, has received significant scholarly attention in recent years,[7] but the contribution that women journalists made to a specifically feminine culture of consumerism has been largely overlooked, even though, clearly, women's pages and women's magazines were the media carrying the consumer message.[8] Women journalists' professional opportunities branched out to meet the varying challenges of serving women readers. On the women's page, they occupied a halfway house between consumer advocacy and advertiser. As this adviser role matured, some journalists became advertising copywriters, while others refined their advocate-informer role by professionalizing their credentials, testing products, and steering readers through the wonderland of advertisers' claims. The two roles seemed to be diametrically opposed, yet the assumption that united them was the creed of mass-consumer society – namely that informed consumption held the solutions to the problems in modern women's lives.

The adversarial relationship which modern commentators assume to exist between the newsroom and the advertising department did not necessarily invade the consciousness of women journalists before the Second World War. Most women writing for the women's section saw themselves, not as handmaidens of the corporate interest, but as public educators performing a service that their readers wanted and needed. One idealistic commentator forecast that the women's page would become the major socializer of the urban working class, teaching basic skills in housewifery and motherhood, cleanliness, nutrition, and home nursing, thus assisting or even replacing the reform efforts carried on in churches and hospitals.[9] The same assimilating function held true for rural regions. Recent immigrants to Canadian farms – women who may never have cooked before, let alone transformed a prairie sod hut into a home – used the women's page as their primer on how to conduct an arduous and isolated way of life. Authoritative information about home finance, new standards of hygiene and efficiency in home management, modern principles of child rearing, and hints about the changing modes of cooking, decorating, and entertaining kept homemakers abreast of the transformations in their occupation. Young businesswomen with some disposable income turned to the women's page for *le dernier cri* in fashion and beauty, while the advancing tide of

Lady Willison (Marjory MacMurchy), president of the Canadian Women's
Press Club 1909–13, c. 1909 (Minna Keene/NA, PA-138849)

women workers in the Canadian labour force could find in the wom-
en's pages encouragement, sympathy, and strategies for coping and
progressing in their chosen field.

It was the homemakers, however, the most numerous and influential
group of women in Canadian society, who, according to Marjory
MacMurchy, most needed guidance. MacMurchy had established her
credentials as an authority on women's issues over a long career in
journalism, which included a series on "Politics for Women" in the
Toronto *Mail and Empire* before the First World War. As the war
accentuated the myriad changes that had transmogrified women's lives,
MacMurchy laid bare the plight of the modern housewife, whose work
in the home, position, and responsibilities had changed so much that it
was difficult for her to determine what her services to the community
were and ought to be. The state did not recognize her role in child
rearing and domestic economy; although housewives spent half the
national income, official agencies ignored their power. While
MacMurchy advocated that the government take action to educate
women for their domestic role, she and her journalist colleagues had
long been providing that service.[10]

The homemaker that MacMurchy and her journalist colleagues pictured was basically a middle-class mother, who herself did much of the work involved in cleaning and decorating her home and clothing, feeding, and caring for her family. In rural papers, the added burdens of the farm wife occupied much space. As with the women's page in general, differences of race and class were subsumed in the overarching category of gender. Newspapers and magazines catering to women projected an image of an "average" woman, who had money to spend and wanted to spend it wisely, and who needed advice about how to run her home and family efficiently because traditional methods of learning her domestic trade were no longer adequate.

What this mythical average woman actually did as part of her daily, weekly, monthly, or annual ritual of home maintenance varied dramatically over the first half of the twentieth century, as well as by region and class. In the nineteenth century, when homes had been lit and heated by coal and gas, a very necessary annual spring cleaning had turned the house from top to bottom in order to eliminate the accumulated grime from soot and smoke. Carpets and draperies had to be removed and beaten outside, walls and wood work scrubbed with borax, windows washed, and furniture polished with linseed oil.[11] By the twentieth century, the electricity available to urban Canadians, cleaner fuel, and household appliances such as vacuum cleaners diminished the rigour of the annual ritual but raised the standard of overall home cleanliness. Similarly, washing day, as described by the journalist and novelist Kathleen Strange, was a back-breaking ordeal that took the entire day: "The boiling sudsy water had to be carried in pails from the stove to wherever my tubs were set. More than once I burned myself severely ... At the beginning I had washed by hand, rubbing laboriously on a board and earning for myself a frightful backache." A hand-turned washing machine reduced some of this labour for Strange, isolated as she was on a prairie farm in the interwar period.[12] For the better-off urban homemaker even before the First World War, laundresses or commercial laundries took much of this work off the housewife's hands.[13] But she had the work back again with the availability of washing machines and electric irons, which also made for the possibility (and expectation) of daily changes of clean-pressed clothes. As servants disappeared, replaced by appliances, the homemaker found herself alone in her domestic workplace, solely responsible for its upkeep. As Veronica Strong-Boag has observed, even with the introduction of goods and services for homemaking, "labour was not so much eliminated as reshaped."[14]

It is little wonder, then, that Canadian homemakers needed information and guidance on how to do their job. Moreover, the need of modern women for advice went beyond the merely practical, encompassing emotional and psychological matters as well. In an era of mobility and rapid change, when generations no longer lived near each other and when mores altered so radically that a mother's advice no longer suited her daughter's dilemma, it would seem that a great many women, and some men too, sought the personal but anonymous counsel of the newspaper oracle. To be sure, the correspondents' query feature was almost as old as the newspaper itself,[15] but there was a degree of intimacy and urgency that distinguished the modern confessional impulse from the more discursive requests for information of earlier times. Personal relationships, as they appeared in the newspaper, seemed to be especially anguished. The women's editor of the Vancouver *World* reflected sadly on the lack of camaraderie between mothers and daughters, which, she said, prompted young girls to seek help from the newspaper.[16] Margaret Currie of the *Montreal Star*, who had built a long career advising the forlorn letter writer, observed the same phenomenon with dismay: "The pathetic little letters that come to me every day, letters you dismiss contemptuously as silly or stupid – prove that mothers aren't on the job of mothering."[17]

Currie's brusque criticism reinforced that of many of her colleagues, who were similarly inclined to blame mothers for the multicausal and widely dispersed changes in women's lives. A full-time career woman with no children, Mrs Eldred Archibald, through her "Margaret Currie's Page," became the archetypal wise mother and homemaker, a guardian of morality who taught thousands of readers how to cook and clean and budget, how to raise their children, save their marriages, and cope with the caprices of life during the seachanging years of the 1920s, 1930s, and wartime. Although she could be critical of individual failings, Currie's advice was free of ethnic and religious discrimination, according to the endorsement of local doctors and ministers, who called her page the single most influential source of "social service work" in the pluralistic society of Montreal.[18]

The lovelorn columns, as these items of personal counselling came to be known, were indispensable to twentieth-century newspapers. They were almost certainly an outgrowth of the volume of unsolicited letters begging the newspaper columnists for advice. Whatever their ostensible function on the newspaper, once women began to be identified as featured personalities, they were plied with letters telling of personal traumas and crises. In author-journalist Stinson Jarvis's view, women had a special aptitude for the role of newspaper counsellor; the number of men, he admitted, who could "really make friends with their readers [was] exceedingly small."[19] Thus, "Margaret

Currie's Page" emerged from quantities of letters addressed to her "Economy Corner" on the women's page of the *Montreal Star*. Similarly, Lally Bernard (Mary Agnes Fitzgibbon) of the Toronto *Globe* did not set out to be a newspaper counsellor; her mandate was commentary about society and current affairs. But although she protested her lack of qualifications, readers persisted in turning to her for comfort. She in turn used their various plights as vehicles for discourse on general social ills. For instance, when "K" sought solace after a blighted romance, Lally Bernard turned this *cri de coeur* into a denunciation of "coming out" ceremonies and the way that young women were forced into the social whirl regardless of their inclination.[20]

In later years, newspaper experts specialized in distinct departments of female life and often had professional qualifications in home economics, nursing, or psychology. But the first generations of newspaper women had to be extremely versatile because they were magnets attracting the enormous public need for advice and information. Their audience expected them, as women, to minister to widely varying demands; whether it was a psychological, scientific, literary, historical, or domestic query, the woman journalist had to become an instant expert on whatever subject was presented.

There was a limit to how much research the women's editor could do herself amidst her myriad obligations. Most of the time she clipped tidbits of information from other magazines or newspapers and lashed them together haphazardly with personal comments and local news items. Whatever her qualifications and experience, she was usually willing to venture an opinion and give information on all aspects of women's responsibilities. In the early years of the century, a teenaged Mary McGaw (later, Mary Barker) offered the housewives of Galt, Ontario, instructions on how to make pickles, crochet baby jackets, and make chairs out of barrels, even though she had never done anything of the sort herself.[21] "Kit of the *Mail*," a single parent living in lodgings to keep her children in boarding school, wrote tips on cleaning silver and making kedgeree with all the confidence of a full-time chatelaine. Lally Bernard would interrupt her discussions of literature or current Canadian issues to advise mothers about dressing their children healthfully or to pass on a recipe for "prune shape."[22] Similarly, Katherine Leslie (Kate Lawson) of the Toronto *World* sprinkled details of current fashions in millinery and notes on making cress sandwiches in the midst of her effusions on Browning.[23] Interestingly, Lawson, as women's editor, was allowed to indulge her flights of erudition even though the *World* catered to an audience of immigrants, many of whom were learning English. In other departments, *World* reporters were explicitly ordered to "write with childlike simplicity from a standpoint that was both impersonal and non-referential."[24] Here, too, the women's department was exempted from rules that governed the rest of the paper.

Occasionally, early women's page writers practised what they preached by experimenting on themselves. Ethelwyn Wetherald, the poet who replaced Sara Jeannette Duncan on the *Globe*'s women's page, felt it behooved her to get first-hand experience of the information she dispensed. When she enrolled in a course in physical fitness and beauty, she felt obliged to explain her uncharacteristic activity to her fellow poet W.W. Campbell: "I can't consistently be everlastingly preaching physical culture to the readers of *Wives and Daughters* without finding out what it is like myself."[25]

CONSUMER ADVICE AND ADVERTISING

While the intended function of the adventures which these early "experts" on feminine subjects undertook as part of their journalistic duty was primarily to serve readers, the claims of another master, newspaper advertisers, intruded on the women's department to varying degrees. At times, the demands of readers and advertisers coincided. Readers wanted specific information about the products which the modern consumer society afforded, and manufacturers and service industries wanted readers to know about their offerings. Indeed, the business side of the newspaper usually assumed a community of interest, linking women readers and advertisers. As the advertising manager of the *Daily Province* affirmed, the advertisements were the most important "news" that female subscribers read, "for they give to the woman information fully as valuable as that she will derive from any other part of the publication."[26] At other times, the women's page specialist faced an ethical dilemma – placating the advertiser versus honestly advising her readers.

Beauty and fashion advice were the perennial leaders in women's page popularity, and they epitomized the conflicting loyalties of the adviser as she tried to orchestrate the calls of readers for more information, the shrill chorus of cosmetic and clothing manufacturers crying their wares, and the quieter voice of her conscience reminding her of her journalistic ethics.[27] Margaret Currie of the *Montreal Star* testified that requests for information about how to improve or change the way they looked were the most numerous pleas from her female correspondents – even more common than letters about romantic predicaments.[28] This should not have surprised her. For young women and girls, anxiety over their love life translated into anguish over their personal appearance. The lessening of family and community strictures about premarital socializing and marital choice in the late nineteenth and twentieth centuries meant greater freedom for courting couples. But women were still the passive "chosen" ones and were more than ever inclined to attribute their success or failure to personal attractiveness. Similarly, new opportunities in the service industries and the business world meant that women were more visible in public than they had ever been. Advice manuals on employment were unanimous in their exhortations to "look your best." Good grooming and a smart professional appearance were an essential part of the apparatus of the young businesswoman. Thus, the modern career woman needed more up-to-date advice about how to present herself in this public world than her own mother could supply.

Fashion, according to its very essence, was constantly changing, and as women's costumes simplified and more ready-to-wear items replaced the laboriously produced garments of earlier years, the pace of fashion change quickened. In the 1890s a well-dressed woman's upholstery began with the corset, often laced as tightly as the ribs could stand. This was followed by a long petticoat and a short petticoat or, alternatively, a lacy chemise or beribboned corset-cover over drawers – or perhaps combinations, which replaced corset-cover and drawers. Although few would glimpse them, a woman's stockings were elaborately decorated, and her day time boots were laced or buttoned, though she might wear more revealing pumps in the evening. There would also be the gown and hat, cloak, gloves, fan, parasol, jewels ... and possibly various costumes for golf and yachting, as well as for that symbol of the "new woman," the bicycle. The practical skirt and shirtwaist, as depicted by *Life* magazine illustrator Charles Dana Gibson, elevated the working girls' costume into high fashion.[29]

The total weight of women's costumes gradually lightened over the years, but conformity did not. From the patriotic militarism of First World War fashions to the revealing shifts of the 1920s, and then to the imposed simplicity of rationed clothing during the Second World War, women in the working world were expected to conform to the broader outlines of sartorial currency, and they expected their newspapers and magazines to relay the latest insights from New York or Paris. To be sure, few could afford to follow *haute couture* at its most *haute.* The daily fashion pattern offered by most newspapers throughout the first half of the twentieth century was a practical acknowledgment that many women continued to make their own and their children's clothing. Full-page department store advertisements with lavish illustrations informed readers about what people in their vicinity might be wearing. Whether women bought "off the rack" or stitched their dresses on their home sewing machines, the fashion world assumed that they wanted to be current and needed advice on what to buy. Intellectual and feminist women might take exception to this frivolous preoccupation with external appearance, but the obsession was merely the most obvious manifestation of the uncertainty women felt as their place in society altered. As they left traditional community support systems behind, they were thrown back onto individual resources such as personal attractiveness. Thus, they looked to the newspaper beauty expert to tell them how to fade their freckles, whiten their hands, or wave their hair. Armed with a flawless appearance, they hoped to face the perilous world with confidence.

At the same time, "their movement into new social roles," as Michael Schudson has observed, made women "more than ordinarily susceptible to the siren call of the marketers. Women were newly public people and needed, more than before, social currencies acceptable in the public world defined by men."[30] The developing cosmetics industry, in particular, capitalized on women's insecurity by cajoling or scolding into taking charge of their own chief asset, their beauty, through the skilful and "scientific" application of new lotions, creams, and make-up. They assured the gullible and the desperate that any woman could become a beauty and that a plain woman had only herself to blame. Promises of love and success they manipulated in remarkably overt terms to assail women's self-esteem. Romance and marital fidelity were the prize for beauty; withdrawal of love was the punishment for failing to attract and hold. Cosmetics, as Veronica Strong-Boag has argued, made feminine loveliness into a "purchasable commodity, the possession of which promised success in the marriage market."[31]

Women's magazines and the women's pages in newspapers were naturally the most lucrative vehicle for this sort of sales pitch. Advertisements from cosmetics manufacturers studded the women's pages. The new department stores purchased whole pages placed strategically near the sections that women might turn to for advice and information. Indeed, these were major underwriters of the whole newspaper enterprise.[32] As Charles Russell, a New York reporter, reflected rather sourly, the newspaper had become "an appendage of the department stores."[33] Since the material on the women's page frequently inflated the importance of personal appearance, the line between advertising and copy was notoriously faint, especially in the specialties of beauty and fashion writing. As early as the late nineteenth century, the connection was obvious to the British woman journalist Evelyn March-Phillipps, who complained that the papers for "ladies" constituted a "species of perambulating shop" and that this had disastrous implications for newspaperwomen's journalistic ethics: "Writers, who would be conscientious if they dared, are perpetually cautioned against neglecting the claims of Messrs. so and so, who threaten to withdraw their patronage unless they receive more glowing criticism, warmer recommendations, more frequent notices and illustrations."[34]

While few records remain to trace directly the coercion that advertisers exercised over early women's page editors, there seems little doubt that the editors were under pressure to flatter important advertising clients in their columns. Mrs Edmund Phillips was evidently yielding to some variety of persuasion when she insinuated in her society column that flowers from Dutton's were indispensable to really elegant entertainments.[35] Meanwhile, Dutton's had a small front-page notice in the Saturday edition of the Toronto *Mail.* And although Faith Fenton of the Toronto *Empire* objected to crimping her editorial space to make way for advertisements, she used her column to pass on to readers fashion insights dictated to her by Murray's department store.[36]

Kit Coleman quite frequently punctured the balloons of extravagant puffery that cosmetic advertisers conjured up. At the same time, her entrepreneurial spirit recognized in advertising writing a promising new field. Judging an advertising-writing contest for the *Mail,* which had invited amateurs to try their hand at writing copy for three of the *Mail*'s advertising clients, she demonstrated her own interest in the field and the close connections between the *Mail*'s sponsors and its women's page: "Advertising is yet in its infancy. There is lots to learn about it and I would strongly advise ladies to keep on writing advertisements." She confessed her own frustrations in trying to find an original ploy only to discover that some "horrid (but clever) American man or woman has been there before you and your original idea is as old as the deluge!"[37]

Whatever the overt or covert collusion between women's page editors and the advertising interests, it was also the case, in the early days of the women's page, that the featured items worked at crosspurposes with the advertising copy. A self-proclaimed expert might rattle off a recipe for a homemade hand cream that could be concocted for pennies even while a manufacturer was advertising the allurements of his product on her page. Mrs Henry Syme filled a whole page two or three times a week in the Vancouver *Province* of 1904 with formulae for beauty remedies, along with exercises accompanied by large illustrations. All the while, various soap and cream manufacturers warned readers that only their products could ensure loveliness.

In later years, as Emilie Peacocke stipulated in her guidebook for women journalists, "the old style of beauty article ... ceased to be marketable. The plea of writers of such articles that these things could be made at home at trifling cost was less than useless; it was damning." Lest Peacocke be accused of pandering to the advertisers, she elaborated the ethical distinction between "the extravagantly worded puff" and the mere avoidance of subjects that might undermine the "pulling power" of advertising space.[38] It was a perilous path the woman journalist had to tread between deceiving her readers and undercutting her paper's sponsors.[39]

The relationship between information and advertisement on the women's page was rather chaotic before the First World War. Where on one day a direct plug for a named product would appear in the midst of an editorial, on another, a critique of current fashions would appear next to the department store advertisement. Just before the war, the "shopping column" in Canadian newspapers began to chart the foggy terrain between journalism and advertising. It differed from market news columns in its motivation and financial foundation. Where market news was intended to guide the consumer to the best quality and prices, the shopping column aimed to deliver the consumer up to the advertiser. As textbook writer Genevieve Boughner described them, with no implied criticism, "The average unobserving reader scans the chatty little items, without realizing often that they are not the reporter's actual opinions, but space 'bought and paid for' ... These departments masquerade typographically as editorial matter."[40]

The shopping column was typical of the kind of quasijournalistic position that women so frequently filled. The market news columnist was paid by the editorial department, but the "shopper" was in the advertising department or, quite commonly, was a freelance journalist paid according to her success in drumming up advertising revenue. On occasion, the shopping columnist even purchased items and sent them to out-of-town readers.[41] Mary Barker, who eventually became one of Canada's more successful advertising writers, was the first female copywriter ever employed by the Ottawa *Citizen*. Beginning in 1918, after a fifteen-year recess from newspaper work, she pioneered the "reader" form of advertising, in which she concocted little stories to dramatize shopping expeditions.[42] Her colleagues in the Ottawa branch of the Canadian Women's Press Club praised her skill effusively: "By a delicate and imaginative style, interwoven at times with touches of poesy and phantasy, she converts the business of selling goods into a high and romantic adventure, as if a trip to the shops of Sparks Street were a golden journey to Samarkand."[43]

Alixe Carson claimed to have imported the shopping column to Calgary. When she lost her job in the "morgue" on the *Calgary Herald*, apparently because someone else would do it for less, she immediately marched down to the advertising department with her idea for a freelance feature, "Round the Shops with Alixe." To earn $3.50 per column, she bustled around the local merchants to persuade them to buy space and then wrote her patrons up in her copy. Her experience opened her eyes to the fundamentally commercial nature of the newspaper business: "I no longer believed the high-blown rhetoric of publishers about their public service."[44] The ingenue now knew that advertising was what made the newspaper world turn. When Carson left the *Herald* for a slightly less venal opportunity as society editor on the Calgary *Albertan*, the tradition she had started on the *Herald* was continued by her successor, Olive Kells, as "Observations by Olive."

FROM PRESSWOMAN TO COPYWRITER

While Carson remained securely in journalism for the rest of her career, a great many Canadian women journalists traded their reportorial role for that of the huckster. Writing advertising copy paid better than newspaper work,[45] and for the really enterprising it could facilitate a kind of independence that journalism rarely gave to women. Edith MacDonald was a pioneer among women in advertising. After a respectable career as women's editor of the Toronto *News*, she began writing for the T. Eaton Company in 1910 and stayed on for fifty years, writing copy even after her official retirement in 1936, until her death in 1960 at the age of eighty-four.

It was to acknowledge the career paths of members such as Edith MacDonald that the CWPC altered the rules of membership to include women who had been journalists but had taken up advertising. MacDonald addressed her colleagues on the subject of "The New Advertising" at the triennial convention of 1913. Knowing that her audience had reservations about the intellectual and moral rigour of the field, she offered her own experiences to prove her case that "advertising and news are first cousins." She explained, "As a member of the editorial staff of an estimable daily newspaper, I was called upon to spend much time and ink in the supplying of cures for freckles and recipes for pumpkin pie, while as an advertising writer it has been my high privilege to expatiate on Cubist pictures and review books by Nellie McClung."[46] The odd mix of hucksterism and information that characterized advertising in its early days allowed MacDonald the creative leeway she evidently relished. For example, a full-page Eaton's advertisement for underwear carried in *Saturday Night*, 15 November 1913, included a boxed article, signed "The Scribe" (MacDonald's pseudonym) about how a family had renovated their farmhouse. The article apparently had nothing to do with the ad copy yet presumably drew readers to the page. MacDonald was working for Eaton's, not *Saturday Night*.

MacDonald's acknowledgment of the uncertain boundary between advertising and news reporting was seconded by the textbook writers, Harrington and Frankenburg, who admitted that much that passed as news was in fact advertising, while advertising conveyed much that was news. Their guideline for discriminating between the two was public service. If the main motive was individual profit, it was advertising; if community benefit was paramount, it was news.[47] After the First World War journalists became more sensitive to the implications of conflict of interest. Miriam Green Ellis, a highly professional agricultural reporter, tried to alert her colleagues to the blurry boundary separating news from promotion: "Then there is the trouble of side-stepping those seeking publicity, often the kind of publicity for which the advertising section expects to get so much per inch. The line between news and publicity is sometimes very fine."[48]

Not all women journalists could afford the high-minded ethical standards that informed the career of Miriam Green Ellis. In her lecture to fellow CWPC members, Edith MacDonald had conceded that advertising work might not attract the idealists whose motive was "making their name" or "following ... an art." The practical issue was earning a living in a field that was calling for writers.[49] Certainly, Madge Macbeth, one of the most entrepreneurial of women writers, needed no prodding to turn her literary abilities to commercial profit. During and just after the First World War, she worked for Frieman's department store in Ottawa, where she staged one-act plays to dramatize the selling of goods. "Notices" of these dramas (most likely written by Macbeth), then appeared embedded in Frieman's full-page advertisements in the Ottawa papers. These notices publicized Macbeth's theories about the art of advertising: "At a time when governments and all the sections and intersections of men within nations make use of propaganda to further the interests which [it] is desirable should be furthered, it is not surprising that a big business house in Ottawa should take a leaf from the book which seems to have been a best seller. The success of propaganda depends upon how cleverly, and often elusively, the subject is put across."[50] Macbeth thus demonstrated her astute perception of the realignment of journalistic ethics in the wake of the war, when governments had co-opted the services of writers and reporters to manipulate the home-front mentality.[51] Not given to soul searching about the ethical implications of publicity and propaganda for her profession, she gave lectures to manufacturers on the "science of advertising."[52] Once her reputation as a personality and woman of letters was firmly established, she cheerfully agreed to the use of her name and photograph for a tobacco advertisement, provided she also wrote the copy.[53]

Women journalists' close connections with advertising and merchandising enabled some of the more enterprising to launch independent advertising sheets. Mona Clark, editor of *Gossip*, a Toronto weekly, was admirably qualified to give the craft lecture to CWPC members on the science of advertising. In a lecture pointedly captioned "Advertising Tells Terse Truth," she found it necessary even as late as 1935 to defend, by emphasizing an upward spiral of progress, the sort of enterprise newswomen were apt to disparage: "Advertising, though once degraded so that the public lost faith in it, is today progressing toward the goal of a recognized profession like law, medicine or science." She urged her audience to take advantage of their sex to get ahead in this lucrative field: "In a world where 94% of all advertising is directed to women why should not our Canadian women writers direct that advertising?"[54] Some journalists followed Clark's lead in other cities across Canada. Myrtle Patterson Gregory, star reporter of the *Vancouver Sun* in the 1920s, put out the *West End Breeze* in the mid-1930s, so that she could continue earning and writing while raising her three children. Similarly, the Winnipeg *Gossip* was one of the many ventures Hilda Hesson undertook as an independent businesswoman. Hesson gained sufficient stature in the community to be elected to the city council by 1940.[55]

Closer akin to newspapers than magazines, though they might be issued on a weekly or monthly basis, these flimsy flyers were rather like a women's section cut loose from its moorings in the regular newspaper. Although advertising was overtly the point, they also carried society news, humorous articles, and general-interest features. The thirties were the heyday of this sort of publication. Given their dependence on consumers and on advertisers of luxury goods at a time when few could afford even bare necessities, their success was somewhat paradoxical. They were, nevertheless, evidence of women journalists' versatility in the Depression years, which stymied so many traditional opportunities. Ida Toffelmeyer had been society editor of the Hamilton *Herald* – a position that furnished her with well-to-do contacts when she launched *Chatter* in Hamilton during the mid-1930s. Similarly, Dorothy Bell had been quite successful as an editor and freelance writer for the Maclean group of magazines. Her confidence was tested to its limit when she introduced to Vancouver her new venture, *About Town*, the very week in the autumn of 1929 that the New York stock market crashed. She admitted that times were often tough, but she and her staff were able to hold on throughout the Depression. A number of Vancouver's more prominent women journalists found opportunities under Bell's wing. Mamie Moloney, in later years a successful columnist, spent some time on *About Town*. So did Gwen Cash, who remembered that the little vignettes about local goods and services were fun to compose but rather hard to sell to merchants who were more familiar with traditional display advertisements in newspapers.[56] Evidently there were sufficient people with the wherewithal to support the news-sheet, which had an average circulation of 3,000 to 4,500 among the moneyed elite and hotel patrons of Vancouver. Bell closed down her operation at the end of 1942 so that she could do war work.[57]

THE NEWSPAPER EXPERT AND THE FEMALE CONSUMER

As advertising emerged as a distinct profession and women began to make their way in its various branches, presswomen writing on the home page began to demarcate the boundary between the roles of the adviser and the advertiser. In the years following the First World War, professional experts on homemaking, consuming, and other domestic interests began to put firm distance between their advice to readers and the newspaper's advertising clients. Although the general tenor of women's page material still tended to foster consumerism in general, copy that promoted any particular firm was no longer encouraged. Thus, Valerie of *Saturday Night*'s "My Lady's Dressing Table," in cautioning her readers that she could not name specific products, coyly deflected responsibility: "You have no idea how stern and strict and absolutely formidable the advertising manager can be."[58] "The Home-Maker" in the Toronto *Globe* published among her rules for readers the caveat: "Difficulties which may be solved by advertising cannot be dealt with in the Home-Maker's Page, nor any trade names or business addresses published."[59]

Conscientiously service oriented, "The Home-Maker" page was, according to one newspaper survey, the single most popular feature in any Canadian newspaper.[60] Readers who admitted that they could not afford to take a newspaper during the lean years of the Depression nevertheless wrote in to tell Mona Purser, the editor, that kind neighbours saved her page to pass on to those who might otherwise miss it.[61] This and similar features specialized in cost-cutting devices, shopping strategies, and alternative recipes designed to help readers cope with the collective stringency of the Depression and war years.

Women's page experts aimed primarily to give their readers the best information at their disposal. This did not necessarily mean that they were hostile to the corporate interest or the advertiser. They recognized that their readers were shoppers, that they needed to buy things

for themselves and their families, and that they wanted to shop as intelligently as possible. Both advertising and newspaper advice helped
women do this. Department store advertisements allowed a woman to
find out what merchandise was being featured at what price, while
market columns allowed her to do price comparisons around her city.
Readers were no longer limited by what their local merchants offered.
Within constraints imposed by family budgets, they had the power to
choose.

Even rural readers became acquainted with what could be had from
the modern retail empires. Women's page editors on farm pages were
more than enthusiastic promoters of labour-saving devices for the farm
home, because they knew how desperately hard worked farming
women were. Mary McCallum, women's editor of the *Grain Growers'
Guide,* actively encouraged the electrification of farm homes and
kitchen gadgets because "time [was] too valuable to use women power
when electricity [was] so easily within reach."[62] Her predecessor on the
Guide, Francis Beynon, had been equally enthusiastic about consumer
goods that could improve the standard of living of prairie women.[63]
Interestingly, Beynon came to journalism from a very early career in
advertising, having been employed by Eaton's.[64] This ardent feminist
and reformer saw no contradiction between promoting women's
rights and promoting consumerism: both represented freedom,
power, and choice.

Freelance contributors were advised that articles extolling the
wonders of household consumer goods were more likely to be printed.
Elise Philipps, in "Reaching the Rural Woman," maintained, "If you can
offer something that will help to tie in with the advertising you have a
better chance than ever of getting a check. By that I do not mean that
you should mention commercial products by name, far from it. But if
you can tell of how some woman made her housework easier by in-
stalling modern conveniences, and perhaps give the story of how she
earned the money to buy those improvements, you are almost sure to
please."[65]

By the 1930s in large metropolitan areas, the consumer advice
function of the women's section had become an essential feature.
Lillian Foster of the Toronto *Telegram* was a zealous advocate on behalf
of her readers, and she assured them that she had seen, felt, or tasted
everything she wrote about. Foster's "Shopper" column described
goods, and readers could write in to find out which shop sold particular
items, but Foster insisted there was "no advertising tie up." Indeed, she
was so single-minded in her pursuit of the practical that she was
reported to have interrupted a conversation about international affairs

with the blunt query, "Yes – but what has that to do with the carrots in my refrigerator?"[66]

Newspaper consumer experts, on the whole, dedicated their efforts towards informing consumers to buy intelligently as individuals, not to mobilizing their economic power collectively. But, during the First World War, Jessie MacIver, editor of the *Woman's Century*, attempted to organize female consumers to use their power to effect feminist social reform. Launching her "Made in Canada" campaign, she wrote to Violet McNaughton, women's editor of the *Prairie Farmer*, "We women are the buyers of the nation and if we insisted on the made in Canada for our homes, and also a certain standard, we would soon make our men sit up."[67] McNaughton, in western Canada, was not as enthusiastic about a movement that was so clearly geared to the interests of the industrialized East. The movement made no particular headway.

Somewhat later, in the early Depression years, when Britain was spearheading an effort to construct an Empirewide trading bloc, Anne Anderson Perry urged her fellow presswomen to get into the fray. Calling for "strong useful information regarding the woman shopper and Empire trade," she argued, "In Canada women constitute about ninety per cent of all retail buyers and there can be no question – even the feminine brain can comprehend it – of their power to influence trade returns."[68] While Perry wanted there to be women at the heads of Board of Trade information bureaux sending material "written by women for women," it was not until the Second World War that women began to occupy such positions.

The momentum of consumer militancy, if not initiated by newspaperwomen, was at least spurred by advice features that acknowledged the intelligence and real concerns of the homemaker-consumers. Helen Gregory MacGill tried to convey this message to the corporate readers of *Marketing* (15 October 1927). While recognizing that women were "the most consistent and thorough readers of advertising," MacGill underlined the fact that women read the advertisements in search of honest information, "because the great majority of them have little to spend and have much to buy. The day is past," she warned the admen, "when the advertiser can make any woman buy something that she does not want."

Newspaper consumer advocates' sensitivity to the limitations and motivations of their readers sharpened during the Depression. While their intended function in the newspaper was to enlighten shoppers, in writing about shopping in all its dimensions, women journalists helped to heighten consumer awareness. At a time when the spectre of hunger and malnutrition stalked many Canadian families, homemakers badly needed to make every penny count in the marketplace. Veronica Strong-Boag has chronicled the mounting hostility between consumers and advertisers in the 1930s when shoppers lashed out at advertisers whom they blamed for misrepresentation and collusion with business to raise prices.[69]

This was a mood that alarmed Mabel Crewes Ringland, who was an active member of the CWPC as well as being president of the Women's Advertising Club. Although her advertising colleagues considered her "an alarmist on the subject of consumer antagonism," she had a healthy respect for the mobilization of women's buying power. After attending a particularly large and vociferous meeting of the Toronto Housewives' Association, she warned "advertising men" specifically not to ignore "this dynamite right under their very noses."[70] Ringland aspired to a reciprocal relationship between the advertising industry and its audience, by which men and women advertisers would listen to the homemaker and in turn educate her to the benefits that "democratic consumerism" and technology could offer. But by and large, the dream-mongers ignored Ringland and her like-minded colleagues.[71]

The separate streams of advertising and consumer-oriented service became somewhat more distinct, then, during the 1920s and 1930s. Women readers came to expect the home page "expert" to have their interests at heart in the columns of practical information. Jessie Allan Brown, who syndicated a practical column of "Hints for Homebodies" around rural weeklies during the 1930s, prided herself on her expertise. She was a trained home economist as well as a Maritime housewife. She believed that she understood rural homemakers' difficulties and had the scientific background to solve them. Brown was thus both annoyed and amused when a Nova Scotia editor accused her of being in the back pocket of the "cod liver oil" interest because she so frequently advised mothers to feed the oil to their children. She ran afoul of other editorial clients by her use of registered trademarks in her column. She protested that "certo" and "thermos" were common parlance and were more easily understood by readers than "pectin" and "vacuum flask."[72] But her sensitivity demonstrated that ethical standards of a professional nature had been refined by this period.

It was in part an acknowledgment of the public-service role played by women's page "experts" that led the Wartime Prices and Trade Board to employ experienced women journalists in their public relations department.[73] Byrne Hope Sanders, seconded from *Chatelaine* to become the director of consumer services, attributed her new job to the power of the female consumer. Claiming that she represented all women buyers, she pronounced, "'We spend eighty-five cents out of every dollar our husbands earn. And have a mighty good idea of where the other fifteen cents goes!"[74]

The newswomen employed by the Wartime Prices and Trade Board relied on their sisters in the press to help them do their government jobs effectively. They were their liaisons with the public, a conduit that passed information about government action in regulating prices and the flow of consumer goods. Women's page and magazine editors in wartime used their sway to mobilize the power of the female consumer to cooperate with government policies. Wilma Tait, editor of the *Canadian Home Journal,* used military metaphors to transmit the official home-front dicta of conservation: "Wise spending is done when a recognized need is carefully planned – for at home, and shopped for with definite aim – the one sure way of getting the best, of avoiding shopping hysteria (one of the worst Fifth Columnists), of spending more and getting less."[75] But they were not merely passive transmitters; women journalists also communicated to the authorities information about how the public was reacting to government policy.[76] For instance, when Marian Casselman, representing the consumer section of the department of agriculture, toured the prairies, she was peppered with questions from the Saskatoon branch of the CWPC. In particular they asked her how rural residents were to deal with weekly rations when they might live twenty miles from the nearest store and had to buy in bulk. Journalists thus became the professional servants of their clients and championed their interest in the public sector.

THE "PROFESSIONAL" NEWSPAPER EXPERT

Another dimension to the increasing professionalization of specialties within the women's department was that of education. In the 1920s, guidebooks on journalism were emphasizing that the would-be specialist in homemaking, fashion, beauty, or interior decorating should prepare herself by getting a degree in home economics. It would be her narrow and academic expertise that earned her a job, rather than the old-fashioned reliance on all-round versatility. The beauty expert would understand physiology and the chemical basis of cosmetics; the fashion writer would be well versed in textiles and design. Writers on childhood would have degrees in psychology, while the food columnist would have dietetics training.[77]

The postwar period witnessed the "professionalizing" of many formerly private family functions, and newspapers acted as funnels to direct the prescriptions of trained experts to the homemaking amateur.[78] Thus, when the *Grain Growers' Guide* initiated its enlarged women's section just after the First World War with features such as "Better Babies" and "The House Beautiful," it added to its staff Margaret Speechly, one of the first graduates of the five-year degree course in home economics at Manitoba Agricultural College. For all her academic background, Speechly was anxious to make use of the practical expertise of working farm women; she wrote to Violet McNaughton, for instance, for specific insights on how to manage the enlarged household duties during threshing time.[79]

When newspapers began to promote columnists with professional credentials, specialized expertise could provide an entry into journalism for women who wanted a career change. Jessie Leitch (Mrs Wilbur Bryan) turned her nursing experience to journalistic use. Trained in Winnipeg, she served had in England and France during the war, and after being discharged she wrote a column on home nursing for the *Dispatch and Pioneer Press* of St Paul, Minnesota. Leitch syndicated these columns, and by the time she came to Vancouver in 1924, she had enough experience to land a position as a general reporter and feature writer for the *World*.[80] Similarly, Charlotte Whitton's extensive experience as a social worker and as editor of the professional journal *Canadian Welfare* enabled her to engage in journalism in order to survive a hiatus in her multifaceted career.[81]

Not only was the "expert" journalist encouraged to have a professional background, but the practice of specialty journalism had begun to change, especially in areas connected with homemaking. No longer was housekeeping advice dressed up in story form, adorned by fine writing, or inserted into chatty essays. The emphasis now was on information and accuracy. There was a decreasing tolerance of haphazardness in the content of informational features. In the trade journal *Editor and Publisher*, a contributor complained that errors in articles addressed to housewives undermined their trust in the accuracy of the entire page, with disastrous consequences for the advertisers and the newspaper enterprise. His example was a budget column, typical in the Depression years when hapless consumers were scolded for extravagance and told they could live on a pittance if they managed their resources efficiently. The journalist's wife had discovered numerous mistakes in arithmetic, as well as omissions and misrepresentations.[82] Such hard-hitting professional scrutiny was an advance on the days when an all-purpose adviser such as Margaret Currie could blithely assure her readers, beleaguered by postwar inflation, that their troubles would be solved if they would substitute lamb shoulder for leg and plain lettuce salads for imported asparagus.[83]

Not long after the Great War, newspapers in the United States began to refine their public-service role and act as professional consumer-information bureaus. New York papers, always leaders in innovation, were setting up their own laboratories to test recipes and manufactured products. College-trained experts were hired to preside over the "lab," with the twofold purpose of serving readers with "scientific" expertise and of attracting advertisers, who valued the endorsement.[84] This idea began with *Good Housekeeping Magazine*, which tested food, laundry products, and household equipment and published the results. The success of this venture and its wide imitation demonstrated renewed faith in journalistic "objectivity" as part of a professionally "disinterested" service to customers. The *Good Housekeeping* seal of approval was esteemed by manufacturers and consumers alike.

Canadian publications took some time to imitate the application of "science" to home consumerism. *Chatelaine* did not establish its version of the *Good Housekeeping* service until 1930,[85] and newspapers lagged even farther behind. The "Edith Adams Cottage and Home-Maker's Service," a *Vancouver Sun* laboratory that specialized in recipe testing and home efficiency schemes, was not initiated until just after the Second World War. Moreover, it was the veteran journalist Myrtle Patterson Gregory who presided, albeit over a staff of university-trained home economists.[86]

It was no doubt the success of American self-help features, widely syndicated in Canada, that had slowed down the progress of Canada's own "professional" experts. By the 1920s, it was already becoming difficult to initiate a specialist feature in a newspaper because individual papers could obtain already popular features comparatively inexpensively. Syndicated child-rearing advice columns such as "Angelo Patrie," or even whole children's pages imported as a piece, eroded the chances for Canadian journalists.

By the interwar period, the lonely hearts field had been cornered by Dorothy Dix, an American journalist whom Canadian editors ignored at their peril. Elizabeth Long of the *Winnipeg Free Press* noted that Dorothy Dix frequently lured male readers to the women's page and thus became a "must" on her women's page.[87] By the same token, Alixe Carson's imperative, "Leave out anything but don't leave out Dorothy Dix," showed the pressure exerted by popular demand.[88] Only where a Margaret Currie (Mrs Eldred Archibald) or Mrs Thompson (Isabel Turnbull Dingman) had already established a loyal following did these made-in-Canada features survive. Elsewhere, according to Norman Mackintosh, features editor of the Toronto *Telegram*, the American syndicates crowded Canadians out of their own market.[89]

Although the basic parameters of domestic life in Canada and the United States were similar, American material did not always suit the Canadian situation. Katherine Middleton, home economics editor of the Winnipeg *Tribune*, argued that American information often conflicted with specifically Canadian circumstances. This was particularly an issue with respect to wartime food distribution. She gave an example of how the Canadian food editors were trying to cope with meat rationing by recommending "meat extenders," recipes that stretched short supplies without absorbing equally meagre supplies of eggs and cheese. Meanwhile, American markets had no shortage of cheese and eggs, and syndicated recipes that encouraged the liberal use of meat substitutes could therefore have a devastating effect on Canadian consumption.[90]

Even though few barriers prevented American material from flooding Canadian markets and suffusing the women's page, Canadian women writers were not able to reverse the flow. It was very difficult to access the huge American market. Ethel M. Porter, a Canadian woman journalist who moved to the United States, reported back to members of the Canadian Women's Press Club that "although a Canadian postmark is not an obstacle," distance was. The editor wanted contact with contributors, and specialized articles on travel, sport, or vacations competed in a heavily filled market. Porter advised that there was still an appetite for short articles on mother and child, on inspiration, and on "systematizing the housework" (provided it could compare with the most up-to-date American standards), but that food and cookery were increasingly the province of the professional experts. The market in Canada was narrow as well. Wilma Tait, editor of the *Canadian Home Journal*, warned an audience of freelance writers, "The market is practically closed to contributors on such subjects as household economics, interior decorating, fashions, beauty, etc. – subjects of a technical nature. Most magazines have a staff editor or contributor who has special training in these fields of journalism."[91]

Despite the apparent narrowing of the range, it was still possible for a woman journalist to build up a multifaceted career as an expert. A really enterprising and trained expert could market her skills independently in a number of venues, sometimes simultaneously. Pearl Clarke used her expertise in food sciences to penetrate both the syndicates and the advertising field. While living in Montreal in the early 1930s, she syndicated a cookery feature as Mary Moore in the *Montreal Standard* and *Edmonton Journal*. She also wrote advertising and publicity for Harriet Hubbard Ayres of Canada Ltd. Then she moved to Hamilton, where she wrote advertising copy and publicity for Mary Miles Fine Foods, all the while maintaining her Mary Moore features.

Kate Aitken speaking on CBC radio series, *Your Good Neighbour,* Toronto (NA, C-66618)

By 1942 she had become accounts executive for the Russell T. Kelly Advertising Agency in Hamilton.

The most expert of all experts, Kate Aitken, exemplified this branch of journalism at its zenith. Although she was not university trained – normal school was the limit of her formal education – Aitken combined prodigious energy and practical experience to achieve a fabulous career in the dispensation of practical advice. Initially, she had been one of the many farming wives who made extra income by selling home produce – eggs, canned fruit, and vegetables. Kate Aitken, however, did it better than anyone else and soon became a lecturer for provincial and federal departments of agriculture, visiting remote Women's Institute groups and sharing her self-taught wisdom. All the while she was raising two daughters and experimenting with breeding and feeding chickens for the poultry division of the Canadian Department of Agriculture.[92] By 1927 she was women's director of the Canadian National Exhibition. That same year, while visiting England with an exhibit of Canadian handicrafts, she was asked to substitute for the suddenly indisposed official delegate to the international wheat conference. Seated next to the Italian representative, Aitken managed to sell a large purchase of Canadian grain to Italy; and when Mussolini vetoed the sale, she bearded the lion in his den, flying to Rome and actually convincing Il Duce himself of the quality of Canadian grain.[93]

Aitken's ability to pinch-hit at a moment's notice provided her next big chance. When a local broadcaster broke his leg, Kate Aitken valiantly stepped in, thereby launching her long career as Canada's best-known female radio personality.[94] Early radio's appetite for a wide variety of practical information for the daytime listening public of homemakers furnished a versatile expert with an ideal platform, despite inhibitions about women's voices on the air.[95] Where most journalists stepped from newspaper writing to advertising or broad-casting, Aitken did the reverse. She had established herself as a homemaking expert by the time the *Montreal Standard* hired her in 1941 to be women's editor of the magazine supplement. When she became branch president of the Canadian Women's Press Club in Toronto, her colleagues noted, "An expert's advice is needed for writing and living in war time."[96] Aitken's admirers would have been well advised to follow her pattern of career management as well as home management. Her earnings have been estimated to be as much as $25,000 from various enterprises by 1941.[97] Being a well-known authority was big business. Moreover, at a time when newspaper experts were keeping their distance from product sponsorship, Kate Aitken, like most of her fellow broadcasters, was employed by major advertisers (in her case, Canada Starch and Tamblyn Drug Stores). Yet her asso-ciation with specific companies did not seem to tarnish her credibility as an all-purpose expert.

At bottom, it was the needs of readers that defined the "expert" phase of women journalists' work on the women's page. The newspaper adviser, whether a heart-throb or a cookery specialist, had to maintain that thread of trust, confidence, and affection that would continue to elicit letters. In the case of the Toronto *Globe*'s "Home-Maker" page, Mona Purser's stamp was so strongly imprinted that the thirty-year-old feature ended with her death in 1954. It would have been unthinkable to carry on "Margaret Currie's Page" without Mrs Archibald or "Mrs Thompson Advises" when Isabel Dingman died in 1960. Their power was based on the projection of a distinct personality with whom readers could identify and to whom readers would commit their dilemmas.

In the early period of their ministry, women journalists had not infrequently treated their power with some levity. Julia Henshaw of the Vancouver *Province* used the furore over the Hetty Green forgery scandal to speculate with mock alarm the damage a bogus version of her own signature might do: "What then might happen, I shudder in my sealskin at the thought, if some mere man, someone who knows naught of beauty, were to write something altogether false, and sign it 'G'wan'? You, seeing the closely imitated signature, might read it with all the loving trustfulness of your simple natures, believing in me, G'wan, as you have a right to believe, and oh! what poison might you not imbibe."[98]

Similarly, Kit Coleman had the stature to be able to rebel teasingly against the tyranny of the never-ending requests from readers, as she did in her Toronto *Mail and Empire* column in 1906:

> I hate to have to write this page,
> I hate work's odious fetters,
> It puts me in a red hot rage
> To have to answer letters.
>
> Such as "Dear Kit, Please tell me now
> – I must decide instanter –
> If I should marry the man with the plough
> Or else the Cuban planter."
>
> Or, "Dear Kit, Is it proper quite –
> To ask a young man in,
> Who sees you home on Sunday night –
> Would you call that a sin?"
>
> It's "I've got a pimple on my nose
> It worries me a lot!"
> And, "What is best to eat and drink,
> Now that the weather's hot?" ...
>
> "Dear Kit, you do know such a lot!
> Please say how may leglets
> A lady centipede has got –
> Who lays – how many egglets?"
>
> I hate to use my head to think,
> I hate to have to eat
> I love to just lie flat this month
> And sleep away the heat.[99]

In contrast to Coleman's aristocratic lassitude, Kate Aitken was always brisk, always took her correspondents' questions seriously, had plenty of energy for their demands, and resisted any temptation towards facetiousness. She thus became the "busiest woman in Canada," answering 260,000 letters a year and giving 600 broadcasts to 5 million listeners, all about baby care, marketing, recipes, and general household lore, and proving that the Canadian appetite for expert advice had no limit.[100]

Women continued to turn to the women's pages of their newspapers or to specialized magazines to find guidance for the increasingly complex problems of running a household, raising a family, and otherwise conducting their lives as women. While the particulars of these lives varied according to context and region, specific and professionalized expertise was becoming increasingly useful to a broad audience – hence the rising significance of the syndicated column and the radio broadcast, both of which tended to reduce opportunities for the local cookery writer or agony columnist.

Much less interchangeable was news about the social landscape. Only a woman enmeshed in the local social scene could accurately chart its hills and valleys for an audience that would never climb the heights but nevertheless wanted to know what the view was like from the top. The society writer was indispensable.

CHAPTER SEVEN

Among Those Present: Chronicling the Canadian Social Scene

Let the Old World, where rank's still vital,
Part those who have and have not title.
Toronto has no social classes,
Only the Masseys and the masses.

B.K. Sandwell, 1952

In 1889 the editor of the Toronto *Mail* vilified the class of newspapers that purveyed "the tittle tattle of drawing-rooms for their readers."[1] That his own paper would ever deal in rumours and fads seemed a preposterous notion. Yet within a few years, "On Dit" appeared in the columns of the *Mail,* coyly dressing up ordinary gossip in pseudo-French elegance. Its author, Mrs Edmund Phillips, admirably conveyed the spirit of drawing-room chit-chat – mostly talk about who was doing what, but also discussions of the plays, recitals, and charitable affairs that fashionable people attended. From then on, the society column was a fixture in the *Mail* and in every other Canadian daily. Yet the society column, page, or even section occupied an uncomfortable niche in the newspaper scene. While newspaper publishers and proprietors knew it to be an indispensable circulation builder, the journalistic fraternity disparaged it, and the women who wrote it were often rueful about their handiwork. Why was it that a newspaper feature that was incontestably popular should be so despised? To be sure, gossip was rarely admired, but the distinction between "gossip" and "news" was rather murky when the media regularly publicized individual private affairs ostensibly to arouse human interest or expose scandal. In the case of the society column, however, the setting was an exclusive quasi-private realm where only women held sway.[2] Men might snigger at the "pink tea circuit," but they valued social prominence and wanted to see their wives' and daughters' names listed "among those present."

Perhaps it was the dissonance between somewhat shamefaced social ambition and resentment of those who dispensed the prizes of social recognition that made the status of society column, and the women who made up those columns in the newspaper, paradoxical. Michael Schudson has written of the department store that it "democratized envy" by displaying luxuries all could see but few could buy.[3] In similar fashion, the society columnist "democratized" envy for social position. By making the names and activities of the well-off familiar to people who would normally have no contact with them and no knowledge of what these kinds of people did, the society column created a flutter of interest and an appetite for more. This chapter examines how and why the society column came to be a regular fixture of Canadian newspapers and how it influenced the experiences of and attitudes towards the women who made social affairs into news.

THE ORIGINS OF THE SOCIAL COLUMN AND SOCIAL REPORTER

Canadians came somewhat later than Americans to pursue social recognition via the daily press. Hence, Canadian newspapers followed conventions established mainly in the United States, though with a deferential nod towards the proprieties established in Britain. Before the 1880s, the conservative tone and small scale of Canadian high society delayed the inauguration of newspaper columns dedicated to its comings and goings. The Toronto *Globe* newspaperman M.O. Hammond, reminiscing in the 1930s, could recall a time when society matrons, unused to the publicizing of private life, would "forbid" the use of their families' names in the columns of newspapers.[4] The names of well-brought-up ladies could respectably appear in the paper only when they were born, married, or died. Anything more was brazen self-advertisement.

It was through familiarity with American newspapers that Canadians gradually became accustomed to the idea that the daily paper was a suitable forum for information about personalities and social life. In the United States, society reporting was already established by mid-century. James Gordon Bennett of the *New York Herald* claimed to have invented the society column in 1840 in order to demonstrate that America's upper-class life was just as brilliant as European aristocratic life.[5] But those Bennett intended to flatter by publicity were not particularly grateful. The proprietor of a "penny paper hawked about the street by a gang of troublesome ragged boys," as one social leader described the *Herald*, had no personal access to the exclusive society his paper chronicled. *Herald* reporters had to invade the parties of the elite and hound the fashionable for personal information.[6] As a result, their write-ups evinced a note of resentment. Bennett's precedent possibly established an adversarial relationship between the press and the exclusive set that figured frequently in American social reporting – a tendency to jeer and fawn simultaneously.

This attitude did not infect Canadian social reporting to any significant degree. The British deference towards birth, title, and protocol pervaded Canadian society news. The Court set the tone of British high society and placed firm restrictions on public access to its functions.[7] But although the British press generally exhibited more deference towards society's principals, it was not far behind the American press in detailing personal trivia about the rich, famous, and well born. England was close on the heels of America when in 1846 the recently founded *Daily News* engaged Lady Blessington at five hundred pounds a year to contribute "items of fashionable intelligence."[8] That her friends and relatives were less pleased than her readers by her excursion into print may account for the relatively short duration of her career as a journalist. During the six months that she divulged society's secrets to the wide world, Lady Blessington's privileged access to the "best circles" constituted her chief value to the *Daily News.*

In the context of a society of formal ties, where title still signified status and where mobility, although possible, was highly regulated, the ideal social reporter was one whose entrée was already established, one whose presence would not too vulgarly jar the sensibilities of the guests. A similar situation obtained in the highest echelons of Canadian society, especially among those who surrounded the governor general's court in Ottawa. Where formal and intricate rules of precedence overlaid all social occasions, it required a knowing eye to interpret the complexities of social arrangement for the satisfaction both of those who attended and of those whose only participation was vicarious. Madge Macbeth, a journalist who had for years observed Ottawa society, quipped "that Ottawa in the twentieth century, was controlled by a social code quite as remorseless in its way as the tribal etiquette which governed the Algonquins when Champlain visited its site, three hundred years before."[9]

To be able to unravel the mysteries of social ritual required a kind of expertise quite outside the usual journalistic training. In Canada as in England, the first social reporters tended to be "to the manner born" with ready-made access to the elite. Emily McCausland Cummings, the first society editor ever employed by the Toronto *Globe*, was the daughter of the Reverend Dr Shortt and widow of a Toronto barrister. In her correspondence she was eager enough to point out her warm personal friendship with Lord and Lady Aberdeen, with whom she stayed when covering Ottawa social events.[10] Lily Barry, who wrote her social notes under the *nom de plume* of "The Hostess" for the Montreal *Family Herald and Weekly Star*, came from a prominent Ottawa civil servant's family. Mrs Edmund Phillips, "On Dit" of the Toronto *Mail*, was the wife of the distinguished organist and choirmaster of the church of St George the Martyr, which had one of the most prestigious congregations in Toronto.[11] At the western extreme of the Canadian social scene, Alexandra of the Vancouver *Province*, Miss Isabel MacLean, the daughter of Vancouver's first mayor, was well placed to record the doings of her city's fledgling social circuit.

That social reporters were born, not made, was the received wisdom that Sara Jeannette Duncan's heroine in *A Daughter of To-Day* learned to her chagrin when she offered to replace the social correspondent on a popular Paris journal. Her informant smiled at her ignorance as he explained that the social reporting was done by "a woman who is invited everywhere in her proper person, and knows 'tout Paris' like her alphabet." He told her, "You would have more chance of ousting their leader writer."[12] Forty years later, a one-time social editor, Lois Reynolds (Kerr), etched the stereotype of the patrician social reporter still deeper with Princess Kerchewffsky, the guileful journalist-heroine of her farce, *A Guest of Honour*.[13]

Well connected as they may have been, it was no accident that the first social reporters were women. In anomalous fashion, the task of society reporting combined high prestige in one context with low status in another. It demanded the best social connections and involved daily contact with the leaders of local society, yet in terms of status in journalism, few departments ranked lower. Trafficking in names and family connections, reinforcing the arbitrary demarcations of social status, and generally exploiting the prying curiosity of the readership were the raison d'être of the society column. These were not the skills that idealistic journalists cherished. Indeed, ethical journalists prided themselves on respect for privacy; to report items learned at a friend's house or in a private club was to transgress the journalistic code of honour.[14]

The stigma surrounding the social page tended to besmirch the dignity of all women journalists in the eyes of their male peers. In 1923 the *Hook*, a short-lived Vancouver weekly, contemptuously dismissed the presswomen who were attending the triennial convention of the Canadian Women's Press Club and upbraided the Canadian Pacific Railway for wasting its funds subsidizing their travel and entertainment: "Most of them live and move and have their being in a sphere of journalism bounded on the north by a pink tea, on the south by a 'pretty bridge was held' and on the east and west by descriptions of how a handful of women in their town are upholstered and decorated when they attend a theatre or a dance or a horse race. We call it a pretty barren prospect for journalism or for travel publicity but the CPR is willing to spend thousands of dollars on it."[15]

Over the years, even as the society column became solidly entrenched in the make-up of most newspapers, its stature as a journalistic department did not improve. If anything, the tasks of society editors and reporters became more routine and more narrowly conventional as they became more specialized. The first society reporters in the late nineteenth century often doubled as general columnists and thus combined with their lists of names, descriptions of dress, and general gossip comments on contemporary artistic and social reform movements. Some popular social editors' columns, such as those of Agnes Scott, The Marchioness of the Ottawa *Free Press,* were closer to editorials than "who's whos." But even when serious issues or cultural events crept into the column, the light touch of trivial banter necessarily defined the tone. Agnes Scott's editor, Lady Gay (Grace Denison), cautioned the overly earnest: "Philanthropy unabridged has ostracized many from the smart set who won't be bored about social questions ... The horse-docking cruelty, the factory acts, the suffrage, have each been a rock to wreck the social ship which ran overfreighted with them into the shallow seas of society."[16]

On smaller papers the newspaperwoman was almost invariably called the society editor regardless of what she did. Sally MacAffrey, who worked on the Woodstock *Sentinel Review* in the early years of the twentieth century, was so labelled even though, in point of fact, she was an all-round subeditor. Her editor admitted to her, "You know, if you weren't a woman, I'd make you city editor." But society editor she remained until she left journalism.[17] Marjorie MacKay had a similar experience on the St Catharines *Standard.* Bowing to the pressure of the local elite, the publisher hired this very young war widow, who had no previous newspaper experience, to cover social and personal events. Her one recommendation was that he had met her at a dinner party – clearly, she knew the right sort of people. Although the publisher had granted MacKay her job as a gesture of beneficence, the demand for her stories soon assured them front-page placement in the small-town paper, and she stayed in that same "temporary" job for forty years.[18]

ONLY A WOMAN WILL DO

The assumption in MacKay's and countless other cases was that only a woman could do society reporting. The exception to this rule was in New York City, where male social reporters held sway. The high prestige of the "Four Hundred" possibly accounted for men deigning to participate in this usually despised department. More important, the refusal of James Gordon Bennett to hire women journalists for this most sacred *Herald* function set a precedent for male dominance on the society pages of most of the powerful New York papers well into the twentieth century.[19] The public setting of New York's high society functions, which in the twentieth century were increasingly held in hotels rather than private homes, provided an atmosphere in which male society reporters could move with ease and authority.[20] Even so, it was significant that many of these New York society watchers camouflaged their identities with female pseudonyms. In this realm, women's expertise commanded more certain trust even if the newspapermen cornered the most lucrative positions.[21]

Elsewhere, women invariably occupied the society desk. An American editor, who had little good to say about women journalists in general, sneered that the only reason publishers employed women to "sound the alarm when Chappie Chrysanthemum changes his cravat" was that women would do it more cheaply, not better, than male reporters.[22] But low status and low salaries are not a sufficient explanation for women's monopoly of the society page. They had expertise and qualifications that male journalists lacked. The most common reason proffered in journalistic realms was that ignorance of fashion disqualified the bumbling male. Katherine Leslie (Kate Lawson Appleby), editor of "The Woman's World" department of the Toronto *World*, lampooned male ineptitude about female attire and suggested that if a comic paper employed a male journalist to cover the "costumes and millinery of society, as is now seriously done by society reporters, his department would rapidly become the funny corner of the paper."[23] Similarly, M.O. Hammond.assumed that when men first ventured into this territory, they soon exposed their incompetence: "It was the turn of men to blush and hesitate as they were assigned to report weddings and balls with the aid of women friends who knew dress materials and costume design."[24]

Dress was an integral part of society reporting at a time when social leaders set the fashions and lesser lights had to garner clues from newspaper descriptions to design the upcoming season's wardrobe. A female critic of overlong accounts of "drawing rooms" implied that the digests of guests' attire were inserted for the gratification, not of the public who would never need such costumes, but for the dressmakers who advertised in the paper.[25] In the days before the fashion industry cut itself loose from the elite and appealed more democratically to a wider consuming public through specialized columns and advertisements for ready-made costumes, mention that Lady So-and-So had worn a certain couturier's dress provided commercially vital recognition for those connected with the clothing trade.

At the turn of the century, Margaret Graham attempted to cut the ties that so closely bound women's journalism and fashion reporting. As she introduced her Ottawa social notes to the readers of the Vancouver *World*, she affirmed that she was going to write about the sacred emotions surrounding social ceremonies, such as weddings, and not merely who wore what. She disarmed any charge of "strong-mindedness" by insisting that she was not seeking to reform things: "I love pretty frocks and hats and am at this moment wearing the most frivolous things I can afford. I am merely protesting against reading and writing about clothes."[26] But her protest only went so far; at the end of her column she reneged on her serious pledge and included details of the gowns and flowers she had gleaned from other journalists' reports. The rubric that social functions were chiefly occasions for the display of feminine consumption was too entrenched to be flouted.

Even when, in later days, society columns ceased to be the main source of fashion enlightenment, verbal pictures of the frocks worn at teas, coming-out parties, and charity bazaars continued to fill column after column. To get every detail correct was an exacting task. Obliging hostesses or proud mothers of brides might furnish advance details of costumes to society news scouts, but no reporter could succeed without an ability to absorb at a glance subtle nuances of style. The burden of describing every gown appearing at the governor general's ball exhausted social reporters in the capital. During the opening of Parliament festivities, they had to attend late-night functions that might not end until 3 or 4 AM and then write through the night in order to file their stories by 7:30 AM. One Ottawa personality, a leading civil servant who was a journalist on the side, called a halt when the plain black dress she had worn for ten years was described yet again and her paste necklace grotesquely misrepresented as "olivine beads." She took care to point out to the society reporter that the public was not likely to take kindly to gorgeous descriptions of a civil servant's attire; readers might think she did not require her salary.[27] There was great relief among Ottawa journalists when the local papers, the *Journal* and the *Citizen*, decided to limit costume descriptions to the governor general's party and debutantes.[28]

In this milieu, the working clothes of the society reporter were a vital factor in her professional success. Particularly in the early days of social reporting, the writer had to appear to be one of the party and not obviously an interloper. A guidebook writer of the very early twentieth century warned the novice journalist away from what she termed "social work," assuming that any woman who needed to support herself by writing would not possess clothes of sufficient style and quality to be able to attend grand affairs or even to quiz dressmakers and milliners about their clients' costumes without humiliating herself.[29] In later years, the burden of personal attire became somewhat less pressing. As society reporters became accepted accessories at fashionable functions, there was more emphasis on their professional appearance than on the elegance of their regalia. When the Vancouver branch of the press club discussed the topic of appropriate dress for social reporters, the consensus was that the reporter should avoid any costume that might upstage that of her hostess or the guests.[30] Nevertheless, in order to comment on the modes of the beau monde, the society journalist had to present herself as a woman who understood fashion.

Few men could claim that distinction. But it was not merely the mysteries of the *toilette* that disqualified male reporters from the society beat; most of them were ignorant of the subtle and not so subtle rules that governed society and etiquette. It was the matrons of society who established the standards of protocol and propriety and upheld them. Even if their husband's position defined their own place in the hierarchy, it was the wives who determined who would be admitted and who excluded from privileged social gatherings. In the financial marketplace or even the political platform, an "unknown" could make his way and establish a place among his colleagues. In contrast, high society took place in private homes, and thus the elite could more certainly manage affairs in their own interest – namely, exclusiveness. In the outside world, businessmen, politicians, and professional men had to rub shoulders with all sorts of "unsuitable" persons, but because the men were not responsible for entertaining and social life, they were not necessarily obliged to invite these people into their homes. Women did not participate in the wider realms of public life; their judgment did not have to embrace business or political considerations. By default, they took charge of the private realm of social life.[31]

For the most part, men needed women to scale the social ladder. As R.A.J. McDonald has observed of Vancouver society before the First World War, even membership in the Vancouver Club, the most prestigious for professionals and businessmen, could not ensure access to the highest stratum. Only through ties "of family and home," which women controlled, could the applicant gain entry to the best circles.[32] Women were thus responsible for raising or maintaining the social status of their families. In purely social terms, a man's standing was measured by his wife's circle of acquaintances. As her name and her parties gained recognition in the local newspaper, the family's social position came to be distinguished from its merely financial status.[33] A businessman could be democratically broad in his extrafamilial social contacts while his wife took on the odium of "snobbery" in her efforts to elevate or protect the family's social status.[34] The conventions that bestowed upon matrons all responsibility for establishing social status still prevailed in the late 1930s, as Alice Harriet Parsons discovered when she conducted an opinion survey among her University of Toronto journalism class. Discussing the currency of the ideal of the "lady" in modern times, she learned that men still valued the ability of a wife to improve their social standing in the community.[35]

On the other hand, according to Mona Clark, a specialist in business and career journalism in the interwar period, a woman's inability to forget social distinctions was a serious impediment to her success in pursuing a business or professional career. In an article for the *Canadian Magazine* in the late 1920s, Clark cited numerous examples of women who had refused to associate with inferiors or to forgive lapses of etiquette and had thus lost valuable clients.[36] Curiously enough, Clark edited a social-cum-advertising sheet, *Gossip*, that exploited precisely these same feminine failings.

The reporter who interpreted the social milieu for the excluded public had to understand its mores, preferences, and prejudices absolutely. As early as 1897 a woman journalist noted, "Women are ever the keenest and best social critics and no editor, in these days of sexual topsy-turvydom, can afford to dispense with their brilliant aid."[37] The proprietor of the South Carolina newspaper where Jean Graham made her debut as a journalist learned this lesson in dramatic circumstances. After his city editor was challenged to a duel on account of a misbegotten wedding write-up, the owner decreed that a woman's tact and talent was imperative. Jean Graham was then a young Canadian schoolteacher with no newspaper experience, but when she took over the society beat she did a better job than the city editor.[38] On her return to Canada she rose quickly, becoming editor of the prestigious society section in *Saturday Night* and then overall editor of the *Canadian Home Journal.*

By this time, the second decade of the twentieth century, women's special expertise in society reporting had gained the textbook stamp of approval. Harrington and Frankenburg's *Essentials in Journalism,* a widely circulated authority, acknowledged that "a certain nice discrimination, more frequently given to women than to men, enabling the possessor to recognize, almost intuitively, relative social distinctions and the varied importance of events, are the chief requisites for success in this work."[39] The emphasis on intuitive understanding rather than acquired expertise somewhat blunted the compliment – if indeed praise was intended – but it certainly reinforced the maxim that only women could do this sort of reporting. Because high society was private life on display, a woman representative of the voyeuristic public had a less offensive presence than her male counterpart.

In cities with pretensions to "good society," newspapers might have difficulty recruiting a social reporter who had the requisite familiarity with the exclusive families and who also took her duties seriously. The widely circulating social butterfly who would submit her gatherings in time to coincide with newspaper deadlines was a rare species. The editor of *Mayfair Magazine* was at his wit's end trying to find a social correspondent who was well enough connected to cover the Ottawa social scene and would do it for the pittance he could afford to pay – a mere twenty-five dollars a column. A Mrs Allan Keefer offered to do the rounds only to let him down because she had to "rest her eyes." To cover for him, he was forced to cajole Madge Macbeth, whose dinner-party circuit was formidable but who, by the 1930s, was a successful enough journalist to be able to dispense with the drudgery of society writing.[40]

Lois Reynolds, given editorial responsibility for an expanded society department on the newly merged Toronto *Globe and Mail,* was delighted when a young debutante, Zena MacMillan, agreed to become her assistant. Reynolds had the journalistic experience for the job, but she lacked that intimate knowledge of Toronto families that would distinguish her department. In enlisting the young socialite, Reynolds launched the career of Zena Cherry, who was to dominate Toronto social news for the next few decades.[41] Alixe Carson, by the same token, was an asset to the energetic upstart newspaper of Calgary, the *Albertan.* Daughter of a prominent lawyer, she was invited to the most prestigious parties, and as a frequent guest of Colonel Woods, who owned the establishment journal, the *Evening Telegram,* and entertained all notables passing through Calgary, she was often able to scoop the society reporter of her host's paper.[42]

Naturally, the experienced journalist resented the advantage that a pre-established position in local society gave the untrained novice. In an article on professional education for women journalists, the author complained that "many editors seem to feel that a knowledge of the pet vanities and jealousies of local personas is a superior qualification to good writing on the part of a neutral and unbiased reporter."[43] Unjust it may have been, but the press had no automatic right of entry into private social functions and thus had to rely on the tact and popularity of insiders. To maintain the correct balance between the role of invited guest and professional reporter and between propriety and interesting copy called forth the utmost discretion from social editors. The *Ladies' Pictorial Weekly* particularly cherished Maud Ogilvy – a novelist who was one of the very first women to contribute social notes to Canadian newspapers – for her ability to "draw the line between privacy and publication, between the incidents and people we may write about and those cases in which publicity would be a breach of good taste ... She culls her facts and fancies with a taste and judgment rarely combined in so high a degree. Consequently her services are called into requisition by people who would hesitate before placing themselves and their entertainments at the mercy of the ordinary newspaper reporter."[44]

STATUS AMBIGUITY: PERSONAL AND PROFESSIONAL

The social reporter's affinity with high society distinguished her from the "ordinary reporter" but also ensured that she could not go about her business in a straightforward professional manner. Indeed, the conflicts potential in her many contradictory roles must often have caused personal anguish. Her position was an invidious one. The society editor moved between two realms: the competitive business world and the society of ladies of leisure. She was not entirely at home in either. Her network of social connections had earned her entry into journalism in the first place, and her professional situation depended on those same doors remaining open to her; but her status as a working woman earning her own livelihood tarnished her status as a "lady," in the early days especially, and undermined her claim to equality with those she circulated amongst.[45] Similar tensions operated in her professional life. She was working as a professional, paid to extract information from individuals, but she had to relate to her informants in quasipersonal, quasiprofessional fashion. She had to maintain the façade of a leisured lady discussing the activities leisured ladies undertook. Advice from a popular guidebook illustrates the contradictions inherent in the social reporter's responsibilities. "Inject a social note," the author counselled the neophyte attempting to establish herself with her city's prominent socialites, "and avoid the appearance of a business solicitation."[46]

In her reports as well as her news-gathering forays, the journalist of high society had to tread daintily. Her hostesses wanted discreet publicity but not infamy, while her readers and therefore her employer wanted bits of spicy gossip and the occasional scandal. The blurring of boundaries between personal and professional roles called for a cool detachment that was often hard to maintain. For instance, when Lotta Dempsey was a very young social editor for the Edmonton *Bulletin* in the late 1920s, she became a personal friend of the premier's wife, Mrs Brownlee. She later recalled her embarrassed discomfort when her paper engaged in a muckraking expedition to uncover the sexual scandal that ruined Premier Brownlee's political fortunes and disgraced his family. Dempsey learned to overcome her own delicacy for the sake of journalistic prowess, but she fittingly entitled her memoirs *No Life for a Lady*. In an earlier period, Mary Agnes Fitzgibbon confronted her identity conflicts by attempting to separate her personal and professional personae. Relating to editor Willison a private conversation she had had with Lord Wemyss, she confided, "I say nothing about this in my letters, for I have made it a rule only to write in a public way, and have my two cards professional and private, and when my professional card is presented then all conversations are for publication, but I am certain that women journalists weaken their value by not respecting the privacy of social intercourse."[47]

Writing about London society and politics in the first years of the twentieth century, when almost any news held the attention of a sentimentally colonial reading public, Fitzgibbon was able to maintain an ethical nicety that many social reporters could not afford. A bit of mischief was often necessary to inject life into the social affairs at home in Canada. The mysterious Amaryllis of *Saturday Night,* also known as "the Marchioness" in the Ottawa *Free Press,* managed to balance discretion and liveliness in the social realm with considerable finesse. In real life she was Agnes Scott, a young lady born to the best circles of Ottawa society, but her father had left his family little beyond a peerless pedigree. For a period of five years Scott observed the doings of Ottawa society, the only social milieu likely to have national interest in late nineteenth-century Canada. In her columns she had scope for acerbic comment and wide-ranging social commentary.[48] Notwithstanding the occasional barb with a personal target, Scott confined her sallies to diffused parodies of contemporary society. For instance, at the outbreak of the Boer War, she slyly noted that war, "relic of barbarism" as it was, at least had the effect of diverting tea-time conversation away from the servant question and one's neighbours, and was altogether more interesting than a peace conference. "So ladies, study your maps!" she teased.[49]

Mrs Alfred Denison, Scott's editor in the society department of *Saturday Night,* was another woman who let her rigorously critical opinions about people and society show occasionally behind her discreet veil of light social prattle.[50] According to Hector Charlesworth, who began his career the same week in March 1891 that Grace Denison started, "in handling social gossip in a manner that titillated curiosity without giving offense, no journalist was her equal."[51] Denison may have been tactful, but she was not without spirit. Charlesworth recalled her bridling when a famous contralto insulted a fellow woman journalist, Faith Fenton of the Toronto *Empire.* She consoled Fenton by suggesting that a description of the singer's "bull neck" might find its way into the *Saturday Night* write-up. In her own right, Denison was probably quite adept at defending her honour and respectability through the subtle and skilful use of publicity.

Charlesworth's evocation of Denison's presence at the *Saturday Night* office illustrates yet another dimension of the interpenetration of the professional and the personal in a social editor's life. Denison was a counsellor and confidante of the debutantes who fluttered in and out of her office. As the daughter of Archdeacon Sandys of Chatham, her social credentials were impeccable. But she was separated from her husband, hardly a respectable state for a nineteenth-century Canadian lady. She had no communication whatever with her estranged husband and may well have been absolutely dependent for her living on her salary from *Saturday Night*.[52] In compensation for her irregular family life, she domesticated her professional life by mothering her contacts. All told, her situation was not likely to be congenial to a proud and strong personality. Denison's successor on *Saturday Night* hinted knowingly at the trials Lady Gay had undergone: "The first woman in Canada to turn her literary ability to what is known as 'society editing' and the difficulties of her early work can hardly be understood today by those to whom the woman's page or the society column is a familiar feature every morning."[53]

To be sure, the frustration evident in the lives of many society reporters had more than a purely personal foundation. Much of Denison's and other society editors' irritation stemmed from the endless trivia they witnessed. Serving up confections of vacuous frivolity laced with snobbery could satisfy only the most abject social sycophant, which Denison evidently was not. Even the *crème de la crème* of Ottawa society was not immune to Lady Gay's censorious pen when it offended her standards of propriety. Covering the viceregal ball at the turn of the century, Denison recoiled in repugnance at the rapacious greed of her companions: "If the sandwiches had been their first meal for a week and their last for a month they could not have been grabbed at more convulsively ... My ears were filled with demands more or less frantic in two languages." [54]

It was also tiresome to have to go through the same charades again and again, as socialites pretended to deflect publicity and scorn those who made their living by writing about the establishment, while in fact they were anxiously scanning the columns for mention of their names and their daughters' dresses. Lois Reynolds (later Kerr), social editor of the *Globe and Mail* in the 1930s, took light-hearted revenge on the dowagers of Rosedale in her popular one-act play, *Nellie McNab*. On the eve of her daughter's coming out, Mrs Stratford, a well-to-do widow, goes through the ritual of brushing off the social reporter's call: "Of course you have chosen a very inconvenient time to call. You must know we are all very, very busy up here." And then she trills out a well-rehearsed litany of detail about the gowns, jewels, and flowers that are to adorn the entertainment, and ends by inviting the social editor and her assistant to come for an advance view.[55]

Although social editors, reporters, and news scouts had their trials, they enjoyed a measure of power in their own circuit. The rise of the popular press made publicity and therefore disgrace possible on a hitherto unprecedented scale. The social reporter could do considerable harm to the reputations of her subjects if she chose. A notice in the Vancouver *Province* of 1900 may have caused some tremors of dismay in certain quarters when social editor Mollie Glenn intimated "that the wife and children of a well-known man in town have been sadly neglected, in fact are in destitute circumstances, while the man in question has been entertaining parties at dinner and acting the part of genial host to all but his worthy family."[56]

Ultimately it was a question of loyalty: Did the society editor ally herself with "good society" or did she cast her lot in with the half-gaping, half-resentful public? Most would have seconded Agnes Scott's vision of her role as a mouthpiece of high society: "All sensible people see that what the public wants, the newspapers are bound to supply ... They are thankful that the important work of telling of the doings of society is placed in competent hands where good judgment and dignified methods will be used. No underhand means are resorted to, no news is sought for at the back door."[57] In other words, those who wished to be exclusive should embrace one of their own, one whose understanding, delicacy, and wisdom could be relied upon.

USES AND ABUSES OF THE SOCIAL COLUMN

Social leaders appreciated the fact that if publicity was required, they were in safer hands with a reporter who identified her interests with their own rather than with a reporter whose motive was merely to amuse the public at their expense. It was also becoming apparent to the socially aspiring citizens of a fluid society that the high society game was often played out in the pages of the newspapers. It was no longer sufficient to be invited to a major social event in order to establish one's acceptance into the elite; if the invitation was to have real currency, it must be widely known that one had been there. While the hostess may have drawn up the guest list, notice in the newspaper increasingly defined the event. Consequently, ambitious newcomers to social prominence might actively court publicity or even try to manipulate the news-gathering process. In her satire of Ottawa social life, Madge Macbeth detailed the stratagem of a thick-skinned arriviste who, uninvited, brazened her way into a major social function and then "helpfully" telephoned the social reporter in order to imprint in a public forum her own presence at the event. The canny reporter was prepared to respond, but with "her tongue in her cheek."[58]

In real life, a young and inexperienced Edna Brown had to parry the wiles of those who tried to vault social hurdles by using the society columns of the Vancouver *News-Advertiser.* A new arrival on the Vancouver scene, Brown had among her contacts a local matron who was widely known as a social climber. Because of her ambition, this woman was a ready source of news, always willing to supply information about her own social events. On one occasion she asked Edna Brown to call at nine o'clock because she was hosting a very important social gathering. When Brown appeared she met a rather chilly reception from the ordinarily effusive socialite, who brushed aside any suggestion of publicity for her private party. The next day, the "gay deceiver" flounced into Brown's office to explain. Her friends had been asking why her parties were always written up in the papers, and she did not want them to think she called in the reports herself. Thus, she had arranged the subterfuge to have Brown call while her guests were present in order to impress them by her established standing. Nonetheless, she did want her party reported. Though humiliated by this exercise, Brown confessed that she was too dependent to risk running foul of an unfailing news source, so she dutifully pandered to her patron's ambition.[59]

Had Brown been more worldly, she might have done some manipulating in her turn. Every social newswriter could choose to ignore or demote the fashionable functions that particular hostesses initiated. There was a hierarchy on the society page. The establishment might warrant a headline and article all to themselves, while the less worthy earned paragraphs of varying length. On the *Toronto Star* it was spelled out: a minor wedding could be dispatched in 150 words, a "good" wedding in 250, while a very important one merited 500. It was left to the discretion of the social reporter to judge the relative weight of each event.[60]

The lower the social standing of an individual, the greater the social reporter's leverage. She had it within her power to confirm or erase the social arrival of marginal players in the local scene. By failing to notice someone's gown or by filing a would-be personage among the "also attended," she could diminish their status. "It is an undoubted fact," wrote Ishbel Ross, who began her career in Toronto before going on to greater triumphs in New York, "that the ambitious have been nursed to social security, or doomed to oblivion by the reiterative paragraphs ... of the conservative society page."[61]

In the CWPC's craft journal, Anne Anderson Perry related as a cautionary tale the story of a society reporter who was altogether "too

clever by half" and ultimately came to no good. Setting her parable in
the years before the First World War, Perry told of a power-hungry
woman who worked for a city editor who was "deeply imbued with
American high pressure methods of news getting." He allowed the
society news editor to have her way in her page, and she exploited her
opportunity to bring ahead her social "pets" and to reduce her ene-
mies: "Many and deadly were the sleep destroying darts she stuck into
the latter by placing them among the 'many others' or 'outs' at this or
that social function which all her friends were comfortably 'in' ...
People learned to fear her ill will and her pointed pen, for women in
particular are not yet aware how easy it is to handle this type of newspaper bully if it is done with courage and despatch. So she throve." But
although the managing editor, a passive decent sort, had allowed the
city editor and social editor complete freedom, not recognizing that
the "sparkle" of the society column came from "hidden dynamite," her
"colored," inaccurate, and unfair reports eventually brought too much
trouble to his paper. "Hers was a job that was lost."[62]

Perry, a vigorously upright and loyally Canadian journalist, attributed this style of social reporting to the "yellow press" in the United
States. To be fair, social editors of respectable American newspapers
were equally offended by scandal-mongering gossip sheets. A Wellesley
College career adviser steered graduates interested in journalism away
from society reporting altogether. She warned that a young woman
entering this line would have to "become absolutely hardened, willing
to forgo people's confidence, to use her friends one and all, to sacrifice
everything to her one purpose of getting the gossipy news in print
first."[63] Genevieve Boughner, writing in a more practical vein a decade
or so later, admitted that vicious slander still characterized some social
reporting in the United States. But she maintained that the harm done
to the paper by libel suits and a generally bad reputation was considerable and that those who traded in lies made life difficult for all social
reporters. She admitted, however, that the popularity which such short-
sighted methods accrued sometimes compensated for the damage they
did to the newspaper.[64]

All in all, the social reporter was, in the end, more dependent than
any other type of journalist on the good will of her respondents. Her
news beat was by definition small, and once excluded from her city's
best society, even a brilliant social satirist would find her niche uncom-
fortably restricted. Given the insecurity of her position, then, a commentator on high society could not wield her power irresponsibly. It
was crucially important to her constituents and her reputation with
them that no mistakes or omissions should occur unintentionally, for

they would certainly be noticed by the slighted victim. Accuracy down to the minutest detail of name, title, relationships, dress, and decoration was essential for the social editor's ongoing success. Nothing was more important, according to the canons of journalistic literature: "The society column is the public highway of the newspaper. It traffics in names, in family connections, and to some extent in personalities. It is an asset to the paper only if these names are correct; otherwise it is a liability."[65]

In Canada, "correctness" meant the formal address of a court gazette. Learning the intricacies of aristocratic nomenclature was a trial principally afflicting Ottawa reporters, but in all settings, a married woman was identified by her husband's name – Mrs J.S. Smith. The eldest daughter would be dignified by a simple Miss Smith, while Christian names fell only to younger daughters. Not for Canadian editors was the cheeky familiarity of nicknames which the social columns of William Randolph Hearst's newspapers affected to vex American hostesses in the early part of the century.[66]

Whatever their attitude towards society and society reporting, all the guidebooks and advice manuals concurred: even small errors were mortal sins on the society page. Dorothy Bell admitted, rather cheerfully to be sure, that she had lost her job on the *Vancouver Sun*'s society page because she had confused two wedding gowns.[67] Because misprints and mistakes carried so heavy a charge, "bloopers" on that page were favourite themes for after-dinner talks in press circles. P.D. Ross of the *Ottawa Journal* regaled his listeners with his paper's misbegotten description of a cabinet minister's wife at the governor general's ball, clad in "crepe de chine trimmed with two bathtubs and a toilet."[68] And Alixe Carson Carter gleefully recalled a *Calgary Herald* report of a wedding "consummated" on the church altar.[69] Doubtless, the happy pair were less enraptured with their coverage in the public press.

The society editor had to bear the wrath of offended celebrities, many of whom would not scruple to use their social prominence as a weapon against her if she transgressed too often or too seriously. Thus, if Beatrice Sullivan, social editor of the Toronto *Mail and Empire*, flew into a rage when any name in her column was misspelled (even though her handwriting was an appalling scrawl), it was "understandable," her colleague explained, "when we recall that mention in that sacred area was the next thing to being presented at court."[70] If the principals happened to be not only socially prominent but also advertising clients, the social editor's job was doubly fraught – as Lois Reynolds remembered, covering the wedding of John David Eaton and Signy Stephenson for the Toronto *Globe*.[71]

CHARTING THE SOCIAL TOPOGRAPHY

The social editor's veneration for accuracy of address underscored the conventional rationale of the society column – that everyone mentioned would certainly buy the paper to see her name in print, presumably to reify her sense of place in the social hierarchy. But even if everyone in the whole upper class of society bought the paper to read his or her name, that would account for only a few hundred sales. The Toronto-born journalist Stinson Jarvis pointed out the illogic of this explanation of the society page's appeal: "The four hundred, if numbered correctly, would purchase just twenty dollars worth of a Sunday paper which sells at a few cents a copy; so that it is perhaps not with a view to selling the papers to the individuals whose names are therein repeatedly mentioned that such attention is paid to the doings of an often uninteresting and minute class."[72] The mass-circulation newspaper had to appeal to the thousands, and the society column was part of that attraction. This was axiomatic to George Bernard Shaw, who attributed the popular appeal of the London *Star* to its discovery that "washerwomen are as keen on society gossip as Duchesses."[73]

The expanded newspaper clientele marked a change from the days when the newspaper-reading public was small and so were social circles. In a restricted social milieu, citizens did not require newspapers to tell them who their principal citizens were. As urban society inflated, it became more complex just at the time when a larger newspaper clientele began to clamour for more local news. One of the draws of the society page may well have been that it identified a recognizable group as the elite. It mapped the social topography for new recruits to the modern city. The fact that they could read about social leaders, even if they might never see them, may have provided the illusory comfort of knowing who was who. The "best families" no longer lived in the house on the hill, visible to all below; they now occupied the society column. Madge Macbeth hinted at this practical function in the *Land of Afternoon*, where a veteran of the Ottawa scene scolds the socially witless heroine: "Why the Society Columns are read to better advantage by the tradespeople, the gas inspector, the telephone operators, the very cab drivers, than you ... Those people almost unerringly place the rest of us in our proper class. They observe the rules of precedence, which you don't."[74]

In New York City, the idea of the Four Hundred gave interpreters of the social scene their cue: "Editors recognized the fact that a definite identification of the members of this charmed circle immediately had aroused and focussed the public interest sharply upon them and their doings."[75] The Four Hundred concept was infinitely elastic; nevertheless, the sense that it encased a limited group imbued those inside it with an aura of glamour. The intimate "between you and me" tone which fashionable reporters began to affect by the turn of the century drew the reader within that magic circle, for the moment at least.

Apart from the vicarious thrill of "being there," the society column helped teach newcomers the rudiments of success in an urban culture. It defined social status by outlining the distinctions that set the elite apart. The way a social columnist described manners and modes taught lessons of etiquette, most of which were utterly inappropriate to the real lives of the ordinary readers. Nevertheless, ambitious readers poised on the fringes of social acceptability lapped up every fragment of insight into drawing-room mores. Especially when the "exclusive set" took on elaborate fads and fancies, such as violet-hued calling cards or primrose kid gloves, which were chiefly intended to distinguish those in "the know" from those outside, the social reporter had to appear *au courant*. For instance, readers of the Vancouver *World* learned in 1902 that the telephone was beginning to revolutionize the ritual of morning calls. As one social personage confessed, through the telephone she could quickly dispense with the less interesting obligations she had incurred: "I make nearly all my calls now over the phone ... Although I may have nothing in particular to talk about, we chatter away for several minutes, and before I ring off I impress upon her the fact that I am returning her call, and that she needn't expect me to come in person."[76] In the same period, the Vancouver *Province*'s social editor instructed readers about informal entertaining at one's summer residence – what could be served, what the butler, maid, or page should wear, and how the hostess should greet and dismiss guests. The detailed instructions had the illusion of giving practical advice to a leisured but rather awkward audience, whereas it is more likely that the editor was merely conjuring dreams for the denizens of a social diaspora.

Beyond the didactic element, an atmosphere of spectacle, sometimes indeed of carnival, hung about the social column. Kit Coleman lampooned this dimension of society reporting in her article "The Vagaries of a 'Woman's Page.'" Masquerading as a society editor, she lectured a fictional assistant who despaired of answering a reader who believed that the hobnobs of New York had diamonds set in their teeth. "What's that? Why, of course they wear diamonds in their front teeth. My dear young lady, so long as you work for this Woman's Page never deprive the members of the Four Hundred of any of their spectacular accessories, and never do anything to cheapen them. If the women were to lose their faith in the Four Hundred, there would be no more women's pages, and you and I would be out of work."[77] It is perhaps significant that Coleman published her little parody in the *Manitoba*

Free Press rather than in her own Toronto *Mail and Empire*. Canadian society was subject to enormous regional variation – in some regions "high society" might include shopkeepers; in others, titled aristocrats. Where one society reporter might curtsy before a duchess, another had to sort the farmers from the ranchers. The women's editor of the Timmins *Daily Press* noted that the high point of social life in her locale was card games. In this mining town, ethnic diversity created a multiplicity of organizations, and it was a complex job for the social reporter to ensure that "the rules of class distinction – already established, although the town is only thirty years old – are observed."[78]

In remote backwaters or raw new cities, reporters sometimes borrowed terminology imported from a more exotic social terrain in order to give the local scene "tone."[79] Often this was inappropriate. For instance, the notion of an "upper ten thousand" hardly suited a city like Vancouver, whose total population barely exceeded that number before the turn of the century. All too often a society editor would try to elevate affairs in the local "cow town" by lifting material from more sophisticated arenas, with painfully laughable results. The editor of the Calgary *Weekly Herald* gleefully exposed the naive pretensions of a nearby small-town society reporter. Borrowing an item from a New York paper, she tried to "localize" her material by attributing to a neighbourhood dinner party a lively conversation on the merits of Botticelli. Now, in that particular town, the Calgary editor remarked, there were not likely to be enough people who knew who Botticelli was to hold a conversation of any description, and most of that town's principal citizens would most likely pronounce the artist "in western parlance, [as] 'a Dago' of some kind."[80]

That such burlesques should taint the sturdy spirit of her dearly beloved West exasperated Emily Murphy. A serious reformer and not one to dabble in high society for all her social prominence, Murphy castigated rural and western readers of urban society pages. In her view, such columns induced rural discontent, persuading the country woman that city life was all balls and outings and that her farmer husband was just "poor prunes." "Real sophisticates," she told her readers, "avoid society."[81] Murphy was an unheeded Cassandra in the burgeoning western cities, where streams of immigrants of all social stripes jostled the establishment's status quo. Fortunes were made and lost in short order; in the turbulent political climate, an election might turn the bottom to the top. In the mid-1930s, young Alixe Carson, as social reporter on the Calgary *Albertan*, found herself cowering behind her desk as a newly elevated personage – the wife of a politician recently elected to the Alberta legislature during the Social Credit sweep – demanded that her daughter's wedding receive front-page attention.

This rankest of outsiders, lacking the sophistication even to discern the strategic patience required to weave together the elements of money, prestige, family, and connections that were prerequisite to social success, tried to bully the social editor into recognizing her claims. On this occasion, the managing editor intervened to remind the matron that he still ran the paper even if her husband's party ran everything else.[82]

It was perhaps in the light of similar incidents, together with the potential ennui of having a limited circle of notables, that Elizabeth Long, who had spent years as social editor for the *Manitoba Free Press*, counselled her successors to "lift her social column from the monotony of parochial events by offering in each issue some item of general interest that is smart, bizarre or entertaining ... the thing readers will choose to discuss at dinner that evening with the feeling they are being bright."[83] The society column was supposed to lift spirits and open horizons, and to stimulate feelings of identification with a glamorous elite elsewhere, even if the reader was marooned on the Depression-gripped prairies.

It was not so necessary to go to such lengths in Ottawa, where federal politics defined society and thus furnished social reports with constantly changing personalities and visiting dignitaries. In the capital, high society and politics were intertwined to a remarkable degree. In treating this milieu, editors who normally might not deign to attend society assignments, took care that leading political lights received the appropriate social coverage. The editor of the *Montreal Standard* solicited Madge Macbeth, the freelance journalist and novelist who was approaching celebrity status herself by the 1920s, to investigate how the newly elected bachelor prime minister, William Lyon Mackenzie King, was going to arrange his entertainments, and to discover who was going to do the honours in the absence of a Mrs King: "You are the only one we could entrust with a delicate article of this kind."[84] The editor chose well. Macbeth divined the innermost workings of Ottawa social life, as she disclosed in her satire *The Land of Afternoon*: "In the Capital success is regarded from only one angle, the Social. Professional, literary, political, all these are but feeders to the main issue."[85]

The intermingling of society and politics was a perennial feature of any nation's seat of government.[86] But in the last decades of the nineteenth century and the first few years of the twentieth, women could play a part only in the social arena. Before women had the vote, politically astute social leaders had to rely on that supposedly all-powerful "influence" which they wielded through their parties and "drawing rooms." The political reporter might not necessarily circulate in this milieu, but the social reporter certainly did. Few social reporters in Canadian history enjoyed the position of trust and intrigue that the

Toronto *Globe*'s editor Emily McCausland Cummings occupied when Wilfrid Laurier made her his go-between in communications with Lady Aberdeen. The wife of the governor general warmly supported Laurier's bid for leadership, but her position enjoined nonpartisanship. Through her emissary, Mrs Cummings, Lady Aberdeen was able to meddle in Canadian politics invisibly.[87] When Laurier at last ascended to power, the Liberal-leaning *Globe* celebrated by sending two women reporters to cover the opening of Parliament. While Jean Blewett mused on the beautiful scenery, the stately visages of the politicians, and the philosophical dimensions of politics, occasionally giving a sidelong glance at the dresses, Emily Cummings did a thorough rendering of the parties and personalities, and their various deckings.

The ability of an Ottawa reporter to penetrate the most active networks depended, of course, upon politics. Yesterday's "best circles" for sociopolitical gossip might be tomorrow's outer fringe. Sara Jeannette Duncan was frustrated to discover this conundrum when she became parliamentary correspondent for the *Montreal Star*. In Ottawa, she found herself excluded from the most noteworthy occasions partly because she was unmarried but mainly because she represented an opposition sheet. But if ostracism from the principal Tory social events stymied her ambition of becoming the Canadian interpreter of affairs in the capital, she drew comfort from Lord Lansdowne's invitations to intimate gatherings at the governor general's residence.[88]

The presence of the viceregal court lent stability and established a certain tone of formality and rigidity which balanced the unpredictability of rising and falling political fortunes in Ottawa. There was less ambiguity in defining who was someone and who was not by association with the governor general's retinue. The ceremonies of protocol – formal entrance announcements, hierarchical seating patterns at banquets, the debutantes introduced by the governor general – clearly indicated descending orders of precedence. Mrs Alexander McIntyre (Frills of the Ottawa *Citizen* at the turn of the century) devoted most of her attention to military and aristocratic titles. She surpassed even her own adulation for rank when she paid a special visit to a prominent colonel's racehorse, whose health occupied most of a column.[89]

In Canada, the odour of colonialism lingered most pervasively around the society page, and anything to do with royalty or aristocracy held absorbing interest. This fascination continued throughout the twentieth century, despite the sanguine hopes of a pro-American writer who believed that the Canadian press and public were becoming more republican in sympathy. In 1891 Walter Blackburn Harte assured American readers that Canadians had no time for the trivial anachronisms of royalty. With the exception of official organs, he wrote, "all the other papers are avowedly democratic, and they do not pretend to treat the Court at Ottawa seriously; in fact, they ridicule its titular precedencies and distinctions ... and they hold stars and garters in very light estimation."[90]

Six years later, the eulogies of Kit of the *Mail* on Queen Victoria's Diamond Jubilee were so popular that she collected them for separate publication as a book, *To London for the Jubilee*. No seasoned name dropper could have excelled Kit's descriptions of the costumes and principals at Lady Devonshire's ball – the climax of the celebrations. Yet her Irish wit and social conscience had the last word. The magic realm she conjured from the jewels, velvet, and satin of each resplendent lord and lady drew her readers step by step into the magnificent ballroom. Then, abruptly, the dream dissolved as the nudge of a policeman's baton urged Kit to move on; so she and her reader shuffled along with the rest of the gaping onlookers. Although Kit had shared a carriage with Prime Minister Laurier as they went to a Buckingham Palace tea, it was typical of her character to identify in the end with Dickens's pathetic Joe of Tom-all-alone's – just one of the crowd.[91]

Such humility was not true to the spirit of the social column, and the irreverent Kit would never have limited herself to its narrow conventions. But in her evocation of imperial glory she struck a resonant chord in Canadian society, with which royal watchers identified whenever they had the opportunity. *Saturday Night* maintained Mary MacLeod Moore in London to relate the affairs around the palace and report notable occasions in the decades before and after the First World War. The "London Letter" included reports of British social reform and cultural affairs, and took note of prominent Canadians who were circulating in London society, but the concentric circles of royal relations were always to the fore.

Coronation reports and royal tours could establish for years the reputations of the women journalists fortunate enough to be sent on these assignments. When Mary Agnes Fitzgibbon represented the Toronto *Globe* at the coronation of Edward VII, she exulted, "I feel as though I had my foot on the first rung of the ladder which leads to literary fame."[92] Her "Coronation Letters" won front-page placement in the *Globe* during July 1902 when the king's illness delayed the ceremony, allowing Fitzgibbon a chance to display her abilities as a social and political commentator. As a result of her success, she became the *Globe*'s special correspondent in London for the next five years, and she returned in 1911 to cover the coronation of George V on the *Globe*'s behalf. Marjory MacMurchy of the Toronto *News* and Louise Birchall of the *Star* were the only other Canadian women correspondents at the crowning.

Royal visits were social events of such magnitude that they transcended the limits of the society page and engaged the attention even
of general reporters, who normally scorned the "pink tea" circuit. In
the 1920s, Myrtle Patterson – already the highest-paid woman reporter
in Canada, earning fifty dollars a week on the Vancouver *News-Advertiser*, added another five dollars a week to her salary by her ingenuity in
discovering the whereabouts of the glamorous Prince of Wales. She
followed his car in a taxi until he entered a West End mansion. Then,
pretending that her car had broken down, she inveigled her way inside
to discover the handsome Prince playing squash in the private
grounds.[93] When this Prince Charming finally renounced his crown for
the woman he loved, the society department of the Edmonton *Bulletin*
went into a romantic swoon and arranged to have a bunch of violets
plucked from a ranch Edward owned in the Alberta foothills to send as
a wedding token. It was headline news on the society page when the
demoted king deigned to have his secretary acknowledge the gift.[94]

Two years later, in 1939, when Edward's brother, King George VI,
crossed Canada, only three women, none of whom were society reporters, were on the press train. On this occasion, male reporters did not
slight a prestigious opportunity even if it did require describing the
queen from head to foot and listing the many dignitaries who were
received across the continent. As the only women included in the
cavalcade, Jessie MacTaggart, Muriel Adams, and Nancy Pyper were the
envy of their fellow press club members. Falsely modest, they affected a
peevish tone at the arduous schedule they endured. "Everyone thinks
we stay up all night drinking Cuba Libras and romancing with famous
newspaper men," Jessie MacTaggart reported. But although she admitted that the porters called the press train "the trunks and the
drunks," no one was having much fun, and she said that the famous
male reporters were just as nervous about getting and filing their stories
as they, the "lesser fry," were.[95]

On less prestigious occasions the routine worries of the social
reporter were of a lower order. Florence Taylor, recollecting her days
on the Victoria *Times*, emphasized the sheer volume of labour the social
whirl generated for those whose vocation it was to chart its course. By
her time, the early 1940s, the social departments of newspapers were
well-organized factories of social intelligence. Telephoning local
hostesses and arranging interviews with visiting celebrities took up most
of her day: "How well I remember the days when the social room desks
were piled high with wedding 'forms' full of details regarding future
weddings which eventually would turn into romantic accounts of yet another nuptial event."[96] Similarly, Alixe Carson's days were spent manufacturing events out of telephone conversations. Carson described how,

despite the bread lines of the Depression years, there was a great deal of entertaining. Calgary was a very social town, she recalled.[97]

Indeed, the Depression did little to crimp social activity insofar as it was projected into the newspaper. By the mid-1930s the Toronto *Globe* frequently had two social pages, which spilled over into the other sections of the newspaper. Most metropolitan newspapers employed social reporters to assist the social editor in charting the fashionable functions of the city. Like the ultraglamorous films of the thirties, accounts of cruises, elegant soirées, and fashion shows diverted the humble reader from her own woes for a moment. During the two world wars, the outside world penetrated to the extent that fashionable ladies organized fundraisers, debutantes visited the troops, and military paraphernalia studded the cast of starred weddings. Occasions when both the bride and groom sported uniforms ignited a conflagration of patriotic fervour on the page.[98] But although the movements of history might provide a changing backdrop for the social pageant, no hint of despair entered the never-never world of the society page.

NEWSWOMEN VIEWING THE SOCIETY PAGE

For journalists whose attraction to their occupation was a desire to be in the centre of things, to feel the pulse of change, the sameness of the society column, disguised only by the most superficial changes in fashion, was deflating. At best, they might categorize it as necessary drudgery, the "dish washing" side of newspaper work – as Florence Sherk, long-time women's editor of the Fort William *Times-Chronicle* put it.[99] Or they might engage in self-ridicule to air the embarrassment and frustration they suffered from constantly chronicling vapid "petticoat gush." In the *Quill Driver*, the private newsletter of the Ottawa branch of the Canadian Women's Press Club, members parodied stereotypes in a mock "agony column." Miss Pix, for instance, would be asked to respond to Flossie, a light-headed society belle, desperate to earn some pin money: "It costs me a fortune to keep my boyish bob in shape. I think I should like to be a Society Editress for I am crazy about teas and things. I can't spell very well but I hear the printers are just lambs and I am sure they would help me out. Would you advise me to go in for this?"[100]

For Anne Anderson Perry, the servitude of women journalists to the dictates of the gossipmongers was not a laughing matter. A strong-minded woman who wanted Canadian women's sections to offer the "big army of business and professional women something worthy of their intellectual steel," Perry felt that the "capital S (of Society) ought to stand for Shackles."[101] Most career journalists were anxious to graduate from the society department if they possibly could. When Lily Laverock, a learned graduate in moral philosophy from McGill and a suffragist, joined the staff of the Vancouver *News-Advertiser* in 1909, she refused the traditional position of society editor and insisted on the more dignified title of women's editor. Gwen Cash, too, prided herself on avoiding the "snob stuff" when she first started out as a reporter on the *Vancouver Sun* in 1917.[102] And Grace McGaw, after her initiation into the challenging "street beat," considered her next appointment, the more traditional social round, a "descent."[103] Conversely, Isabel Black, who had been society reporter for the *Province* and then the *Sun* in Vancouver in the early 1920s before she left journalism for marriage and motherhood, sighed to her former colleague, Myrtle Patterson, that all her newspaper career had added up to was "secretary's reports," and she had no regrets when she abandoned it.[104]

Lois Reynolds Kerr looked back on her days as society editor on the Toronto *Globe* more charitably. She remembered the glamour and the many perks, such as tea at the Yacht Club, a treasured event in the bleak Depression days.[105] Kerr's abiding ambition, however, was to be a playwright. She treated her newspaper job as an apprenticeship, one that gave her access to all manner of people and situations. Ultimately, she used her days on the society page to furnish background material for four of her plays, *Nellie McNab*, *Among Those Present*, *A Guest of Honour*, and *No Reporters Please*.[106]

Given the contempt or at best patronizing tolerance that so often fell to the society reporter, relations with other women journalists could be cool if not positively frigid. June Callwood, who was just beginning her career on the *Brantford Expositor* during the Second World War, defined her own professional identity in opposition to the resident society reporter, Ethel Raymond: "Miss Raymond was a perfect character. She wore gloves and I think sometimes typed with them on, and she always kept her hat on in the office. She was a stoutly corseted woman who couldn't spell and the managing editor … hated her with a passion and he then concluded he hated all women."[107] In the United States, the antipathy between society writers and other women journalists escalated to crisis point, and in 1932 the former withdrew from the Women's National Press Club and formed their own Newspaper Women's Club.[108]

No parallel schism developed in the Canadian Women's Press Club. At least publicly, Canadian newspaperwomen maintained a front of solidarity, recognizing that social reporting was an inescapable fact of life for many of them. Thus, while Dora Dibney was president of the club, even though she had never been a social editor, she defended those members of her flock. In a mock-diatribe on the ills afflicting women journalists, she railed, "For long, long years, city editors, managing editors and news editors have relegated women, as a whole, to the society desk where they have done right nobly. In fact I don't know how they stick to it at all. Seems like a swell training ground for a diplomatic post. I'd never make the grade I know."[109]

One aspect of social reporting that did salvage something for the ambitious woman journalist was its discipline. The emphasis on accuracy and thorough observation was probably more acute in this department than any other. The society reporter had to learn discretion and tact, and she had to learn how to coax information from sometimes unwilling subjects and not to alienate them in her reports. For this reason, guidebook writers concurred that, for all its apparent tedium, there was probably no better all-round training open to the journalist, male or female.[110] A good society reporter could undertake any kind of reportorial duty. The most logical move onwards was, paradoxically, a sideways step into club reporting, where the journalist would meet many of the same contacts she had wooed in society but would treat their activities in the more serious vein of social reform.

CHAPTER EIGHT

The Women's Press Gallery:
Club Reporters, from
Partisans to Publicists

St Peter met her at the gate,
And took her by the fin
Said He: some sins we all must rue,
But you did clubs one winter through,
And that is hell enough for you -
Come in.

J.P. McEvoy

In the era before women won the vote, their parliaments were the clubs they formed for intellectual, philanthropic, or social reform.[1] The journalists who followed club activities for the newspaper-reading public were, in a sense, the women's press gallery. In the club movement, serious and idealistic newswriters found their professional and personal goals converging. The drive to be at the centre of community affairs and to make a vital contribution propelled the clubwoman and journalist alike. Covering clubs gave ambitious presswomen a chance to practise the kind of reporting that had informed their ambition to become journalists in the first place. Under the auspices of club reporting they could engage in the debates resounding through their times, grapple with social problems, and experiment with new ideas.

It was in this facet of their gender-specific work experience that many women journalists came to make the news they would also report. In the early days of the women's club movement, presswomen were not merely observers recording the news as it happened. They were at the very heart of the reform era, as committed clubwomen themselves – aware of the social problems in their environment and optimistic that organized voluntary activity could surmount them. The unity of purpose that bound clubwomen and journalists together would eventually unravel as some journalists became "objective" disengaged observers of women's clubs and others became "professional" public relations officers in the paid service of clubs. This chapter focuses on the transformation of the club reporter's speciality from the climax of women's achievement as amateur reformers before suffrage to the falling off of voluntarism and encroachment of professionalism in the arena served by women's clubs.

IN SOLIDARITY

From the outset, the relationship between clubwomen and presswomen was a mutually self-serving alliance. Newswomen owed their jobs partly to the club phenomenon. When newspaper owners acknowledged that club news might be a way of drawing female readers, they hired female reporters to cover meetings. Predictably, club reporting was not a specialty valued highly by male editors in the days when organizations of women were a novelty. To the male establishment, there was something comical or unseemly in the coming together of women to discuss ideas and issues. Ishbel Ross, who began her career on the Toronto *News*, recalled a time when city editors habitually greeted club reporters with the query, "Were they funny or did they fight?"[2] The lines of doggerel penned by the American editor J.P. McEvoy, quoted above, encapsulates the satirical scorn that many editors directed at women's organizations.

Given an antagonistic attitude on the part of the media, women's club leaders were often unwilling to bear the full light of publicity on their first experiments in public speaking. But in the safety of an all-female forum, women could practise the mechanics of politics – how to conduct meetings, how to command attention from large gatherings, how to translate aspiration into action, and in general how to take part in the life of the nation. The reluctant or patronizing attention of the press was not conducive to confidence building, and club leaders were therefore inclined to eject the reporters sent to scrutinize their efforts. These precautions were understandable but were not gauged to win a favourable reception for their cause. But who was to know that the serious young lady taking notes at the Elm Street Methodist annual mission meeting was Garth Grafton of the Toronto *Globe*, sent down to replace a rejected male reporter? The real Sara Jeannette Duncan squirmed a little in her disguise when a kindly soul beside her in the audience, watching her zealous note taking, commended her dedication to mission work. Nevertheless, Garth Grafton's write-up, though light-hearted and humorous, applauded the conduct of the women-only meeting.[3] Sympathetic treatment at the hands of a woman reporter could only serve to increase the confidence of club leaders and, ultimately, their cooperation with the press.

Clubwomen soon learned that publicity was crucial to the success of their projects. If the point of organizing was to validate women's participation in community life, newspaper reports ensured that the general public knew about it. Many of the club leaders were socially prominent women who used their status to influence wider society. The publicity that presswomen provided to women's clubs elevated the status of what well-to-do women of leisure were doing with their time. The same woman who poured at such-and-such a tea or who looked so charming in her crêpe de Chine gown might be president of the local Council of Women, the Women's Canadian Club, or a Political Equality League. In addition to local recognition, reports in the press furnished a vital communications network linking the widely dispersed local branches of nationally organized clubs. Committed club leaders were increasingly motivated to facilitate the club reporter's job by keeping her abreast of their meetings, projects, and achievements, because she was their lifeline. Only through publicity would the public become aware of what organized women were thinking and doing. The Women's Canadian Club of Winnipeg, for instance, regularly reserved a special table at its luncheons for the women of the press.[4]

By the same token, the stories that clubwomen created by their activities, whether it was the routine occurrence of a regular meeting or a dramatic gesture such as a parade or demonstration, were often the "hardest" news on the women's page. Unlike the columnist or expert adviser who conjured up her material from her own well-spring of ingenuity or quasiplagiarized clippings, the club reporter recorded news as it was happening. Presswomen anxious to make their mark as serious reporters were often attracted to club work because it replicated in the women's department the city editor's domain.

Certainly, club reporting seemed to be a more promising route into mainstream journalism than the oft-despised social circuit or the more literary feature writing. Many an all-purpose women's page editor, whose raison d'être on the paper was the "Social and Personal" column, expanded and dignified her paragraphs by emphasizing the cultural and civic activities of her city's social leaders, since the reporter who covered the ball and the fete also attended the lecture and meeting. Reporting the talks of visiting speakers or enlarging on clubwomen's earnest resolutions enabled early social editors to inject an intellectual note into an otherwise frothy roster of dowagers, debutantes, and their dresses. The meeting of the international Women's Congress gave the first social editor of the Toronto *Globe*, Mrs Willoughby Cummings, an opportunity to report on how women were contributing to the Chicago world's fair of 1893. So inspired was she by her experiences that she returned to help found the National Council of Women in Canada.[5]

According to their intellectual perspective, women journalists emphasized one or the other dimension of their beat. In 1904 Margaret Graham, who sold her work to papers as widely dispersed as the Vancouver *World* and the Halifax *Herald*, introduced her column on social life in the capital with the promise to concentrate on the way that women in Ottawa, through clubs, were influencing legislation. But she was not averse to the "necessary frivolities of life," she said, and she assured her readers that she would keep them informed about the glamorous affairs in the capital: "Because women today must needs keep pace with the progress of the world – nay, is herself an indispensable factor in that progress – shall we banish social pleasure and be ever on serious thought intent?"[6]

Women's clubs – idealistic, civic minded, and forward looking – were integral to the diversity and seriousness of the women's page. They furnished women journalists with opportunities to grapple with current social issues rather than confining their attention to domestic affairs and fashion. Not surprisingly, then, women journalists enthusiastically publicized the activities of women's organizations, introducing and explaining them to a larger audience than any club, however entrepreneurial, could hope to embrace in its membership. Even a large and well-established club such as the National Council of Women of Canada, with branches in all the major cities of the dominion, still needed the kind of reasoned elucidation of its raison d'être that Lally Bernard (Mary Agnes Fitzgibbon) provided during a national convention in 1903. Given the editorial privilege of her own column, Lally Bernard was able to explain the origins and intentions of the national council more thoroughly than the usual tersely worded club report could. In rather grandiose language, she invested the council with lofty philosophical and educational functions. Affirming that "the 'humanities' are what mainly concern a women's council," she contended that the National Council of Women made its business "the practical application of humane principles." In national conventions, such as the one she was presently attending, or local branch meetings, the women's council studied practical ramifications of the laws made by men and especially scrutinized the effects of legislation on the helpless. Fitzgibbon thus validated a uniquely female relationship to the legislative and reform process.

In these early days of the club movement in Canada, journalists were more intent on promoting the club idea to women than in advertising its legitimacy to men. The Marchioness (Agnes Scott) of the Ottawa *Free Press* hinted that her notes on the National Council of Women might well attract men to her column, "for the male sex, though professedly above the vice of inquisitiveness, has a fondness for knowing what it is all about."[7] But on the whole, club reports and editorials on the women's page about various organizations tried to dispel the fears of potential members that they might be neglecting their families or becoming less womanly by taking up an interest outside the home. "The Rocking Chair," a weekly feature of the Winnipeg *Saturday Post*, saluted "the modern club woman" as, at one and the same time, "the most advanced of those feminine progressives" and a demure back-bencher in worldly affairs. Marking the occasion of the fourth anniversary of the Winnipeg branch of the Women's Canadian Club, the author (probably Effie Laurie Storer) defused any notion that it was composed of strong-minded harpies bent on selfish independence: "It was formed to supplement the Men's Canadian Club in that fashion in which women most ably supplement men's work everywhere and along all lines, chiefly through home influences."[8] Its dedication to the cause of patriotism, the author claimed, should interest everyone, including dedicated homemakers who confined their interest to husband and children, busy wage earners, and the more leisured clubwomen.

These modest introductions of women's clubs to the wider community of newspaper-reading women appeared on the threshold of that period when almost all organizations of women were rallying their constituencies to demand the franchise. As the twentieth century got underway, a spirit of confidence and assertiveness seemed to grip clubwomen as well as the journalists who wrote about them. Neither were content to be furtive about the extent of their activities and ambitions. The philosophical and strongly feminist Lily Laverock embraced a mission to uplift the intellectual, cultural, and moral horizons of Vancouver women when she assumed her duties as women's editor of the Vancouver *News-Advertiser* in 1909. At a time when clubwomen were perceived as being among the most forward-looking and intellectual of women, Laverock, the first female graduate in moral philosophy from McGill, could most certainly meet her sisters in clubdom on their own level.[9] She made it her business to broadcast their serious interests and achievements. Her colleagues in the Vancouver newspaper scene took heart from the kind of changes Laverock wrought in the local setting. Amy Kerr, owner of the *Western Women's Weekly*, venerated Lily Laverock as one who raised the status of a "mere society page to the dignity of a woman's page filled with a broader vision and foreshadowing the bigger suffrage movement."[10]

What Laverock achieved on the *News-Advertiser* was matched in varying degrees in the other Vancouver papers. The women's pages in Vancouver newspapers were only just emerging at the turn of the century at the same time as Vancouver branches of nationally organized clubs were in formation. There was a special excitement attending the activities of women in what was still a new city in Canada. Ethel G. Cody Stoddart, an active clubwoman and journalist who wrote as Lady Van for a variety of West Coast periodicals, proudly displayed the distinguished cast of Vancouver leaders and their achievements in a survey of the local club scene in 1910.[11] Mabel Durham and Beatrice Nasmyth of the *Province,* Clare Battle of the *World,* and Lily Laverock of the *News-Advertiser,* despite the rivalries of their respective papers, shared a sober-minded fervour that materialized into an unusually marked emphasis on social reform in the women's pages of Vancouver newspapers during that lively decade of female activism before and during the First World War.[12]

Indeed, there was sufficient activity among Vancouver clubwomen to convince two newspaperwomen, Laverock first and then Kerr, to cut themselves loose from bondage to the daily press in order to launch independent women's newspapers. Lily Laverock's *Chronicle* had lofty intellectual goals that were not, unfortunately, supported by a solid financial foundation. One can only wonder whether, had she possessed a personal fortune like that of Viscountess Rhondda, the *Chronicle* might have approached the feminist majesty of *Time and Tide.* In the event, the *Chronicle* closed down within a year of its birth in 1910.[13] That Amy Kerr's *Western Women's Weekly* lasted longer, from 1917 to 1924, was due in part to her business acumen but also, in large measure, to the support of the local women's clubs, whose activities formed the main substance of the weekly. Kerr launched her paper at the height of the club movement when women's organizations had more members and more prestige than at any time in their history.[14]

By that time, a decade or more of constructive achievement and sometimes controversial activism on the part of clubwomen had roused the Canadian public into a recognition that reform-minded women were intent upon success for their issues. Press reports were indispensable to that end, as a contributor to the *Western Women's Weekly* testified in her letter, "On the Importance of Club Reporting": "I have great faith in the power of the press as an educator, and education is better than agitation. Our women's organizations are doing good and noble work but there is a large number of women who do not belong to any of them ... I trust that through the medium of your columns you will be able to arouse women to a sense of their responsibilities. "[15]

Positive publicity fuelled the momentum of community leaders' ambition. The tender treatment they received from newswomen increased their confidence to tackle yet more projects and become yet more newsworthy. Furthermore, newspaper reports attracted new members and provided a communications network for clubwomen that was especially valued in national organizations, where conventions were infrequently spaced and only a few delegates could represent distant regions. In the pages of *Saturday Night*, clubwomen became big news. During "club" month – usually June – presidents of national organizations were featured on the front page of the women's section in glamorous oval-shaped studio shots and introduced to a nationwide audience.

As the reading public's interest in the club movement climaxed, even the most hidebound newspapers were obliged to follow the various clubs' activities. Women journalists appreciated the profuse copy that politically engaged clubwomen supplied. For instance, when the Imperial Order of the Daughters of the Empire (IODE) sponsored British suffragist Barbara Wylie on a speaking tour in western Canada, the *Edmonton Journal* featured the club in the lead article on the women's page and used the occasion to underline the aims and achievements of the IODE.[16] As Isabel MacLean of the Vancouver *Province* crowed:

Feminism itself has opened a tremendous area to the woman journalist ... She cannot afford to neglect this area, for here the great battles – other than political – are waging, often silently but none the less decisive; and important contributions to life and literature will yet spring out of its soil. The feminist page now embraces the live issues of the day and many problems, common to all humanity, which it is impossible to enumerate here – problems of social service, education, immigration and so forth.[17]

Club reporters were grateful to their informants for helping to make the women's section one of the liveliest departments in the newspaper. However, their enthusiasm for the club movement was not confined merely to their own writing careers. That missionary zeal to reshape society in a moral feminist mould informed the women journalists just as it did the clubwomen. The feminists of the age believed that in whatever corner women worked, their presence would cleanse and renew.

PARTISANS

During the first decades of the twentieth century, women journalists were doubly engaged, advancing both their own careers in the press and the causes they cherished as committed clubwomen. Right from the beginning, Canadian newspaperwomen had been involved in the major reform activities of Canadian society. The incidence of active club membership among women journalists was remarkable, though not altogether surprising given their general level of awareness and enterprise.[18] Being an active clubwoman could also provide an entrée into journalism. Just as an established social position was an asset to the would-be social reporter, a network of connections among local clubs was invaluable, especially in the period when clubwomen tended to be shy of publicity. Lily Laverock, for instance, was one of the founders of the Vancouver Women's University Club. It was the quality of the reports she submitted to the local press that won her a job on the Vancouver *World* in 1907. Years later, Abbie Lane was recruited for the Halifax *Chronicle* precisely because she was active in most of the clubs in the city. "My only qualifications for the job," she said, "were that I knew everyone in town and could type."[19] Organizations such as the Women's Canadian Club and the National Council of Women, with mandates to mobilize women's energy to improve society, accorded with the professional public service mentality of many women who were ambitious for a career in the press. Journalists, as individuals, were prominent members of both, and the Canadian Women's Press Club was among the official affiliates of the National Council of Women from 1909 to 1926. Women journalists, particularly those employed by reform-minded papers or who enjoyed a degree of editorial autonomy, were in a highly strategic position to promote their clubs and causes.

At the same time, circulation managers were anxious to align themselves with prominent reform activists in order to build subscriptions among a female readership. Violet McNaughton achieved so much prominence through her activism in the Women's Grain Growers' Association that without applying for a newspaper job, she was actively pursued by a variety of agricultural papers to conduct a women's page. The editor of the *Saturday Press and Prairie Farm* did not hide his motives for recruiting her: "We should ... have to judge of the success of the page by the effect it produced in the way of subscriptions." She was offered two dollars a week, plus 50 per cent of subscriptions raised.[20] She was then solicited by the Regina *Leader-Post* to conduct a "Women's Grain Growers' Corner," an offer which, because of wartime newspaper shortages, came to nothing. Mary McCallum of the *Grain Growers' Guide*, called McNaughton "the mainstay of the club women's page,"[21] while the editor tried to recruit her for subscription drives on the grounds that "the women who read *The Guide* are the most active in the farm women's associations."[22] McNaughton eventually accepted a position with the *Western Producer* where she stayed for a quarter of a century.

But if newspapers were using McNaughton for her revenue-raising potential, she was also dually motivated in accepting the positions. For any Saskatchewan farmer, a source of regular income was welcome; but

for Violet McNaughton, access to the public press for promoting the
issues she embraced so passionately was even more to the point. She
would be using her weekly editorial and her extensive circle of writing
friends to agitate for causes ranging from suffrage to female immigration schemes, rural nurses and local hospitals, farmer's cooperatives,
help for the disabled, old age pensions, and, most consistently, pacifism. For McNaughton, the role of the press in forwarding women's
causes would continue to expand even after the franchise was won. She
spoke thus to the women's section of the Saskatchewan Grain Growers'
Association : "We must now remember that we have entered a fuller and
more complex life, and prepare ourselves accordingly. The publicity
that the press gives to our conventions enables us to mould public
opinion now in a manner that we could not do before we were enfranchised."[23]

Presswomen, then, did more than join existing societies; they used
their public role in the press to act as agents of organization and
recruitment for women's clubs. Since their job was to write about
women, they were more likely than any other group to discover the
areas of neglect and injustice that blighted many women's lives.
McNaughton and her friend and colleague Annie Hollis knew from
personal experience as farm wives the soul-destroying isolation that
women's clubs did something to abate.[24] Other women journalists were
similarly committed to reaching out to the farm wife and embracing
her in a circle of mutual self-help. Mae Clendenan, for instance, as
women's editor of the *Farmer's Advocate,* did not merely write about the
gadgets and hints that would lighten the burdens of her clientele of
farm women. She went out to meet the farm women, billeting in one
sod shack after another, so that she could find out first-hand about rural
women's lives and organizations.[25] In 1921 Violet McNaughton's remote Saskatchewan farm was one of her stops. Clendenan was able to
joke about her mission with her friend, urging her to be "practicing
some soulful expressions to spring on the poor reporter when she
comes to interview you."[26] Eleanor McLennan, women's editor of the
Calgary Herald in the years before the First World War, used her page to
publicize philanthropic societies and their achievements and in
addition made a point of visiting a poor family every day. At Christmas,
her column raised two thousand dollars for gifts.[27]

The crusade to both publicize and ameliorate the female predicament prompted some women journalists not only to join clubs but to
found them too.[28] Lillian Beynon, women's editor of the *Manitoba Free
Press,* set about connecting beleaguered prairie farm wives by initiating
the Homemakers' Clubs. In this effort her sisters in the press were right
by her side. At the first Homemakers' Club convention, held in Regina

in 1910, Florence Lediard Clutton of the *Farmer's Advocate* and Mary Mantle of the *Northwest Farmer* were among the organizers. Fellow members of the Canadian Women's Press Club took part as well; Nellie McClung and Cora Hind gave addresses, while Annie Perry, Mae Currie, and Isabel Armstrong registered as delegates. Although these women participated as members, their engagement did nothing to inhibit their write-ups in their respective papers. Indeed, Isabel Armstrong requested permission of the Regina *Leader* to begin a regular page of information and communication among Homemakers' Club branches. The women's section of the Grain Growers' Association had a similar history. Lillian's sister Francis Beynon, women's page editor of the *Grain Growers' Guide*, was the driving force here. As with the Homemakers' Clubs, a constellation of newspaperwomen, led by the stellar Cora Hind and including Mae Clendenan, both Beynon sisters, Nellie McClung, Irene Moore, and Jean Grant, addressed the first convention in 1913.[29]

In organizing the farm women of the prairie provinces, journalists worked on behalf of other women; in campaigning for the vote, women journalists worked for all, themselves included. As Mary Ford pointed out, while mildly berating her readers for failing to sign the petition circulated through the *Grain Growers' Guide* "Remember that the vote or equal suffrage question does not only benefit the present generation, but will mean the uplift and the betterment of humanity mentally, morally, physically and politically for all generations to come."[30] Journalists and writers were strongly represented in the suffrage societies, constituting nearly one-quarter of the leadership.[31] For instance, the founder of the Ottawa Equal Suffrage Society was Mrs J.J. McNulty, a journalist who disguised her identity by writing as A. O'Reilly.[32] In Vancouver, suffrage leaders Helen Gregory MacGill, Alice Ashworth Townley, and Lily Laverock were founding members of the local branch of the Canadian Women's Press Club. Another early Vancouver press club member, Beatrice Nasmyth, went on to manage the campaign of the first woman ever elected to the Alberta legislature.[33] In Winnipeg, ten members of the local CWPC branch got together to form the Political Equality League.[34] At the top of the national organization was Flora MacDonald Denison, president of the Canadian Suffrage Association 1911–14.[35] From 1909, Denison devoted a page in the Toronto *Sunday World* specifically to the women's movement. As Nellie McClung acknowledged gratefully, prosuffrage presswomen lavished space on "the cause."[36]

As illustrated earlier, there was a tradition among women in newspaper work not only to write the news but to make it. Women journalists put this flair for self-generated publicity to work for their organizations.

The best-known instance of newsmaking for a cause was the Winnipeg Political Equality League's "Mock Parliament." Frustrated by the stubborn unwillingness of the incumbent Manitoba government to take seriously their demands for the vote, the suffrage society staged a protest designed to attract attention. In the skit that made the Winnipeg Political Equality League famous and Manitoba premier Sir Rodmond Roblin infamous, newspaperwomen took the leading roles. Kennethe Haig of the *Manitoba Free Press* played the attorney general, Isabel Graham of the *Grain Growers' Guide* was speaker, while Genevieve Lipsett-Skinner, political correspondent for a variety of papers including the conservative *Winnipeg Telegram*, became minister of economy and agriculture. The Beynon sisters, Lillian Thomas and Francis, acted as members of the opposition, while Nellie McClung clinched her place in women's history by her cheeky portrayal of the fatuous manner of the premier himself. Directing the whole production was Harriet Walker, editor of *Curtain Call*.[37]

If, as committed suffragists, the women journalists of Winnipeg were biased in their approach to the "woman question," in equally partisan fashion they repaid their debt to the party that enfranchised women. In 1917 the Winnipeg branch of the CWPC organized a voluntary committee to work for the government in the forthcoming election. Its members prepared leaflets addressed to new women voters and, quite unselfconsciously, dedicated their women's pages to promote the fortunes of the incumbents.[38] Here, as in other instances, they chose the journalism of engagement over objectivity.

It was fitting that at the height of the women's club movement and the integration of women's journalism with social reform through the club movement, Emily Murphy should preside over the CWPC. In Murphy's career the boundary between her journalism and her social activism was invisible. Her Janey Canuck pieces qualified her for membership in the CWPC, which was specifically a professional women's organization, but she used her writing and ultimately her organizations to promote the causes she favoured as a social reformer.[39] Murphy's enmeshed motives accorded with the tradition of the CWPC to that date; the club had frequently behaved as if it were as much a reform society as a professional women's association. In Regina, for example, the CWPC worked hand in glove with the National Council of Women to lobby for the dower law.[40] Murphy was particularly adept at guiding reforming zeal and generating publicity. A headline in the *Edmonton Journal* of 1914 typified the Murphy style: "Press Women Pray for Suspension of Liquor Licenses." Murphy had led fellow journalists in a public prayer for one of her most cherished causes.[41]

Murphy's tenure as president of the CWPC was extended throughout the First World War, when virtually all women's organizations mobilized in a frenzy of patriotic fervour. Newspapers reflected the shift. Erin (Mary Josephine Trotter) noted in the *Canadian Courier,* "Our world has changed, in little more than a month, so that we hardly recognize the old round of interests, in which we talked of chiffon and suffrage."[42] Women journalists were at the centre of activity, both personally and professionally. Almost every branch of the CWPC embarked on one or another scheme to raise money for "our boys overseas." Within weeks of the outbreak of war, the Winnipeg branch had written and produced *The Knapsack,* a collection of essays, poetry, and stories, which sold out its print run within a week and raised around a thousand dollars to purchase Christmas presents for Canadian barracks overseas.[43] Hour upon hour of collective sewing and knitting united the clubwomen of Canada, while the presswomen tallied up the mounting piles of "soldier comforts," some of which, like the wristbands which soldiers used to clean their boots,[44] were poignantly useless. The cross-country knitting jag inspired journalist and poet Katherine Hale (Amelia Warnock Garvin) to compose the poem "Grey Knitting," which instantly established her fame. Her central stanza underscored the dissonance between the wartime experiences of men and women:

> Whispers of women, tireless and patient
> "Foolish, inadequate!" we hear you say;
> "Grey wool on fields of hell is out of fashion,"
> And yet we weave the web from day to day."[45]

DIVISIONS

Although the war saw the majority of newspaperwomen and clubwomen welded together in a common cause, it also ignited quarrels, some of which never subsided. Among journalists, the most doleful schism came where togetherness had once been most solid. The women who made Winnipeg famous in their satirical sketch for suffrage were divided over the war. At one extreme was the archpatriot Cora Hind, who believed that Canada should support Britain without question and who "spent both time and money unstintedly in the interests of 'the boys' at home and overseas."[46] At the other extreme was the pacifist Francis Beynon, who found herself at odds with the women whose causes she had for so long embraced as her own in the *Grain Growers' Guide.* Beynon opposed the position taken up by Nellie McClung that foreign-born women should be denied the franchise.[47] As a newspaper-

Emily Murphy, president of the Canadian
Women's Press Club 1913–20, at home in
Edmonton in 1923, photographed by her
friend Miriam Green Ellis (NA, C-895760)

woman she was silenced when her opposition to war alarmed her
employer. In 1917 Beynon resigned from her paper and entered
voluntary exile in New York, where she joined her sister Lillian Beynon
Thomas, whose husband Vernon had similarly run afoul of his paper's
wartime belligerence.[48] In her novel *Aleta Dey*, Beynon took revenge on
the narrow-minded war fever of the do-good clubwoman in the character of a "commanding society woman" of the Women's Canadian
Club. This termagant reproves Aleta's doubts about virtue being all on
one side with a viciousness that encapsulated the bigoted spleen that
passed for patriotism at the time: "You must see yourself, young lady,
that there is a vast difference between crucifying a white man and
hanging a coloured one."[49] In between these hostile poles of patriotism
and pacifism stood Nellie McClung, lamenting the war as a "crime
committed by men" but eventually siding with the national effort and
even supporting conscription.[50] Yet the war effort, however painful, saw
the women's club movement reach the peak of its prestige and the
fruition of many aspirations. By the end of the war women had won the
vote, liquor sales were controlled by government regulation in most

provinces, and a federal Department of Health took official responsibility for many of the family issues clubwomen had raised.[51]

Perhaps inevitably, on the crest of organized women's triumph, the seamless web of alliance between women journalists and clubwomen began to fray. Some women journalists became more inclined to analyse their function as club reporters, and although they usually remained supportive of philanthropic goals, they were not always uncritical champions of the conduct of clubwomen. Marjory Mac-Murchy, who had had a varied career in journalism in the early years of the twentieth century and enough stature by the beginning of the war to be appointed to the Reconstruction Committee, first laid down the gauntlet in the midst of the war years.[52] As a respected public servant, MacMurchy was no longer directly dependent on the cooperation and benevolence of the clubs she scrutinized and could therefore take a stern look at how women's clubs actually served women and national unity.

MacMurchy published her critique in a book with a rather wry title, *The Woman – Bless Her: Not as Amiable a Book as it Sounds.* Looking at a range of women's organizations at a time when the stringency of wartime tested their efficiency and utility, she found them wanting. Modest and single-minded missionary societies got full marks, as did the Women's Institutes and the Homemakers' Club, which she felt amply demonstrated the worth of their contribution to their members and to Canadian society. But other large organizations, she implied, were not accomplishing much and expected far too much credit for what they did achieve. Some of her frustrations as a journalist surfaced as she upbraided the leaders for self-aggrandizement. They attached too great importance, she observed, "to having placed on record, especially in the public press, that they were the first to begin the movement for some remarkable reform, that they bore the heat of labour of the day, and that in fact no one else is entitled to any credit."[53] There was an irony in MacMurchy's reflection: the journalists had succeeded all too well in luring once- shy club leaders into the limelight.

MacMurchy also disparaged the omnibus approach to reform and welfare taken by the huge national clubs. Rather than casting their net widely and, she implied, ineffectually, MacMurchy challenged the really large organizations (no doubt she had the National Council of Women in mind) to concentrate on specific problems affecting women's lives – for instance, infant mortality, consumer education, women's employment, and public health – and solve them. She also expressed misgivings about the fact that many women's clubs had less than fully democratic structures and were not teaching women how to cooperate with each other and ultimately with men. They would have to integrate their movement with the mainstream of society, she said, if they were to become a potent factor for change.[54] Published at a time when prairie women were winning the provincial franchise and all Canadian women would soon have the federal vote, her book was one last sober lecture before women were initiated into the rights of full citizenship.

Suffrage success brought a multiplicity of divisive issues to the fore. The attempt to form a Woman's Party fractured the suffrage alliance along the fault lines of region and class. The *Woman's Century*, official organ of the National Council of Women, rejected an article that Violet McNaughton wrote criticizing the platform of the Woman's Party and the imperialist assumptions of the eastern club leaders who were promoting it.[55] Western women journalists such as Cora Hind, Mary McCallum, and Violet McNaughton were already wary of the "made in Canada" drive promoted through *Woman's Century*, which seemed to suit the interests of eastern Canada better than those of the West.[56] Before long, rural and western women's organizations would cease their affiliation with the National Council of Women.[57]

PROFESSIONAL JOURNALISTS OR PROFESSIONAL PROMOTERS?

As the women's club movement entered its crossroads, leaving the shadowland of persuasion and entering the world of real political power, the path of the club reporter forked as well. New directions and career possibilities beckoned in the postwar era. Some newswomen turned towards a professional commitment to community service by applying their journalistic skills to public relations. For others, club reporting was an avenue leading towards politics either as observers or as participants. And even for those who remained in the traditional groove of women's club reporting, a different relationship began to emerge between club and reporter. Where once a warm mutual regard sustained both clubwoman and presswoman, in the postwar era, women journalists became sensitive to possible conflicts between journalistic "objectivity" and the crusading spirit of the engaged reformer.

Miriam Green Ellis, for one, made it a point of honour never to join any organization that she might cover as a professional journalist: "I wished to feel free to observe without any 'loyalty drag' that would have attached to membership." On this point she took issue with her fellow agricultural reporter, Cora Hind, whose commitment to reform through the women's club movement never faltered during her long life. Hind exercised the privilege of membership and spoke her mind freely even at meetings she attended in her professional capacity as a newspaperwoman.[58] Her colleague on the *Winnipeg Free Press* candidly acknowledged Hind as a crusader: "Once she had made up her mind on a question she was ceaseless in her advocacy. In this way she accumulated causes. 'Love me, love my causes.' She lived for them."[59] In the aftermath of war, however, when women's clubs had achieved public recognition for their service to the community, most journalists felt it less necessary to nurture them. Mary McCallum, as she prepared to cover the Women's Institute convention for the *Grain Growers' Guide* in 1919, disclosed an independent frame of mind. "They are now a strong organization," she wrote to Violet McNaughton, "and I am not going to hesitate to criticize where criticism is necessary."[60]

Journalists continued to be active as individuals in women's clubs, and as long as they didn't overstep the bounds of newspaper policy, there was considerable tolerance for club promotion on the women's page. Open partisanship of good works schemes could only entrench the newspaper's reputation as an organ of community service, and women journalists were often charged with this branch of their own paper's corporate citizenship. For instance, Beatrice Phipps, society editor of the Toronto *Evening Telegram*, was given special charge of publisher John Ross Robertson's pet project – the Hospital for Sick Children. Newspapers persisted in mounting well-publicized charitable fundraisers, combining their community service role with the promotion of the paper itself. Even the unsentimental political reporter Judith Robinson, together with Mona Purser and C.G. Mary White, co-operated in a newspaper crusade to raise funds for a home for unemployed single men.[61] In rural areas, a weekly newspaperwoman was still expected to be an integral member of her community. Grace Wright, who ran the Charlottetown *Confederate*, emphasized that a journalist in her position "usually finds herself at very least, a member if not president, secretary or treasurer of such organizations as the Women's Institute, the hospital auxiliary, and church society and Red Cross."[62]

Particularly in urban settings, however, the postwar era saw a shift in women journalists' relationship to clubs, which for some represented a new career frontier. Beyond the casual promotion of clubs and causes under the auspices of their newspapers, a considerable number chose to migrate from newspaper journalism to the relatively new and often better-paid opportunities that beckoned in the public relations field. This exodus raised questions about professional identity which the most philosophically rigorous newspaperwomen tried to sort out. Writing for the war effort, as most journalists, male or female, had done in one way or another, often blunted scruples about objectivity. "Propaganda" was not a term of opprobrium when it was patriotic to "do your bit" for the war effort.[63] Then wartime fever subsided and left journalists disconcerted; they had been duped and had in turn duped others in a context of public hysteria. Elizabeth Bailey Price recalled with some chagrin, "What victims of propaganda we were in the Great War ... and how the war news was censored and controlled and how atrocities were played up to fan the fires of hatred."[64] Now a renewed enthusiasm for professional ethics gripped newspaper circles. Journalists became more wary of overtones of hucksterism or boosterism, especially as advertising and public relations developed as specialties in their own right.[65]

Even so, the fact remains that, for women, opportunities for advancement in "pure" journalism were in short supply, and the kind of writing women had been doing for years as club reporters promoting philanthropic clubs and literary societies had honed their skills as press agents and fundraisers. Hence, some women journalists blithely adapted their skills in order to professionalize the publicity function of large-scale women's organizations. As former newspaperwomen, they knew that the most effective publicity was that which disguised its overt propagandistic purpose and aroused public curiosity. A skilful journalist would know how to dress up her notices in the guise of "real" news so that they would be more likely than routine press releases to win space in the paper. As Elizabeth Bailey Price reported to Mary McCallum of the *Grain Growers' Guide,* the Federated Women's Institutes had abandoned the idea of an "official organ believing that a good live press agent is better." McCallum commented wryly, "As a matter of fact that displays an unlooked-for amount of sense."[66]

In urging women writers to consider public relations as a lateral career move, guidebook author Ethel Brazelton observed that there was an inherent congruence between women's altruism, their "natural partisanship," and the work of a professional welfare writer.[67] Public relations writing so aptly suited the contemporary estimation of feminine talent, as well as the professional and voluntary experience of women journalists, that those who made the transformation from supposedly objective reporter to committed propagandist did so with little regret.

For some newspaperwomen, public relations could even seem an upward career move. Mary H.T. Alexander, a writer who had turned her hand to everything, from music criticism to beauty articles, became editor of the *Canadian Red Cross Magazine* and publicity director of the Canadian Red Cross in 1927. It was the best job she had ever had, and she wrote to her friends about her satisfaction in having so much appreciation and power. She had a good salary and her own office and secretary – no newspaper opportunity would have given her so much status and support. But it was largely her former newspaper career that made her valuable as a publicity agent, for what Alexander did to garner publicity for the Red Cross was to cajole her former colleagues into writing features about their local branch of the Red Cross. In other words, her job was to get her friends to supply valuable publicity for the cause for which she was being paid, by inserting as news items material that furthered the aims of the Red Cross. The degree to which her friends were able to comply may or may not have been a factor in Alexander's relatively short tenure in the position.[68]

More enduring was the career of Mary Agnes (Mrs O.C.) Pease, who had been a freelance writer and contributor to the *Montreal Star* from 1913 until she became editor of the IODE journal, *Echoes*, a post she held from 1921 until her death in 1948. Mild and unchallenging as the editorial duties may have been, the job must have seemed desirable enough to attract Zoe Trotter, one of Canada's most widely experienced reporters, who became Pease's successor at *Echoes*. Trotter had been one of the first female telegraph operators on the *Calgary Herald*, and she had also been an early legislative reporter in Alberta. During the 1920s, Trotter had written a special political column for women and thus had wide experience with women's clubs and the political education of women. She used her connections to become one of the first women to run an independent public relations agency, with the IODE as her chief client.

Although skills acquired as a newspaperwoman were an asset to the publicity agent, the professional aims of the newswoman and the press agent did diverge, however "good" the cause. The responsibility of the former was to ensure that community events received balanced coverage in a format attuned to general interest. If a newspaperwoman's involvement with specific organizations was more than voluntary, her employer might take exception. In 1924 Beatrice Green became mired in conflicting loyalties when she accepted a salaried position as publicity representative of the Society of the Macabees while at the same time acting as society editor for the Vancouver *Province*. Her employers considered her to be abusing her position by inserting free promotion for the Macabees into her column. It would seem that her fellow women journalists agreed that she had overstepped an ethical boundary. It was a notice in Amy Kerr's *Western Women's Weekly* that drew public attention to the fact that there was glowing publicity about all Macabee functions in the *Province* while other local charities and patriotic organizations were ignored by the paper.[69] Beatrice Green lost her job.

Elizabeth Bailey Price was acutely sensitive to the ethical borderlands separating newswriting from public relations writing because her career straddled the two territories and spanned the reform and postwar eras. By combining her two callings, writing and philanthropy, Price cobbled together a living during the lean years of the 1930s. She syndicated columns of Women's Institutes' news among prairie papers and then became the official press agent of the WI. On a number of occasions she represented the Women's Institutes at international meetings, most auspiciously at the International Conference of the Pan-Pacific Women's Association in Honolulu in 1934.

An ardent pacifist, Price was particularly anxious that women's peace work gain maximum publicity. She confronted head-on the reticence of the International Pan-Pacific Women's leaders who were nervous about the diplomatic repercussions of their pacifist discussions and therefore intended to bar the press from all but the most general sessions. As Price arrived in Honolulu, relations between the conference conveners and the local press were tense, the latter threatening the conference with the "thunder of silence" if it insisted on keeping them out. It did not help that Price's landing inspired headlines such as "Canadian Women's Press Club Head Here." Eventually, in a private meeting with the president of the Pan-Pacific Women's Association, Price was able to allay fears that the society's motives would be misrepresented. She launched into a headlong defence of the press and, in particular, of the club reporter's role as the only medium through which an organization could make direct contact with the masses of the people. If they wanted to promote international peace and freedom, Price urged, they should use their funds for press releases and cable tolls instead of on reprints of long reports for members' eyes only.[70]

As an insider in both camps, Price could mediate between the timidity of clubwomen about negative publicity and the clamour of the press for unrestricted access. The stand-off Price negotiated was symptomatic of the distance that had grown between clubwomen and journalists. In the years following the First World War, when women had ostensibly graduated into full citizenship and therefore responsibility, club reporters began to subject women's organizations to more searching critiques than they had done in the decade before the war. This was in part a case of inflated expectations. In the immediate wake of the suffrage victory, there was a tendency to overestimate the power of women's clubs. Previously, these clubs had stood for a cluster of far-reaching social and moral reforms that were supposed to represent the aspirations of the female community. Now that women had the vote, surely they would begin to build their utopian "New Day" in Canada. The tone of an editorial in the Vancouver *World* in 1921 was only half-mocking when it implored male subscribers to be sure to monitor the activities of Vancouver women by reading the women's page, for only thus could they learn what plots newly enfranchised women were hatching to reduce still further the status of men.[71]

In the same period, Cornelia (Lucy Doyle) of the Toronto *Telegram* viewed with deadly seriousness the League of Women Voters' debate about whether to cooperate with the International League for Peace and Freedom. Devoting a long editorial to this problem, Cornelia lashed out at the leaders – leading lights such as Jane Addams and Carrie Chapman Catt – whom she blamed for undermining the allied cause during the war. She took care to point out that MP Agnes Macphail was a pacifist attending the convention and that misguided Toronto women were helping to spread "pacifist propaganda."[72] Cornelia made reference to the Chicago *Tribune*'s conspiracy theory, which traced all pacifist organizations, however innocent they appeared, back to Moscow. No doubt she saw the figure of Lenin's henchwoman, Alexandra Kollontai, as the spider at the centre of this dastardly web of peace-mongering women.[73]

Lucy Doyle was well known for her peppery style. As the Vancouver *Province* of 2 September 1923 put it, "Miss Lucy Doyle does not belong to the wishy washy school of journalism. If kind words are merited, nobody is more generous with them, but if a woman's organization needs to be jerked up about its shortcomings, Miss Doyle can do this to the king's taste."[74] A loyal colonialist, Doyle's sentiments echoed the kind of knee-jerk patriotism that prompted the IODE during the war to question the National Council of Women's affiliations with "enemy" women's clubs. It also suited the conservative traditions of her paper. In any event, she need not have worried about the radical tendencies of the League of Women Voters; the Toronto club folded within six years of its birth.

Even as newswomen began to move away from uncritical boosterism of club and cause, club reporting remained an essential matrix for their professional development as journalists. In some cases a foundation in club reporting facilitated promotion to other departments of the newspaper. Annie Mathewson, for one, was able to use her expertise as a club editor to jump into legislative reporting for the Fredericton *Gleaner*, and by 1941 she had become one of the few women city editors.[75] Meanwhile, the cooling off in relations between women journalists and women's clubs continued. The number of presswomen had expanded dramatically during the war, and many of the new recruits may not have participated in the movement and shared the reformist vision that had united journalists and clubwomen in prewar days. Significantly, in 1926 the Canadian Women's Press Club decided to sever its affiliation with the National Council of Women on the grounds that, as a club of journalists, it could not necessarily endorse the positions which the council ordained.[76] But even among the established newspaperwomen of the "fighting days," faith in the new world order of moral womanhood began to wither. For Mary Lowry, club reporter for the *Toronto Star*, the disillusion set in early. In 1922 she was sent to Baltimore to cover a convention of the Pan-American

League of Women Voters. When a row broke out behind the scenes at the convention, Lowry was too loyal to her sex to exploit the fracas and thus missed a major news story. All the other papers revelled in the scandal.[77]

The high hopes, generated during the heyday of the women's club movement, that women with political power would bring important social issues to the fore deflated as it became clear that voting women did not apparently make any difference at all. Anne Anderson Perry, a feminist of the feisty prewar Winnipeg circle, expressed a general sense of discomfiture in her article "Is Woman Suffrage a Fizzle?" when she asked, "Where, indeed, [is] any clear indication that the woman voter is thinking either constructively or nationally as a practical politician along the lines of economics, education, health conservation, child-welfare, or of those other great 'causes' which so long have held her interest in her innumerable clubs and societies?"[78] Even though Canadian women were "better organized" than in other lands, said Perry, the club movement had failed to put forward female leaders who could point the way to the mass of women voters. Instead of using hard-won political power to practical purpose, she observed, we women "continue to go round and round in circles in our manifold organizations, passing much the same hardy perennial crop of resolutions as in pre-voting days, and registering smiling satisfaction at our rate of progress towards goals set long before women had the franchise, a rate of progress which cannot be described otherwise than as laborious and much camouflaged standing still."[79]

It was irritating to engaged feminists such as Perry that the energy that had sustained the large women's organizations before the success of suffrage was now diverted into the "women's auxiliaries" of existing political parties.[80] Perry found it particularly galling that neither press nor party paid more than a passing glance at the labour women lavished on election campaigns that were almost totally dominated by men. A younger journalist, Harriet Parsons, aimed similar barbs at the torpidity of women's clubs in the postsuffrage era. "In Great Britain and the United States, the winning of the suffrage was only the beginning of women's political activity. In Canada, it would be not far from the truth to say that it was the end."[81]

THE SPRINGBOARD TO POWER

If ultimately voting women disappointed the hope of many early feminists that the women's movement could organize a moral and reforming democracy, for a handful of journalists, women's clubs furnished a springboard to careers in government and politics.[82] Indeed, journalism provided an unusually good preparation for women whose political ambitions were ignited by the suffrage struggle.[83] Two women journalists who became magistrates, Emily Murphy and Helen Gregory MacGill, were both thoroughly familiar with the law because of their club and suffrage activism.[84] The career of Violet McNaughton also illustrates the versatility that both journalism and politics demanded, for she carried on both simultaneously, running the women's section of the *Prairie Farmer* and *Western Producer* while acting as a leader in both the farm women's movement and the suffrage movement. She was not at first overly optimistic about how far women would get in politics even after the suffrage victory. As she wrote to Margaret McWilliams, "Re parliamentary career. Personally, I do not expect to see women get real recognition for several years yet ... You know I am a member of several bodies where I am the only woman. I am treated awfully well, my opinion is sought ... but I feel the dear men do not quite put me on a par when it comes to administrative or legislative matters. And I could knock spots off some of them."[85] She persevered though and went on to become one of the founders of the Saskatchewan Progressive Party. In 1934 McNaughton was awarded the OBE, and during the Second World War she was recruited by McWilliams to serve on the National Committee on Reconstruction.[86]

Like Violet McNaughton, her friends Mary McCallum and Amy Roe combined rural journalism with the work of government. For McCallum, a wartime ordeal of frenetic activity as women's editor of the *Grain Growers' Guide* was rewarded by appointment to the Council of Agriculture.[87] Amy Roe's years working with and writing about prairie women's organizations for the Manitoba Grain Growers and the *Country Guide* laid a solid foundation for official positions on the Manitoba Welfare Supervision Board, the Manitoba Rural Housing Committee, and as adviser to the attorney general.

After the war, Valance Patriarche similarly graduated from journalism to government service when she was appointed censor of motion pictures for the province of Manitoba. She became the only woman censor in Canada. In contrast to her former colleagues in journalism, who may have found some satisfaction in effecting change as government officers, Patriarche found that her new "official capacity" was in fact a "life of dumb seclusion." As one producer told her, "It is not your business to think: you must cut out a little here and there and then keep quiet about it."[88] Writing to Florence Randal Livesay, Patriarche complained, "I don't seem able to get the logic of this contention that the people who are professionally connected with some branch of public work and have correct information are to be gagged in order the outsiders may talk platitudes."[89] Her background as a journalist had qualified her for her new job, but the narrowness of her mandate frustrated the reform aspirations that had fuelled her journalism.

While women's editors and club reporters were winning recognition for their expertise in welfare issues by appointment to various government boards, other women journalists were seeking direct political responsibility – an even more formidable challenge. Not many were successful. Amy Roe's former companion in journalism and the Homemakers' Clubs, Isabel Armstrong, attempted the move into public life after she returned to Ontario. Having been president of the London branch of the Women's Canadian Club as well as the Canadian Women's Press Club, Armstrong was well versed in local women's issues. She believed that women had a "political duty" and was optimistic that a newly enfranchised female public would advance her political ambitions. In the Ontario election of 1921, she ran as a Liberal candidate but lost.[90] In Manitoba, Genevieve Lipsett-Skinner ran for office as a Conservative and also lost. Annie Hollis of Saskatchewan attempted the leap to Ottawa, but she too failed to win election, as did Mildred Low in Ontario.

More successful was Nora Frances Henderson, whose solid career in municipal politics branched out from her experience as a reporter and enterprising club member.[91] A crusading journalist from the time she started in 1918, Henderson had used her position on the women's page of the Hamilton *Spectator* to draw attention to persistent social problems and the efforts of women's organizations to address them. She was also active in the Hamilton Council of Women, which urged her to turn her talent as a dramatist to social purposes. In 1930 Henderson staged a play, *The Pageant of Motherhood*, to stimulate public action on the high maternal mortality rate in Canada. By the 1930s, though remaining a loyal clubwoman, she was feeling that the traditional womanly gestures – holding conventions and passing on resolutions to the government – were ineffectual. Women, she believed, had to assume positions of real authority and not rely on mere suasion. Through her column, Henderson urged the women of Hamilton to take to the hustings. When no one heeded her call, she put herself forward for the city council and in 1930 led the field of aldermanic candidates. Within a few years, she had become acting mayor and held a seat on the Board of Control. Then, in 1935, the Nora Frances Henderson League mobilized bands of women of all political persuasions to abandon party in order to get women represented – specifically, in this case, to send Henderson to Ottawa. At this point, Henderson gave up the daily editorial she had continued to write for the women's page of the Hamilton *Spectator*, fearing that her political engagement might be incompatible with editorial impartiality. In fact, she never did get to Ottawa, but she continued to be a major force in Hamilton until her death in 1949.

Nancy Hodges was among the most successful of the journalists-turned-politician. The women's page editor first of the Kamloops *Sentinel* in 1912, then of the Victoria *Times* for more than twenty years, she was far more interested in club work than journalism. As her colleague Elizabeth Ruggles MacDonald recalled, "She did the society page ... practically with her hand tied behind her back; it was just something to put bread on the table and she wasn't enamored with it. She was much more interested in her other organizations."[92] Hodges used the expertise and connections she had garnered from her years as women's page editor and as an enthusiastic member of women's organizations in Victoria to vault into a political career in the British Columbia legislature. Having run unsuccessfully for the Liberals in 1937, she was elected in 1941 and in 1943 was appointed Speaker of the House, the first women in the British parliamentary history to achieve this position.[93] In chronicling Mrs Hodges's achievements, the *Globe and Mail* of 29 December 1943 observed that her first job was "that of cook and housekeeper" and that she always made the beds and cleaned the dishes before writing her Victoria *Times* daily column or attending the legislature.

Somewhat later, Margaret Aitken found her political ambitions favourably furthered by her links with women's clubs in Toronto. Aitken was a columnist rather than a club reporter, but she had ample opportunity to "plug women's organizations" (as she put it) in her column "Between You and Me" in the Toronto *Telegram*. When she ran as a Conservative candidate in the federal election of 1954, she had a ready-made network of organizations to host teas and fundraisers for her campaign.[94]

CRITICS IN CLUBLAND

Although a sprinkling of women graduated from the voluntary good works of the club to the responsibility and power of the legislature, their numbers disappointed the high hopes raised during the suffrage campaign. As Harriet Parsons observed with regret, "True we have one woman Member of Parliament and one woman Senator, and we have had a woman delegate to the Disarmament Conference and several delegates to the League of Nations – but women didn't put them there. Few women run for office, and those who do are not overconfident of women's support."[95] Elizabeth Bailey Price went further and specifically pointed at clubwomen as culprits in her analysis of women's uninspired political record. Despite the fact that energetic and talented candidates had emerged from the club movement, they could not count on the support of their sorority, she said: "The intolerance among them [clubwomen] is appalling. Should she smoke in public, or take cocktails even in moderation, it is regarded by many as an offense to 'womanhood.'"[96]

Moreover, after the gargantuan efforts of the war years, the club movement lacked direction. In the 1920s clubwomen seemed to be immobilized, and journalists found them less satisfying sources of news. Jessie Robson Bothwell, writing for *Saturday Night*'s women's page, a page that had for years relied on women's clubs for its most newsworthy items, put forward the notion that most women's clubs should simply be abandoned. "Count up the number of meetings you have attended this year: how much of this time was used in real accomplishment? Frankly was there not more time spent in election of officers, amendments to constitutions, etc than in the work itself?"[97]

By this time, the largest organizations were on the decline. With the riveting struggle for the vote over, women's page editors devoted less space to club activities. Moreover, clubdom's aging membership and "old-fashioned" issues such as temperance – unfashionable in jazz-age society – were not particularly newsworthy. The partnership that had once bound clubwomen and journalists together in promoting their shared causes was not much in evidence in the 1920s. Thus, Evelyn Caldwell, in her first years as a women's page reporter for the *Vancouver Star*, recalled with some glee the time she had outsmarted a woman's organization that did not want a particular meeting publicized – she had eavesdropped on their proceedings from the women's washroom.[98] Plainly, identification with her trade figured more strongly than solidarity with the women's club movement.

Similarly, for Nancy Bissett of the *Winnipeg Free Press*, the idea of identifying personally with clubwomen was ludicrous: "I visualized a club woman as being a total amazon; wearing neck ties and flat-heeled shoes, carrying a briefcase of important papers and having the voice of a booming cannon. I pictured all club women as being always bright and efficient and authoritative, if-you-know-what-I-mean." That she might voluntarily attend "hen banquets" to listen to women giving speeches, or even – ultimate horror – give a speech herself was unthinkable. Flippant and superficial as her comments were, they revealed a widely held vision that clubwomen were old fashioned, unglamorous, and boring.[99] Dragging her heels, Bissett succumbed to pressure and visited a well-known women's club because her boss insisted that "it would be good for her brain." Brains were not unduly emphasized in the perky chit-chat that too many women dispensed as journalism once the feminist controversies were no longer fashionable. Bissett and her ilk represented a tendency of young career women to distance themselves from the strong-minded women of first-wave feminism. As Peter Filene has observed of American professional women in the 1920s, the focus on individual career advancement precluded collective goals.[100]

This was not the case with a journalist such as Elizabeth Bailey Price, who earned her trade in the shadow of energetic western reformers such as Emily Murphy. Price remained forever committed to the goals of feminist altruism, but even she recognized the difference between the aspirations of the reformer and the specific career goals of journalists. When she became president of the journalists' own club for professional development, she rejected any notion that it take on philanthropic projects: "The Canadian Women's Press Club is not organized to save babies, be kind to animals, fight tuberculosis etc. Our services to these causes are given through the publicity we do for them. We are primarily a selfish organization, banded together to save ourselves first."[101]

Price aimed to clarify where the responsibilities of the CWPC lay – specifically to its members and not to society in general. By the same token, club reporters were trying to establish who they were serving and how best they should do it. An item in the "Newspacket" addressed this issue, emphasizing the distance that ought to figure between the journalist and the subject in club reporting. The article pointed out that the reporter was there as an impersonal recorder of what was said or done: "He is merely an onlooker and is reporting the course of events, not for the benefit of those at the meeting but for the whole community." The example the author gave was that of a reporter at a temperance meeting who was asked to give his opinion of the liquor question and rightly refused to do so because he was representing his paper, not the temperance federation.[102]

Mary James, a *Globe and Mail* reporter for forty years, subscribed to this kind of professional detachment while playing a crucial part in the dissemination of club news in Toronto. In modestly disclaiming her own importance, James accentuated her journalism rather than her altruism: "My role has been a very minor one. I just sat quietly at press tables and reported speeches as I heard them."[103] But according to *Globe and Mail* editor Richard Doyle, James's accomplishments went far beyond "the needs of her beat," which required only "polite little stories about women's activities." James took on such meaty issues as discrimination against women in the workplace, the exploitation of nurses in training, and the all-round scarcity of career options for women.[104] At her retirement party, representatives of most of the women's organizations in Toronto saluted her integrity and her devotion to duty. Her newspaper credited her achievements and her recognized place in community affairs, stating: "It was a tribute to the best kind of professional journalism, and one this newspaper is glad to endorse."[105]

The ideal club reporter was as intellectually ambitious as her prewar counterpart, but in this more self-conscious age she cast a critical eye at the clubs she observed, sensitive to their strengths and shortcomings alike. For the veteran journalist Anne Anderson Perry, club work was not above criticism just because it promoted worthy endeavours. In a "craft talk" for her fellow press club members, she contrasted a "sensational" club editor with one who used her intelligence. The former, she said, "coloured" her reports with "cheap patriotism" rather than "any real civic consciousness." The latter was "no uplifter but a student of good government." And while "women's clubs doubtless often annoyed her with their futilities or stupidities," she saw their "invaluable side in the lives of contemporary womanhood." The model journalist used her editorial page to "show hard thinking, urbane intentions by constructive interest in what mattered in her community, province and country."[106]

Just as the clubwoman had to suppress the frivolous titillation of "slumming" if she was to minister sincerely to the needs of her community, the journalist had to guard against pandering to the prurient curiosity of her readership if she was to inform them properly. All the same, the club reporter had to shed any fastidious avoidance of unpleasantness if she was to execute her responsibilities effectively. Genevieve Lipsett-Skinner delved into the heart of Winnipeg's North End, where new immigrants festered in one of the worst slums in prewar Canada. She saw newborn babies covered in flies, interviewed a German mother who had lost seven of her ten children, and talked to an abandoned mother in a rat-infested slum.[107] It was no doubt her knowledge of the mean streets that prompted her to study law and run for political office. Later, as a member of the press gallery in Ottawa, she took up the challenge of enticing women readers, with tantalizing bits of gossip, to become informed voters.[108]

In contrast, Lotta Dempsey, who began her career on the *Edmonton Journal* in the middle 1920s, at first recoiled from the sordid realities of child abuse, drug addiction, domestic violence, and other issues that women reformers confronted. But as she became acquainted with the older generation of women activists, including Emily Murphy, Irene Parlby, Nellie McClung, and Henrietta Muir Edwards, her mentors reproved her immature attitude: "You are young ... but know and care about these things if you are going to be a good reporter, and, more important, a worthwhile human being."[109] Dempsey learned her lesson quickly, and not many years later, when she had advanced to the head of the women's section of the *Edmonton Journal*, she had little patience with the innocence of young Jessie Potter, her assistant, who botched a report on the Farm Women's Convention. The central controversy was the sterilization of the mentally disabled, but naive young Jessie missed the point because she did not know what sterilization meant.[110]

In the interwar era it would seem that for every journalist who sharpened her skills and intellect in order to follow the important causes the women's clubs embraced, there was a club that declined into either passivity or triviality. Having won the great battle for the vote, the diverse spectrum of women's clubs in Canada could find no focus of equivalent importance that was not at the same time controversial and divisive. During the Depression, when myriad social and economic problems seemed to overwhelm national life and when international friction rubbed away at the confidence of pacifists, women's clubs seemed either disengaged or, if they did tackle controversial causes, diffident about publicity. This impasse was an abiding vexation to those newspaperwomen who were ambitious for themselves and for their sex to make a mark in the world.

If Canadian clubwomen could not find common causes during the late 1920s and 1930s, neither could they find the kind of leadership they had thrived under during the prewar period. Those leaders who did come forward were older, often born in the nineteenth century.[111] For club reporters who longed to grapple directly with pressing social and political issues that were integral to women's lives, it was galling to look over the border and see how newspaperwomen had become insiders in the highest political circles. In the United States, the wife of the president had become the figurehead of women's volunteer organizations and was giving them prestige and momentum. And as a special boon to newspaperwomen, Eleanor Roosevelt held a briefing session every week, open only to the women of the press, at which she kept them up to date with plans and policy. A two-way tutelary relationship was thus established. Roosevelt imparted valuable information and thus elevated the status of Washington newspaperwomen, while they in turn taught her the value of publicity and how to establish rapport with the press. American presswomen so valued Mrs Roosevelt's patronage that they honoured her every injunction, even when their adulation conflicted with reportorial objectivity.[112]

Canadian newspaperwomen enjoyed no parallel opportunity. The doldrums of the women's club movement in Canada during the 1930s were rarely relieved. The fact that Canada's prime ministers during these years – Mackenzie King and R.B. Bennett – were both bachelors did nothing to improve things. Nor did the royal representatives of the period lend their prestige to women's clubs in Canada. Much as the newspaperwomen of the 1930s adored Lady Tweedsmuir and welcomed her into their club as a fellow writer, she did not act as the masthead of women's social activism as Lady Aberdeen had done at the turn of the century. When the momentum of women's clubs gave way to inertia, the enthusiasm of even the most ardent club reporter palled.

It was perhaps fitting that Elizabeth Bailey Price – loyal clubwoman and charter member of numerous national club branches, who had built a career in publicity for major women's organizations – should assess the malaise of women's clubs most cogently. As president of the Canadian Women's Press Club from 1932 to 1935, she lashed out at the National Council of Women, which, she said "calls itself the Women's Parliament of Canada" and then carries on its most controversial and newsworthy discussions in camera, barring presswomen from these sessions.[113] Later, in an article for *Chatelaine* in 1939, Price catalogued her thoughts about women's clubs. She noted the aging membership, the flight of the young and energetic, and the overlap of mandates. She particularly berated clubwomen for holding tedious meetings – a cry from the heart of a journalist who had had to cover so many. Clubwomen were often ill-informed, Price charged, yet they felt obliged to put on record their often vacuous opinions. Most important of all, she blasted her contemporaries for side-stepping the most telling issues of the day. Although most clubwomen were over forty, they seemed to draw a virginal blank on problems such as birth control, sterilization, venereal disease, and abortion; and when they did discuss any contentious issues, they barred the press from these sessions, an interdiction which Price particularly resented as ungenerous, given the unstinting cooperation presswomen had always shown the National Council of Women.[114] It was the desire for personal aggrandizement, having their pictures in the paper and being noted as good citizens, that motivated most clubwomen today, Price lamented. But in their hunger for publicity for its own sake, they were no longer newsworthy – the ultimate transgression from the newswoman's perspective.

All told, women's clubs were not supplying the press with the kind of copy that had fertilized the cooperative relationship of the past. Journalists were often disillusioned by the behaviour of club leaders, whose motives were not always purely altruistic; social ambition and authoritarianism were sometimes hard to bear. The Scribe (Mary H.T. Alexander) exposed the banal side of club work when she interviewed the editor of a local weekly who recalled a set-to she had had with an aspiring society matron who was attempting to use her "welfare work" to earn recognition in social circles. This would-be personage had burst into the editor's office to complain that she had been left off the list of guests at a recent function: "I'll have you know I was there in my prettiest frock, none of your mail-order catalogue kind either, but a real gown with a genuine Paris label on it. No madam, you can't get away with any of your mean tricks for everybody knows me as the best – absolutely – the hardest welfare worker in this town. Nobody in this whole burg works harder than me."[115] This sort of manoeuvre was so common that newspaperwomen's guidebooks warned readers to beware of the unsolicited and unauthorized club news that might issue from the ambitious social climber anxious to short-circuit the established route to social position.[116]

At the same time, the principals of locally prominent societies could be as autocratic in their public roles as they were in their private social lives. They used their club work as an accessory to enhance their overall social prestige and had lost sight of the goals that once inspired their organization. The Vancouver branch of the CWPC felt obliged to intervene on behalf of one of its members who had been badly treated by a local clubwoman. On the occasion of President Harding's visit to Vancouver, the long-time journalist Lily Laverock was snubbed by the president of the Women's Canadian Club, which was hosting the event. It was ironic that it was Laverock, one of the staunchest supporters of the women's club movement in the suffragist decade, who was subjected to a humiliating experience by an overbearing club president.[117]

The fact that clubs in the interwar decades had routinely used press convenors, whether paid or volunteer, in order to control the kind of image projected in the public press made interaction with the professional journalists responsible for club coverage increasingly contentious. To be sure, public relations officers made the club editor's job easier; rather than trotting from one meeting to the next, she could fall back on a nicely polished press release. Conversely, the tempting ease of the predigested promotional piece presented new problems to the club editor who wanted to retain power over her own page. It was up to her to decide what would appear and what would be discarded. Knowing this, publicity agents tried any number of ruses to gain attention and influence. As illustrated earlier, those who had once been journalists came to promotional work with a network of connections in the newspaper world. Club editors understandably became impatient with press agents who attempted to exploit personal friendships or, worse, to use their influence with the editor's superiors to get their copy in print. Georgina Rodden used expertise accumulated from her years as women's club editor of the *Montreal Daily Star* when she issued to clubwomen a list of guidelines intended to formalize the interchange between the club and the press.[118] Chief among Rodden's injunctions was her insistence that if clubwomen wanted to get publicity, they had to merit it. "The most important copy you can submit is that covering some measure of reform your group is sponsoring within the community," Rodden stipulated, adding sardonically, "It makes even better copy when something is actually done."[119]

Nevertheless, the symbiotic relationship that bound clubwomen and newswriters together still obtained: clubs had to have publicity if they were to garner community recognition and support, and newspaper writers still needed liaisons with women's clubs in order to make up their community notes. Club stories were an essential back-up for the hard-pressed daily columnist.[120] But just as the society reporter had to flatter and cajole, so too did the club editor require discretion and tact to elicit the live news from the dead wood of self-promotion.

It is little wonder, then, that club editors occasionally vented their frustrations in critical articles. The more idealistic and ambitious the reporter, the more vexing it was to find her most challenging and potentially interesting opportunity suffocated by pettiness, egocentricity, and torpor. From being one of the swiftest currents in the mainstream of national life, women's clubs had become a backwater eddy. The national organizations in particular had ceased to be the busy intersection where women met the wider world of politics, welfare, economics, and international relations. Elizabeth Long, herself an active clubwoman but also a hard-headed journalist, noted that newsworthy women were not necessarily to be found in the established clubs: "The last few years has seen the rise of the little club. Women everywhere are joining small study circles and conversation over the teacups is apt to centre on these rather than on larger organizations which reached their zenith about the close of the war."[121]

It was the next great war that gave a final fillip to women's organizations and to the clubs department of the newspapers. Once again the home-front war effort gave both a compelling raison d'être – the former to organize fundraisers, parties to entertain the troops, and the endless knitting; the latter to rally the volunteers and tally the results. Leslie Johnstone of the *Ottawa Journal* found her workload increasing almost within days of Canada's entry into the war. While she reported that some women's organizations disbanded, many more were formed to do war work.[122] However, while existing and spontaneously organized women's clubs did the lion's share of volunteer war work, this time there was a top-down approach as the government recognized the vital importance of women's unpaid labour in the war effort. The Women's Voluntary Services division of the Department of National War Services coordinated many of the volunteer services that women contributed to the home front.[123]

This war, moreover, saw more women inducted into professional and paid work. Press coverage concentrated as much on the phenomenon of a Canadian "Rosy the Riveter" as on the stalwart volunteer. It was a harbinger of the shape of things to come. The kind of work women had once done on a voluntary basis was gradually becoming institutionalized, and paid professionals were taking the place of amateurs. This process had begun in the interwar period with the rise of the professional press agent. Government assumption of certain "club causes," such as social welfare, had also begun before the Second World War and accelerated afterwards.

The fact that important issues were taken seriously enough to be incorporated into government business was due in large measure to the clubs of dedicated amateurs and to women's page publicity. But paradoxically, once these causes became "essential services" after the war, the women's section was considered too slight a venue to promote them. In an ironic reversal of the editor's dilemma of the interwar period, when clubs failed to engage in the kind of discussion she wanted to write about, a director of child-welfare services advocated that women's pages should be abolished, or at the very least that welfare issues should not appear there, because then men did not read about them. Arguing that social welfare was big business, he maintained "We can no longer afford to leave it in the hands of a few starry eyed dreamers."[124] It was a telling comment on the declining status of the women's page when the causes that had justified it and given it substance came to resent its company.

CHAPTER NINE

On and Off the Beat: Women
Journalists on the News Side

The clever woman is she who aims to get off the beaten track in which her sex is travelling ... In getting off the beaten track you must expect opposition. Family and friends are usually conventionality itself ... It is useless to go off beaten tracks without determination to cut out a path for yourself. It is easier to glide along well worn roads than to be a pioneer, but there is neither the excitement nor the reward that follows pioneering.

Alice Mason, *Manitoba Free Press,* 3 February 1910

In her column for *Saturday Night* in 1912, Lady Gay (Grace Denison) celebrated the spirit that motivated young women to try their hand at journalism: "The girl who is too enterprising to turn to nursing; too independent to long for marriage, too full of strength and life and curiosity and a certain devil-may-care daring and faith in her lucky star, to accept sports and the conventional pursuits as an adequate outlet for her eager spirit, turns to journalism as a flower to the sun. She wants to jump into the interests that sweep along in the river of life, not to wade or paddle upon the shore; she goes in up to her neck, and also, alas, sometimes, over her head."[1] The "girl journalist" was still a novelty even after a generation of women writing for the newspapers. But by 1912 Lady Gay's daring soul might have found the women's section of the newspaper too restricted to contain her spirit. Certainly, her first motive may have been to earn her keep, even though writing for newspapers and magazines was a risky and gruelling route to financial independence; there were more comfortable and acceptable ways for a woman to earn a livelihood. But for the woman who chose journalism, the risks, danger, and scope for adventure were the real bait. Those with a wanderlust wanted a chance to get off the beaten track; a reporter's notebook gave the travel-adventurer a professional excuse for going to the ends of the earth. Journalism was also a route for the ambitious woman who wanted to get on the inside track – to participate in the world of politics, business, international relations, and even war. As a newspaper reporter, a woman could wade into the political fray, walk the waterfront at night, or hobnob with cattle ranchers if that was her bent. No other occupation could so magically open these aggressively masculine chambers to the feminine voyeur.

Moreover, according to an American newswriter, it was a feminist imperative to combat limitations on the opportunities open to women in journalism. "I look with growing unease," wrote Virginia Cook in 1932, "at the apparent willingness of newspaperwomen to abandon their struggle for the right to cover news of real import ... The attitude that women journalists should specialize exclusively in those fields in which men are disqualified by their sex, for example, child training, beauty and shopping columns, may be penny wise but it is pound foolish ... It plays into the hands of the male journalists and puts us exactly where they would like to have us."[2]

This chapter looks at the exploits of some newswomen who established careers in conventionally male specialties: war, politics, economics and finance, and general reporting. But although these women carved out a space for themselves, their personal success did not permanently open the gates to women who followed their paths. In their special fields they were the "firsts," but unlike the first generation of women journalists whose creation of women's pages made journalism as a gender-segregated career more plausible for the women who followed them, these "firsts" remained anomalies for reasons that were as individualistic as their career paths. Indeed, this individualism, dedication to personal ambition, and belief that hard work and talent would gain its reward may, as journalism historian Linda Lumsden has argued, have obscured for them the structural barriers and collective discrimination they experienced because they were women.[3]

GENERAL REPORTERS

Perhaps the most difficult track of all for a woman to succeed in was the most ordinary – the general news department. Women had been trying to break into the city beat since the turn of the century, and in ones and twos they had made it. But according to the journalist and newspaper historian Ishbel Ross, even by the end of the 1930s, women had not made substantial gains in any newspaper milieu: "It is a fact that in New York not more than half a dozen women go out on straight news stories in competition with the men reporters, and I doubt if twenty take orders direct from the city desk ... The crimson rope always seems to be strung across the city room when the girl reporter approaches."[4] Despite that invisible crimson rope, the attraction of women to the "news side" did not subside. It was the city room that enchanted the weavers of newspaper legend. That was where the "real" newspaper work happened, for the work of a "real" reporter was to record the hum of daily urban life. Women who were attracted to the press for adventure, not for literary work, were most vulnerable to the mystique of the street beat.

By the 1920s and 1930s, popular literature had imbued the newspaper "game" with seedy glamour.[5] What aspiring journalist had not seen one or another version of Ben Hecht's play, *The Front Page?* The image of the city editor hunched among banks of telephones and piles of paper – his hard-edged face scowling under a green visor, a cigarette wedged into one side of his mouth while his commands are barked out of the other, causing reporters to scatter as one story after another washes over the city desk – was among the more hackneyed by-products of urban culture. By the 1930s the intrepid "girl reporter" had joined the cast. Superman comics supplied Lois Lane of the *Daily Planet* as a kind of mascot, and Hollywood put forward a string of movies in which women got to do what men did mainly because they were "front-page girls."[6] The public lapped up the gender-scrambled images projected by Katherine Hepburn and others, whose femininity was only enhanced by man-tailored suits.

Women might play at the newspaper game, but by and large the tough, cynical, streetwise legman was just that – a man. He might be ill-paid, he might be unpolished, but his worldly masculinity was unquestioned. Alice Harriet Parsons knew something of the backstreet beat when she wrote a potboiler story about the press. Parsons had established a reputation for ingenuity as a reporter on the Cleveland *Plain Dealer* before she returned to Canada. Drawing on her experience but also on stylized stereotypes, in "By-Line" she rehearsed the formulaic image of the journalist whose veins "run with printer's ink."[7] She chose a male protagonist as the vehicle for hoary newspaper lore, enshrining in him the addiction that is supposed to enthral all journalists – the lure of the front-page scoop. Parsons's hero was in fact a plodder, capable only of police reports, and he got a front-page story only on the day his paper closed in the grip of the Depression. But through all his disappointment, the love of the life of the professional busybody – the conceit that he had his finger on the pulse of the city – sustained him.

Had he been a woman, he would not have got or kept his job; as Ishbel Ross testified, men might spend their whole lives merely gathering news and never write a line, but a women could survive only by ingenuity and by the excellence of her style.[8] Formidable hurdles stood between the woman reporter and the city beat. The late nights, dangerous assignments, and urban scenes of squalor were not thought appropriate for female employees. As well, newspaper folk believed that women had too little of the aggressive persistence thought necessary to get the story. Even when, after the First World War, the sphere of acceptable activities for women widened, cities did not get less dangerous. Then there was the chemistry that gender brought to every newsgathering occasion: the woman on the beat could not be invisible. For the would-be general reporter, getting the chance to show what she could do on the street was usually the most challenging obstacle she faced.

Ishbel Ross was herself a successful "front-page girl." After her debut on the Toronto *Daily News*, her abilities as a reporter had been tested in the most competitive of all settings, New York City, and she had not been found wanting. Indeed, her city editor on the *Tribune*, Stanley Walker, a man who harboured serious misgivings about most women journalists, became one of her staunchest champions: "Her lack of giddiness, her clear and forthright mind, her amazing and unfailing stamina on the toughest assignments, and her calm judgments, seemed to come closer than any of the others to *the man's idea of what a newspaper woman should be* [my italics]."[9]

Walker used the opportunity of praising an exceptional woman to air his condemnation of most newspaperwomen who, he said, "wanted to do a man's work, to be treated as men" but were "slovenly, incompetent vixens, adept at office politics, show offs of the worst sort, and inclined to take advantage of their male colleagues."[10] To make it on the news side, the woman reporter thus had to fulfil "the man's idea of what a newspaper woman should be" – to mould herself into a male-defined archetype, designated "objective," and to suppress aspects of her personality that might seem feminine. The "sob sister" routine was more or less passé and would do little to advance the career of a serious contender in the city room.

Ishbel Ross made the grade, but like other women who won acceptance into the male-dominated beat, she was an exception. And even after her stunning success, she was not altogether sure that it was the best place for a woman: "I happen to be an old front page fan myself, with a taste for fire engines and other gaudy doings in the daily press, but I must say that after the first ten years of that, the physical machinery begins to jitter a little, if not the mental processes. I suppose it's true – that we simply are not gaited to perpetual front page effort."[11] There was no denying that the city reporter held an exceedingly strenuous job. It was also a job that emphasized the sordid, shocking, and pathetic examples of human existence as the most "newsworthy." It was from this side of the city beat that paternalists wanted to shield delicate female sensibilities. At the same time, it was believed that the supposed feminine capacity for empathy could enhance the woman reporter's ability to gather the news. Edna Brown, as a nineteen-year-old novice on the Saint John *Sun* in 1908 was sent to cover a double murder. The only woman in the courtroom, she was able to get an interview with the young Sicilian convicted of the crimes. The man had no friends or family, and he opened up to the young reporter almost certainly because she was a woman. He asked her to come to his funeral and to buy herself a pearl ring with the small amount of money he would leave. Her paper had assigned her to cover the hanging as well, and she fulfilled all these missions. But the memory stayed with her.[12] Edna Brown, coming to Vancouver, escaped with some relief from this kind of "reality" into the gentler territory of the women's section.

Because there were relatively few front-page girls in Canada, CWPC members were understandably proud of Mary Dawson Snider who, they claimed, was "quite equal to a man and possibly far more brilliant."[13] Snider began her career in typical fashion, creating features that would entice women readers of the Toronto *Telegram*, such as "Market Day Hints," which she instituted in 1906. In 1908 she married the city editor, Jerry Snider, and continued to work for the *Telegram*. By then she was twenty-eight.[14] Possibly her husband's confidence in her gave her the break that made her name when she managed to get an exclusive for the *Telegram* by getting in to interview the *Titanic* survivors, even though the pier where they landed had been closed to the press by harbour authorities. Even though she was married to the city editor, Snider evidently felt she had to prove worthy of her paper's trust. Later she explained how she had done it: "I did not throw myself in front of an ambulance ... but just stopped in front of it sudden like – just held it up and persuaded the doctor in charge that if I failed in the assignment, all Canadian newspaperwomen would be discredited and my paper would think it, on account of my sex, that I had been repulsed. Canada sounded a long way off to that practitioner on that grey morning – 'Jump in' he said, 'but mind, you're a nurse.'"[15]

That urgent sense of looming failure – that "my paper would think it, on account of my sex, that I had been repulsed" – and the idea that the chances of all newspaperwoman hung on her success spurred on journalists such as Snider to heroic feats when male reporters would more easily have accepted the equality of universal rejection. Snider earned a byline for her pains and, as a kind of oblique acknowledgment of merit, no particular recognition that she was a woman reporter. This was in marked contrast to Kit Coleman's treatment just over a decade earlier, when her female identity and point of view had been the headliners in the Toronto *Mail and Empire*. The *Telegram* treated Snider's story in the same fashion as those of the male reporter they had sent to the scene, except that a modest sidebar indicated her singular triumph.[16]

Snider rose to the challenge again in 1919 during the Winnipeg General Strike. She was one of the few to get her story through when workers honouring the strike suspended publication of local papers, cut off telegraph lines, and shut down the trains.[17] Canadian Press telegraphers went out, and their colleagues in Calgary and Edmonton refused to accept messages originating in Winnipeg.[18] Yet day after day Mary Dawson Snider's byline appeared from Thief River or Noyes, Minnesota, where she had gone to send out copy about the Winnipeg situation. Writing for an arch-Conservative paper, Snider's reports were decidedly slanted against the strikers and especially against the leader, William Ivens, whom she labelled the "Dictator of Do-Nothing."[19] Yet she had some sympathy for the telephone workers which emerged as she contrasted their lot with that of the society girls who, for a lark, replaced them on the switchboard. The young women outside on the picket line were grey with dirt and exhaustion: "They could not be motored home for the refreshing bath, change of apparel and appetizing luncheon enjoyed by many volunteer girls. Life had never seemed so easy for them. They expected the dawn of a better day May first."[20] Now, weeks later, they straggled back to work in ones and twos, as Snider believed they should, but she acknowledged their dejection. Snider maintained her career throughout her marriage. She had no children and continued to write for the *Telegram* and other publications until her death in 1932. But in spite of a litany of accomplishments and special stories, her obituary in the *Telegram* emphasized that her specialty was "home-making."[21]

In the scramble for the scoop, newspaperwomen faced head-on the frenzied rivalry between newspapers. They were competing for their jobs in this line not with other women but with men. One can only wonder how the lone woman reporter fared in the swarm of reporters around the assignment book each day. Was she routinely given the flower show or the zoo story and other minor assignments? Did male reporters accuse her of unfair "pull" if the city editor sent her on a significant story? Doris Milligan was one who triumphed in the fray. She insisted that discrimination did not form a large part of her experience. Perhaps she had learned from experience to follow Ishbel Ross's maxim. "The women who have gone farthest in journalism are not those who have yipped most loudly about their rights," said Ross. Nothing has done more to keep women reporters in the shade. Peace at any price is the city room philosophy."[22] Milligan concentrated on building up her credentials. Her career literally spanned the country.

She began on the Regina *Post* in the women's department in 1922, went on to the Moncton *Transcript,* but returned to the *Post* when it offered her a general assignment and the city hall beat. In 1929 she moved to Vancouver and took a job on the *Star.*[23] But she left the *Star* because she perceived an atmosphere that discriminated against women. At the *Vancouver Sun,* where she spent the rest of her career, she claimed not to have experienced any differential in pay.[24] As guild secretary of the Vancouver local of the newspaper union, she was well aware of the differentials endured by other women journalists.

Doris Milligan did not marry, and she was unswerving in pursuit of her calling. But even this very serious woman was not always taken seriously. For instance, on a human-interest assignment to cover the local beach scene, she was dismayed to be asked to model a bathing suit herself.[25] On another occasion she was exasperated to find that her own paper, the *Vancouver Sun,* had ignored a story she had filed by telephone at deadline as the drama was unfolding before her eyes. She had happened upon a violent bank robbery – she stepped over the teller's blood to receive a full disclosure from the police. It was a very big story for the Vancouver scene of the early thirties, and she was so sure that the afternoon *Sun* would come out first that she passed on her news to the rival paper's reporter, who had not made the scene. Thus, Milligan was more than dismayed when her paper ignored her story, which was front-page news in the next morning's *Province.* She had "scooped" herself. Embarrassed and aware that she might lose her job for such a gaffe, Milligan did not let on that it was she who had given the story to the *Province's* reporter. Nevertheless, she was resentful that "they didn't hold the paper for a minute and yet they knew there was something quite horrendous happening." In contrast, the *Province* had delayed its deadline for half an hour to accommodate its male reporter's version.[26] Despite these initial adversities, Milligan persisted and progressed, eventually becoming the first woman in Canada to be assistant city editor, and occasionally acting as full city editor.[27] This was the ultimate test of the street-beat reporter; for women, the city editor's desk was a bastion stormed only in wartime.

Women such as Milligan, who were prepared to play the game according to the rules even when the rules were not applied neutrally, were able to succeed. An American headliner, Anne McCormick, first woman to win the Pulitzer Prize, was more forthcoming about the barriers. Women reporters rarely make the headlines, she maintained, because they were not given the headline-winning assignments, which routinely fell to men.[28] Describing the way her generation of women had advanced, McCormick implied that it was by suppressing their otherness: "We had tried hard not to act like ladies or to talk as ladies are supposed to talk – meaning too much – but just to sneak toward the city desk and the cable desk and the editorial sanctum and even the publisher's office with masculine sang-froid."[29]

This observation describes a problematic dimension of the situation that women reporters experienced. They were not to act like "ladies" – but neither could they act like men. The first woman to become city editor in her own right, Margaret Healey of the *Halifax Mail*, understood that she had to operate in gender-neutral fashion, and she was convinced that only a single-minded dedication, which precluded the distractions of marriage, could ensure success. As she put it, "I married business."[30] When she was promoted to the chief's chair on 14 May 1943, her press club colleagues obliquely hinted at the usual quasi-authority of women "editors" when, in pleased astonishment, they insisted, "No one should get the idea she isn't a full-fledged editor with all the rights, privileges and adjuncts appertaining thereto."[31] Healey had earned her position by seniority and versatility. She had been on staff longer than anyone except the managing editor, and through eleven years of service she had covered every beat except sports and the legislature. Her credentials and track record were faultless. Still, as city editor, Healey did not bark out orders like a man. She stepped carefully, and lest she bruise sensitive egos, she made a point of "asking rather than ordering when making assignments."[32]

Another stellar reporter, Jessie MacTaggart, advanced to a position of genderless anonymity when she became head of a wire service. "I don't know of any job that could bring more satisfaction to a woman who wants to work without consideration of sex," she reported to her friends in the Toronto branch of the CWPC. "You aren't a woman, or even a person, but only a point on a wire. Outside of the Northwest, I don't think anyone even in the AP knew that AP Tacoma was a woman."[33] By that time, MacTaggart had proved her mettle as a person who was absolutely determined to succeed. To land her first job, she had co-authored a book on the Nicaraguan insurrection with the *New York Times* foreign correspondent Harold Denny.[34] She had then returned to Canada to work on the Toronto *Mail and Empire* covering the morgue and the police beat, which were usually cited as the most grisly assignments. A story told of McTaggart illustrates her reportorial sang-froid. She was at the scene of a major railway accident near London, Ontario, which ended in the death of her own father, engineer Malcolm MacTaggart. Urging her family to rush off to the hospital with the ambulance, Jessie stayed behind to report the tragedy to her paper.[35] In her mid-thirties she married an American newspaperman and moved to

Tacoma, where she became bureau chief for Associated Press during the war.

It was from the broad experience of general reporting that a few women were able to make it into the ranks of executive authority on newspapers. Although most women did not take this giant step, there were still many lateral moves that could widen their career possibilities. From a thorough grounding in general reporting, for instance, specialization might be the next step. This was a logical procession according to Miriam Green Ellis, who advised that general work could provide a useful safety net if special fields dried up.[36] But it was as specialists that she believed women could most indelibly make their mark. Moreover, she had faith that specialist journalists would do much to encourage the overall achievement of women in various careers in Canadian society – in sports, for example. "I feel sure," she commented, "that women in sports have achieved a much surer place in the sun, since women sport writers got into action."[37]

Her assumption here was probably not accurate. Women's achievements in sports had preceded and far exceeded women's representation in sports reporting. Women's sports were regularly covered in newspapers in the 1920s and 1930s but usually by male staff reporters. When a very few women did begin to report sporting events, they were confined to women's sports, and most of them were athletes first, rather than journalists. Of the four women who made a reputation as sports reporters in Canada, three had won fame in association with Canada's path-breaking Olympic team of 1928. Track stars Myrtle Cook and Fanny (Bobby) Rosenfeld were rewarded first with medals and then with jobs on the *Montreal Star* and the *Globe and Mail*, respectively. Alexandrine Gibbs, who debuted as the *Toronto Star*'s sports reporter in those same Olympics, went over to Amsterdam as team manager. Only Phyllis Griffiths began as a reporter, but she landed her sports column, "The Girl and the Game," on the Toronto *Telegram* after she had won the University of Toronto's top award for women's basketball.[38] It seems unlikely that the legions of male sports reporters had to prove themselves as sports champions to qualify for their jobs.

COMMERCIAL REPORTERS

The increasing importance of Canadian women in the commercial arena was not matched by an equal presence of women specialists in financial journalism. By the twentieth century, women's economic power as consumers was generally acknowledged. Furthermore, individual women were becoming prominent in their own businesses and were eagerly following the financial pages. Yet only three women in

Canada made their names in commercial news reporting: Cora Hind and Miriam Green Ellis, who covered agriculture, and Ella Johnson, the marine and financial editor of the *Vancouver Sun*. There were more women associated with war correspondence, presumably the most thoroughly male refuge, than with financial specialization in Canada. A similar situation prevailed in the United States, even though there were vastly more women employed as journalists. When Ferdina Reinholt did a survey of women employed in representative American papers in 1925, she found that only one of the 459 respondents worked in the business field, an oil reporter in Oklahoma.[39]

In Canada, E. Cora Hind was the shining exception that disproved every prejudice the newspaper community harboured about women's capabilities in journalism. She won an international reputation for her coverage of the agricultural scene. At the age of seventy-four she capped her brilliant career by setting off on a prolonged tour, during which she reported on agricultural conditions around the world. Visiting Czechoslovakia she was puzzled to be welcomed as a celebrity rather than as the working journalist she saw herself to be. A Czech official explained, "You write of bread. Many of the countries you have visited, when their harvest fails, must import wheat. Therefore we always have our eyes on the wheat fields of the world ... Year by year, we have awaited your reports ... It may have been world markets to you. It was our people's lives to us."[40]

Agriculture was the most important industry in Canada, and Cora Hind was the most important newspaper expert on Canada's principal export. Perhaps because she was a larger-than-life character with unbending integrity, strong feminist views, and outspoken judgments, her champions took especial pains to emphasize her "femininity." Grant Dexter, her protégé, writing her obituary, observed, "She was perhaps the most misunderstood person of prominence in the country. She was not all journalist and crusader. Off the beat she was wholly and charmingly feminine. Her maternal instinct was strong."[41] Her good friend and colleague Miriam Green Ellis took the opposite tack. Reporting that Hind was rather vain about her dainty lingerie and neat ankles, she commented, "The rest of us were proud of her head equipment."[42]

Hind's outstanding achievements have been recorded in numerous biographies.[43] In contrast, Miriam Green Ellis, whose achievements were comparable if more local, subsided into obscurity after her death. She had a long and distinguished career which seems to have satisfied her inborn thirst for exploration and adventure. At the end of that career, the seventy-two-year-old western editor of the Montreal *Family Herald and Weekly Star* could boast a beat that stretched from "the head of the lakes to Vancouver Island and sometimes slop[ped] over to

Toronto and Chicago."[44] Her white pompadour and walking stick were familiar to every farmer and rancher who cared to attend those annual rituals of Canadian agriculture – the country fairs. Ellis believed that her role was to act as a conduit between farmers and scientists, governments, and manufacturers; her mission was not only to popularize technical and scientific information for the farming community but also to air the farmers' point of view. She once reported that her paper received 94,000 letters of inquiry. This was the reason farmers bought the paper – "to find out what the other fellows are doing."[45] And that is what she reported. She agreed with Hind that agriculture was the most important sector in Canada. "If agriculture is not prosperous, nothing else is for it is the biggest new source of wealth."[46] Both women made their reputation as peerless authorities in this most vital Canadian industry.

Like Cora Hind, Ellis took some time to find her niche in life. Although Hind went straight after her goal of newspaper work, approaching the editor of the *Manitoba Free Press* as soon as she arrived in Winnipeg in 1882, twenty years passed before she was finally accepted by the new editor, J.W. Dafoe. By that time she was forty years old and had already established a reputation for omniscience among local agronomists. Ellis was slower to realize her vocation. As a child on her grandparents' farm in Ontario, she had come to love the farming life, but her first career goal was medicine. This ambition ran afoul of her highly conventional family. Young Miriam Green had to study more appropriately feminine subjects like music – which she did, and with some success, even though she did not find it congenial.[47] Still following the path of convention, she became Mrs Ellis. At some point she apparently had a stillborn child, and the husband who figured so minimally in her life disappeared.[48] In 1904, when her parents moved to Edmonton and then Prince Albert, Miriam went too. Thus began her lifelong identification with western Canada, the vast territory whose potential drew out her latent talent and ambition. It was at this point, when she was well into her thirties, that Miriam Green Ellis shook loose from the bonds of family conformity and began to establish her own identity.

An unpublished novella gives some hints about the conflicts Ellis may have experienced in her early days. Her child-character Helen struggles against a family that tries to make a tomboy into a "lady." In her story Ellis laments what was likely a major feature of her own young life – conflict with a mother who seemed intent on forcing a lively child into a model of staid femininity: "If mothers could only let their little girls play naturally, and not try to make them conform to what every other little girl is doing, there might be fewer repititions [*sic*] of the old saying: 'I wish I were a man.'"[49] Letters she preserved in her files demonstrate the disappointment her mother experienced on the other side of the relationship: "Miriam," her mother once wrote to her, "if you were only pure and good I would give a million dollars if I had it."[50] For the fictional Helen, skirts were a "special abomination" as the girl tried to climb trees, ride horses, or tramp through the woods. The mature Miriam Green Ellis did all these things and more. She must have taken special pleasure in shocking the Ontario agricultural community when she and her friend Cora Hind tramped into the bull ring of the Royal Winter Fair wearing breeches.[51] Some farmers' wives refused to receive them. By then, Miriam Green Ellis was indifferent to the strictures of convention. Skirts were entirely unsuitable for the life she was leading.

Shortly before the First World War, Ellis began to contribute to the *Prince Albert Herald*, and in 1916 she moved south to Regina, where she landed a job as a cub reporter on the *Post*. She was thirty-seven. Just two days into the job, she was sent to report the city council meeting, to cover for the male reporter who was off on drunk leave. Although she had not even known who the mayor was or anything about local issues, she stayed up all night perfecting her copy. The mayor was so pleased with her "unbiased" reporting that he asked that she be assigned to the city hall beat. In the course of that year Ellis covered the legislature, the grain growers' companies, the board of trade, mortgage companies, various conventions, and even curling. Occasionally she slept at the office, working around the clock. Even so, she was fired before the year was out.[52]

Moving to the Edmonton *Bulletin*, Ellis had the satisfaction of rejecting telegraphed pleas from the Regina *Post* to return. In Edmonton she met her mentor, Frank Oliver, who steered her into the specialty that made her career. Like the "Hon Frank," Ellis believed that "agriculture was the basic industry." And unlike "the boys" who wanted to cover the police court, Ellis was happy to write about the agricultural fairs.[53] It was Oliver who came to respect her as "the best damn man I've got."[54] But she admitted that he was never comfortable with women in the office, though he did not discriminate against them. Moreover, he seemed to expect all women to be alike. The contrast between Ellis, who spent her vacations knocking about hunting and fishing, and Marion Seymour, the society editor who went abroad shopping, was more than he could fathom. But he gave Ellis the chances she needed to develop her knowledge of Canadian journalism and agriculture.[55]

Even though Ellis revered her boss, she was feisty enough to challenge him when he impinged on her journalistic ethics. In 1917 she was assigned to cover a speech Oliver made during the conscription crisis. Oliver was a Liberal loyal to the anticonscription stance his chief, Laurier, had assumed. Ellis worked hard on the story and next morning

Miriam Green Ellis during her trip to the Arctic Ocean (J.F. Moran/NA, PA-102597)

was dismayed to find a paragraph altered. When she then confronted
Oliver with the rewrite, he asked her why it was out of bounds for him to
edit his own speech in his own paper. Ellis's response encapsulated her
reportorial creed: "This is a newspaper .. and the two thousand people
who were there ... know you did not say that ... The responsibility for
that report is on me."[56] It was this "holy zeal," as she put it, that distinguished Ellis's career as an honest reporter. From time to time, Oliver
sent her out of the city, often in a horse and buggy, to find out about the
new ventures in ranching and farming that were opening up the
Northwest, including the frontier settlements of the Peace River. Even
this did not quench her adventurous spirit. In 1922, when she was forty-
three, Miriam Green Ellis set off to follow the Mackenzie to Aklavik.
Very few white women had ever been this far north before, though the
people there rememberd one woman journalist who had preceded
Ellis. Agnes Deans Cameron had offended some of her northern hosts
by failing to return some photos she was lent.[57]

As had been the case with Agnes Deans Cameron, Ellis's arctic
journey gave her an international audience. She left the *Bulletin* for a
stint of freelance lecturing and writing, selling her stories all over
Canada and the United States. It was this renown, as well as her agricul-

tural expertise, that won her the position that would occupy her considerable energy for the rest of her career – western editor of the Montreal-based *Family Herald and Weekly Star*. As an agricultural specialist, Ellis took on an exceptionally varied territory, intellectually as well as physically. In one year she might do a story on the techniques of harvesting blueberries in the Fraser Valley of British Columbia, write another about the isolated homesteads of northern Saskatchewan, interview scientists developing new strands of wheat, investigate the bacon board, examine drought cycles, and report the many fairs and conventions of the agricultural calendar. She would visit huge farms that stretched many kilometres and others only a few hectares in area. As one of her colleagues recalled, Ellis could call most pure-bred bulls by their first names.

Ellis won acceptance by an exclusively male society of farmers and ranchers, agricultural businessmen, and fellow journalists. Only Cora Hind surpassed her in worldwide fame. She rejoiced in her own versatility in traditionally male skills, whether it was hunting and fishing or nursing her old car over the the rough tracks of Canada's homesteads. She did not record any prejudice against her personally, but she could be wry about collective discrimination. Her speeches were peppered with asides that testified to her combative feminism. For instance, she loved to remember the hazards of driving in the days before the First World War: "Of course there were not many women driving in those days; like taking up the collection in church, it was really a man's job."[58]

At the end of her career, Ellis was feted and celebrated by the farmers and ranchers she had served, but media attention was less welcome. As she recorded in her diary, "Am disturbed over proposed story by CP [Canadian Press]. They are apparently not concerned over my work but whether I wore Breeches, had a piano, how old I am, whether I smoke etc."[59] Having spent her career in a male domain, Ellis had to parry questions that would never have been asked of a man. Thus she was subject to the paradox that awaited many prominent women journalists, as the historian Susan Henry has observed: "Because she is made to appear more human than her male counterparts, she also appears less professional."[60] For the historian, the understanding of such attention is useful; for Ellis, who passionately embraced the ostensibly neutral reporters' creed, the attention on her as a woman and on the way she defied female conventions was entirely unwelcome.

The other woman who made a career in commercial reporting was even less constrained by the strictures of convention. As one of her colleagues recalled, "She invaded this strictly masculine field with characteristic disregard for accepted conventions and it never bothered her when she had to delve into sordid details."[61] Eleanor Walker

Johnson did a great many things women were not supposed to do – all of which demanded strength and considerable bravado. Before the 1914–18 war, she had been one of the first women to drive a taxi in Canada, with her own cab in Victoria. Apparently, she warded off potential harassers with a monkey wrench. She became a timber cruiser and then a timber broker in British Columbia's most important industry. She also worked as a real estate agent and insurance broker. A handy carpenter, she built her own house in Burnaby and then ran her own cement construction company, winning contracts for the first sewers in Burnaby and for a roundhouse for the Canadian Pacific Railway. Alongside all these adventures, Ella Johnson had done some district reporting for the Vancouver *World* around the turn of the century.[62] Thus, having personal experience in many of the industries of the developing port city, she was she was ably qualified to become the financial and marine editor for the *Vancouver Sun* just after the war. She wrote masterfully about a variety of economic topics, giving no hint that "E.W.J." was a woman. For instance, in one week in July 1919, her editorials on the financial page commented on labour attitudes, free trade, small investors, and Canada's need to maintain its navy.[63]

Yet despite her mastery of economics, hers was not an office job. It involved an intimate familiarity with the waterfront scene, "which she knew as few people ever knew it."[64] Ella Johnson walked with confidence around the backstreets – she was a large, athletic woman who once swam the turbulent waters between Kitsilano beach and West Vancouver. She was on good terms with some of the more colourful characters of the Vancouver scene, including both the Japanese and Chinese communities – rather unusual in those times of strained race relations in western Canada. Edith McConnell (Murray), who at the time was writing features for the *Sun*'s women's section, recalled how Johnson trotted her round the waterfront to get a story on a sea captain who was in port with his Chinese wife and son. The "King of the Bootleggers" – whom Johnson called a "fine chap who keeps half the people around the harbour from starving in the winter" – rowed the two women out from Coal Harbour to the Chinese junk so that McConnell could get her story.[65] Johnson's connections with the Japanese community led to the biggest scoop of her career. Her contacts tipped her off about the purpose of a high-ranking Japanese delegation that was passing through Vancouver en route to Washington just after the First World War; apparently, the United States was withdrawing from the tripartite naval agreement with Britain and Japan. It was thus Johnson who broke this story to the world.[66]

In later years, when she ran for office in provincial politics as a Liberal, Johnson seemed to have betrayed whatever trust she had won in the Japanese community and succumbed to the anti-Japanese sentiments of her would-be constituents. Asked by a reporter in 1933, "Do you think Japanese women should be fed?," she replied that "every man, woman and child should be fed" but that "Canadian women" should be fed first. Then she boasted that she had recently ensured that thirty Japanese "girls" would be discharged so that "white women might get the jobs they were filling."[67] Johnson was defeated in 1933 and again in 1937. She then tried and failed to win a Burnaby municipal commissionership.

Given the potential dangers of her waterfront beat, it is not surprising that Johnson carried a loaded revolver on her rounds. But she seems to have had some extraordinary fears about her life and property. According to one of her former colleagues, she was obsessed with the idea that she might be robbed. She was a passionate gambler,[68] and perhaps she had acquired some unsavory contacts. No one knew why, in 1941, overnight she sold her New Westminster home and her car and disappeared. She apparently explained to the buyers that she required an operation urgently and was going to the Mayo Clinic in Rochester, New York. Maybe so – she was over sixty – but she lived on for another decade. Someone claimed to have recognized her characteristic figure in a newsreel about Mexico City. Then, in 1951, a woman calling herself Edna Jepson of Seattle died in a hotel in Douglas, Arizona. She had retained her initials but had jettisoned her identity. It was her lifetime railway pass that connected Edna Jepson to the one-time financial editor of the *Vancouver Sun*.

In life as in death, Johnson was a mystery. Journalism was only one phase in her constantly changing career path. While she was remembered with some fondness as one of the mavericks of early Vancouver, her colleagues struggled to classify her. The male columnist P.W. Luce assumed that Johnson had been "at odds with life" and must have "yearned to be a man"! She seems to have been a valued member of the Vancouver branch of the Canadian Women's Press Club, though the author of the "Pen Portraits of Club Members" could not resist a jest at Johnson's formidable size: "In the office and the Club her opinion carries weight."[69] Although Johnson was on friendly terms with her female colleagues, Myrtle Patterson (Gregory) and Edith McConnell, she did not maintain her membership in the all-female world of the CWPC for long. Perhaps she was more comfortable in a gender-neutral environment. Unlike E. Cora Hind, who insisted that her female identity be acknowledged when an editor tried to pass her off as E.C. Hind, Ella Johnson's signature under the "Latest News of the Financial World" in the *Vancouver Sun* was ambiguous. As noted above, she used her initials only, or "E.W. Johnson" for her market summaries.

With these trailblazers so prominently on the scene, women's eligibility for financial journalism should have been accepted by the late 1930s. But Rosa Shaw discovered to her chagrin, on a cross-Canada tour she undertook for the Montreal *Gazette*, that whenever one of her pieces happened to land on the financial page, the byline was always missing. "Why?" she asked. "Perhaps the feeble female intellect isn't supposed to be able to grapple with stories about wheat and mining, even if it does succeed in turning them out and getting good-sized headlines on them."[70] Ella Johnson, Cora Hind, and Miriam Green Ellis were to remain the exceptions for some time to come.

POLITICAL CORRESPONDENTS

As with business reporting, women were notably scarce in political reporting, despite the brave new world of equality projected by the suffragists of the prewar generation. When women were barred from voting, their exclusion from mainstream political commentary was predictable. Even so, on the women's page, newswomen had been writing commentaries and critiques of contemporary politics for years. Violet McNaughton's "Welfare Page" in the *Saturday Press and Prairie Farm* regularly editorialized on federal and provincial politics. Once women were enfranchised, it was natural to suppose that women reporters would routinely cover the political scene. But the number of women reporting politics after gaining the vote was nearly as small as before. There were some who had covered city hall either as specialists or as part of the general reporter's beat, though Winnifred Stokes was still considered "one of the few" in 1935 when she covered Niagara's city hall and court for the Niagara *Evening Review*.[71] Even fewer women covered provincial legislatures, though Alberta had had two notable legislative reporters – one presuffrage, the other postsuffrage. Katherine Hughes covered the Alberta legislature for the Edmonton *Bulletin* from 1906 to 1908, before taking a government job as the first archivist of Alberta; Zoe Trotter joined the Alberta press gallery as the representative of the Calgary *Albertan* in the mid-1920s.

The ultimate goal of the political reporter was the Ottawa press gallery. As Sir John Willison commented, "No greater distinction comes to a Canadian journalist than to be chosen to represent an influential newspaper at Ottawa."[72] According to Peter Desbarats, this elite corps was more like an intimate club than a "distinctive national force." Even after the Second World War, it still had only sixty-four members.[73] Many women claimed to be the first to breach this exclusive enclave. But the door opened, admitted one, and then closed, so each time the woman felt the pride of entry – and the loneliness of isolation.

Eve Brodlique had sat in the gallery for the *London Advertiser* before the turn of the century, joined briefly by Sara Jeannette Duncan. Two decades later, Katie Snider was sent by the Toronto *Telegram* to sit in the gallery for one parliamentary session during the First World War. She claimed to be first woman accredited to it. The "lone female among a covey of male writers and correspondents from all over the world," she recalled that "no provision had been made at that time for a female." The lounges were off-limits, but once the men "finally accepted" her, they left the door to their exclusive comfort zone open so that at least she could hear the music played on their Victrola.[74] She loved living at the Chateau Laurier and found parliamentary reporting less arduous than the general work she had done previously. But a more conventional fate beckoned. As soon as she came home to Toronto she married George Martin, a reporter with the *Globe*, and followed his dream of returning to his home town, Kitchener, where he became editor of the local paper. Although she helped out from time to time, there was no professional place for her in this very conservative town. From a promising beginning, her independent career withered.

A more enduring breach of the all-male bastion was accomplished by Genevieve Lipsett-Skinner. She was extremely well qualified to take her place in the gallery. By the time she came to Ottawa, she had worked for the *Winnipeg Telegram* for more than a decade and had earned a reputation for versatility and perseverance, which prompted the kind of contorted compliment that so often fell to women journalists in unconventional beats. Florence Sherk wrote that Lipsett-Skinner could "take a survey of labor conditions, or of judicial proceedings and give a story of causes and results that any editor might be proud to publish anonymously in the hope that it might be credited to a man."[75] In Winnipeg, Lipsett-Skinner had been a founding member of the Political Equality League and had taken part in the Mock Parliament at which Nellie McClung had played Premier Roblin. She had been the first married woman to qualify for a law degree in Manitoba and had taken honours. She had also run, unsuccessfully, as a Conservative candidate in the Manitoba election of 1920. But by 1921 there was nothing to keep her in Manitoba – her mother had died, her marriage had ended, and she wanted a fresh challenge.

Understandably, she was dismayed when her former editor appointed a "new man" as the paper's Ottawa correspondent. "Why didn't you offer that job to me?" she demanded as she listed her qualifications. "I understand our constitutional development and I know how to get news."[76] Her editor's response defined her challenge: "You are a woman and you would not be admitted to membership in the Parliamentary Press Gallery." The editor recalled that there had been a woman

Genevieve Lipsett-Skinner, first official member of the Parliamentary Press
Gallery, featured in the souvenir booklet for the triennial in Vancouver, 1923
(City of Vancouver Archives CVA 396, vol. 1, file 8)

there earlier – in the late nineties (most likely Brodlique) – "but she was
never regarded as a member." Lipsett-Skinner plotted her strategy
carefully. Learning that the defeated Conservative leader, Arthur
Meighen, was calling to Ottawa a caucus of all candidates, elected or
defeated, or their proxies, she dredged up a hospitalized acquaintance
who had been defeated and secured his proxy. She then sallied forth to
Ottawa, armed with an entry into "at least one official political circle." It
was, she added, "the first and last of my career – because the caucus is
sacred to members of Parliament and senators." She then began a
careful study of the "stuff" that other political writers produced and
decided that, rather than reproducing a roster of "straight comment on
the day's political events," she would introduce the human element.

A *Saturday Night* article described Lipsett-Skinner's technique of
"sugar-coating her pill of knowledge with such gossipy insider information as the price of a Senator's limousine or the cost of his chauffeur's
gloves." [77] She believed that a new angle would help her sell her copy to
newspapers across the country. Her brother Robert Lipsett, a member
of the Parliamentary Press Galley, was a valuable ally as she pursued her
goal. She used his desk in the morning to send articles to the most

important papers in Toronto, Winnipeg, Calgary, Edmonton, Vancouver, Montreal, and Calgary. Everywhere she sent her copy it became news – except Winnipeg: "The city where I had grown up, and had worked as a journalist all my days was the only city that wouldn't use my Ottawa copy. Whether it was good or bad, there were thousands of Winnipeg readers who would read anything that bore my byline, for they had been accustomed to me for years. Neither the *Free Press* nor the *Tribune* would use one article at space rates."[78] One Halifax paper printed her articles but never paid, so she abandoned that avenue. But the Vancouver *Province, Calgary Herald, Edmonton Journal, Toronto Star,* and *Montreal Star* all became regular customers. Now she was established. She and her brother rented a house and entertained MPs. "In this manner, I learned that the private thoughts of most men in public life, are different from the thoughts expressed in public."

At this point Lipsett-Skinner began to experience some setbacks. At first, she had found the thirty-three members of the press gallery "quite pleasant," but this did not last: "Came a day, when somebody going over the files in the reading room, saw Genevieve featured in several important dailies. Then an early frost set in. One old fellow took a solemn vow never to say good morning to me again. Others sat around in groups and discussed 'this terrible thing which has come upon poor old Bob Lipsett – his sister breaking into this Gallery.'" Although she had been sitting in the press gallery and doing the job of an Ottawa correspondent, she did not yet qualify as an active member, and when she applied for formal membership in the gallery, she was refused it. Despite the fact that five papers were taking her copy, she had not been "sent" by any one of them. When she pointed out that the president of the gallery was out of work, with no newspaper job at all, she met yet more obfuscation – oh but he used to have several. "Ah," retorted Lipsett-Skinner. "I have been laboring under a misapprehension, I thought this was a place provided by the taxpayers of Canada for working journalists, but I was mistaken. It is a refuge for men who once had good jobs on newspapers."[79] Although she was defeated in this instance, she was not out.

Her next assault was more direct. She travelled to the West Coast, where the open-minded publisher of the *Vancouver Sun,* Robert Cromie, agreed to send her as his paper's official correspondent – even though she had not previously sent her copy to the *Sun.* He also agreed that she could sell her copy anywhere outside Vancouver. With this official accreditation, Lipsett-Skinner found the next three years in Ottawa more than satisfactory. Most of the men "were quite agreeable." Most of the time her reports on Parliament were sober accounts of House of Commons affairs, but her puckish wit lurked beneath the

surface. Reporting on Arthur Meighen's speech as leader of the opposition in 1924, she commented, "He was in his best form, and his claim as
the world's champion 'optimist' can be disputed successfully by Edgar
Allan Poe ... and Charles Baudelaire ... When Mr Meighen finished we
all felt as if we had been the actors in a natural deathbed scene."[80] Her
reports to the *Vancouver Sun* were always on the front page and always
signed "Genevieve Lipsett-Skinner (Special Sun Representative)."

During her fifth year in the gallery, she discerned that the new
president of the press gallery was vying for her position with the *Sun* in
addition to the eastern paper he already represented. Quite without
warning, Lipsett-Skinner was informed by the chief page that her desk
had been assigned to a new man from Toronto and that there was no
place for her. Not to be outmanoeuvred, she insisted that the page give
her the key to her old place, and life again passed without incident.[81]
Then, after five years in the gallery, four of which she had passed as an
officially accredited member, Lipsett-Skinner moved on, taking a job
on the editorial staff of the *Montreal Star.*

Later, when addressing her fellow CWPC members, Lipsett-Skinner
took pains to emphasize that she really had made the grade as a parliamentary correspondent; she had not been a lady visitor or a temporary
member. Yet Canadian newspapers did not seem to recognize her
achievement. She fumed at an article she had read in a Canadian
newspaper which celebrated a woman in the press gallery in Washington, dismissing the status of Canadian women in Ottawa as "precarious." On the contrary, she insisted, she had had "all the rights and
privileges enjoyed by the 33 men in the Gallery." But she acknowledged, "I have had no successors, and it seems a pity."[82] That was in
1933 – the year her portrait was the first woman's to hang in the Parliamentary Press Gallery.[83] In future, no one would be able to forget that
a woman had sat there. Within a year of this honour, Lipsett-Skinner
was in distress, reduced to petitioning her press club's Beneficiary Fund
when a painful illness prevented her from working.[84] By 1935, at the age
of forty-nine, this lively, intelligent woman was dead – and a couple of
decades later, press club members had difficulty piecing together her
biography.

Genevieve Lipsett-Skinner had first appeared in the Parliamentary
Press Gallery on the very day in March 1922 that Agnes Macphail made
her debut as the lone woman in the House of Commons.[85] In the
postsuffrage era, there seemed to be an obvious correlation between
successful women politicians and women political reporters. Would
women reporters sit with more authority in the press gallery if there
were more women in the House? Would the presence of female parlia-
mentarians oblige editors to send more women to cover politics?

Miriam Green Ellis assumed the reverse: women would succeed in politics only after women political reporters encouraged them. Writing on special fields for women journalists, Ellis remarked, "It does seem a bit pathetic that such a good fight was made to secure franchise for women and that we have two women members of parliament in all Canada and one woman senator ... In times of crisis we really need to draft the best minds and I believe that women writers by their support of women candidates and by fitting themselves for the positions of authority and confidence, could develop women's place in public life."[86]

But no armies of female correspondents arrived in Ottawa to replace Genevieve Lipsett-Skinner; and only one woman, Martha Louise Black – elected to fill the seat her husband temporarily vacated in 1935 – joined Agnes Macphail in the chamber below. The next woman in Ottawa's Parliamentary Press Gallery was doomed to repeat the triumph and loneliness of being the "first." Evelyn Tufts arrived in Ottawa ten years after Lipsett-Skinner left. She became the first woman ever to be elected an honorary life member of the press gallery.[87] For more than fifteen years she sat there, the only woman with permanent status. It was little wonder that she became somewhat obsessed with women's failure to make headway in politics, either as participants or as observers like herself. She was constantly urging her fellow CWPC members to take on the field. As a member of the memorial awards committee, she bemoaned the absence of political articles submitted, even though it had been a particularly active year in international and national political events. She assumed the reason was that male editors would not give women journalists the chance to write about politics: "Apparently the men still pre-empt this field, as they do the Press Gallery. They still stick to the old cliché about a 'woman's angle' when they hand out the assignments; whereas we all know that all angles, today, are women's angles, in politics as elsewhere. However, they are starting to give the squaws [*sic*] the vote, see, so perhaps it might be a good time for all us girls to go off the reservation."[88] Tufts's friends claimed that she never let the subject drop. In her defence, she bristled, "How can I help it, sitting there day after day looking at all those men, without one woman's face to break the monotony. Women are the civilizers of the world. They always have been, and there should be a few of them in the government."[89]

Tufts had built an extraordinary career from rather obscure beginnings. Married to an ornithologist with the Dominion Parks branch, she raised her daughter and submitted the occasional book review to the Halifax *Chronicle Herald*. She had a finely developed literary aesthetic and cultivated ties with the Canadian poetry community.[90] She seemed headed for a conventionally feminine career in literary journalism, but instead she became famous for some sensational scoops. In the summer 1935 the *Chronicle-Herald* gave her the chance to travel on Northern Airways to Great Bear Lake and the Eldorado Mine with Lord Duncannon, son of the governor general. She then managed to join a judicial party flying to a remote arctic village, where an Inuk was being tried for murder. Since she was the only reporter covering the case, her story in its romantic location was carried by papers all over North America.[91] She then happened to be on holiday in New York when the trial of Bruno Hauptmann, accused of kidnapping and murdering the Lindbergh baby, convened. The *Chronicle-Herald* sent her down to New Jersey to cover the trial. She was the only Canadian reporter there, working beside some of the most famous journalists in America. Her features proved to be so outstanding that the *Chronicle-Herald* offered her a full-time job, and within a year she was representing the paper in the press gallery in Ottawa.[92]

Evelyn Tufts brought a different style to the all-male bastion. Rather than trying to blend into the crowd of men, she emphasized her femininity, wearing colourful and fashionable clothes and remarkable hats.[93] Meanwhile, she did the job brilliantly, bringing an amazing memory and down-to-earth wit to bear on day-to-day political reporting. But like many another woman journalist, it was the "story behind the news" that interested her and feature writing that she most enjoyed.[94] The plight of miners and fishermen during the Depression, the tragic illogic of a system that saw mountains of apples rotting in the Annapolis Valley while fishermen's wives struggled to buy fruit for their children – these were the stories that moved her. During the Second World War, she was the first woman to get an overseas assignment – promoting the Queen's Canadian Fund for the *Chronicle-Herald*. She crossed the Atlantic on a clipper ship via Lisbon and then spent three tense months in Britain before returning to Canada on a crowded troopship.[95]

Although Tufts had a brush with the scene of war, she did not seek official accreditation as a war correspondent. She was amply occupied with Canadian politics and war work. As we have seen, a number of women found that war furnished them with opportunities they might never have seized otherwise, as they took over positions vacated by men. The men were away covering the biggest story in the world. Some women wanted to be at that scene too.

WAR CORRESPONDENTS

Overall, not many more women went overseas as war correspondents in the Second World War than in the First. Official accreditation was tediously elusive, even though Canadian women had been writing about wars and had been officially accredited since the turn of the century. Each time a woman achieved official status, she had to overcome the same arguments. War was quintessentially a man's business, she was told. Women had no place on the battlefield; there were no facilities for them there, and in their vulnerability, they would endanger men's lives. Kit Coleman had disproved these allegations in the Spanish-American War of 1898. She was still Kit Watkins when, by charm, talent, and sheer audacity, she had become the world's first woman war correspondent.[96] Unfortunately, her travails in getting to Cuba delayed her so long that the main battles had been fought before she arrived. What she did see horrified her. Her reports emphasized the seamy, pathetic side of war – neglected men dying of their untended wounds, ill with malaria.

In her vehement reaction against what she had seen in Cuba, Kit perhaps fulfilled the fears of those who wanted to exclude women from the battlefield. Although her resourcefulness in fending for herself invalidated the perennial excuse that a woman would have to be protected in a war zone and would thus endanger herself and her protectors, her presence was disquieting; for there were regions in the psyche of warfaring men that were vulnerable to the penetrating gaze of a woman reporter. Would a woman, immune to the mystique of war as a glorious male apotheosis, puncture the illusion that kept young men signing up and fighting? Would the physical proximity of a woman on the battlefield undermine the mystified images of "womanhood as homeland" that buoyed up soldiers' zeal for sacrifice? To be sure, the generals and the journalists usually had an uneasy relationship, but in the case of the Spanish-American War, dream child of the sensational press in the United States, glory was the headline of the hour. Kit may have kept the worst of her reflections to herself, but she did nothing to fan the flames of heroism.[97]

Kit claimed that her experiences as a war correspondent had cured her of curiosity, and she warned other women off.[98] Nevertheless, looking at war from the underside continued to attract women. Almost as soon as the Spanish-American War flickered out, the Boer War began, and this time Canadians were directly involved. No Canadian woman managed to repeat Kit Coleman's feat in gaining official accreditation, but the opportunity to go as a teacher of Boer children in the British camps allowed Florence Randal of the *Ottawa Journal* and Nan Moulton, a freelance writer from Winnipeg, to gain a distant view. However, the next war provided a far more varied chance for women to write about it.

One of the first women to exploit the First World War as a journalistic opportunity was not initially a journalist at all. Rosamund Boultbee was a society woman with an ample stock of connections in Liberal Party and government circles. She had no particular expertise or even ambition to become a newspaperwoman, and she did not at first need the income. What she did have was curiosity and the leisure to travel. When one of her many jaunts to Europe coincided with the outbreak of the war, she jokingly suggested that if she wrote letters to her friend Lady Willison (Marjory MacMurchy), Willison's husband could publish them in the *Toronto Daily News* and then one letter would do for all her friends.

Sir John Willison took her idea seriously and promised that he would both publish and pay for any letters she cared to write.[99] At first she had the background "colour" field all to herself. In Paris she entertained soldiers on leave and wrote up their stories. Exhilarated by her early successes, she took on the much more dangerous challenge of travelling to Russia. Willison, as a family friend, advised her against this venture, but as a newspaper editor, he confessed that he would be glad of her letters. Russia in the last days of the Tsar was full of sensational news, but Boultbee was stymied by the censors. These barriers were just as impenetrable to male reporters. Indeed, one male war correspondent, when denied access to Russian troops on the Eastern Front, joined up as a private.[100] This route was not open to Boultbee. But in the end, by ingratiating herself with the head of the censorship department, she got her stories sent directly to the *News*. Her trip to Russia and then to Romania, where once again she interviewed the major personalities, exhausted her, but they made her name.

Next, she proposed to cover the war in Italy. Here her "connections" did not serve her so well; to get a passport, she needed formal accreditation from a newspaper willing to acknowledge her as a staff member. It was the *Toronto Star* that came to her aid. Managing editor Bone was quick to see the newsmaking potential of having the *Star's* own woman at the front. Once again, Boultbee plied her talent for insinuating herself into the best circles and was taken directly to the front by the Italian colonel in charge of the press. This martinet, as he proved to be, insisted that the reporters in his retinue visit battle sites by day and write up their stories immediately by night, a routine that left Boultbee prostrate.

Curiously, despite her genteel delicacy, Boultbee's reaction to war was not in the least ladylike. Unlike Kit Coleman, who had been sickened by the scenes of carnage, Boultbee's experiences ignited in her a strong desire to kill.[101] But unlike the gallant Kit, who endured endless hardship, Boultbee frequently collapsed in nervous exhaustion, vowing to give up journalism. Having fallen into journalism by accident rather than design, she viewed her vocation as a kind of addiction she could not shake off. Although she did not like taking a livelihood from someone who needed to earn, she needed a raison d'être for her own mental health.[102] All told, she was inclined to lament her lot, complaining, "I wonder if it is realized how hard journalists have to work sometimes."[103] Nevertheless, her stock with the *Toronto Star* continued to rise. She was urged to cable rather than mail her articles on the Italian situation and was subsequently posted to Switzerland to visit camps of interned prisoners. Boultbee's difficulties persuading Swiss officials that she was an accredited correspondent for the *Star* touched off a nervous breakdown, and she spent most of her stay in Switzerland convalescing rather than writing articles. For her final tour of duty, she joined the fray of journalists around the Paris Peace Conference, where she was entirely frustrated by the difficulty of getting stories. So she came home.

More successful in mining gold out of the peace conference was Beatrice Nasmyth. She was the only woman reporter to witness the signing of the Treaty of Versailles.[104] She had been in London covering the home front and the aftermath of war in Britain when the Vancouver *Province* sent her to Paris in 1919. Originally the women's editor of the *Province,* Nasmyth had taken a job as publicity secretary to John Reid, agent general for Alberta, in order to get overseas when the war broke out. She took advantage of her situation to explore every journalistic opportunity that came her way. At a time when Viscountess Rhondda was not allowed to occupy her inherited seat in the House of Lords, Nasmyth managed to get access to the press gallery of this ancient bastion of exclusion – the first woman to do so.[105]

When Alberta women won the provincial vote, Nasmyth was determined that a woman serving with the armed forces would stand for election. "I thought that to be really worthy of the name suffragette," she wrote to her father, "I should have a woman candidate in the field for our overseas elections."[106] Roberta MacAdams, an army nurse, was flabbergasted at first by Nasmyth's suggestion that she run but then agreed to do so, and with Nasmyth engineering a vigorous campaign for the soldiers' vote, MacAdams became the first woman elected to the Alberta legislature.

Towards the end of the war, Britain's Society of Women Journalists demanded the right to visit the front. Nasmyth was one of four Canadian women journalists who demanded that they too should be allowed access to "that mysterious place where hundreds of thousands of our men had been swallowed up."[107] Four British women were allowed to cross the channel, and a few weeks later, in December 1917, four Canadians went behind the Canadian lines in France. Other women who went to France with Nasmyth capitalized on their prominence as well. Mary MacLeod Moore, after her early years with the *Montreal Herald*, was entrenched in London as *Saturday Night*'s resident correspondent; and Elize Montizambert, who had been in Paris as correspondent for the *Montreal Star* and the *Canadian Gazette* when war broke out, spent most of the rest of her career in London writing for various British newspapers and magazines.[108]

Margaret Bell Saunders saw the war from a far less comfortable perspective, having volunteered as a nurse in order to get to the front. In the fall of 1915 she was wounded during a German air raid of the Belgian town where her relief unit was stationed.[109] Having established her credibility as a witness on the firing line, she spent the rest of the war doing background war stories. Writing as Margaret Bell, she won a byline in the Toronto *Globe* on 15 July 1916 for her three-column story on spies, which focused on the devious female spies who had exploited the king of Belgium's order for clemency.

Even though a number of Canadian women made their names during the war, and even though women became firmly established as journalists in the following years, it was no less difficult for women to cover the battles of the Second World War. There were practical reasons for this, including the fact that war was even more dangerous for reporters; there were no stable fronts, and the modern technology of war had no particular respect for the sanctity of noncombatant life. Moreover, by this time, the relationship between press and military had become more formalized. The military had become sophisticated in its use and control of the press, aware of the importance of public opinion and determined to mould home-front morale by structuring media access. War correspondents attached to the American army received a set of privileges that defined their dependent relationship with the military; they were assigned to press camps, issued uniforms, jeeps, and drivers, and provided with teletype and radio transmission, and resident censors. General Eisenhower wanted the reporters to be "quasi staff officers" as a form of protection should they be captured.[110] The military accommodated the press and in twice-daily briefing sessions gave more than broad hints about what would become news.

The problem for women was that this privileged access was mostly out of bounds. Before the Americans entered the war, women trying to cover the conflict in an official capacity were bluntly rejected. The British military establishment, especially General Montgomery, was vehemently opposed to the intrusion of women war correspondents. Canadian women journalists were deflected by the Wartime Information Board on the grounds of danger and cost. Flying was said to be too dangerous for women, so they had to travel by ship, which was certainly not a safe option during the Battle of the Atlantic. During the voyage, each woman had to be accompanied by a male in case of torpedo attack. As a result, sending women abroad to cover the war would have cost at least $1,500 per person.[111]

Since the Americans were more welcoming to women war correspondents, British and Canadian women journalists usually sought accreditation from the U.S. military.[112] But before the United States entered the war in 1942, the women determined to cover the biggest story in the world had to go to the front on their own. They had no official status if captured, and they generally worked solo, unlike male correspondents, who were more inclined to collaborate with one another.[113] The official press hotels and the shared insights and gossip that went along with semicommunal living were off-limits to freelance writers. Some of these women became scornful of male news-gathering techniques, which so often were done in bars while they themselves were out in the streets collecting material first-hand.[114]

Even when women gained official accreditation, they were rarely allowed to travel with the press camps. Mostly they had to remain with the women's military services or the field hospitals – which, ironically, might be closer to enemy lines than the press camps.[115] The lack of toilet facilities – the most mundane but vexing problem for the woman "warco" – was the usual excuse for barring women from the front lines. One of the first women to make it to North Africa as the American forces landed was International News Service's Dixie Tighe. Tighe was one of the "glamour girl" American warcos who gloried in her visibility in the all-male environment. According to her colleague Iris Carpenter, when Tighe was greeted by a party of officers coming to brief her, she interrupted them in order to catalogue her needs: "First I'll need a little girl's room and a sentry. Guess you'd do," she said, pointing to the nearest sentry.[116] After ensuring her celebrity status with her self-publicized exploits – the only women to fly on an operational mission – Dixie Tighe came back to North America to warn other women off. Addressing the Canadian Women's Press Club, she preached that women really did not belong at the front, that it was ridiculous to expect the army to provide facilities for women, and that "men in the forces are embarrassed to have women around in the hellfire of the front. Back a bit from the front lines, well, that's different."[117]

Back with the female services, newswomen had facilities as women, but there were no particular services for them as journalists. They had to be very ingenious to send out even the acceptable stories on nurses, WAACs, and wounded men.[118] If they chose to defy orders and cover other stories, they had to risk their lives and their official accredited status, if they had it, or even face court martial.[119] The death-defying exploits of such adventurous journalists as Americans Martha Gellhorn and Ann Stringer, both of whom ignored the rules and witnessed military violence first-hand, were not repeated by the Canadian women who wrote about the war. The Canadian newswomen were assigned to background colour stories, not the battles. In terms of conventional hard-news values, they were on a lower track. But in a war in which civilians were strategic targets, where occupation was a fact of life for millions of people, and where women were in active service, the difference between the "hard" news of war and the "soft" human-interest features was murky. Journalism historian Anna Sebba acknowledged that women reporters were more likely to write about refugees and orphans but suggested that it was the male reporters, obsessed with the technology of warfare and the numbers of planes shot down, who took the "soft option."[120] It was less harrowing to write about the big picture than to go into the streets and talk to women who had lost their children, families whose homes had been destroyed, and people who were dealing hourly with hunger, cold, and fear.

Women who wrote about the war, even those with official military accreditation, were expected to limit their coverage to civilians and women in uniform. In any case, not very many Canadian women were granted official status or had the backing of major news organizations. Around one hundred newswomen were granted official accreditation from the American armed forces.[121] The Canadian journalists Mollie McGee and Margaret Ecker Francis were among this elite company, while Gladys Arnold, as Paris correspondent for Canadian Press in the late 1930s, was already in the right place at the right time. Arnold had travelled to France on her own in 1935, with her life savings of five hundred dollars and no particular grasp of the language but full of what she called "political curiosity."[122] For five years before that she had worked for the Regina *Leader Post* as social editor, but she had found Saskatchewan too parochial to satisfy her quest for ideological insight. When she learned that Canadian Press (CP) had no correspondent in Paris, she sent off a barrage of articles to CP in Toronto, for which she received no pay and no reply. She was on the brink of insolvency when CP finally gave her official status, and for the next four years she foraged for the "Canadian angle" in French news.

When war appeared imminent, Arnold went home to Canada to visit her parents, but she fully intended an immediate return, expecting to be Canada's first war correspondent on the Continent."[123] CP editor Giles Purcell warned her that CP could not be responsible for her, but when she assured him that she would be responsible for herself, he gave her a raise. She also had official blessing from the Canadian government, and since she was the only Canadian war correspondent in Paris at the time, she immediately won wartime accreditation from the

French Commissariat of Information and Censorship. In the twilight of the "phony war," there was an equality of frustration as all journalists in Paris were "scratching for war-related stories." But Arnold was well aware that she was "not part of the small charmed circle of the Big League." "Stick to human interest stories," she was told. "The boys in the London Bureau will look after political and military stuff." Her credentials gave her access to most press conferences but not to briefings at the War Office. This exclusion was not, she insisted, because she was a woman but because she was a Canadian.[124] The fact that it was Canada, not the United States, that was at war did not alter Canadian stature in the eyes of French officialdom, and she found it galling to think that Canadians might have to see France and the war through American coverage.[125] In any case, her rounds of pleading with officialdom were soon cut short, for the German invasion overwhelmed everyone. As the male war correspondents disappeared to find the front, Arnold witnessed the mass exodus from Paris. The "human interest" was the big story here as Belgians and northern French civilians packed the roads so thickly that military transport could not get through.

Once the war heated up, Gladys Arnold was not able to get official war correspondent status, so she had to leave France or face internment. With great difficulty she sailed for London. Her experiences in France over the last months provided plenty of copy to issue from the London office of CP, and interviews with nurses and women's volunteer work in Britain kept her busy. But having left her friends behind in France, she was numb with grief and guilt at having taken "the easy way out." When she learned that General de Gaulle was in London, she immediately asked to interview him, and she was given the assignment – no doubt because de Gaulle's quixotic bid to represent the fighting spirit of France was considered a second-string story. Arnold's meeting with de Gaulle proved to be a defining event that affected the rest of her wartime work. Recognizing her commitment to the cause, de Gaulle made her an "honorary Brigadier in the Free French Auxiliary Force."[126]

As part of her human-interest work for CP, Arnold was next assigned to one of the ships carrying British children to Canada. Despite her protests that she did not want to leave, she was ordered to do the story. Even though CP assured her that it would arrange for her to return on a troopship, she did not get back to Europe until the very end of the war. Once back in Canada, Arnold continued with CP, but her imagination had been ignited by de Gaulle's movement. In the fall of 1941 she left CP and, with de Gaulle's former secretary, set up the Free French Information Service. Her motive was patriotism rather than careerism: she believed that German-controlled radio in occupied France was sabotaging the Canadian war effort.[127]

A few years later, Mollie McGee was able to secure the official war correspondent status that had eluded Gladys Arnold. Attached to the *Globe and Mail*, McGee was the first woman to gain accreditation from the Canadian Army and the supreme headquarters of the Allied Expeditionary Force (in August 1944).[128] In typical fashion, she had paved the way for herself by first gaining official status with the United States Army – the first Canadian woman to be so honoured.[129] McGee was prepared to play the game by the rules: "I don't want to go forward to the front line with the armed forces. All I want to do is go and report where other women are driving, nursing, doing canteen work."[130] McGee applied her feminism with a light touch. As an elderly woman, she recalled that "at first the boys wouldn't let me put my typewriter in with theirs" and that she had "fought her way in." In general, she seems to have used humour to make her points. She remembered her days as a CP correspondent in Ottawa when Mackenzie King tried to have her fired for organizing a beauty pageant for the MPs.[131]

McGee had been born in Australia and was still a child when her family moved to Montreal in 1907. As a young woman she studied occupational therapy at the University of Toronto and was a superintendent in Hamilton. But medical work did not satisfy her adventurous spirit. She turned to journalism and got her break in 1933 with the *Montreal Herald* when she did a story on women attending the imperial conference in Ottawa. She had a varied career on *Herald*, writing a column, doing society features, and covering the occasional murder. She then moved to CP for a while before freelancing in Britain. Her coverage of the coronation of George VI and the royal tour of Canada earned her a job with the *Globe and Mail*. McGee returned to Britain as the *Globe and Mail*'s war correspondent posted to the Ministry of Information in London.[132] There was plenty to write about without going to the Continent – the Dunkirk evacuation, the blitz, the first bombing raid on Berlin, the debacle at Dieppe. For McGee, the woman's angle was not a lower flight: "Men and women both are in this war so every story has a woman's side to it. There should be a woman covering every field of activity in which women are taking part ... During the blitz in England, women workers, ambulance drivers, ARP wardens, stood the ordeal as well as men."[133]

McGee was satisfied to cover the war from a woman's point of view; her style was distinctively personal and dramatic. Unlike the distant third-person accounts that characterized much of the reporting, McGee's reports registered an immediate human response to what she was witnessing. Her *Globe and Mail* story of 2 June 1940 stood out from the other front-page accounts of the heroism of Dunkirk: "For two nights and one day I have stood at the backdoor of battle, watching the living and the dead come home from Flanders ... I now know, far better than I ever knew before, that as long as dirty, tattered, blood-stained men can smile with unshaken courage, that no invader can bring this England to her knees." In 1944 McGee was one of the first women to enter the liberated city of Paris. The hotel where she and her military escorts slept had been Gestapo Headquarters, and a hundred Germans were still resident just above her. Much of her writing detailed the ordeals and gratitude of the Parisians, but she also visited two thousand political prisoners, their heads shaved as collaborators. She saw the Gestapo torture chambers and heard the testimony of French Resistance fighters who knew Gestapo methods first-hand.[134]

Margaret Ecker (Francis) was also present in the newly liberated Paris. She was the only woman that CP actually sent overseas as a war correspondent. She had begun her career as a general reporter on the Vancouver *Province* in 1936 and was sufficiently impressive that British United Press gave her a job on the news staff – the first woman it had so honoured. She then moved to Montreal.[135] Even though she had recently married Bob Francis, who became city editor of BUP, she continued to sign her bylined articles Margaret Ecker. In 1942 she joined CP to cover the servicewomen in Ottawa, but within a year she was sent to CP's London bureau. After D-day, Ecker went across to Normandy with the nurses. She covered the liberation of Paris and then went on assignment with the RCAF in Holland and Belgium. The liberation of the Netherlands had a special significance for her, since she had frequently written about Princess Juliana in Ottawa. Now she toured with Queen Wilhelmina during the triumphant return of the Dutch royal family. There was a special affinity binding Canada and the Netherlands during the war years, and the Dutch were eager to show their gratitude to the country that had sheltered some of their royal family and played such a major role in evicting the occupying Germans. For her part in arousing Canadian sympathy, the Dutch made Margaret Ecker Francis one of the few women ever to be included in the Order of the House of Orange.

Ecker's honours continued to roll in. She was among seventeen reporters and the only woman chosen by General Allen, Supreme Headquarters chief of press relations, to witness the signing of unconditional surrender at Reims.[136] A few days later, when the accredited correspondents drew lots, she was one of two reporters allowed to be present on the ship at Flensburg when the German general staff was abolished.[137] By this time she was an experienced correspondent with a considerable reputation in Canada at least. But still she could not blend into the crowd in that all-male setting. Even though General Eisenhower was not averse to women war correspondents,[138] upon seeing the

Margaret Ecker (Francis), the sole woman in the company of
Canadian Press war correspondents (NA, RD-967)

lone woman journalist he allegedly asked, "What's that child doing here?"[139] Margaret Ecker Francis was thirty years old at the time.

˙ Did the women who made it in this most prestigious arena go on to establishment careers? Curiously, few of the women who made it as war correspondents in either world war stayed in newspaper work. Beatrice Nasmyth married at the end of the First World War and did freelance journalism and publicity for the rest of her career; she was known more for the "rhyming menus" she produced for children travelling on the Canadian Pacific Railway than for path-breaking news stories.[140] Rosamund Boultbee wrote her memoirs but otherwise seems to have disappeared from journalism. By the end of the Second World War, Gladys Arnold had found her niche, and she stayed on as an information officer at the French embassy in Ottawa. Margaret Ecker Francis left daily newspaper work for freelancing and working with her husband in a family-run public relations firm – Inside Canada.[141] Mollie McGee dedicated the rest of her career to serving the Roman Catholic Church. During the war she had perceived an antipapal tilt among foreign correspondents. Wishing to counter this, she lived the rest of her life a few blocks from the Vatican and wrote articles on church affairs for Canadian, American, and Australian magazines.[142]

The reasons these women left the hectic mainstream of frontline journalism were as individualistic as their reasons for entering it in the first place. While they rose to the challenges they had set themselves, their competence did not radiate beyond their own achievements. Their experience bore out what Julia Edwards observed of the American war correspondents: "Society accepted each woman's feat as a celebration of the unique, not as evidence of women's capacities."[143]

These women left no evidence that the beats they covered were too tough or too unwelcoming. Not one of them left any hint that she had retreated from mainstream journalism because of what she had endured in the war zone. Their reports sounded the insistent patriotism of the times, plus the news values they had absorbed as part of their induction into these male-dominated specialties. Unlike Kit Coleman, whose news value was precisely that she was a women in a war zone and who was therefore encouraged to react as a woman to what she saw, later war correspondents were channelled into the "woman's angle" but were not expected to write specifically as women. In terms of their private lives as women in journalism, in the 1920s, 1930s and 1940s, women were unlikely to publicize incidents of sexual harassment.[144] Perhaps, setting out to do what women usually did not do, they did not feel entitled to complain when gender became an issue. Or perhaps, like the professional women Mary Kinnear analysed, they were simply "delighted to be accepted."[145]

For these women and for their colleagues in political reporting, financial journalism, and general reporting, journalism was a career that accommodated their love of adventure. At a time when most professional women journalists were confined to women's work, the reporter's notebook gave an unusual few the licence to do things conventionally unheard-of for women. Moreover, having made it in departments of male-dominated journalism, the language available to them to encapsulate their experiences reflected those mainstream conventions. Zoe Trotter reflected newspaper dogma when she reminisced, "If I could choose and live it all over, I'd be a newspaper reporter again. The little triumphs that seemed so big at the time, being the first woman to represent a daily in the Alberta leg. [legislature], one of the 1st women telegraph editors in Canada, etc. have faded into insignificance, with the years, but the big thrill of a difficult story well done, the soldier's widow who came in to thank me for an Armistice day bit, the Yugoslav miner who wept because my story about his bride was on the front page, the political 'scoop,' are golden memories."[146] Despite all her "firsts" in fields where women rarely found a place, Trotter ended her career in conventional territory doing public relations work for such women's clubs as the Imperial Order of the Daughters of the Empire.

Ishbel Ross, the front-page "girl" from Toronto who made it in New York, reminded her former colleagues of the way Arnold Bennett, at the beginning of the century, had labelled all women journalists a separate species. Speaking before the Second World War, she noted that "no amount of careful work" had "served to uproot" the male editor's prejudices against women in the newsroom. Even when women like herself did prove themselves, the light of their achievement did not reflect on other women: "He values the women who happen to have succeeded in his own organization, but he thinks of them always as the exceptions. He has not yet been able to accept the species without reservation."[147]

Epilogue

Are women writers today, when they write so much, influenced by a masculine pattern and masculine prejudices? Our literature and our social ideas would gain enormously if we had more women writers with the confidence and originality to force their readers to open their eyes on a new picture of life – its values, joys, sorrows, and sensations as they are experienced in the lives of women.

Vera Brittain

In 1954 the members of the Canadian Women's Press Club celebrated their Golden Jubilee – fifty years as a club of professional women writers. For this occasion they scoured their files and memories to piece together a history of the early days of the club, the pioneers who had chartered it, and the achievements of notable members. There was much to applaud – the record was studded with the names of women who had won personal fame or authority within the newspaper hierarchy. The triumphs of individuals notwithstanding, the club was a collective of women journalists dedicated to their mutual advancement in their field. Inevitably, in the aftermath of self-congratulation came self-examination. How much progress had women made in the seventy-odd years of their active participation as journalists? Had they achieved their goal of "improving the status of journalism as a profession for women"? Did women have anything approaching a fair chance of succeeding on equal terms with men?

In numerical terms, there had been a big advance; there were more women journalists than ever before. In 1931 only 464 women had officially been counted as authors, editors, and journalists; by 1941 this had climbed to 713 and by 1951 there were 1,621 women working in this category.[1] Even so, discrimination against women as journalists remained entrenched, even though individuals had proved time and again that women were capable of taking on assignments as challenging as those the best male journalists undertook. The stereotypes died hard. In 1949 Doris Milligan noted that there were "two measuring rules for reporters: pay cheques and assignments they get." She added that women were "tops in neither."[2] Milligan was one of the stalwarts who had broken through the barrier. After years on the street beats, she had been one of the first to become an assistant city editor. Well aware of the prejudices that hobbled the progress of her fellow press club members, she buttonholed her boss to pinpoint his objections to women journalists. His litany of complaints was familiar:

1 Sick more than men
2 Skim over things
3 Don't write so impersonally as men
4 Too wordy
5 Quibble
6 Not so wholehearted on the job
7 Generally marry and put husband and home ahead of job
8 Insufficient physical stamina for tough jobs
9 Plead off stunts
10 Emotional outbursts.[3]

Only four years after the end of the war, when city editors had been keen enough to recruit women to replace scarce men, the same old saws had re-emerged to blight the hopes of the new crop of aspirants. There seemed to be no way to dislodge the figment of the flighty "sob sister."

While employers retreated into easy platitudes about women journalists, the confidence of postwar newswomen seemed to falter. The propaganda effort to propel women back into the home after the war appeared to be affecting the messengers themselves. Although undiluted feminists such as Kennethe Haig and Dora Dibney had protested against plans to "get rid of the women" as this attitude began to coalesce even during the war,[4] the domestic revival after the war and the "feminine mystique" that accompanied it appeared to cloud the judgment of newswomen as they contemplated themselves. Even the stout-hearted Miriam Green Ellis, who had scorned the judgment of convention and met her male rivals as an equal on "their" turf, seemed to acknowledge that other presswomen would yield rather than compete: "Press women, like other women, will probably continue to back away if they see their men wanting a job. Yes, they'll still be women – God bless them."[5]

The "Newspacket," which had trumpeted the progress of its members during the war, now became rather frivolous, more inclined to record branch parties than the sober achievements of members. Parties had always been a time for larking and venting frustrations, but in the postwar years there was more emphasis on light-headed femininity. Where earlier, women journalists had called themselves presswomen or newspaperwomen, they now seemed content with such coy nicknames as "newsies," "paper dolls," and "news hens."[6] Moreover, no one wanted to come to the parties any more – according to Evelyn Gowan Murphy – largely because they were drab: "We can't get away from Cocktail and drinking parties which I loathe."[7]

The CWPC seemed to have lost the earnest goals and intimate atmosphere that previous generations of members had treasured, without evidently providing sufficient attraction to lure the rising generation. The founders of the club had dedicated it to uplifting the profession, promoting a Canadian national spirit, and encouraging one another's achievements. By the second half of the twentieth century, the aggressively commercial enterprises that were metropolitan newspapers may have seemed less fertile ground in which to cultivate moral or literary missions. Aspiration for full-fledged professional status remained elusive. At the same time, the CWPC seemed ineffectual in its self-appointed mandate to advance the status of women within the world of journalism. It had no sway with newspaper owners, and as the war had demonstrated, it had very limited powers of persuasion with government officials. It would be in the union, which CWPC members had helped to organize, that women would seek recognition of their status and, over the long term, air some of their specific issues as women in journalism.

In the short term, younger women journalists seemed not to feel any particular need for a women-only association. Earlier generations of newswomen had been isolated from their colleagues by their "separate sphere" of newspaper work – and often from one another, too, when newspapers habitually hired only one "lady" journalist. They had needed the solidarity of their women's press club. Perhaps later generations, working in larger women's departments or even in the newsroom, did not feel the need to club together for mutual support. Thus, it was not surprising that when the president of the London branch canvassed local newspaperwomen to become members, she was told that the London City Press Club had what they wanted – "a lounge, liquor and men. Who needs the CWPC?"[8]

Witnessing the flow of successful newspaperwomen away from the women-only club towards the apparent egalitarianism of their local mixed press clubs, the CWPC executive felt helpless and ineffectual. Eva Fletcher, president in 1968, resented the amount of work involved in being on the executive of an organization whose members did not seem to care about it: "It seems to your national executive that the CWPC is at a point in its history when it must take a sober look at itself, find out where it is going, what services it should be providing to members. Personally, I don't believe I have ever been as frustrated in any position I've held as the present one."[9] Long-time member and Ottawa branch president Alixe Carson Carter chimed in, observing that since newspaperwomen had become a minority among a membership of freelance, public relations, and advertising writers, it was not really a press club at all. Should we call ourselves a "communications club?" she asked. "Perhaps we should disband and amalgamate with the men's press clubs. But are they worth joining? How professional are they? Are they not merely social clubs with everyone and his dog and his flea belonging to pay the bills?"[10] In the end, the members of the Canadian Women's Press Club decided to adapt to the times. Recognizing that they were no longer a press club, they changed their name in 1971 to the Media Club of Canada and opened their doors to qualified male members.[11] In smaller centres, men joined the Media Club, but in cities the flow was the other way as newswomen joined the formerly all-male clubs.[12]

Although social egalitarianism was now more visible, thoroughgoing integration remained elusive. Women still dominated the lower-status "soft news" categories.[13] When the CWPC surveyed women journalists in 1964, it found that although most of them were mature career women who had an average of fourteen and a half years in the business, two out of three felt underpaid for what they did and one-third were anxious for promotion.[14] Few of them realized their ambition. Gertrude Robinson reported in 1977 that women constituted less than 1 per cent of day and night editors, managing editors, and chief editors.[15]

In 1982 Andrea Nugent analysed the malaise of women in Canada's communications industry. As she justified her attention to media women, she unconsciously echoed what Charlotte Whitton had urged half a century earlier. In 1923 Charlotte Whitton had encouraged the women of Canada to pay special attention to the status of presswomen because of their importance in raising the public profile of women. Nugent's concern was more egalitarian: "It is important to know what is happening to women professionals in communications because this industry has an impact on virtually everyone in Canada ... The status of women in this field should be investigated not only in terms of better job opportunities, but in terms of their potential ability to redefine reality by influencing media content."[16] Her conclusions reflected soberly on the link between media perceptions of women and the status of women in media-related jobs, which remained stubbornly low.

The story of the women who continued the struggle for acceptance in the news world after the Second World War warrants further study. What emerges from the fragments of analysis available is a sense that women entering the field in the second half of the twentieth century made their way without any sense of a female tradition in journalism. They had to cut their paths anew – as a new generation of pioneers as if no other women had come before. Observing newswomen of the 1950s and 1960s, historian Julia Edwards commented, "Aspiring journalists did not know enough of the achievements of women in their profession to build on them or even to approach the job market with any confidence."[17]

There seemed to be little reverence for women already in journalism among the crop of young newspaperwomen entering well after the war. Heather Robertson, starting out on the *Winnipeg Free Press,* shuddered as she surveyed her companion on the rewrite desk – "a gaunt, weathered, sad-eyed woman with bright orange hair, bright orange lipstick on one side of her mouth and a cigarette in the other." Discovering that the older woman was employed by the newspaper out of charity because her *Free Press* husband had been killed in the war did little for Robertson's confidence as a newswoman: "The newsroom was full of these people, widows, old girlfriends, meek, battered women who came and went so silently, so humbly, their presence, or absence, was scarcely noticed. Was this where I would be in forty years.?"[18] This was the newspaper of Cora Hind, Kennethe Haig, Lillian Beynon, and Dora Dibney. Leaving the *Free Press* "freaks" behind, Robertson's initiation on the Winnipeg *Tribune* was more fun but no more heartening to an ambitious youngster: "It had been customary to measure the talent of female staff members at the *Tribune* by the size of their bra cups."[19]

Women such as Heather Robertson were convinced that her generation was utterly different from the newspaperwomen of the past: "We were cool, university-educated daughters of the middle class ... Refugees from marriage and the tedious female professions of school teaching and social work ... We were the first of the formidable feminists."[20] They revelled in the excitement of the newsroom and emulated the bohemianism that newsmen had always cultivated. Most of all, they were grateful to escape the "jealousies of the Woman's editor."[21] Yet they were aware of the pitfalls that lay in wait for women – "Goody Two-Shoes assignments ... being a hearse chaser or a vamp" – and they nurtured the ambition to "change the script," to make newspaper work a profession in which women could advance without becoming "one of the boys."[22] It was a noble ideal, to be sure, and one that bore a striking resemblance to the conviction of an earlier generation of well-educated feminists, who also had been fleeing female professions or failed marriages, that they could and would "improve the status of journalism as a profession for women." The women of 1904 had wanted to change the script too.

When the notion of a section devoted to women's interests was still novel, some presswomen had eagerly seized the chance to serve a female readership. With the power and authority of the press behind them, they believed that their journalism would advance the status of all women by promoting and publicizing what women were doing. As women gained political rights, the newswomen hoped to educate this constituency, interpreting public affairs in ways that uniquely suited women readers. Even the society column, despised as it was in some quarters, underscored the social power of women, while the economic power of women was made obvious by the attention advertisers lavished on the women's section and the volumes of advice journalists doled out to guide female consumers. Although women's page editors laboured under numerous burdens, not least of which was lack of respect from their colleagues, the women's sections were often the most interesting departments of the newspaper, because they potentially allowed for in-depth stories on issues that fascinated a great many people.[23]

Notwithstanding the vital work that women's page editors accomplished in some jurisdictions, the shortcomings of traditional women's sections disappointed some presswomen, while the constraints stifled others. Newswomen ambitious to make their way tried to avoid or escape work on the women's page, as if it would somehow taint their reputation. The sense that "real" news was what broke from the city room or took place overseas perennially lured the most adventurous away from the women's department. Time and again, those who evaded the women's section had to prove themselves up to the task as defined by newsmen and learn to apply news values developed by newsmen. For the most part, they kept quiet about whatever dilemmas they encountered by being both a woman and a successful journalist. Thus, the heritage of their experience was lost to the women who came later, who charted the same territory but without signposts and, as one American journalist put it, "adrift in history."[24]

Musing on the occasion of the CWPC Vancouver branch's fiftieth anniversary, reporter and columnist Nikki Moir noted that "there was nothing that the press women of today" did that women such as Edna Brown, who covered a hanging in New Brunswick in 1909, had not done before them.[25] It was a familiar refrain among the oldtimers. As one CWPC historian sighed, "We are really glutted with pioneers in our profession."[26] Her conclusion added a sobering note: "All our honorary members were very famous *at the time*. Yet who remembers them now?"[27]

Notes

AO	Archives of Ontario
CEA	City of Edmonton Archives
CVA	City of Vancouver Archives
CWPC	Canadian Women's Press Club
GFC	Glenbow Foundation, Calgary
HPLSP	Hamilton Public Library, Special Collections
MCC	Media Club of Canada
MTLBR	Metropolitan Toronto Library, Baldwin Room
NA	National Archives of Canada
PAM	Provincial Archives of Manitoba
QUA	Queen's University Archives
SAB	Saskatchewan Archives Board
UA	University of Alberta, Bruce Peel Special Collections Library
UBSCP	University of British Columbia, Special Collections
UWSP	University of Waterloo, Special Collections

CHAPTER ONE

1 National Council of Women, *National Council of Women of Canada Yearbook* 1923, 118.
2 See, for instance, Massey, *Occupations for Trained Women in Canada,* and MacMurchy, *The Canadian Girl at Work.*
3 Canada, Dominion Bureau of Statistics, *Sixth Census of Canada, 1921* (hereafter *Census of Canada*), vol. 4, table 1, "Occupations of the Population, 10 Years of Age and Over by Sex," for Canada 1881, 1891, 1901, 1911, and 1921.

4 Ibid. The total number of "Editors and Reporters" enumerated in 1921 was 1,914. In that same census 49,795 female teachers were recorded and 21,162 nurses and nurses in training.

5 Strong-Boag, *The New Day Recalled,* 42.

6 Nancy Cott observed that the presence of women in professions, where they became "arbiters of custom and convention," was perhaps even more strategically important than the attainment of political rights (*The Grounding of Modern Feminism,* 215). For a thorough and thoughtful analysis of women's experience in the professions in Manitoba, see Kinnear, *In Subordination.*

7 See Prentice et al., *Canadian Women,* chapters 5–11, for an overview of changes in the situation of Canadian women from the late nineteenth century to the first half of the twentieth century.

8 Ibid., 115.

9 Fetherling, *The Rise of the Canadian Newspaper,* 102.

10 Considering how famous some of these women were in their own day, it is surprising that a only handful of biographical studies of Canadian women journalists have appeared, most of them very recent, and most puzzling is the paradox that their once-famous subject have been forgotten. See, for instance, Downie, *A Passionate Pen;* Fowler, *Redney: A Life of Sara Jeannette Duncan;* Freeman, *Kit's Kingdom,* as well as numerous studies of Nellie McClung and Emily Murphy, whose contributions to journalism formed part of a larger commitment to reform. See also Burkholder, *"Kit" Kathleen Blake Coleman;* Cochrane, *Kate Aitken;* Ferguson, *Kit Coleman, Queen of Hearts;* MacGill, *My Mother the Judge;* and the biographies of E. Cora Hind cited below. Bannerman's *Leading Ladies: Canada 1639–1967* includes a number of women journalists in the company of other Canadian women.

11 Journalists comprised fully one-quarter of the suffrage leadership (Bacchi, *Liberation Deferred?* 6, table 1). Although Bacchi does not analyse the contribution of journalists per se to reform movements, other historians do. See Gorham, "Flora MacDonald Denison: Canadian Feminist," and Cook, "Francis Marion Beynon and the Crisis of Christian Reformism." Jackel analyses a consciously constructed network of prominent women journalists in "First Days, Fighting Days: Prairie Presswomen and Suffrage Activism 1906–1916." Women journalists involved in peace activism are analysed by Roberts, "Women against War, 1914–1918: Francis Beynon and Laura Hughes," and Gorham "Vera Brittain, Flora MacDonald Denison and the Great War: The Failure of Non-Violence." Barber notes the engagement of Winnipeg women journalists with immigration and the welfare of servants in "The Servant Problem in Manitoba 1896–1930." Western women journalists were also the subject of Gorham's "Pen and Buckskin: Women Journalists Who Knew Wheat and Justice."

12 Comparatively little research has been done on the history of women in journalism in any nation, but a significant body of work has been assembled on American women journalists in recent years. See Marzolf, *Up from the Footnote*, and Beasley and Gibbons, *Taking Their Place*. For an overview of some British and American reporters, see Sebba, *Battling for News*. Australian women journalists are surveyed in Clarke, *Pen Portraits*.

13 Wendy Mitchinson summarizes the body of literature on women and industrialization thus: "the general conclusion being that it segregated them" ("Women's History," 214).

14 Female names are absent or figure only in the most minor way in the histories and memoirs written by most male journalists of the late nineteenth and early twentieth centuries. A standard source on Canadian newspaper history, written under the auspices of the Canadian Press Association (Craik, *A History of Canadian Journalism*, vol. 2) barely mentions a single woman's name – though this is perhaps understandable, since the Canadian Press Association by the twentieth century represented publishers, and very few women published daily newspapers. The more readable work, Kesterton's *History of Journalism in Canada*, spends less than two pages on the "women's pages," significantly just before giving a similarly brief discussion of advertising. Women's names appear only in lists of columnists associated with particular papers. Great men of the press rarely focused on their female colleagues as they reflected on their careers. J.S. Willison, for example, employed some of the best newspaperwomen in Canadian history for the *Globe* and *News*, and his wife, Marjory MacMurchy, was among the most famous women journalists of her day, yet he hardly mentions a female name in his memoir, *Reminiscences Political and Personal*. Orlo Miller in *A Century of Western Ontario: The Story of London, "The Free Press," and Western Ontario, 1849–1949*, mentions Grace Blackburn only in passing and completely ignores Susan Blackburn, despite the fact that both women regularly wrote the editorials and that Grace singlehandedly ran the women's section and wrote the art and theatre reviews of the family-run paper. Stuart Keate ignores most of the women he worked alongside in Vancouver and Toronto, except for a female sportswriter whom he snidely assumes to have had "a direct pipeline to the executive suite" (*Paper Boy*, 21). The invisibility of women in conventional journalism history inspired the title of Marion Marzolf's pioneering history of women in American journalism, *Up from the Footnote*.

15 Empire building forms the main preoccupation of biographical studies of the great men of Canadian newspaper history. See, for instance, Harkness, *J.E. Atkinson of the Star*, in which the many women Atkinson worked are very much bit players. The once-famous Elmira Elliott (Madge Merton) is important only when she marries Atkinson. Similarly, Mary Dawson Snider, an enterprising reporter in the early part of

the century, is introduced primarily as the wife of C.H.J. Snider, editor
of the Toronto *Telegram* (Poulton, *The Paper Tyrant*, 201). Robert Fulford
does not mention that his first mother-in-law was the very successful
journalist Isabel Turnbull Dingman in his memoir, *The Best Seat in the
House*. Nor do presswomen figure in I. Norman Smith, *The Journal Men*.

16 Good, *Acquainted with the Night*.

17 Biographies of E.Cora Hind began to appear shortly after her death, the
first by her good friend and fellow journalist, Kennethe Haig, *Brave
Harvest*. See also Carlotta Hacker, *E. Cora Hind*.

18 Covert, "Journalism History and Women's Experience," 4.

19 Scanlon, *Inarticulate Longings*, 10.

20 Boyce et al., *Newspaper History*, 13.

21 For an account of the rise of mass-circulation newspapers, see Baldasty,
Commercialization of News, Lee, *Origins of the Popular Press in England*,
Schiller, *Objectivity and the News*, and Schudson, *Discovering the News*.
While women do not figure significantly in any of these studies, they es-
tablish the social and intellectual context of women's entry in journal-
ism.

22 The most comprehensive analyses of the transformation of the Canadian press are Rutherford, *A Victorian Authority*, and Sotiron, *From Politics
to Profit*. For a lively overview, see Fetherling, *The Rise of the Canadian
Newspaper*.

23 Desbarats, *Guide to Canadian News Media*, 1.

24 Rutherford, *Making of the Canadian Media*, 60.

25 Heilbrun, *Writing a Woman's Life*, 40.

26 Rutherford, *Making of the Canadian Media*, 54–8. For a discussion of
objectivity as an ideology and mythology, see Schudson, *Discovering the
News*.

27 Desbarats, *Guide to Canadian News Media*, 123

28 Ibid., 121.

29 This was the title of Ackerman's 1949 lecture on the complementary
roles of men and women in newspaper work (reprinted in Beasley and
Gibbons, *Taking Their Place*, 177–8).

30 Jackel, "First Days, Fighting Days."

31 The concept of "subpowers" exercised by ostensibly oppressed groups
provides a possible way of understanding the limited autonomy of
women journalists in their own women's departments. See Iacovetta and
Valverde, *Gender Conflicts*, xviii.

32 Beasley and Gibbons, *Taking Their Place*, 2.

33 Cited by MacEwan, ... *And Mighty Women Too*, 171.

34 Desbarats, *Guide to Canadian News Media*, 97. The same assumptions operate in the United States. See Richards and Young, *Women on the Deadline*, xiii.

35 Marjory MacMurchy, "Journalism and Literature: Books of the Year by Canadian Women," in Weaver et al., *The Canadian Woman's Annual and Social Service Directory*, 200.

36 Rutherford, *Making of the Canadian Media*, 45. For an overview of Canadian magazines, see Sutherland, *The Monthly Epic*.

37 In order to chart the evolution of women's pages in Canadian periodicals, a small sample of urban dailies that hired significant numbers of women and represented both the popular and "highbrow" styles were surveyed for four weeks per year, twice per decade, according to the duration of the women's section in each. These include the Toronto *Globe* (later *Globe and Mail*) and *Toronto Star*, the Vancouver *Province*, and the *Vancouver Sun*. Other newspapers and magazines that hired significant numbers of women were scanned extensively but less systematically (see bibliography). Clipping files in the papers of individual journalists were also a useful source of the writing they produced.

38 The task of reconstructing an individual biography from clues planted in newspaper columns is a daunting one. Fowler (*Redney*), Freeman (*Kit's Kingdom*), and Downie (*A Passionate Pen*) all rely on their subject's newspaper writing for want of more straightforward biographical information. Freeman is particularly alert to her subject's literary "self-creation," while the others are inclined to extrapolate biographical "fact" from what might well be posturing. Deborah Gorham's fascinating study of the life of Vera Brittain, a well-known British novelist and journalist, is made possible by Brittain's extensive body of self-reflective work. Gorham sensitively tests Brittain's autobiographical creations against her diaries, letters, and fiction to showcase a consciously self-constructed life (*Vera Brittain: A Feminist Life*).

39 Howard Good analyses the autobiographical impulse among a number of American journalists in *The Journalist as Autobiographer*, but the only women in his survey share a chapter. Among the Canadian women journalists who have written memoirs are Arnold, *One Woman's War*, Boultbee, *Pilgrimages and Personalities*, Carter, *Stop the Press!* Cash, *Off the Record*, and Dempsey, *No Life for a Lady*. Madge Macbeth packaged her life in rather glamorous and amusing terms in *Boulevard Career* and *Over My Shoulder*. Hewlett's *A Too Short Yesterday* changes the places and names associated with her early life as a prairie bride writing for various newspapers. Francis Beynon's *Aleta Dey* is a novel that reconstructs some of the more dramatic episodes of her career as a journalist in Winnipeg.

40 Heilbrun, *Writing a Woman's Life*, 13. Heilbrun also notes (24–5) how women's letters offer a contrasting narrative to the lives they present to a wider public.

41 Quoted by Rex, *No Daughter of Mine*, 63.

42 Kinnear (*In Subordination*, 152) points out the difficulty of trying to create a composite type out of the variety of professional women's lives.

43 *Census of Canada, 1921*, vol. 4, table 1.

44 In small centres where not many journalists worked, librarians and journalists were, for some reason, classed together. For instance, ten women were given as librarians and editors in Halifax in 1921 (*Census of Canada, 1921*, vol. 4, table 40).

45 See "Introduction to the Seventh Census of Canada," *Census of Canada, 1931*, vol. 5, xv, which excludes "own account" workers, employers, and unpaid workers from its category "wage earners." The category "wage earners," however, probably included the small number of women who worked as editors for publishing houses and were not strictly "journalists."

46 Margo Anderson discusses the general ideological inconsistencies in historical statistics about women, in "The History of Women and the History of Statistics," 14–36.

47 *Census of Canada, 1941*, vol. 7, table 5, shows that 88.7% of the 1,330 librarians, 81.45% of the 1,251 social workers, and 90% of the 26,473 graduate nurses were single. As well, 91.6% of 384 female professors and college principals and 93% of 64,465 female teachers were unmarried – not surprisingly, given the restrictions on married women teachers. Women in male-dominated professions were less overwhelmingly unmarried: of the 384 female physicians and surgeons, 62.7% were single, as were 71.3% of the 129 female lawyers.

48 Based on figures from series D107–22, *Historical Statistics of Canada*, 2nd edn, ed. F.H. Leacy (Ottawa: Statistics Canada 1983).

49 In 1931, 142 of the 2,880 male journalists were over sixty-five, compared with 24 of the 464 female journalists (*Census of Canada, 1931*, vol. 7, table 41). By the time of the 1941 census (vol. 7, table 5), 188 of 3,434 male journalists were over 65 compared to 36 of 713 female journalists.

50 *Census of Canada, 1941*, vol. 7, table 5. Of 713 gainfully employed women authors, editors, and journalists, 297 (41.7%) had thirteen years or more of education. Of the men, out of a total of 3,434 1,394 (40.5%) were in school thirteen or more years.

51 *Census of Canada, 1931*, vol. 6, table 28.

52 *Census of Canada, 1941*, vol. 6, table 6.

53 See bibliography for private manuscript collections consulted for the project.

54 Desbarats (*Guide to the Canadian Media*, 105–6), suggests that the reluctance of journalists to submit to investigation stemmed partly from the competitiveness of the business.

55 In 1971 the Canadian Women's Press Club changed its name to the Media Club of Canada and admitted men into the membership. The

National Archives of Canada catalogues the records of the club under its modern name. In 1993 the dwindling membership decided to return to its original name, the Canadian Women's Press Club (Rex, *No Daughter of Mine*, 271).

56 Cited by Ruth Roach Pierson, "Experience, Difference, Dominance, and Voice in the Writing of Canadian Women's History," 91.

57 Kinnear, *In Subordination*, 24.

58 Henry, "Private Lives: An Added Dimension for Understanding Journalism History," 98–102.

59 In order to qualify as a member, the applicant had to demonstrate that she had been employed on a newspaper for at least twelve months or had published at least ten articles and had been paid at the standard rates by established periodicals. She then served a probationary period of one year. Newspaper illustrators, poets, and authors of recently published books were also eligible if they were sponsored by two newspaperwomen who already were members. By the 1920s, advertising and public relations writers could belong, but they had to have been journalists first. Members had to fill out workforms to maintain their membership, demonstrating that they continued in employment or continued to place the minimum number of articles every year. Membership records identified the category of employment or achievement at regular intervals, usually every three years. For the purposes of this study, a worksheet on each member who qualified and completed her probationary year between 1904 and 1945 was compiled. On the whole, the records are accurate; but inevitably, given the voluntary nature of the club and the magnitude of the national scope it embraced, mistakes and omissions occurred.

60 National Archives of Canada (NA), MG28 I232, Media Club of Canada (MCC), Canadian Women's Press Club (CWPC) Triennial Report 1942, 37.

61 Census figures compared with CWPC membership files lead to a comparison that is less than rigorous because in both cases individuals are included who were not strictly journalists. In 1911 the census enumerated 69 female editors and reporters, whereas CWPC listed 173 active members (including authors and periodical illustrators); the 1921 census counted 248 editors and reporters, while CWPC recorded 302 active members (which now included advertising writers); the 1931 census listed 464 gainfully employed and 357 wage earners (including authors), while CWPC records for 1929 showed 357 active members; the 1941 census listed 713 gainfully employed and 528 wage earners (including authors), while CWPC for 1942 gave 309. The Second World War saw an influx of women into paid writing, but there is little way of knowing how many remained career journalists.

62 Women who had been active members of the club for fifteen or more years could apply for associate membership when they retired. They are designated as such in membership rolls.

63 For women working in socialist periodicals, see Newton, "The Alchemy of Politicization."

64 For the careers of two early francophone journalists, see Boivin and Landy, "Francoise et Madeleine." See also Hamel, *Gaetane de Montreuil,* and Beauchamp, *Judith Jasmin.*

65 Mary Shadd Carey edited a paper for African Americans fleeing the United States. See Bearden and Butler, *Shadd.*

CHAPTER TWO

1 "Louis Lloyd's Letter," *Week,* 14 December 1888.

2 Duncan dispelled the doubts of an uncertain correspondent in the Toronto *Globe,* 23 September 1886.

3 Kroller, *Canadian Travellers to Europe.*

4 E.E. Sheppard, "Around Town," *Saturday Night,* 6 September 1890, 1.

5 Tausky notes that by 1903, *A Social Departure* had sold 16,000 copies in the United States alone (*Sara Jeannette Duncan: Novelist of Empire,* 54).

6 *Census of Canada, 1921,* vol. 4, table 1, includes a retrospective account of "Occupations of the Populations, 10 years of Age and Over by Sex," for Canada 1891.

7 National Council of Women, *Women of Canada,* 76.

8 *Saturday Night,* 6 September 1890, 1. Fowler (*Redney,* 51) refers to this incident. At this point, Duncan was still Sarah Janet Duncan.

9 Chenier, "Agnes Maule Machar," and Roberts and Tunnell., *A Standard Dictionary of Canadian Biography,* 314–15.

10 Vancouver *News-Herald,* 17 May 1934.

11 National Archives of Canada (NA), MG28 I232, Media Club of Canda (MCC), vol. 23, file 2, "Newspacket," 8, no. 3 (15 May 1942): 2.

12 Ibid., 1 March 1938, 2. This article also tells the story of Frances Ann Turner Gowan, who carried on her husband's Brockville paper while he was attending sessions of Parliament in Ottawa and Toronto.

13 Well-known examples include Nicholas Flood Davin, founder of the Regina *Leader* and later a Conservative MP; Andrew Patullo, publisher of the Woodstock *Sentinel-Review* and member of the Ontario legislature. In the West, Francis Carter Cotton sat in the B.C. provincial legislature for most of the years he was proprietor of the Vancouver *News-Advertiser.* Civil service appointments allowed literary newspapermen to thrive. See Fetherling, *The Rise of the Canadian Newspaper,* 74.

14 Charlesworth, *More Candid Chronicles,* 144.

15 Cited in Fowler, *Redney,* 267.

16 "Woman's Kingdom," Toronto *Mail and Empire*, 1 December 1900.

17 Rutherford *(A Victorian Authority)* and Sotiron *(From Politics to Profit)* analyse these changes and the rise of newspaper entrepreneurs.

18 Fetherling, *The Rise of the Canadian Newspaper*, 75–7.

19 J.E. Atkinson made the *Toronto Star* into one of the biggest and richest papers in Canada precisely by following this formula (Cranston, *Ink on My Fingers*).

20 Cited by Downie, *Passionate Pen*, 161.

21 Schudson, *Discovering the News*, 26.

22 "Around Town," *Saturday Night*, 6 September 1890, 1.

23 Charlesworth, *Candid Chronicles*, 89; Willard and Livermore, *American Women*, 761.

24 "Prominent Women, no. 17: Madge Merton," *Ladies' Pictorial Weekly: A Newspaper for the Women of North America*, 16 July 1892.

25 *Canadian Printer and Publisher*, May 1892, cited in Chalmers, *A Gentleman of the Press*, 52.

26 "The Old Organ Grinder," *Saturday Night*, 10 August 1889, 8; "The French Revolution," *Saturday Night*, 17 August 1889, 3.

27 Charlesworth, *Candid Chronicles*, 95.

28 NA, MG29 D112, Kathleen Blake Coleman Papers, vol. 1, file 4, Wilfrid Laurier to Kathleen Blake Watkins, 24 July 1907.

29 Ferguson, *Kit Coleman, Queen of Hearts*, 11. Kit's department was swamped with letters from readers and soon took on an agony column function in addition to her feature articles and essays.

30 Roberts, "'Rocking the Cradle for the World.'"

31 In 1881 Sarah Anne Curzon was associate editor of *Canada Citizen*, a prohibition paper. Sarah Anne Herbert began *The Olive Branch* even earlier for similar motives.

32 Mitchinson, "The W.C.T.U."

33 Provincial Archives of Manitoba (PAM), Florence Randal Livesay Papers, folder 4, scrapbook of South Africa, contains clippings of her weekly letters to the *Journal* during 1902 and 1903. See also Gwyn, *The Private Capital*, 371–9.

34 Archives of Ontario (AO), M.O. Hammond Papers, box 2, "Ninety Years of the *Globe*" (typescript), 196.

35 White, "A Decade of American Journalism."

36 W.C. Brann, "Women in Journalism," *Iconoclast* [c. 1890s]; reprinted in *Matrix* 17, no. 6 (August 1932): 13.

37 Alden, "Women in Journalism," 209.

38 Ross, *Ladies of the Press*, 17.

39 See Banks, *Campaigns of Curiosity*, 215–24 for a defence of yellow journalism. Banks, a mainstream journalist who dallied briefly among the tabloids, relished doing stories about the sweat shops and factories of the

east side. Ultimately, she argued, her "descent" into yellow journalism made her grow in charity and "out of the narrow minded creeds she had been brought up in."

40 For instance, the *Montreal Star* in 1883 cooperated with the city police to expose a notorious clothing shark racket (Mahaffy, "The Tradition Makers," 10–11).

41 Downie, The Passionate Pen, 9.

42 "Prominent Women no. 17: Madge Merton," *Ladies' Pictorial Weekly,* 16 July 1892.

43 Cranston, *Ink on My Fingers,* 83–4.

44 Ella S. Atkinson (Madge Merton), "Nondescript," *Canadian Magazine,* May 1896, 181.

45 Marzolf, *Up From the Footnote,* 23–4.

46 Goodwin, "The Early Journalism of Sara Jeannette Duncan," 48.

47 Mahaffy, "The Tradition Makers," 10–11.

48 *Journalist,* 29 May 1886, cited in Goodwin, "The Early Journalism of Sara Jeannette Duncan," 44.

49 Charlesworth, "The Canadian Girl," 191.

50 Tausky, *Sara Jeannette Duncan: Selected Journalism,* 50.

51 Ibid., 49–50.

52 Roberts and Tunnell, *A Standard Dictionary of Canadian Biography,* 228.

53 Willard and Livermore's entry on Wetherald noted, "Although a Canadian by birth and citizenship, she is, by training, intellectual development and literary clientage, quite American" (*American Women,* 762).

54 AO, Sanford Papers, correspondence, Mary Elizabeth McOuat to Mary Bouchier Sanford, n.d.

55 Harte, "Canadian Journalists and Journalism," 433.

56 Bayard, "Eve Brodlique," 516.

57 White "A Decade of American Journalism," 850–62.

58 Eggleston, *While I Still Remember,* 144.

59 Harte, "Canadian Journalists and Journalism," 433.

60 Low, *Press Work for Women,* 51.

61 Chenier, "Agnes Maule Machar."

62 AO, Sanford Papers, Laura Durand to Mary Bouchier Sanford, 1 April 1897.

63 Ibid.

64 Harkness, *J.E. Atkinson of the Star,* 44.

65 Gilbert and Gubar, *No Man's Land,* vol. 1 (New Haven: Yale University Press 1987), 241, cited by Heilbrun, *Writing a Woman's Life,* 110.

66 AO, Sanford Papers, Mrs J.C. Croly to Mary Bouchier Sanford, 8 February 1891.

67 National Council of Women, *Women of Canada,* 80. Sandra Gwyn pursues

the elusive Amaryllis in far more entertaining and enlightening fashion (*The Private Capital*, 471–83).

68 Haig, *Brave Harvest*, 51–2.

69 Schudson (*Discovering the News*, 73–5) describes how the idea of "scientific observation" underlay the reporter's creed of objectivity, and he notes that some of the best turn-of-the-century American novelists, including Willa Cather, Jack London, and Theodore Dreiser, sought journalistic experience. Sara Jeannette Duncan has been identified as the most "prominent defender and proponent of literary realism in Canada" (Gerson, *A Purer Taste*), 52.

70 Tausky (*Sara Jeannette Duncan: Novelist of Empire*) traces how the topics of Duncan's journalism foreshadow themes she developed in her novels.

71 "How an American Girl Became a Journalist," in Tausky, *Sara Jeannette Duncan: Selected Journalism*, 6–13. There is no place or date of publication for this manuscript, so it is impossible to determine at what stage in her career Duncan wrote it.

72 During her travels in 1889, Duncan met Everard Charles Cotes, who at the time was working as an entomologist for the Indian Museum at Calcutta. She married him in 1890 and spent most of her life in India.

73 Stevenson, "From Fort Garry, West," 68.

74 Queen's University Archives, QUA, Campbell Papers, box 9, file 3, Ethelwyn Wetherald to W.W. Cambell, 10 February 1896.

75 "Reminiscences of the Poet," in Garvin, *Lyrics and Sonnets*, xvi.

76 O'Hagan, "Some Canadian Women Writers," 713.

77 [Professor James A. Spencelevy] in Roberts and Tunnell, *A Standard Dictionary of Canadian Biography*, 34–5.

78 QUA, Pierce Papers, box 1, file 11, Arthur Stringer to Lorne Pierce, 14 February 1924.

79 Miller, *A Century of Western Ontario*, 227.

80 Grace Blackburn seems to have kept her two identities separate since, in a letter to fellow writer and journalist Madge MacBeth, she had to explain that "Grace Blackburn the poetess and Grace Blackburn the newspaper woman are one and the same person" (NA, MG30 D52, Macbeth Papers, vol. 1, Grace Blackburn to Madge Macbeth, 30 July 1917).

81 AO, Sanford Papers, Laura Durand to Mary Bouchier Sanford, 1 April 1897.

82 "Mrs. Blewett has the truest and most sympathetic touch of any Canadian woman writer of to-day" (O'Hagan, "Some Canadian Women Writers," 793). O'Hagan omitted any mention of Durand, which may have accounted for her contempt for his opinions.

83 Bayard, "Eve Brodlique," 517–18.

84 Bannerman, *Leading Ladies*, 84.

85 See Mitchell, "Careers for Girls: Writing Trash," 109–13, for an amusing

account of how girls who wanted to write for a living were advised away from journalism and into serial story writing by turn-of-the century British advisers.

86 PAM, Livesay Papers, folder 3, diary 1904, 15 September 1904.
87 AO, Sanford Papers, Mary McOuat to Mary Bouchier Sanford, n.d.
88 [Mack], "Salaries Paid to Journalists in Canada," *Saturday Night*, 14 October 1899, 7.
89 Katherine Hale, "A Well Loved Journalist," *Canadian Courier*, 22 May 1915.
90 NA, MG29 D112, Coleman Papers, vol. 2, file 33, *Edmonton Journal*, 21 May 1915.
91 Marjory MacMurchy, *Toronto News*, 17 May 1915. Although MacMurchy does not name her, the journalist referred to was almost certainly Eve Brodlique, who so often praised Kit in her columns for the Chicago *Times-Journal.*
92 See NA, MG29 D112, Coleman Papers, vol. 2, files 13–18, for a manuscript of her unfinished "Irish novel."
93 AO, Sanford Papers, Kathleen Blake Watkins (later Coleman) to Mary Bouchier Sanford, 22 March 1897.
94 NA, MG30 D29, Willison Papers, vol. 3, file 63, Kit Coleman to John Willison, 13 October 1899.
95 NA, MG30 D29, Willison Papers, vol. 3, file 29, Jean Blewett to Willison, 28 August 1905.
96 Cranston, *Ink on My Fingers*, 34.
97 AO, Hammond Papers, env. 2, Ethelwyn Wetherald to M.O. Hammond, 23 February 1928.
98 QUA, Thomson Papers, box 34, file 16, E.W. Thomson to Wetherald [c. 1896].
99 "Earnings of Newspaper Writers," *Saturday Night*, 22 June 1889, 3, reported stratospheric sums earned by American writers.
100 Bok, "Is the Newspaper Office the Place for a Girl?" 18.
101 "Reminscences of the Poet," in Garvin, *Lyrics and Sonnets*, xvi.
102 Rutherford, *A Victorian Authority*, 81.
103 "Woman's World," Toronto *Globe*, 25 January 1887.
104 Ridley, "The Dual Struggle," 2.
105 "Driftwood," Toronto *Globe*, 7 May 1904.
106 NA, MG30 D29, Willison Papers, vol. 14, file 112, Mary Agnes Fitzgibbon to J.S. Willison, 30 November 1906.
107 "Newspacket," 9, no. 5 (November 1942): 2.
108 Having moved to Victoria, she was once again begging Willison for work, hoping that she could make $20 a week with steady employment (NA, MG30 D29, Willison Papers, Fitzgibbon to Willison, 24 August [c. 1908]).
109 Vancouver *World*, 22 June 1895. The social correspondent (probably

Sara McLagan) described Cummings as "a widow lady who earns her livelihood by her pen."

110 Metropolitan Toronto Library, Baldwin Room (MTLBR), Burpee Papers, Kate Simpson Hayes to Lawrence Burpee, 29 November 1898.

111 MacAree, *The Fourth Column*, 296.

112 NA, MG30 D29, Willison Papers, vol. 9, file 73, Kit Coleman to J.W. Willison, 1 Dec 1901.

113 NA, MG29 D112, Coleman Papers, vol. 1, scrapbook, Stinson Jarvis, "Newspaper Women," *Frank Leslie's Weekly*, 23 June 1892, describes an unnamed newspaperwoman who had raised the circulation of her newspaper by at least one-third. The journalist was almost certainly Kit, for the article was included in Coleman's personal clippings scrapbook with the passages describing her heavily scored. Wollock ("Did Stinson Jarvis Hypnotize "Kit of the Mail?") speculates about the relationship between these two journalists.

114 Brown, *The Correspondents' War*, describes the newspaper context of the Spanish-American War.

115 Rowland, "Kit Watkins," 15.

116 Most estimates of Kit's salary assume that $35 per week was her peak, but exact figures must be treated cautiously since little evidence supports various speculations. See the discussion and sources culled by Freeman, *Kit's Kingdom*, 10.

117 QUA, Lorne Pierce Collection, Garvin Papers, box 32, file 8, Kit Coleman to Katherine Hale [Mrs Garvin], n.d.

118 Toronto *Mail*, 27 December 1890.

119 NA, MG29 D112, Coleman Papers, vol. 2, file 34, "'Kit': Kathleen Blake Coleman, Pioneer Canadian Newspaperwoman," pamphlet prepared by Hamilton Branch of CWPC, 12.

120 Low, *Press Work for Women*, 3.

121 There is some inconsistency with dates. Most sources indicate that she began on the Toronto *Globe* in February 1894. Yet Durand was already established on the *Globe* by 1893, according to a letter that Constance Boulton wrote to Mary Bouchier Sanford, 12 June 1893 (AO, Sanford Papers). In 1897 Laura Durand sent Sanford a character estimate from John Willison which testifies to seven years' experience on the *Globe* (AO, Sanford Papers, Laura Durand to Sanford, 22 April 1897).

122 AO, Sanford Papers, Mrs Willoughby Cummings to Sanford, 17 November 1897.

123 AO, Sanford Papers, Laura Durand to Sanford, 22 April 1897, enclosing endorsement by Willison.

124 AO, Sanford Papers, Constance Boulton to Sanford, 12 June 1893.

125 AO, Sanford Papers, Laura Durand to Sanford, 22 April 1897.

126 Ibid., 10 March 1897.

127 Ibid.

128 Morgan, *Types of Canadian Woman*, 99.

129 Wachter, "Ethel M. Arnold."

130 Low, *Press Work for Women*, 12.

131 AO, Sanford Papers, Durand to Sanford, 1 April 1897.

132 NA, MG30 D29, Willison Papers, vol. 12, file 102, Laura Durand to John Willison, 9 March 1901.

133 Ibid., Willison to Laura Durand, 6 April 1901.

134 Ibid.

135 QUA, Thomson Papers, box 34, file 16, E.W. Thomson to Ethelwyn Wetherald, 27 January 1911.

136 Rutherford, *Making of the Canadian Media*, 54.

137 Harte, "Canadian Journalists and Journalism," 466.

138 Stursberg's *Extra!* extends the tradition into the 1930s.

139 NA, MG30 D29, Willison Papers, vol. 22, file 168, Marie Joussaye to Willison, 9 June 1902.

140 Sheppard, *Saturday Night*, 6 September 1890, 1.

141 G.H.P., "Young Women as Journalists," 396.

142 Dougall, *The Madonna of a Day: A Study*.

143 Ibid., 12.

144 Bok, "Is the Newspaper Office the Place for a Girl?" 18.

145 Scanlon, *Inarticulate Longings*, argues that Bok opposed women's rights in general and women in the paid labour force in particular.

146 AO, Sanford Papers, Mary Elizabeth McOuat to Sanford, n.d.

147 AO, Sanford Papers, Constance Boulton to Mary Bouchier Sanford, 12 June 1893.

148 Ferguson, *Kit Coleman, Queen of Hearts*, 2.

149 Freeman (*Kit's Kingdom*, 29–32) describes Kit's irreverent exploitation of her reader's speculations about herself.

150 AO, Hammond Papers, "Ninety Years of the Globe," (unpub. mss) 172.

151 NA, MG30 D29, Willison Papers, vol. 14, file 112, Fitzgibbon to Willison, 19 September 1902.

152 Toronto *Globe*, 4 April 1903.

153 NA, MG29 D112, Coleman Papers, vol. 2, file 40, contains a genealogy of Coleman which Robin Rowland obtained in 1978. Kit's personal myth making is a major theme in the biography by Freeman (*Kit's Kingdom*).

154 Brown, *The Correspondents' War*, 210–11.

155 Toronto *Mail and Empire*, 18 May 1898.

156 Toronto *Globe*, 11 June 1898.

157 Bennett, *Journalism for Women*, 11.

158 "Driftwood," Toronto *Globe*, 7 May 1904.

159 *Montreal Star*, 25 January 1888, reprinted in Tausky, *Sara Jeannette Duncan: Selected Journalism*, 49–50.

160 *Manitoba Free Press,* 28 February 1890.

161 NA, MG29 D112, Coleman Papers, vol. 1, scrapbook, "Newspaperwomen," *Frank Leslie's Weekly,* 23 June 1892.

162 [Mack], "Salaries Paid to Journalists in Canada," *Saturday Night,* 14 October 1899, 7.

163 Vancouver *World,* 6 April 1895. Douglas Fetherling reinforces this journalist's assumption that the byline was a way of minimizing the owner's responsibility for every opinion printed in his paper. But before the First World War it was an unusual practice for the work of male reporters (*The Rise of the Canadian Newspaper,* 75).

164 Rutherford, *Victorian Authority,* 85.

165 NA, MG29 D112, Coleman Papers, vol. 2, file 37, Mrs. Balmer Watt to Katherine Hale [Amelia Warnock Garvin], [c. 1934].

CHAPTER THREE

1 Sixteen women travelled together to St. Louis. Two more from British Columbia were invited but travelled separately. There were many more women than this active in journalism at the time. The 1901 census listed fifty-two women journalists (*Census of Canada, 1921,* vol. 4, table 1).

2 The only other man admitted to this privilege played a similar guardian angel role towards the end of the club's history as an all-female organization. Dr. Ephraim Herbert Coleman oversaw the passage of the club's formal national incorporation through the Senate in 1958 and was rewarded with honorary membership. The Canadian Women's Press Club became the first and only nationally incorporated association of journalists in Canada on 15 August 1958 (National Archives of Canada [NA], MG28 I232, Media Club of Canada [MCC], vol. 25, file 12, Madeleine Levason to Ted Barr, 26 August 1958).

3 Rex, *No Daughter of Mine,* is an anecdotal sketch of the club and its more prominent members.

4 See above, 000n61, for roughly comparative figures.

5 Marzolf, *Up From the Footnote,* 26, and Beasley, "The Women's National Press Club," 113.

6 Marzolf, *Up From the Footnote,* 26. A Federation of Women's Press Clubs began in Boston in 1891 (Beasley and Gibbons, *Taking Their Place,* 10), but it is not clear whether these organizations existed continuously after their founding.

7 Membership in the Canadian Press Association was initially open to everyone who worked on periodicals in Canada, according to J.H. Cranston, and its purpose was mainly social – to promote understanding and fellowship in the "great journalistic fraternity" (Cranston, *Ink on My Fingers,* 59–60). A few women's names figure on the early lists; most of

these women were editors of very small periodicals, such as Jane Wells Fraser's religious publication, *East and West*. After 1919, when the Canadian Daily Newspaper Association broke away, the concentration on the business interests of proprietors became more pronounced.

8 NA, MCC, vol. 17, file 4, Edna Baker to Kay Mather, 22 May [no year given].

9 "Woman's Kingdom," Toronto *Mail and Empire*, 11 February 1905.

10 Provincial Archives of Manitoba (PAM), Livesay Papers, folder 1, diary, 1902–7.

11 NA, MG29 D112, , Coleman Papers, vol. 1, scrapbook, unidentified clipping [c. June 1906].

12 NA, MG28 I2, Canadian Authors' Association Papers, vol. 2, Price file 39454, Mrs Elizabeth Bailey Price to Mr Kennedy, 20 May 1935.

13 The first printed annual report and all subsequent reports include the constitution, which begins with these objectives. See NA, MCC, vol. 1, file 6, Annual Report 1907–8.

14 See Kinnear, *In Subordination*, for a general discussion of women's entry into professional occupations.

15 Bayard, "Eve Brodlique," 516.

16 Kinnear, *In Subordination*, and Cott, *The Grounding of Modern Feminism*.

17 See, for instance, Smith, *A Woman with a Purpose*, Backhouse, "To Open the Way for Others of My Sex," Hallett, "Nellie McClung and the Fight for the Ordination of Women in the United Church of Canada," and Kinnear, *In Subordination*, for a general overview of women's experience in male-dominated professions in the universities, medicine, and law.

18 See Danylewycz et al., "The Evolution of the Sexual Division of Labour in Teaching," Coburn, "I See and Am Silent," and Struthers,"Lord Give Us Men," in addition to Kinnear, *In Subordination*, for the experience of women in the female professions.

19 Haig, *Brave Harvest*, 14.

20 Archives of Ontario (AO), Sanford Papers, Mary McOuat to Mary Bouchier Sanford, [c. 1893].

21 Bayard, "Eve Brodlique," 517.

22 Dorr, *A Woman of Fifty*, 96.

23 Alden, "Women in Journalism," 209.

24 "The Daily," *Canadian Magazine*, June 1896, 102.

25 For a general discussion of the evolution of the ethos of "objectivity," see Schudson, *Discovering the News*, and Schiller, *Objectivity and the News*.

26 Marzolf, *Civilizing Voices*, 47.

27 Victoria *Colonist*, 21 January 1906, cited by Pazdro, "Agnes Deans Cameron," 116.

28 For instance, the pioneer of the "new journalism" in Britain, W.T. Stead,

suggested the idea of endowed newspapers entirely free of commercial motivation so that journalists could pursue the public interest rather than profit (Boston, "W.T. Stead and Democracy by Journalism," 97). Marzolf, *Civilizing Voices*, surveys the various schemes put forward in the United States to uplift the press, including endowed newspapers, the licensing of journalists, and legal or governmental control.

29 Craik, *A History of Canadian Journalism*, 78.

30 Hamilton,"Canadian Journalism," 19.

31 Lippmann, *Liberty and the News* (New York: Harcourt, Brace, and Howe 1920), cited in Schiller, *Objectivity and the News*, 188.

32 Toronto *News*, n.d., cited in Cranston, *Ink on My Fingers*, 159. Joseph Atkinson was the publisher of the *Toronto Star*. Robinson spoke from personal experience, engaged as she was in trying to keep her own paper, "a shoestring experiment in journalistic honesty," afloat. Ultimately, the *News* closed on 13 April 1946.

33 Sotiron, *From Politics to Profit*, 161.

34 Ibid., 163. Cranston, who knew Atkinson well, was apt to be more understanding than the austere Judith Robinson. Interestingly, Cranston attributed the loss of Atkinson's public-service goals and his submission to Mammon as a consequence of the death of his wife, the journalist Elmira Elliott Atkinson.

35 Rutherford, *A Victorian Authority*, 88.

36 *Week*, 30 September 1886.

37 NA, MG29 D112, Coleman Papers, vol. 3, file 1, scrapbook, undated clipping. The report was in all likelihood written by one of the band in June 1906.

38 NA, MCC, vol. 47, file 9, scrapbook (presented by Pat Groves 1928,) undated clipping, 67.

39 NA, MCC, vol. 1, file 7, Triennial Report 1913–20, "How Foreign News Is Collected in Canada," 62. This "triennial" report encompassed far more than three years because there was no meeting during the First World War.

40 Ibid., "On Interviewing," 61.

41 Ibid., 69.

42 NA, MCC, vol. 1, file 7, Triennial Report 1920–23, "The Ethics of Journalism," 31.

43 Mrs Reginald Smith and Mrs Nease moved the recommendation (NA, MCC, vol. 1, file 7, Triennial Report 1923–26, 10).

44 NA, Ottawa Women's Press Club, vol. 3, scrapbook, *Ottawa Citizen*, 14 November 1928.

45 NA, MCC, vol. 1, file 8, Triennial Report 1929–32, president's address, 32.

46 NA, MCC, "Newspacket," 10, no. 1 (August 1943): 2.

47 E.K.J., "The Women's Quiet Hour," *Western Home Monthly*, July 1906, 85.

48 City of Vancouver Archives (CVA), CWCP, Vancouver Branch Papers, vol. 2, scrapbook no. 1, unidentified clipping, [c. 1923].

49 University of Alberta (UA), Ellis Papers, folder 5, "Canadian Business Women," speech to the Regina Quota Club.

50 NA, MCC, vol. 1, file 7, Triennial Report 1913–20, "On Interviewing," 62.

51 "Guest Editorial," in "Newspacket," 17, no. 6 (March 1953): 3.

52 NA, MCC, vol. 1, file 8, Triennial Report 1935–8, 72.

53 CBC broadcast, 28 September 1944, quoted in "Newspacket," 11, no. 2 (November 1944): 3.

54 NA, MCC, vol. 1, file 6, Constitution of the Canadian Women's Press Club, article 5, section 3.

55 NA, MCC, vol. 1, file 7, Triennial Report 1913–20, 47.

56 PAM, CWPC, Winnipeg Branch Papers, box 1, minute book 1915–22, minutes of the annual general meeting, 20 September1917. Nothing much came of the motion since the Winnipeg branch did not have the power to reject members at the local level. Only the national executive could rule on the membership.

57 Cook, "Francis Marion Beynon and the Crisis of Christian Reformism," 208n40.

58 CVA, CWPC, Vancouver Branch Papers, vol. 1, minute book 1917–21, minutes of meeting 24 June 1921. There was some suggestion that Mrs. Green tyrannized her assistants at the Vancouver *Province* as well as offending her fellow press club members.

59 CVA, CWPC, Vancouver Branch Papers, vol. 1, CWPC Triennial Convention 1923; Vancouver program and promotion booklet, edited with an introduction by Annie Dunn, "All of Us for Each and Each of Us for All."

60 NA, MCC, vol. 1, file 7, Triennial Report 1920–23, 12.

61 Alan J. Lee makes the point that market forces ultimately determined the conduct of newspapers (*The Origins of the Popular Press in England*, 117).

62 PAM, CWPC, Winnipeg Branch, box 6, "On Thinking It Over," unidentified clipping [c. 1958].

63 "To Land's End" [c. 1932], City of Edmonton Archives. Murphy Papers, box 2, cited by Penner, "Emily Murphy and the Attempt to Alter the Status of Canadian Women," 36.

64 NA, MCC, vol. 4, file 31, executive circular, vol. 11, no. 10, 11 December 1935.

65 NA, MCC, vol.6, file 12, Florence Randal Livesay to Mrs James Nairn, 13 January 1947.

66 "Newspacket," 2, no. 2 (February 1936): 2.

67 "Newspacket," 11, no. 3 (March 1945): 1.

68 NA, MCC, vol. 1, file 8, Triennial Report 1932–35, president's address, 52.

69 CVA, CWPC, vol. 1, minutes, 27 May 1921.

70 "Newspacket," 4, no. 4 (September 1938): 3.
71 Ibid., 1.
72 CVA, CWPC, Vancouver Branch, vol. 2, scrapbook, 8.
73 NA, MG30 D29, Willison Papers, vol. 10, file 78, "Journalism," an address delivered before the Political Science Club, University of Toronto, 23 November 1899, 6.
74 "Journalism and the University," *Canadian Magazine,* July 1903, 216.
75 Charles Hands's report on "The Lady War Correspondent and How She Proved Herself One of 'the Boys,'" London *Daily Mail,* 13 June 1898, is cited by Brown, *The Correspondents' War,* 210–11.
76 The British Institute of Journalists attempted to construct an entrance examination that would sort incoming members, but the attempt to regulate new recruits to the field in this fashion ultimately failed (Bainbridge, *One Hundred Years of Journalism,* 54–6).
77 Hosmer, "The Future of the Newspaper Woman," 411.
78 Emilie Peacocke was on the University of London's journalism course committee. She reported university practice in her guidebook, *Writing for Women,* 102–3. A sociologist of education, Ferdina Reinholt, found that U.S. schools of journalism were also considering quotas of female students ("Women in Journalism," 38–41). See also Beasley and Gibbons, *Taking Their Place,* 12–13.
79 James, "What Journalism Schools Teach Women," 3. Helen Wadleigh observed that university education gave excellent training but would not make much difference in salary for women ("Why Go to a School of Journalism," 11).
80 NA, MCC, vol. 1, file 7, Triennial Report 1910–1913, "The Equipment of the Woman Journalist; and Keeping Up with the Times," 20.
81 Courses in various aspects of journalism began to be taught in the 1920s through the Extension Department of the University of Toronto. Dorothy Bell and Harriet Parsons were among the first teachers of these night-school courses.
82 Beasley, "Women in Journalism Education," 11, 14.
83 CVA, CWPC, Vancouver Branch, scrapbook 2, 41.
84 NA, MCC, vol. 45, file 24, Jo-ann Price articles, "Start To Cry ...," paper for Medill School of Journalism, Northwestern University.
85 Desbarats maintains that even today journalists have little faith in college preparation for the job (*Guide to the Canadian News Media,* 110).
86 Stewart, *Young Canada Goes to Work,* 98.
87 Stursberg, *Those Were the Days,* 91.
88 Dempsey, *No Life For a Lady,* 29.
89 "Newspacket," 16, no. 1 (August 1949): 1. According to the *Vancouver Sun,* 23 June 1949, Dingman was the only female journalism lecturer in the British Empire.

90 NA, MCC, vol. 1, file 8, Triennial Report 1935–38, reports of round table conferences: newspaper and editorial, 72.

91 NA, MG30 E256, Whitton Papers, vol. 82, "CWPC: Members' Memorial Award," 1. Whitton was paraphrasing the substance of the debate in her report; the scholarship was in fact awarded to students of English at McMaster.

92 *Ottawa Journal,* 7 September 1973.

93 "Newspacket," 5, no. 3 (1 May 1939): 2.

94 See the 1941 census, vol. 7, table 5. Stuart Keate maintains that the *Ubyssey* was "about the only avenue to the downtown Vancouver press in the mid 1930s" (*Paper Boy,* 9).

95 In response to my many questions, Edith MacInnes McCook described her career and generalized about journalism in her letter of 24 May 1987.

96 Rutherford, *A Victorian Authority,* 79.

97 Stursberg, *Extra!* 33.

98 Keate, *Paper Boy,* 9.

99 PAM, CWPC, Winnipeg Branch, minutes, 11 May 1911.

100 In 1931 journalists, authors, and editors together accounted for only 0.4% of female professionals in Canada; in 1941 the percentage climbed to a mere 0.6% (Department of Labour of Canada, "Women in the Professions in Canada," in *Women at Work in Canada,* 35, table 26).

101 MacPherson, "Careers of Canadian University Women," 29. Eleven universities cooperated with her study.

102 Ibid., 31–3.

103 Alice Harriet Parson, "Careers or Marriage," *Canadian Home Journal,* June 1938, 3.

104 "Newspacket," 7, no. 3 (1 May 1941): 3.

105 NA, MCC, "Historian's Report," Triennial Report 1913–20, 24.

106 UA, Ellis Papers, speech to the Winnipeg Branch of the CWPC, 1938.

107 "Newsletter," 8 October 1930, 1.

108 Donald, *The Imperial Press Conference in Canada* [c. 1920].

109 "Newspacket," 1, no. 2 (February 1935): 4.

110 NA, MCC, vol. 21, file 37, W.A. Craik to Isabel Armstrong, 17 November 1937.

111 Stursberg, *Extra!* 73.

112 NA, MCC, vol. 1, file 8, Triennial Report 1942–46, 18.

113 "Newspacket," 7, no. 1 (November 1940): 2.

114 NA, MG30 D85, Dora Dibney Papers, file 3, 6 November 1941.

115 See chapter 9.

116 NA, MCC, vol. 9, file 27, Ann Donnelly to Nora Elliott, 19 June 1944. See chapter 4 for the Claire Wallace story.

117 "Newspacket," 10, no. 3 (February 1944): 2.

118 NA, MCC, vol. 19, file 19-1, historical columns on the CWPC, 1966–68, "The Morning Star of Memory ..." by Jean Sereisky-Dickson, historian and archivist.

119 NA, MCC, vol. 25, file 25-12, Kay Mather, "CWPC: Its Route and What It Offers."

120 "Newspacket," 9, no. 7 (May 1943): 2.

121 Beasley and Gibbons, *Taking Their Place,* 15–16.

122 "Newspacket," 10, no. 2 (November 1943): 2.

123 O'Neill, "The Playwrights' Studio Group," 90.

124 "Newspacket," 17, no. 1 (December 1951): 4.

125 Desbarats, *Guide to Canadian News Media,* 106.

126 For an analysis of literary stereotypes, see Good, *Acquainted with the Night.*

127 PAM, CWPC, Winnipeg Branch, box 1, minute book 1930–40, "A Toast to the Ladies of the Press!" by a Mere NewspaperMAN, unidentified clipping, 21 June 1938.

128 The opposition between labour-leaning journalists and aspiring professionals divided the British community of journalists into two rival organizations, the National Union of Journalists, founded in 1907, and the Institute of Journalists, which was given its Royal Charter in 1890 (Lee, *Origins of the Popular Press,* 114).

129 PAM, CWPC, Winnipeg Branch, box 1, minutes of the annual general meeting, 9 May 1939.

130 NA, MCC, vol. 1, file 7, Triennial Report 1913–20, 55.

131 Ibid., E.B. Price, "Report of the Press Women's Conference, Alberta and Saskatchewan," 70.

132 Ibid., 69.

133 Saskatchewan Archives Board (SAB), McNaughton Papers, folder 2, 22 November 1938.

134 NA, MCC, vol. 1, file 7, Triennial Report 1913–20, 70.

135 The three brave souls were Edna Brown, Fanny Cromar Bruce, and Amy Kerr, who was self-employed (CVA, CWPC, Vancouver Branch, scrapbook 2, 1909–30, 25).

136 Ibid. Myrtle Patterson was on the executive in 1928. Mae Garnett was the only woman to become president, elected in 1933 (University of British Columbia, Special Collections [UBCSP], Barry Mather Collection, box 1, crapbook of the B.C. Institute of Journalists).

137 The guild originated in the United States in 1933 as an independent craft union for reporters and editorial workers. By this time, according to Susan Craig, it was obvious that professional associations afforded little protection for newspaper folk when so many were unemployed ("Solidarity Is a Sometimes Thing," 2).

138 Interview with Norman Hacking in Stursberg, *Extra!* 76.

139 "Newspacket," 4, no. 1 (November 1937): 3.
140 "Publishers Reject C.I.O. Guild," *Globe and Mail*, 2 July 1937. This position more or less parallels the position taken by the newspaper industry owners in *Editor and Publisher*, 3 March 1934, as cited in Schiller, *Objectivity and the News*, 196.
141 Cranston, *Ink on My Fingers*, 154.
142 Ibid., 162–3, describes how *Star* employees were subjected to individual pressure either not to join or to resign if they had joined. Harkness (*J.E. Atkinson of the Star*, 279) describes how, as the union foundered, the people who had led the move to organize were fired on the slightest pretext. An unnamed individual was fired because he wrote on the side for a local magazine – he committed suicide a few days later. Jessie MacTaggart, years later, indicated that sentiment figured in the collapse of the *Star* local. When rumours circulated that the elderly Atkinson had suffered a heart attack because of the strike call, the union called off job action. A remarkably healthy Atkinson greeted the would-be strikers with triumph but not malice; working conditions and pay did improve (Craig, "Solidarity Is a Sometimes Thing," 4).
143 Harkness (*J.E. Atkinson of the Star*, 281–3), claims that by 1941 bad strategy on the union's part, combined with the *Star*'s offer of a five-day week and wages of $40 a week for experienced reporters, had deflated the local.
144 "Brilliant Columnist," Vancouver *Province*, 26 August 1943.
145 Harkness, *J.E. Atkinson of the Star*, 281.
146 Siggins, *Bassett*, 33. Ironically, when organized Toronto *Telegram* workers negotiated their first contract in 1953, publisher Bassett proved to be surprisingly cooperative (Clark, "Solidarity Is a Sometimes Thing," 5).
147 Stephen Gold, "Columnist's Career Recalled," Ladysmith-Chemainus *Chronicle*, 6 September 1988.
148 In response to my letter, Mamie Boggs explained her role in the Vancouver local, 13 April 1989. The Vancouver union was not at first affiliated with the American Newspaper Guild but was independent, with its own charter from the Trades and Labor Congress. See Craig, "Solidarity Is a Sometimes Thing," 3.
149 Stursberg, *Extra!* 76–7.
150 "Newspacket," 8, no. 3 (15 May 1942): 2.
151 Stursberg, *Extra!* 78.
152 NA, MCC, vol. 29, file 49, "Proposed Resolution at Triennial Meeting of Canadian Women's Press Club, June 1945." The triennial did not occur in 1945 because of transportation difficulties during wartime. When the delayed triennial did convene in 1946, the union issue was not raised.

153 NA, MCC, vol. 1, file 8, Triennial Report 1935–38, "Address by Ishbel Ross," 82.

154 CVA, CWPC, Vancouver Branch, scrapbook 2, clipping from the first annual report of the branch founded in 1910, 60.

CHAPTER FOUR

1 National Archives of Canada (NA), MG28 I232, Media Club of Canada (MCC), "Newspacket," 1, no. 2 (February 1935): 3.

2 Gail Cuthbert Brandt's review article "Postmodern Patchwork" suggests the image of a "crazy quilt" to understand the diversity of women's experience in history.

3 Creese and Strong-Boag, *British Columbia Reconsidered*, 1.

4 Edith MacInnes McCook to Marjory Lang, 24 May 1987.

5 Harte, "Canadian Journalists and Journalism," 14.

6 Stewart, *Young Canada Goes to Work*, 99.

7 In a letter to me describing the career of Bessie Forbes, Florence Taylor generously supplied details of her own experience, July 1988.

8 "Newspacket," 2, no. 4 (1 August 1936): 4

9 NA, MCC, vol. 15, file 12, Margaret E. Ness, "Western Rainbow Rises to Fame in Canada's Rosy East," *Women* [c. 1948].

10 "Brilliant Columnist," Vancouver *Province*, 26 August 1943.

11 In a letter to Lorne Pierce, Robinson described her affliction (Queen's University Archives [QUA], Pierce Papers, box 9, file 5, Judith Robinson to Lorne Pierce, 17 December 1942).

12 NA, MCC, vol. 1, file 8, Triennial Report 1932–35, "Address by Ishbel Ross," 77–8.

13 "Newspacket," 11, no. 3 (March 1945): 3.

14 Stephen Gold, "Columnist's Career Recalled," Ladysmith-Chemainus *Chronicle*, 6 September 1988.

15 City of Vancouver Archives (CVA), CWPC, Vancouver Branch Papers, vol. 2, scrapbook, *Vancouver Sun*, 29 September 1959.

16 Ibid.

17 "In Our Early Days," *Saturday Night*, 11 December 1937, 1, 3.

18 "Around Town," *Saturday Night*, 6 September 1890, 1.

19 "Canadienne," and "Something about Salaries," *Saturday Night*, 26 April 1913, 29.

20 Ibid.

21 Mack, "Salaries Paid to Journalists in Canada," *Saturday Night*, 14 October 1899, 7. The salaries newspapermen acknowledged in their memoirs more or less bear out Clark's estimates. J.E. Atkinson, before he became the publisher of the *Toronto Star*, was earning $15 a week as a

reporter, rising to $17 when he won the prestigious post of parliamentary reporter for the *Globe* in 1888.

22 Provincial Archives of Manitoba (PAM), Livesay Papers, folder 3, diary 1904, n.d.

23 Eggleston, *While I Still Remember*, 86, 134, 153, 191.

24 Edith MacInnes McCook to Marjory Lang, 24 May 1987.

25 Lawrence's remarks were quoted by Anne Anderson Perry, "Our Quarterly Craft Talk: Is Yours Just a Job or a Profession?" in "Newsletter," May 1931, 3.

26 "What Canadian Women Journalists Might Do," "Newsletter," January 1933, 1.

27 *Census of Canada, 1931*, vol. 6, table 32. Hind was just shy of seventy.

28 According to statistics compiled by the Department of Labour, 10% of the female labour force fourteen years and older was married in 1931, rising to 12.7% in 1941. These figures included the permanently separated (Department of Labour, *Women at Work in Canada*, table 10, 15). Just under 25% of women journalists had married at some time in their lives, including the separated and widowed (ibid., table 6).

29 National Council of Women, *Women of Canada*, 73–7. The list is not exhaustive and not entirely accurate about the marital status even of those it includes. For instance, "Miss" Atkinson, born Elmira Elliott, was the wife of Joseph Atkinson, soon to be publisher of the *Toronto Star*. Predictably, the council's list does not specify how many of the married women were widows or separated self-supporting women.

30 PAM, CWPC, Winnipeg Branch Papers, reel 3, minutes of annual general meeting, 26 October 1911.

31 NA, MCC, vol. 1, file 7, Triennial Report 1913–20, "Historian's Report," 30.

32 Edith Bayne, "Genevieve Lipsett-Skinner, LL.B.," *Maclean's*, December 1918, 113–14.

33 Ibid.

34 Genevieve Lipsett-Skinner, "Why Girls Leave Home," in "Newsletter," May 1933, 2.

35 Charlesworth, *Candid Chronicles*, 93–4.

36 "Lady Gay's Page," *Saturday Night*, 16 November 1912, 30.

37 Sanders, *Emily Murphy, Crusader*, 65.

38 PAM, Livesay Papers, folder 6, Ruth Cohen Collie to Florence Randal Livesay, 30 July 1934.

39 White, "It's Good, It's Bad," describes the contradictions that caused married women to accept and be grateful for exploitative opportunities.

40 NA, MG30 D52, Macbeth papers, vol. 1, correspondence, 18 September 1918.

41 NA, MG30 D52, Macbeth Papers, vol. 1, correspondence, Price to Macbeth, n.d.

42 "Women and Their Work: Madge Macbeth Won Success as Writer,"
     Maclean's, 1 January 1924, 50–1.

43 "Trials and Triumphs of a Free Lance Writer," *Saturday Night,* 19 April
     1913, 29, 31.

44 Canadienne, "Something about Salaries," *Saturday Night,* 26 April 1913,
     29.

45 See chapter 9 for analysis of the careers of women who succeeded in
     male-dominated specialities.

46 Cash, *I Like British Columbia,* 4.

47 Read, *The Great War and Canadian Society,* 68.

48 Kerr, "Lois Kerr," 37.

49 Good, *The Journalist as Autobiographer,* 82–3.

50 Redditt, "She Loves Murder and Kiddies Love Her," 64.

51 Kinnear, *In Subordination,* 17.

52 *Among Those Present,* performed first on 27 May 1933 at the Hart House
     Theatre in Toronto. She later rewrote and published it in *The Curtain
     Call,* October 1938.

53 Kerr, "Lois Kerr," 35.

54 Linda Hale and Marjory Lang interview with Lois Reynolds Kerr, 27
     April 1988.

55 Ibid.

56 Kerr, "Lois Kerr," 35.

57 Kessler-Harris, *Women Have Always Worked,* 63–4; Prentice et al., *Cana-
     dian Women,* 230.

58 From Macbeth's autobiography, *Over My Shoulder,* quoted in Sutherland,
     Monthly Epic, 177.

59 Vipond, *Listening In,* 96.

60 NA, MG30 D52, Macbeth Papers, vol. 12, scrapbook 1918–25, *Ottawa
     Citizen,* 8 February 1922. The article was originally published in the *New
     York Times Book Review.*

61 NA, MG30 D52, Macbeth Papers, vol. 4, Sherk to Macbeth, 19 November
     1926.

62 PAM, Livesay Papers, file 5, Valance Patriarche to Kilmeny (Florence
     Randal Livesay), 27 March 1940.

63 Gertrude Pringle, "Is a Business Career Possible for a Married Woman?"
     Canadian Magazine, March 1927, 30.

64 NA, MG30 D52, Macbeth Papers, vol. 4, Mary Barker to Madge Macbeth,
     24 April 1931.

65 Hewlett, *A Too Short Yesterday,* 113.

66 Saskatchewan Archives Board (SAB), Buck Papers, vol. 4, file 21, A.E.M.
     Hewlett to Ruth Buck, [c. 1970].

67 SAB, McNaughton Papers, A1 E88, A.E.M. Hewlett to Violet McNaugh-
     ton, 17 May 1942.

68 NA, MCC, vol.6, file 10, A.E. May Hewlett to Dora Dibney, 21 March 1944.

69 "Lone Scribes," Newspacket," 5, no. 1 (1 November 1938).

70 SAB, McNaughton Papers, A1 D27 , Violet McNaughton to Annie Hollis, 21 March 1941, Hollis to McNaughton, 9 April 1941 and McNaughton to Hollis, 14 May 1941. Ironically, Hewlett also felt that Dibney "did not like my stuff" (Hewlett to McNaughton, 17 May 1942). Otherwise she and Dibney had a good relationship.

71 SAB, McNaughton Papers, A1 D27, George Hollis to McNaughton, 8 July 1942.

72 NA, MG30 D85, Dibney Papers, file 3, correspondence 1945, J.W. Dodd to Dora Dibney, 13 October 1945.

73 Not surprisingly, there were quite a few journalist couples – Joe and Elizabeth Bailey Price, Mary Dawson and C.H.J. Snider, the Balmer Watts, and Margaret and George Murray are some better-known examples.

74 Edith MacInnes McCook to Marjory Lang, 24 May 1987.

75 "Newspacket," 1, no.1 (November 1934): 14.

76 NA, MCC, vol. 45, file 24, articles of Jo-Ann Price,"Start to Cry ...," paper for Medill School of Journalism, Northwestern University, 27 November 1944.

77 "Newspacket," 10, no. 4 (May 1944).

78 NA, MCC, vol. 18, Price file, Jo-Ann Price to Kay Mather, 24 May 1954 .

79 Keddell, *The Newspapering Murrays.*

80 Watt, *A Woman in the West,* 43. This represents a collection of columns she wrote between 1905 and 1907 for the Edmonton *Saturday News.*

81 Doyle, *Hurly-Burly,* 21.

82 Carter, *Stop the Press!* 40.

83 Stursburg, *Extra!* 35.

84 "Newspacket," 1, no. 2 (February 1935): 4.

85 Stursberg, *Extra!* 22.

86 NA, MCC, vol. 1, file 8, Triennial Report 1942–46, "Historian's Report," 44.

87 "Newspacket," 11, no. 4 (June 1945): 4.

88 Mamie Boggs described how she managed the "dual struggle," in her letter to me dated 13 April 1989.

89 The "princely salary" of $75 a month which she received in the early 1930s was slashed by 10% three times until for most of the Depression she earned only $60 a month (Stursberg, *Extra!* 74).

90 James Craig, "It's Never Too Late to Bring Justice," *Vancouver Sun,* 19 August 1989.

91 NA, MCC, vol. 41, file 3, "Newsletter," Spring 1934, 6.

92 Lotta Dempsey's second husband, Richard Fisher, brought two sons into the marriage, and she had a child in 1939. With domestic help she was

able to carry on, but as she complained to fellow press club member Jean Sweet, illness and trouble with the maid could cause her carefully constructed domestic routine to go awry (NA, MCC, vol. 9, file 23, Lotta Dempsey Fisher to Jean Sweet, 6 April 1939).

93 Dempsey, *No Life for a Lady*, 27.

94 CVA, CWPC, Vancouver Branch Papers, vol. 1, Marie Lapsely Anderson to Myrtle Patterson [later Gregory,] 8 January 1928.

95 "Newspacket," 8, no. 2 (March 1942): 3.

96 NA, MCC, vol. 46, file 14, "Membership List, Triennial Report for 1932–35. See table 5.

97 "Keeping Up Our Club," in "Newsletter," October 1932, 1.

98 "We Were Wondering," in "Newspacket," 8, no.3 (May 1942): 3.

99 NA, MCC, vol.6, file 10, Mary H.T. Alexander to Ann Donnelly, 4 June 1942.

100 Ibid., 1 June 1942.

101 NA, MCC, vol. 6, file 10, Myrtle Patterson Gregory to Ann Donnelly, 10 June 1942.

102 See Pierson, *They're Still Women After All.*

103 Glenbow Foundation, Calgary (GFC), Dibney Papers, file 5, *Winnipeg Free Press*, 9 July 1966.

104 "The Merry-Go-Round," in "Newspacket," 11, no. 1 (August 1944): 1.

105 Ibid., 4.

106 Ibid.

107 University of Waterloo, Special Collections (UWSP), Wallace Papers, file 172, "The Truth," unpublished ms. This is Wallace's own account of the affair. She was responsible for writing, and researching, editing, and broadcasting her programs as well as the commercials. She also made as many as ten public appearances a week, travelling across the country. The pace was so frenetic that her assistant resigned.

108 UWSP, Wallace Papers, file 172, "The Affair Financial" file, which contains a clutch of clippings from newspapers across the country.

109 Ibid., "Patriotic Sin," St Catharines *Standard*, reprinted in Galt *Reporter*, 16 March 1944.

110 Ibid., "Tax-Ridden Canadians Snicker at 'Claire Wallace' Brand of Patriotism," unidentified clipping.

111 Ibid., Palmerston *Observer*, 6 April 1944.

112 Like many another highly visible "personality," Wallace had to keep her private self hidden for her own psychological protection. The facts of her first marriage (which ended in divorce) and her son were not widely known. She married again in 1942. See Crean, *Newsworthy*, 88.

113 In her own account, "The Truth" (UWSP, Wallace Papers, file 172), she claims that she was subjected to sneers in the streetcars, as well as getting harrassing phone calls at her office and home. She never publicly ex-

plained her side, partly for strategic reasons: the government was so grateful to her for her discretion that it offered her $1,000 in compensation. Wallace took some satisfaction in returning the cheque.

114 UWSP, Wallace Papers, file 172, "Candid Comments by Observer," Rossburn, Manitoba, *Review*, 1 January 1943.

115 PAM, Livesay Papers, file 5, Valance Patriarche to Florence Randal Livesay, 27 March 1940.

116 UWSP, Wallace Papers, file 172, "Phony Dollar a Year Woman Draws Thousands for Expenses," *Hush*, 17 June 1944.

117 NA, MCC, vol. 1, file 7, Triennial Report 1913, 8.

118 NA, MCC, vol. 4, file 31, executive circulars, 8 August 1934.

119 "Newspacket," 1, no. 4 (1 November 1935): 1.

120 NA, MCC, vol. 25, file 1, Beneficiary Fund 1956–60, 4 December 1958.

121 *Globe and Mail*, 31 May 1955.

122 "Newspacket," 3, no. 3 (May 1937): 2.

123 NA, MCC, vol. 18, files 18–21, "Historian-Archivist's Report," 1962–25, in memoriam.

124 Haig, *Brave Harvest*, 126.

125 NA, MG30 D85, Dibney Papers, file 1, Grant Dexter, "The Unconquered," unidentified paper, n.d.

126 Miriam Green Ellis left an estate of $125,830 in 1964. She left $1,000 to the Beneficiary Fund (PAM, CWPC, Winnipeg Branch Papers, box 6, *Manitoba Free Press*, 30 December 1964).

127 "Newspacket," 14, no. 7 (October 1948): 3.

128 "Newspacket," 1, no. 2 (February 1935): 3.

129 NA, Newton MacTavish Collection, reel 5563, item 449, Jean Graham to Newton MacTavish, 4 October 1911.

130 "Home Editor Retires," *Country Guide*, August 1957.

131 "Newspacket," 10, no. 3 (February 1944): 1.

132 "A Nose for News or the Editor's Opportunity for Service," unidentified and undated clipping, but the author signed herself "The Scribe," which was a pseudonym used by Mary H.T. Alexander; she does not name the interviewed journalist (CVA, CWPC, Vancouver Branch Papers, vol. 2, scrapbook 1, 47.

133 AO, McKanday Papers, "Them Wuz the Days," typescript, 41.

134 Rutherford, *The Making of the Canadian Media*, 39.

135 "Newspacket," 2, 4 (1 August 1936), 2.

136 Hutchison, *The Far Side of the Street*, 318.

137 "Newspacket," 2, no. 3 (1 May 1936): 2.

138 NA, MCC, vol. 1, file 8, Triennial Report 1929–32, 15.

139 "Newspacket," 2, no. 4 (1 August 1936): 2.

140 AO, McKanday Papers,"Them Wuz the Days," 41. See also, Cranston, *Ink on My Fingers*, 174.

141 Examples include Jennie Fraser, co-editor with her brother of the New Glasgow *Eastern Chronicle*, and Annie Helena Derrett who bought the Pincher Creek, Alberta, *Echo* in 1920 having worked on it since 1913; Mabel de Wolfe ran the Consort, Alberta, *Enterprise* from 1914 to 1920; Grace Wright was owner-writer for the Mount Forest, Ontario *Confederationist*; Hazel McCrea and her mother ran the family newspaper, the Hanna, Alberta, *Herald*; Margaret Lapp edited the Brighton *Ensign* for her mother, while Dorothy Taylor managed the *British Columbian* in New Westminster.

142 "Newspacket," 7, no. 1 (November 1940): 1.

143 George Johnston, *The Weeklies*, 94.

144 One of the few but not the only one: Hazel McCrea ran the *Herald* of Hanna, Alberta, with her mother. See n141 above.

145 NA, MCC, vol. 11, membership file 36, Margaret Lapp, "... From a feminine angle...," *Canadian Weekly Newspaper Association Bulletin*, n.d.

146 "Newspacket," 5, no. 3 (May 1939): 1.

147 In the nineteenth century, advertisements on the front page were the norm. Urban dailies had shed this form by the last decades of the nineteenth century.

148 "Newspacket," "Golden Jubilee Issue," 1954, 31.

149 NA, MCC, vol. 11, file 41, Kay Daughen, "Woman Publisher Kept on the Go Producing Prize-Winning Weekly," unidentified clipping, April 1951.

150 Johnston, *The Weeklies*, 92. In 1966 Marston won the Jack Sanderson Award for editorial writing.

151 Margaret Pennel, "How Two Women Are Making a Success of Publishing a Newspaper," *Canadian Magazine*, September 1927, 30, 25.

152 Ibid., 25.

153 "Newspacket," 8, no. 2 (March 1942): 3.

154 NA, MCC, vol. 1, file 8, Triennial Report 1935–38, 82.

155 NA, MCC, vol. 1, file 8, Triennial Report 1929–32, president's address, "Loyalties," 32.

CHAPTER FIVE

1 "A Retrospect," *Country Guide*, 2 December 1929, cited in Rasmussen, *A Harvest Yet to Reap*, 220.

2 Ibid.

3 Ibid.

4 National Archives of Canada (NA), MG28 I232, Media Club of Canada (MCC), "Newspacket," 16, no. 1 (August 1949): 1.

5 "Born in a Pullman," *Press Woman*, September 1943, 3.

6 Jerrold, "That Woman's Column!" 188.

7 Toronto *Globe*, 30 November 1886.

8 Steele, "Ladies' Papers," 105.

9 "A Mirror for Fools," *Saturday Review,* 7 November 1903, 570–1.

10 Quilter, "A Question of Courage," 994.

11 Archives of Ontario (AO), Sanford Papers, Mary Elizabeth McOuat to Mary Bouchier Sanford [1897].

12 NA, MCC, vol. 1, file 7, Triennial Report 1910–13, "Historian's Report," 8.

13 NA, MCC, "What Canadian Women Journalists Might Do, in " "Newsletter," January 1933, 2.

14 For instance, J.S. Cranston began as a sport writer on the Woodstock *Sentinel-Review* and eventually became editor of the *Star Weekly* (Cranston, *Ink on My Fingers*); Stuart Keate, a sportswriter for the Vancouver *Province,* rose to become publisher of the Victoria *Daily Times* and then the *Vancouver Sun* (Keate, *Paper Boy*).

15 Smith, *The Journal Men,* 91–2.

16 "Craft Corner," in "Newsletter," January 1933, 1.

17 "The Readers' Viewpoint," in "Newspacket," 10, no. 3 (February 1944): 4.

18 Wilfred Eggleston got his first *Star* front-page story covering an elephant at the Toronto zoo (Eggleston, *While I Still Remember,* 92–3).

19 Bennett, *Journalism for Women,* 54.

20 Cranston, *Ink on My Fingers,* 114. Cranston mentioned no names, probably because he did not remember the individuals. Three female *Toronto Star* employees left at this time: Isabel Armstrong, who advanced to a long and reputable career on the *Ottawa Citizen*; M. Iola Plaxton, who went into advertising in New York; and Kate Hawes Miles, who disappears from press club records after 1922.

21 Ibid.

22 Bridle, "One of the Oddest of Editors."

23 Cited by Ferguson, *Kit Coleman, Queen of Hearts,* frontispiece.

24 Toronto *Mail,* 25 January 1895.

25 Freeman (*Kit's Kingdom,* 65) describes Kit's pleasure in her male fans and an exchange with a female reader who felt that men's letters should be excluded from women's sections.

26 AO, Hammond Papers, box 2, "Ninety Years of the Globe," typescript [c. 1934], 173.

27 Toronto *Globe,* 11 October 1886.

28 Carter, *Stop the Press!* 37.

29 Dempsey, *No Life for a Lady,* 3.

30 Carter, *Stop the Press!* 34.

31 Frank Chamberlain, "A Week in Radio: Finest Girl Reporter of the Air," *Saturday Night,* 28 August 1943.

32 Edith MacInnes McCook to Marjory Lang, 24 May 1987.

33 Linda Hale and Marjory Lang interview with Lois Reynolds Kerr, 27 April 1988.

34 Edith MacInnes McCook to Marjory Lang, 25 February 1989.
35 University of British Columbia, Special Collections (UBCSP), Mather Collection, clipping, Vancouver *Herald,* 4 December 1954.
36 Crean, *Newsworthy,* 30. Atkinson's attitude towards the women's section had been underlined a few years earlier when he "demoted" Jessie MacTaggart to the women's department to cover weddings as a reprimand for her organizing activities with the embryonic Toronto local of the American Newspaper Guild (Craig, "Solidarity Is a Sometimes Thing," 4).
37 NA, MCC, vol. 1, file 7, Trienniel Report 1920–3, 10.
38 "Advertising for Women, by the *Province* Ad Man," Vancouver *Province,* 2 October 1898.
39 Harrington and Frankenburg, *Essentials in Journalism,* 113.
40 Baldasty, *The Commercialization of News in the Nineteenth Century,* 126.
41 AO, McKanday Papers, clipping from "The Inside Story" (*Globe* staff newsletter), n.d.; "Them Wuz the Days," typescript.
42 Brandenburg, "Research Shows Reader Preference," 30.
43 "Newspacket," 6, no. 4 (August 1940): 2.
44 "Newspacket," 9, no. 6 (February 1943): 2.
45 Jackman, "Chances for Women in Journalism," 1492.
46 AO, Sanford Papers, Mary Elizabeth McOuat to Mary Bouchier Sanford [c. 1897].
47 AO, *Toronto Star* Papers, Directory of Employees, June 1927.
48 "What Canadian Women Journalists Might Do," in "Newsletter," January 1933, 2
49 The hierarchy of authority on the *Toronto Star* is apparent from the instructions Needham gave to his three female employees. See University of Waterloo, Special Collections (UWSP), Wallace Papers, file 23, Richard Needham to Miss Wallace, Miss Tedman, and Miss McMillan, 6 June 1934.
50 "What Canadian Women Journalists Might Do," in "Newsletter," January 1933, 2.
51 CVA, CWPC, Vancouver Branch Papers, vol. 2, scrapbook, 8.
52 Florence Taylor worked under Bessie Forbes's direction in the early 1940s (letter, Florence Taylor to Marjory Lang, 1 July 1988).
53 Boughner, *Women in Journalism,* 6.
54 Baldasty (*Commercialization of News,* 59–80) analyses how advertisers determined the content and form of newspapers in the United States in the late nineteenth century.
55 Edith MacInnes McCook to Marjory Lang, 25 February 1989.
56 Linda Hale and Marjory Lang interview with Lois Reynolds Kerr, 27 April 1988.
57 Perkins, *Vocations for Trained Women,* 228.

58 "The Women's Page," in "Newspacket," 3, no. 1 (November 1936): 3.

59 AO, Toronto *Globe* Papers, assignment book, 1901.

60 See Jackel, "First Day's, Fighting Days," and Gorham, "Pen and Buckskin," 22–3.

61 Edith MacInnes McCook to Marjory Lang, 25 February 1989.

62 Ibid.

63 Saskatchewan Archives Board (SAB), McNaughton Papers, A1 E23, A.P. Waldron to Violet McNaughton, 25 April 1925.

64 Waldron apologized to McNaughton on a number of occasions for these changes (SAB, McNaughton Papers, A1 E23, Waldron to McNaughton, 27 May and 5 October 1926).

65 Taylor, "Window on the World," 63–8.

66 Ross, *Ladies of the Press*, 427.

67 NA, MCC vol. 1, file 7, Triennial Report 1910–13, 4.

68 Toronto *Globe*, 28 February 1887.

69 Downie, *Passionate Pen*, 142.

70 See chapter 8.

71 NA, MG30 D52, Macbeth Papers, vol. 1, Correspondence, Florence Sherk to Madge Macbeth, 30 Nov 1926.

72 "Newspacket," 5, no. 1 (1 November 1938): 1.

73 Toronto *Globe*, 1 September 1936.

74 *Toronto Star*, 14 April 1910.

75 *Canadian Courier*, 22 October 1916.

76 SAB, McNaughton Papers, *Saturday Press and Prairie Farmer*, 19 August 1916.

77 "The Home-Maker," *Globe and Mail*, 2 February 1943.

78 Rutherford, *The Making of the Canadian Media*, 59.

79 Dempsey, *No Life for A Lady*, 120.

80 "Newspacket," 5, no. 4 (September 1939): 4.

81 *Manitoba Free Press*, 9 November 1922.

82 Ibid.

83 Ibid.

84 "Newspacket," 2, no. 4 (1 August 1936): 4.

85 *Printer and Publisher* 19, no. 6 (1910): 47

86 "What Canadian Women Journalists Might Do," in "Newsletter," January 1933, 2

87 "Newspacket," 10, no. 3 (February 1944): 4.

88 "Newspacket," 7, no. 3 (May 1941): 2.

89 Cited by Rica McLean Farquharson, "Miss Foster, Reporter," *Saturday Night*, 19 April 1949, 31.

90 NA, MCC, vol. 45, file 18, Elizabeth Bailey Price, "Pioneer Lady" scrapbook, *Peace River Standard* [c. 1915].

91 Quoted in Rex, *No Daughter of Mine*, 62.

CHAPTER SIX

1 Toronto *Globe*, 22 September 1886.
2 Ibid., 8 September 1886.
3 Emily Pointon Weaver, "Pioneer Canadian Women: VII: 'Kit,' the Journalist," *Canadian Magazine*, August 1917, 275.
4 Schudson, *Advertising, the Uneasy Persuasion,* explores the connections that facilitated the creation of the mass-circulation newspaper, the advertising industry, and the consumer society.
5 Strong-Boag, "Keeping House in God's Country," provides a sophisticated analytical framework for understanding the shifting relationship between the production and consumption sides of women's work in the home.
6 Scanlon, *Inarticulate Longings*, 13.
7 Wright's article "Feminine Trifles of Vast Importance" begins to chart this territory in Canada. See also Benson, *Counter Cultures*, and Lancaster, *The Department Store.*
8 Scanlon provides an insightful analysis of the careers of a handful of women who wrote advertising copy for the J.Walter Thompson Agency (which advertised heavily in the *Ladies' Home Journal*) but not for the women who wrote editorial material in the *Home Journal* (*Inarticulate Longings*, 169–95).
9 Marvin, "Newspaper Work for Women," 234.
10 MacMurchy, *The Woman – Bless Her,* 110–28.
11 Strasser, *Never Done*, 62–3.
12 Kathleen Strange, *With the West in Her Eyes: The Story of a Modern Pioneer* (Toronto and New York 1937), 220–1, cited by Strong-Boag, "Keeping House in God's Country," 131.
13 Strasser, *Never Done*, 104–16.
14 Strong-Boag, "Keeping House in God's Country," 131.
15 Hendley, "Dear Abby, Miss Lonelyhearts, and the Eighteenth Century."
16 Vancouver *World*, 26 April 1904.
17 Currie, *Margaret Currie: Her Book*, 68. This volume reprinted the most popular columns Mrs Archibald had written over the years.
18 Helen Murphy, "Mrs Eldred Archibald," in "Newspacket" 12, no. 2 (November 1945): 2.
19 Stinson Jarvis, "Newspaper Women," *Frank Leslie's Weekly*, 23 June 1892.
20 Lally Bernard [Mary Agnes Fitzgibbon], "Driftwood," Toronto *Globe*, 30 May 1903.
21 Gertrude Pringle, "Is A Business Career Possible to a Married Woman? How Mrs Mary Barker, Advertising Expert, Solved this Problem Successfully," *Canadian Magazine*, March 1927, 30.
22 "Driftwood," Toronto *Globe*, 25 April 1903.

23 "Woman's World," Toronto *World*, 19 April 1899.

24 Fetherling, *The Rise of the Canadian Newspaper*, 75.

25 Queen's University Archives (QUA), Campbell Papers, box 9, file 3, Ethelwyn Wetherald to Campbell, 4 January 1893.

26 "Advertising for Women," Vancouver *Province*, 2 October 1898.

27 Barbara Freeman explores the conflict between women journalists' mandate to chronicle fashion and personal misgivings about restrictive and unhealthy clothing in "Laced in and Let Down."

28 National Archives of Canada (NA), MG28 I232, Media Club of Canada (MCC), vol. 42, file 4, *Quarterly News Sheet*, May 1930.

29 Blum, *Victorian Fashions and Costumes*, 227.

30 Schudson, *Advertising*, 182.

31 Strong-Boag, *The New Day Recalled*, 86. Note in particular the examples of contemporary advertisements Strong-Boag includes which typify the crudely admonishing tone directed at women. See also Vipond, "The Image of Women in the Mass Circulation Magazines of the 1920s."

32 Fetherling, *The Rise of the Canadian Newspaper*, 76.

33 Schudson, *Advertising*, 152.

34 March-Phillipps, "Women's Newspapers," 664.

35 "On Dit," Toronto *Mail*, 8 March 1897. Nevitt argues that this practice was commonplace in nineteenth-century British newspapers ("Advertising and Editorial Integrity," 155–7).

36 Toronto *Empire*, 26 June 1895 and 20 January 1894, cited in Freeman, "Laced In and Let Down," 11.

37 "Woman's Kingdom,"Toronto *Mail*, 22 November 1890.

38 Peacocke, *Writing for Women*, 93–5.

39 Baldasty, *The Commercialization of News*, analyses the way that advertising influenced all parts of the newspaper, including the suppression of news that might reflect badly on a particular sponsor. Male reporters were pressured, sometimes bribed, to write flattering copy. Nevertheless, the women's section was where the relations between advertising and information were most intimate, indeed incestuous.

40 Boughner, *Women in Journalism*, 233.

41 The *Toronto Star* shopping column offered this service to readers; see notice in the *Star* of 10 January 1910, for instance.

42 According to Baldasty (*Commercialization of News*, 67–9), this ploy was rife in American newspapers at the end of the century.

43 NA, MCC, vol. 32, file 8, "Our Mary," *Quill Driver*, 17 January 1928, 2.

44 Carter, *Stop the Press!* 37–8.

45 Beasley and Gibbons (*Taking Their Place*, 14) cite the findings of Iona Robertson Logie's study, *Careers for Women in Journalism: A Composite Picture of 881 Salaried Women Writers at Work in Journalism, Advertising, Publicity, and Promotion* (Scranton, Pa: International Textbooks 1938), 69–70.

46 NA, MCC, vol. 1, file 7, Triennial Report 1910–13, "The New Advertising,"
    24.

47 Harrington and Frankenburg, *Essentials in Journalism,* 42.

48 NA, MCC, vol. 1, file 7, Triennial Report 1913–20, "On Interviewing," 60.

49 NA, MCC, vol. 1, file 7, Triennial Report 1910–13, "The New Advertising,"
    24.

50 NA, MG30 D52, Macbeth Papers, vol. 12, scrapbook 1918–25, *Ottawa
    Citizen,* 25 September 1920.

51 For analysis of how the experience of working in government service
    during the war altered journalists' faith in "objectivity," see Schudson,
    Discovering the News. Buitenhuis investigated the use of men and women
    of letters as pen warriors in *The Great War of Words.*

52 NA, MG30 D52, Macbeth Papers, vol. 12, scrapbook 1918–25, Toronto
    World, 26 February 1920.

53 NA, MG30 D52, Macbeth Papers, vol. 4, Madge Macbeth to B.L. Thomp-
    son, 14 October 1931.

54 NA, MCC, "Newspacket," 11, no. 1 (1 November 1935): 2.

55 University of Waterloo, Special Collections (UWSP), Wallace Papers,
    scrapbook 122, script for "They Tell Me" interview with Hilda Hesson, 2
    February 1945.

56 Cash, *Off the Record,* 44.

57 Doris Milligan, "'About Town' Folds for Duration as Editor Goes into
    War Work," *Vancouver Sun,* 13 December 1942.

58 *Saturday Night,* 24 July 1920, 28–9.

59 "The Home-Maker," Toronto *Globe,* 27 June 1935.

60 NA, MCC, vol. 1, file 9, Triennial Report 1954–56, "Historian's Report."
    Globe and Mail editor Richard Doyle also refers to the survey (*Hurly-
    Burly,* 32).

61 Toronto *Globe,* 26 June 1935.

62 *Grain Growers' Guide,* 12 September 1917, cited by Marchildon, "Improv-
    ing the Quality of Rural Life in Saskatchewan," 90.

63 Ibid.

64 Cook, "Francis Marion Beynon," 190.

65 *The Editor,* 31 January 1931, 91.

66 Rica McLean Farquharson, "Miss Foster, Reporter," *Saturday Night,* 19
    April 1949, 31.

67 Saskatchewan Archives Board (SAB), McNaughton Papers, "Woman's
    Century Correspondence," 1 March 1915.

68 NA, MCC, "What Canadian Women Journalists Might Do," in "Newslet-
    ter," January 1933, 2.

69 See Strong-Boag, *The New Day Recalled,* 118–19, for an account of the
    increasingly antagonistic relationship between consumers and advertis-
    ers in the 1930s.

70 "'No Consumer Movement in Canada!' Oh, No!" *Marketing*, 26 February 1938, 7.

71 For one of the few serious studies of women's role in the Canadian advertising industry, see Dodd, "Women in Advertising."

72 "Newspacket," 5, no. 1 (1 November 1938): 3.

73 Among the CWPC members who served the government during the war were Byrne Hope Sanders, Thelma Craig, Harriet Parsons, and Kate Aitken.

74 UWSP, Wallace Papers, "They Tell Me," Broadcast 79, 4 December 1942.

75 *Canadian Home Journal*, May 1942.

76 Sanders acknowledged how the execution of her job depended on her sisters; see "Newspacket," 8, 3 (15 May 1942): 3.

77 See Boughner, *Women in Journalism*, or Brazelton, *Writing and Editing for Women*.

78 Professional child psychologists were among the most aggressive, especially since mothers were so vulnerable to the charge of perpetrating psychological damage. See Strong-Boag, "Intruders in the Nursery," and Lewis, "Creating the Little Machine."

79 SAB, McNaughton Papers, *Grain Growers' Guide* correspondence, Margaret Speechly to Violet McNaughton, 11 June 1921.

80 City of Vancouver Archives (CVA), CWPC, Vancouver Branch Papers, vol. 2, scrapbook 1, 88.

81 Rooke, "Public Figure, Private Woman," 421. As editor of *Child Welfare*, Whitton qualified for membership in the CWPC and was among the most prominent members, even during the most active periods of her career in social work.

82 Milliman, "Writer Warns of Glaring Errors in Articles for Food Pages," 42.

83 "Rent versus Food," *Montreal Star*, reprinted in Currie, *Margaret Currie. Her Book*.

84 Boughner, *Women in Journalism*, 67.

85 Strong-Boag, *The New Day Recalled*, 118.

86 CVA, CWPC, Vancouver Branch Papers, vol. 2, scrapbook 1, 78.

87 NA, MCC, "Newspacket," 3, no. 1 (2 November 1936): 4.

88 Carter, *Stop the Press!* 49.

89 NA, MCC, vol. 1, file 7, Triennial Report 1923–26, "Syndicating for Profit," 24.

90 "Newspacket," 10, no. 1 (August 1943): 2.

91 "Newspacket," 2, no. 1 (November 1935): 2.

92 NA, MG30 D206, Aitken Papers, vol. 35, clipping file, Toronto *Mail and Empire*, 17 February 1928.

93 Gordon Sinclair, "The Busiest Woman in the World," *Maclean's*, 15 April 1950, 67.

94 Cochrane, *Kate Aitken*, 29.
95 Vipond, *Listening In*, 92, 94–5.
96 "Newspacket," 9, no. 6 (February 1943): 2.
97 Cochrane, *Kate Aitken*, 35.
98 "From a Woman's Point of View," Vancouver *Province*, 2 May 1904, 11.
    Hetty Green was an American millionaire whose signature was forged.
99 "Pot-Pourri," Toronto *Mail and Empire*, 25 August 1906.
100 Gordon Sinclair, "The Busiest Woman in the World," *Maclean's*, 15 April
    1950, 8–9, 64–7.

CHAPTER SEVEN

1 Toronto *Mail*, 23 August 1889.
2 Leonore Davidoff's *The Best Circles* established the raison d'être of
   upper-class women who ruled high society. While the function and
   elaboration of the game varied in different contexts, the rules remained
   fundamentally consistent.
3 Schudson, *Advertising*, 151.
4 Archives of Ontario (AO), Hammond Papers, box 2, "Ninety Years of the
   Globe," manuscript [c. 1934].
5 Schudson, *Discovering the News*, 28.
6 Ross, *Ladies of the Press*, 429.
7 By mid-century the newspapers began printing the names of those
   presented to the sovereign, but the author of the Court Circular was not
   allowed into the Tapestry Chamber. He was merely allowed to stand by
   the window and copy down the names of those who left their presentation cards on the table of the queen's page (Davidoff, *The Best Circles*,
   25).
8 Smith, "Women's Work in the London and Provincial Press," 14.
9 Macbeth, *Land of Afternoon*, 58. (She wrote this book under the pseudonym Gilbert Knox and apparently took some pains to keep her identity
   secret.)
10 AO, Sanford Papers, Mrs Willoughby Cummings to Mary Bouchier
    Sanford, 17 November 1897.
11 "Edmund Phillips," *Saturday Night*, 14 June 1931, 7.
12 Duncan, *A Daughter of Today*, 53–4.
13 Performed at Hart House Theatre, Toronto, 1936.
14 Marzolf, *Civilizing Voices*, 58.
15 City of Vancouver Archives (CVA), CWPC, Vancouver Branch Papers, vol.
    2, scrapbook 1, 36, *Hook*, 28 September 1923.
16 KoKo (Grace Denison), "Overdoing," *Saturday Night*, July 1899, 8.
17 Read, *The Great War and Canadian Society*, 67.
18 National Archives of Canada (NA), MG28 I232, Media Club of Canada

(MCC), vol. 11, file 39, "Held 'Temporary' Job Forty Years," St Catharines *Standard*, 30 March 1959.

19 Ross, *Ladies of the Press*, 442.

20 Meyer, "Society Reporting among the '400,'" 11.

21 Boughner, *Women in Journalism*, 1–2.

22 W.C. Brann, "Women in Journalism," *Iconoclast*, [c. 1898], reprinted in *Matrix*, August 1932, 13.

23 Toronto *World*, 22 April 1899.

24 AO, Hammond Papers, box 2, "Ninety Years of the Globe," 196.

25 March-Phillipps, "Women's Newspapers," 663.

26 Vancouver *World*, 30 April 1904.

27 NA, MG30 D46, Thompson Papers, vol. 1, diary, note beside clipping from *Ottawa Journal*, March 1929.

28 NA, MCC, "Newspacket," 5, no. 2 (February 1939): 4.

29 Low, *Press Work for Women*, 12.

30 CVA, CWPC, Vancouver Branch Papers, vol. 2, scrapbook 1 [Myrtle Patterson], "Message from the Vice President for B.C."

31 The most penetrating analysis of how women ruled high society in Victorian England in order to perpetuate aristocratic pre-eminence is still Davidoff, *The Best Circles*. The general outlines of her argument explicate other social contexts, including "good society" in late-nineteenth-century and early-twentieth-century Canada.

32 McDonald, *Making Vancouver*, 165.

33 McDonald, "Vancouver's 'Four Hundred.'"

34 In New York society, which set the pace of fashionable behaviour, it was the energy and finesse of women that propelled a family from prosperous obscurity into the haute monde. See Jaher, "Style and Status," 258–8 4. See also Davidoff, "Mastered for Life."

35 Alice Harriet Parsons, "Should a Girl be a Lady?" *Canadian Home Journal*, April 1938, 8, 9, 69, 74, 85.

36 Mona E. Clark, "A Woman in Business is Still at Heart a Woman," *Canadian Magazine*, January 1928, 27.

37 Smith, "Women's Work in the London and Provincial Press," 15.

38 *Canadian Printer and Publisher* 19, no. 6 (1910): 47.

39 Harrington and Frankenburg, *Essentials in Journalism*, 113.

40 NA, MG30 D52, Macbeth Papers, vol. 2, J. Hubert Hooper to Madge Macbeth, 18 March 1932.

41 Lois Reynolds Kerr, interview with Linda Hale and Marjory Lang, Vancouver, B.C., 23 April 1988.

42 Carter, *Stop the Press!* 39.

43 Wadleigh, "Why Go to a School of Journalism?" 11.

44 "Prominent Canadian Women, no. 11: Miss Ogilvie," *Ladies' Pictorial Weekly*, 4 June 1892, 355.

45 Pederson, "The Victorian Governess," shows how similar contradictions operated in the identity of the governess, whose occupation depended upon her being a "lady" at a time when "ladies" did not have occupations.

46 Boughner, *Women in Journalism*, 13.

47 NA, MG30 D29, Willison Papers, vol. 14, file 112, Fitzgibbon to Willison, 24 November [c. 1903]. Her "letters" were published in Willison's *News*.

48 See Sandra Gwyn's account of her career in *The Private Capital.*

49 "Notes by the Marchioness," Ottawa *Free Press*, 21 October 1899.

50 Kroller (*The Canadian Travellers in Europe*, 77) describes how Denison's capacity for social critique surfaced in her travelogue, *A Happy Holiday.*

51 Charlesworth, *Candid Chronicles*, 92.

52 Apparently she was so remote from her husband that she had no idea he was ill until he died (ibid.).

53 J.G.(Jean Graham), "A Brilliant Journalist," *Canadian Courier*, (21 February 1914, 20.

54 "The State Ball at Ottawa," *Saturday Night*, 20 May 1899, 6.

55 Kerr, *Nellie McNabb*, 11.

56 Vancouver *Province*, 17 March 1900.

57 Cited in Gwyn, *The Private Capital*, 472–3.

58 Macbeth, *The Land of Afternoon*, 135.

59 Eva Reid, "Newspaper Woman Recalls Early Days in Profession," Calgary *Albertan*, 17 October 1957.

60 See the directive given by Richard Needham, women's page editor, to the *Star*'s three social reporters (University of Waterloo, Special Collections [UWSP], Wallace Papers, file 23, 6 June 1934).

61 Ross, *Ladies of the Press*, 442.

62 NA, MCC, "Newsletter," May 1931, 3.

63 Marvin, "Newspaper Work for Women," 235.

64 Boughner, *Women in Journalism*, 28.

65 Ibid., 9. See also Hyde, *Journalistic Writing*, 240.

66 Ross, *Ladies of the Press*, 444.

67 CVA, CWPC, Vancouver Branch Papers, scrapbook 2, Dorothy Bell to Edna Brown Baker, 10 June 1955.

68 Smith, *The Journal Men*, 63. Madge Macbeth must have heard this anecdote and used it for comic relief as she related the newspaper description of a wedding guest in *The Land of Afternoon*, 316: "Lady Elton looked exceptionally charming in a dull blue chiffon over three lavatories and two swimming baths."

69 Carter, *Stop the Press!* 43.

70 AO, McKanday Papers, "Them Wuz the Days," typescript.

71 Lois Reynolds Kerr, interview with Linda Hale and Marjory Lang, Vancouver, 23 April 1988.

72 "Newspaper Women," *Frank Leslie's Weekly*, 23 June 1892.
73 *Sixteen Self Sketches* (London 1949), 110, cited by Goodbody, "The *Star*," 148.
74 Macbeth, *The Land of Afternoon*, 200.
75 Meyer, "Society Reporting," 11.
76 "The Week in Society," Vancouver *World*, 12 April 1902.
77 *Manitoba Free Press*, 9 June 1906.
78 Ethel Rood Kinsey, "The Lone Scribes," in "Newspacket," 6, no. 3 (1 May 1940): 2.
79 See McDonald, "Vancouver's 'Four Hundred,'" for a discussion of the varying social milieux in western Canadian cities.
80 *Weekly Herald*, 5 February 1903. My thanks to Jeremy Mouat for the reference.
81 NA, MCC, vol. 24, file 1, Emily Murphy Scrapbook, unidentified clipping [c. 1921].
82 Carter, *Stop the Press!* 41. At this point the Social Credit Party was attempting to buy the Calgary *Albertan*, but it fell short of payments and had abandoned the effort by 1937 (Kesterton, *A History of Journalism in Canada*, 114).
83 "The Woman's Page," in "Newspacket," 3, no. 1 (November 1936): 3.
84 NA, MG30 D52, Macbeth Papers, vol. 2, Correspondence 1922, R.A. Cochrane to Madge Macbeth, 23 February 1922.
85 Macbeth, *The Land of Afternoon*, 197.
86 See "The Influence of Society on Politics," *Busy Man's Magazine*, June 1910, 95–6 for a discussion of how English social leaders manipulated the political milieu.
87 Gwyn, *Private Capital*, 281.
88 Tausky, *Sara Jeannette Duncan: Novelist of Empire*, 39.
89 "Ottawa's Vanity Fair," *Ottawa Citizen*, 2 April 1900.
90 Harte, "Canadian Journalists and Journalism," 414.
91 Coleman, *To London for the Jubilee*, 153–4.
92 NA, MG30 D29, Willison Papers, vol. 14, file 112, Fitzgibbon to Willison, 24 October 1902.
93 "The Memories Are Now History," Vancouver *Province*, 18 April 1973.
94 "The Social Round," Edmonton *Bulletin*, reprinted in the "Newspacket," 1, no. 4 (2 August 1937): 3.
95 "Newspacket," 5, no. 4 (September 1939): 1.
96 Florence Taylor to Marjory Lang, 1 July 1988.
97 Carter, *Stop the Press!* 42.
98 The military authorities were particularly anxious to demonstrate the marriageability of female volunteers and therefore employed official military photographers to document the event and distribute photos to the press (Pierson, *They're Still Women After All*, 160).

99 NA, MCC, vol. 1, file 7, Triennial Report 1913–20, "Historian's Report," 25.

100 NA, MCC, vol. 32, file 7, *Quill Driver*, 17 December 1924), 2.

101 NA, MCC, "What Canadian Women Journalists Might Do," in "Newsletter," January 1933, 2.

102 Cash, *Off the Record*.

103 CVA, CWPC, Vancouver Branch Papers, vol. 1, scrapbook 1, Grace McGaw to Edna Baker, 10 June 1955.

104 CVA, CWPC, Vancouver Branch Papers, vol. 1, Isabel Black Tyrwhitt to Myrtle Patterson, 13 December 1927.

105 Lois Reynolds Kerr, interview with Linda Hale and Marjory Lang, Vancouver B.C., 23 April 1988.

106 See the checklist of her plays in O'Neill, "The Playwrights' Studio Group," 96.

107 Crean, *Newsworthy*, 30–1.

108 Beasley, *Eleanor Roosevelt*, 54.

109 D.D., "Gripe column," "Newspacket," 9, no. 7 (May 1943): 2.

110 Peacocke, *Writing for Women*, 24.

CHAPTER EIGHT

1 The National Council of Women specifically used this title to validate its commanding role in the Canadian women's club movement. (Strong-Boag, *Parliament of Women*).

2 Ross, *Ladies of the Press*, 19.

3 Toronto *Globe*, 1 October 1886. On an earlier occasion a less sympathetic Duncan took exception to the florid emotionalism of a temperance meeting (*Globe*, 15 July 1885).

4 *Canadian Courier*, 28 January 1919.

5 Strong-Boag, *Parliament of Women*, 73–5.

6 Vancouver *World*, 30 April 1904.

7 "Notes by the Marchioness," Ottawa *Free Press*, 16 October 1899.

8 National Archives of Canada (NA), MG28 I232, Media Club of Canada (MCC), vol. 23, file 1, scrapbook of clippings, "Effie L. Storer," "The Rocking Chair," Winnipeg *Saturday Post* [c. 1911].

9 Weiss ("As Women and as Citizens," 251) found that 38% of Vancouver clubwomen had university degrees.

10 *Western Women's Weekly*, 21 August 1920.

11 "The Feminine Side of the Western West," *Man to Man*, December 1910, 1071–7.

12 Lang and Hale, "Women of the *World*."

13 No copies of the *Chronicle* remain, but Laverock's contempories lavished praise on it. See City of Vancouver Archives (CVA), CWPC, Vancouver Branch Papers, vol. 2, scrapbook 2, 8.

14 Prentice et al., *Canadian Women*, 205.

15 Jennie Smith, *Western Women's Weekly*, 13 December 1917; cited in Weiss, "As Women and as Citizens," 112.

16 *Edmonton Journal*, 13 January 1913.

17 NA, MCC, vol. 1, file 7, Triennial Report 1913, Isabel MacLean, "The Equipment of the Woman Journalist; and Keeping Up with the Times," 20. The fact that her mother, Mrs M.A. MacLean, was the first honorary president of the Women's Canadian Club branch in Vancouver gave Isobel a special intimacy with the ambitions of clubdom.

18 Susan Jackel argues that women journalists consciously constructed a power base within women's clubs through which they both initiated and publicized reform activity ("First Days, Fighting Days").

19 Lane, cited by Fergusson, *Alderman Abbie Lane of Halifax*, 20.

20 Saskatchewan Archives Board (SAB), McNaughton Papers, A1 E55, T.M. Straser to McNaughton, 4 April 1916.

21 SAB, McNaughton Papers, A1 E23, McCallum to McNaughton, 14 November 1917, McNaughton Papers.

22 SAB, McNaughton Papers, A1, E23, George Chipman to McNaughton, 20 January 1919.

23 SAB, McNaughton Papers, "Annual Report," Women's Section of the Saskatchewan Grain Growers' Association, 1917, 10.

24 Taylor, "Should I Drown Myself Now or Later?"

25 NA, MCC, Violet McNaughton, "Memories of Mae," in "Newspacket," 2 February 1955, 6.

26 SAB, McNaughton Papers, A1 E55, Mae Clendenan to McNaughton, 14 March 1921.

27 London Public Library, vol. 1, Literary Scrapbooks, 79, unidentified clipping [c. 1912].

28 Hale, "The Welcome Wagon," shows how presswomen advised their readers to join local societies in order to combat despair and loneliness.

29 Mary P. McCallum, "Women as an Organized Force," *Grain Growers' Guide*, 26 June 1918. See also SAB, McNaughton Papers, pamphlet file, Saskatchewan Grain Growers' Association, "History of the Women's Section of the Grain Growers' Association."

30 *Grain Growers' Guide*, 7 February 1912.

31 Bacchi (*Liberation Deferred?* 6) finds that journalists and writers comprised nearly 25% of the suffragist leadership.

32 Provincial Archives of Manitoba (PAM), CWPC, Winnipeg Branch, reel 3, scrapbook of clippings, Charlotte Whitton, "On Thinking It Over" [c. 1958]. Her maiden name was Anna O'Reilly. The fact that her husband was a civil servant may have motivated her decision to obscure her identity.

33 Jameson, "Give Your Other Vote to the Sister," 10–16. See chapter 9.

34 PAM, CWPC, Winnipeg Branch, reel 3, scrapbook of clippings, Charlotte

Whitton, "On Thinking It Over" [c. 1958]. See also Cleverdon, *The Woman Suffrage Movement in Canada*, 55–6.

35 Gorham, "Flora MacDonald Denison." Denison was probably not paid for her journalism and was never a member of the Canadian Women's Press Club.

36 McClung, *The Stream Runs Fast*, 118.

37 Ibid.

38 PAM, CWPC, Winnipeg Branch, minutes, 22 November 1917. Anne Anderson Perry, Florence Livesay, and Kennethe Haig volunteered to prepare the pamphlets, while Perry, Cornell, Haig, and Clendenan agreed to use their women's pages to boost government candidates.

39 Jackel suggests that Murphy and McClung deliberately penetrated the CWPC in order to garner the power of the press and presswomen for their reform causes ("First Days, Fighting Days").

40 PAM, CWPC, Winnipeg Branch, scrapbook of clippings, 92.

41 NA, MCC, vol. 24, file 2, scrapbook of Emily Ferguson Murphy, 1913–33. At the CWPC triennial of 1923, the club resolved to ask the federal government to appoint Magistrate Murphy to the League of Nations International Conference on Narcotic Drugs. Drug abuse was another of Murphy's causes (NA, MCC, vol. 1, file 7, Triennial Report 1920–23, 8).

42 *Canadian Courier*, September 1914, 14.

43 PAM, CWPC, Winnipeg Branch, reel 3, scrapbook, Winnipeg *Tribune*, 23 November 1914.

44 The president of the Edmonton Branch mildly scolded the Alberta soldiers for this habit (PAM, CWPC, Winnipeg Branch, reel 3, Margaret Beaufort to the Alberta Soldiers at Salisbury Plain, 16 November 1914).

45 Garvin, *Canadian Poets*, 325.

46 CVA, CWPC, Vancouver Branch Papers, vol. 2, scrapbook 1, Vancouver *Province*, 24 September 1923.

47 *Grain Growers' Guide* 27 December 1916.

48 Cook, "Francis Marion Beynon and the Crisis of Christian Reformism,"198. Cook suggests (207n68) that Beynon's stance on the war permanently alienated her from her former friends in the CWPC. Francis Beynon does not figure in the postwar records of the club, even though she eventually returned to Canada. For a thorough analysis of Beynon's pacifist views, see Roberts, "Women against War" 48–65. According to Beynon, A.V. Thomas was dismissed for shaking hands with an anti-conscription politician (SAB, A1 E23, McNaughton Papers, Francis Beynon to Violet McNaughton, 20 February 1917).

49 Beynon, *Aleta Dey*, 213. The incident referred to was most likely the widely publicized atrocity story of the Canadian soldier supposedly "crucified" by the Germans in Belgium.

50 McClung made her feminist views about war plain in her tract *In Times Like These* (1915). She discussed her sorrow about the divisive effect the war had on her "old crowd" in Winnipeg in *The Stream Runs Fast,* 139.

51 Prentice et al., *Canadian Women,* 263.

52 Her appointment was assistant secretary to the Government Commission on Employment, specifically charged with investigating women's unemployment.

53 MacMurchy, *The Woman – Bless Her,* 28.

54 Ibid., 30–2.

55 SAB, McNaughton Papers, Jessie MacIver to Violet McNaughton, 13 December 1918. Earlier "the Countrywoman" [McCallum] had outlined many of these objections (*Grain Growers' Guide,* 16 October 1918).

56 McCallum, "The Call of Protection," *Grain Growers' Guide,* 5 March 1919.

57 Strong-Boag, *The New Day Recalled,* 192.

58 Miriam Green Ellis recollected her friendship with Cora Hind in a "Guest Editorial" for the "Newspacket," 17, no. 6 (March 1953): 2.

59 NA, MG30 D85, Dibney Papers, file 1, Grant Dexter, "The Unconquered," unidentified clipping.

60 SAB, McNaughton Papers, A1 E23, 18 March 1919.

61 "Newspacket," 5, no. 2 (February 1939): 4.

62 "Newspacket," 6, no. 2 (February 1940): 2.

63 For an analysis of the way writers were inducted into the propaganda industry during wartime, see Buitenhuis, *The Great War of Words.*

64 NA, MCC, vol. 45, file 23, "Publicity: A Peace-Making Factor," address to the General Federation of Women's Clubs, Kansas, 16 May [1938?].

65 See the discussion of how the postwar development of public relations professionals sharpened journalists' sense of their own mission, in Marzolf, *Civilizing Voices,* 106–18, and Schudson, *Discovering the News,* 122–50.

66 SAB, McNaughton Papers, A1 E23, McCallum to Violet McNaughton, 24 September 1919.

67 Brazelton, *Writing and Editing for Women,* 69.

68 Alexander held the job during 1928 but was back to cobbling a variety of freelance jobs together after that (NA, MCC, vol. 1, file 7, Triennial Report 1926–29, membership list).

69 CVA, CWPC, Vancouver Branch Papers, vol. 2, scrapbook 1, 41, "Newspaper Woman Made Press Agent to Maccabees B.A.," *Western Women's Weekly,* [c. 1924].

70 Price recounted her success at the CWPC convention (NA, MCC, vol. 1, file 7, Trienniel Report 1932–35, "President's Address," 50).

71 Vancouver *World,* 12 May 1921.

72 "Woman about Town," Toronto *Telegram,* 10 May 1924.

73 Ibid.

74 Vancouver *Province,* 24 September 1923.

75 "Newspacket," 14, no. 7 (October 1948): 3.

76 NA, CWPC, Ottawa Branch Papers, vol. 3, scrapbook 1916–30, Toronto *Mail and Empire,* 25 June 1926.

77 Cranston, *Ink on My Fingers,* 138.

78 *Maclean's,* 1 February 1928), 7.

79 Ibid.

80 Strong-Boag, *The New Day Recalled,* 196–7.

81 Alice Harriet Parsons, "Women of Canada ... Wake Up!" *Canadian Home Journal,* November 1934, 12.

82 A number of press club members had political careers besides those noted below: Margaret McWilliams, Nellie McClung, Alice Ashworth Townley, Elsie Bell Gardner, and Abbie Lane.

83 MacPherson ("Careers of Canadian University Women," 34) cited the testimony of a woman journalist who maintained that newspaper work was "perhaps the most valuable preparation one can have, after a good education, for the public and semi-public work which women must more and more undertake."

84 MacGill, *My Mother the Judge.* Helen Gregory MacGill wrote a number of books on the law as it affected women and children, including *Daughters, Wives, and Mothers in British Columbia* (1913) and *Laws for Women and Children in British Columbia* (1925).

85 SAB, McNaughton Papers, A1 D48, 23 June 1923.

86 SAB, McNaughton Papers, A1 D48, McWilliams to McNaughton, 26 March 1943.

87 SAB, McNaughton Papers, A1 E23, McCallum to McNaughton, 2 April 1921.

88 Patriarche, "Motion Pictures and Community Standards," proceedings and papers of the Fourth Annual Canadian Conference on Child Welfare, Winnipeg, 1923, 125.

89 PAM, Livesay Papers, folder 6, Valance Patriarche to "Kilmeny", 11 March 1922.

90 "Newspacket," 17, no. 1 (December 1951): 4.

91 Hamilton Public Library, Special Collections, Henderson Papers, vol. 1, scrapbooks, 1924–46, biographical notes by Grace Elton Hemingway, 29 April 1949.

92 Stursberg, *Extra!* 40.

93 When Hodges won her position, the Vancouver *News-Herald* headlined its news item "Nancy Hodges Becomes First Woman Speaker in the World" (13 December 1949). The Victoria *Colonist* (14 December 1949) qualified its interpretation, noting that Mary Ellen Smith had acted as speaker in 1928.

94 Aitken, *Hey Ma! I Did It,* 16.

95 Alice Harriet Parsons, "Women of Canada ... Wake Up!" *Canadian Home Journal,* November 1934, 12.

96 NA, MCC, vol. 45, file 19, E.B. Price scrapbook, "Have Canadian Women Failed in Politics?" *Liberty,* 29 February 1936, 28.

97 "The Vanity and Vexation of Too Many Clubs," *Saturday Night,* 5 May 1923.

98 Stursburg, *Extra!* 36.

99 *Winnipeg Free Press,* 20 March 1943, reprinted in "Newspacket," 9, no. 7 (May 1943): 3.

100 Filene *Him/Her/Self,* 123.

101 NA, MCC, vol. 1, file 7, Triennial Report 1932–35, "President's Address," 52.

102 "Newspacket," 8, no. 2 (15 March 1942): 2.

103 "Newspacket," 27, no. 1 (December 1960): 4.

104 Doyle, *Hurly-Burly,* 35.

105 "Newspacket," 27, no. 1 (December 1960): 4.

106 "Newsletter," May 1931, 3.

107 Lipsett-Skinner's reports for the Winnipeg *Tribune* of July 1913, cited by Berton, "Hard Times in the Old West," 12.

108 "Women in the Public Eye: Genevieve Lipsett-Skinner," *Saturday Night,* 25 July 1925, 23.

109 Dempsey, *No Life for a Lady,* 100.

110 Ibid., 107.

111 Strong-Boag, *The New Day Recalled,* 194. Strong-Boag draws special attention to the activity of women's clubs in the West, where local networks thrived, even as the huge nationals stagnated.

112 Beasley, *Eleanor Roosevelt and the Media.*

113 NA, MCC, vol. 1, file 7, Triennial Report 1932–35, "President's Address," 53.

114 Elizabeth Bailey Price, "What Is Wrong with Women's Clubs?" *Chatelaine,* January 1939, 50.

115 CVA, CWPC, Vancouver Branch Papers, vol. 2, scrapbook 1, The Scribe, "A Nose for News: or, the Editor's Opportunity for Service," unidentified clipping.

116 Brazelton, *Writing and Editing for Women,* 39.

117 CVA, CWPC, Vancouver Branch Papers, vol. 1, minutes, 17 September 1923.

118 UWSP, Long Papers, box 80, no. 3, n.d. "Women's Clubs and the Press" was written specifically by Rodden to help members of the Canadian Association of Consumers with publicity.

119 Ibid.

120 "Newspacket," 5, no. 4 (1 September 1939): 4.

121 Elizabeth Long, "The Woman's Page," in "Newspacket," 3, no. 1 (2 November 1936): 4.

122 "Newspacket," 6, no. 1 (1 November 1939): 1.

123 Rica McLean Farquharson, "Calling All Women!" *Canadian Home Journal*, November 1943, 8, 9, 59, 69, 73.

124 PAM, CWPC, Winnipeg Branch Papers, reel 3, scrapbook of clippings, Mr Critcheley, *Winnipeg Free Press*, 20 February 1967.

CHAPTER NINE

1 Grace Denison, *Saturday Night*, 16 November 1912, 30.

2 Virginia Cook, writing for *Matrix*, journal of the Theta Sigma Phi fraternity of female journalism students, cited by June Handeland Lee, "The Birth of a Notion, " *Landmarks: Magazine of Northwest History and Preservation* 3, no. 3 (Fall 1984): 21.

3 Lumsden, "'You're a Tough Guy, Mary.'"

4 National Archives of Canada (NA), MG28 I232, Media Club of Canada (MCC), vol. 1, file 8, Triennial Report 1935–38, "Address by Ishbel Ross," 87.

5 Howard Good analyses the stereotypes in *Acquainted with the Night*. Douglas Fetherling notes how ubiquitous these popular culture images were in Canada by the 1920s (*The Rise of the Canadian Newspaper*, 108–9).

6 *Sob Sister* (1931), *Dance, Fools, Dance* (1931), *The Final Edition* (1932), *Fly-Away Baby* (1932), *Front Page Woman* (1935) (Lumsden, "You're a Tough Guy Mary," 918).

7 *Macleans*, 15 May 1937, 12–13, 65–7.

8 Ross, *Ladies of the Press*, 11.

9 Stanley Walker, foreword, in Ross, *Ladies of the Press*, xi.

10 Ibid.

11 NA, MCC, vol. 1, file 8, Triennial Report 1935–38, "Address by Ishbel Ross," 86.

12 Aileen Campbell, "The Memories Are Now History," Vancouver *Province*, 16 April 1973.

13 "So Many Words Ago: Mary Adelaide Dawson Snider," in "Newspacket," July 1961, 2.

14 Archives of Ontario (AO), C.H.J. Snider Papers, file 1, Biographical and Family 1896–1976.

15 NA, MCC, vol. 24, file 1, Emily Murphy Scrapbook, 1913–33.

16 Toronto *Evening Telegram*, 19 April 1912.

17 "So Many Words Ago: Mary Adelaide Dawson Snider," in " Newspacket," July 1961, 2.

18 Fetherling, *The Rise of the Canadian Newspaper*, 109.

19 Toronto *Telegram*, 29 May 1919.

20 Ibid.

21 Toronto *Telegram*, 6 September 1932.

22 Ross, *Ladies of the Press*, 9.

23 City of Vancouver Archives (CVA), CWPC Vancouver Branch, vol. 2, scrapbook 1, 87.
24 Stursberg, *Extra!* 36.
25 Ibid., 35.
26 Ibid., 65.
27 The Vancouver *Province*, 25 May 1974.
28 Robertson, *The Girls in the Balcony*, 18.
29 Ibid., 42.
30 NA, MCC, "Newspacket," 10, no. 1 (August 1943): 3.
31 Ibid.
32 Ibid.
33 "Newspacket," 16, no. 1 (August 1949): 2.
34 Bannerman, *Leading Ladies*, 387.
35 Ibid.
36 University of Alberta, Bruce Peel Special Collections (UA), Ellis Papers, speech to the CWPC triennial 1932, "Special Fields."
37 Ibid.
38 Rex, *No Daughter of Mine*, 38. Griffiths's more singular achievement was as Canada's first and, for a long time, only photograph editor (Kesterton, *A History of Journalism*, 89).
39 "Women in Journalism," *Journalism Quarterly* 2 (1925): 38–41
40 Kennethe Haig, "Tribute to a Great Canadian," in "Newspacket," 9, no. 5 (November 1942): 1.
41 NA, MG30 D85, Dibney Papers, file 1, "The Unconquered," unidentified clipping.
42 UA, Ellis Papers, speech to the CWPC, 27 June 1956, 30.
43 See MacEwan, ... *And Mighty Women Too*, Hacker, *E. Cora Hind*, Haig, *Brave Harvest*.
44 UA, Ellis Papers, "Farm Patchwork," lecture to Quota Club, June 1941.
45 UA, Ellis Papers, speech to the Regina Livestock Association, 25 March 1943.
46 Ibid.
47 UA, Ellis Papers, box 2, folder 5, unidentified newspaper clipping announcing "the favorite Toronto Soprano, Mrs Miriam Green Ellis" to appear at Heintsman Hall on Friday, Nov. 18 [no year].
48 Suggestion made by Douglas Waterston, who worked with Miriam Green Ellis on the *Family Herald and Weekly Star* in the 1940s (Douglas Waterston to Linda Hale, 19 September 1988).
49 UA, Ellis Papers, box 2, folder 1.
50 UA, Ellis Papers, box 2, folder 5, Reminiscences, undated letter from her mother.
51 Ruth Bowen, "Among Pioneers," *Edmonton Journal*, 28 November 1964.
52 UA, Ellis Papers, speech to the Regina Livestock Association, 25 March 1943.

53 NA, MCC, vol. 2, file 28, "'Turn in the Road' Announces Miriam Green Ellis Upon Eve of Retirement from Newspaper Work," Winnipeg *Tribune*, 27 December 1952.

54 MacEwan, ... *And Mighty Women Too*, 171.

55 UA, Ellis Papers, "Hon. Frank Oliver," typescript for CBC broadcast, 4 June 1941.

56 Ibid. The ellipses are in the original typescript.

57 Ellis recalled how some of the northerners she encountered rebuffed her because Cameron had forgotten to return photos she had been lent (UA, Ellis Papers, folder 4, speech to CWPC, 27 June 1956, 14).

58 "MGE looks back," Montreal *Family Herald and Weekly Star*, 19 June 1940, 7.

59 UA, Ellis Papers, box 1, Memory Book, 7 January 1953.

60 Henry, "Private Lives," 101.

61 P.W. Luce, "At Odds with Life," *Vancouver Sun*, 3 November 1951.

62 Edith McConnell Murray, "Let's Go Shopping," Vancouver *News Advertiser*, 5 October 1951, and Luce, "At Odds with Life."

63 "Just Who Is the Profiteer?," *Vancouver Sun* 3 July 1919; "Throw the Gates Wide Open," *Vancouver Sun*, 4 July 1919; "Encourage Small Investors," *Vancouver Sun*, 5 July 1919; "Canada Should Have a Navy," *Vancouver Sun*, 6 July 1919.

64 Luce, "At Odds with Life," *Vancouver Sun*, 3 November 1951.

65 Murray, "Let's Go Shopping, Vancouver *News-Advertiser*, 5 October 1951.

66 Luce, "At Odds with Life." The rift was later healed by the Washington Conferences' agreements which, for a time, limited the naval strength of the major maritime powers.

67 *Vancouver Sun*, 27 Oct. 1933.

68 Ibid.

69 CVA, Vancouver CWPC, souvenir booklet, triennial 1923.

70 "Newspacket," 5, no. 3 (May 1939): 3.

71 *Saturday Night*, 28 December 1935, 16.

72 Quoted by Eggleston, *While I Still Remember*, 153.

73 Desbarats, *Guide to the Canadian News Media*, 123.

74 A fragmentary memoir by Katie Dawson is included in her brother's papers (AO, C.H.J. Snider Papers, file 1, Biographical and Family 1896–1976).

75 NA, MCC, Triennial Report 1913–20, "Historian's Report," 25.

76 Genevieve Lipsett-Skinner, "Why Girls Leave Home," in "Newsletter," May 1933, 1.

77 "Women in the Public Eye: Genevieve Lipsett-Skinner," *Saturday Night*, 25 July 1925, 23.

78 Lipsett-Skinner, "Why Girls Leave Home," in "Newspacket," May 1933, 2.

79 Ibid.

80 *Vancouver Sun*, 4 March 1924.

81 Lipsett-Skinner, "Why Girls Leave Home," in "Newsletter," May 1933, 1.
82 Ibid.
83 "Newspacket," 1, no. 2 (February 1935): 2.
84 NA, MCC, vol. 4, files 4-31, executive circulars 1934–38.
85 Ibid.
86 Ellis, "Special Fields," in "Newsletter," October 1932, 8.
87 At the time of her election in 1952 there were only two other life members, plus the honorary life president (NA, MCC, vol. 17, file 2).
88 NA, MCC vol. 15, file 15-12, Evelyn Tufts to Memorial Awards Committee Judges [Elsa Herwig and Bernice Coffey], 9 October 1948.
89 Meg McLaughlin, "Ottawa's Ball of Fire," *Saturday Night,* 10 January 1950, 30.
90 See her correspondence with Charles Bruce, in which she discusses her identification with other writers a decade before her career as a reporter took off (Dalhousie University Library, Charles Bruce Papers, 189, Evelyn Tufts to Charles Bruce, 15 January 1924).
91 Meg McLaughlin, "Ottawa's Ball of Fire," *Saturday Night,* 10 January 1950, 30.
92 "Newspacket," 8, no. 2 (15 March 1942): 3.
93 Bannerman, *Leading Ladies,* 385.
94 Ibid.
95 "Newspacket," 8, no. 2 (15 March 1942): 3
96 See Freeman, *Kit's Kingdom,* 105–21.
97 Freeman, pp. 118–20.
98 Rowland, "Kit Watkins," 19.
99 Boultbee, *Pilgrimages and Personalities,* 68–9.
100 "War Correspondent Talks to Canadian Club Women," *Vancouver Sun,* 2 November 1923.
101 Boultbee, *Pilgrimages and Personalities,* 223.
102 Ibid., 69, 230.
103 Ibid., 270.
104 "Writer, Rights Champion Beatrice Furniss Dies at 92," Vancouver *Province,* 28 Oct. 1977.
105 CVA, CWPC, Vancouver Branch Papers, vol. 2, scrapbook, 13.
106 Beatrice Nasmyth to her father, 16 August 1917, cited by Jameson, "Give Your Other Vote to the Sister," 12.
107 Mary MacLeod Moore, "London Press Women," *Saturday Night,* 26 June 1920, 21.
108 NA, MG30 D29, Willison Papers, vol. 30, file 225, Montizambert to Willison, 9 November 1925.
109 Margaret Bell, "Nothing Ventured, Nothing Won: How Canadian Women Welcomed the New Year in Belgium," *Canadian Courier,* 11 December 1915, 9.

110 Wagner, *Women War Correspondents*, 3, 22.
111 "Newspacket," 10, no. 3 (Feb 1944): 1.
112 Sebba, *Battling for News*, 169.
113 Ibid., 148.
114 Ibid., 139.
115 Wagner, *Women War Correspondents*, 22.
116 Sebba, *Battling for News*, 154.
117 "Newspacket," 11, no. 3 (March 1945): 4.
118 Ibid.
119 Edwards, *Women of the World*, 149.
120 Ibid., 4.
121 Edwards, *Women of the World*, 5.
122 Arnold, *One Woman's War*, 3–4.
123 Ibid., 4.
124 Ibid., 16.
125 Ibid., 19.
126 Ibid., 85.
127 "Newspacket," 8, no. 2 (15 March 1942): 2.
128 "Newspacket," 11, no. 1 (August 1944): 2.
129 "Newspacket," 10, no. 3 (February 1944): 3.
130 Ibid.
131 *Globe and Mail,* 11 December 1991.
132 Desmond, *Tides of War,* 343.
133 Ibid.
134 "I'll Always Remember: My Two Weeks in Paris," *Chatelaine,* November 1944, 11, 62–4.
135 "Newspacket," 8, no. 2 (15 March 1942): 2.
136 Desmond, *Tides of War,* 402.
137 NA, MCC, vol. 17, file 2, biographical notes on Margaret Ecker Francis, 5 March 1954, and vol. 1, file 8, Triennial Report 1942–46, 53.
138 Edwards, *Women of the World,* 151.
139 NA, MCC, vol. 11, file 22, *Globe and Mail,* 7 April 1965.
140 "Writer, Rights Champion Beatrice Furniss Dies at 92," Vancouver *Province,* 26 October 1977.
141 NA, MCC, vol. 17, file 2, biographical notes on Margaret Ecker Francis, 5 March 1954.
142 *Globe and Mail,* 11 December 1991.
143 Edwards, *Women of the World,* 4.
144 June Callwood, who began her career in the 1940s, had the consciousness-raising advantage of the second-wave women's movement behind her when she confided her experiences with the unwanted advances of George McCullagh of the *Globe and Mail* (Crean, *Newsworthy,* 33–4).
145 Kinnear, *In Subordination,* 152.

146 NA, MCC, vol. 11, file 53, "Who's Who: Toronto Branch," information sheet filled in by Zoe Trotter.
147 Ross, *Ladies of the Press*, 11.

EPILOGUE

1 Department of Labour, *Women at Work in Canada*, 35.
2 NA, MCC, "Newspacket," 16, no. 1 (August 1949): 2.
3 Ibid.
4 Dora Dibney's editorial in the "Newpacket," 9, no. 7 (May 1943), insisted that women be part of the postwar planning process. Later she argued for paid maternity leave, free pre- and post-natal care, and scientifically run creches to protect women's right to work ("Newspacket," 11, 1 [August 1944]: 1). Kennethe Haig made a plea for single women, especially farm women, who might never marry and wanted to keep their jobs after the war ("Newspacket," 12, 1 [August 1945]: 3).
5 UA, Ellis Papers, folder 3, "Response to Toast to the Club," 10 April 1945.
6 "Newspacket," 16, no. 1 (August 1949): 1.
7 NA, MCC, vol. 8, file 5, Evelyn Murphy to Kay Nairn, 21 January 1962.
8 "Newspacket," 30, no. 3 (April 1968): 1.
9 "Newspacket," 30, no. 4 (June 1968): 1.
10 Ibid.
11 "Newspacket," 33, no. 4 (August 1971): 1.
12 Carter, *Stop the Press!* 213.
13 Robinson, "The Future of Women in the Canadian Media," 128.
14 "Status of Newspaperwomen," in "Newspacket," June 1964, 2. The survey found that two-thirds of the respondents were over forty.
15 Robinson, "The Future of Women in the Canadian Media," 128.
16 Nugent, "Canada's Silenced Communicators," 123–4.
17 Edwards, *Women of the World*, 244.
18 Robertson, "The Last of the Terrible Men," 129.
19 Ibid., 133.
20 Ibid.
21 Ibid.
22 Ibid.
23 Pelrine, "Whatchamacallit and Why," 8.
24 Thomas, "Sagas of Women Journalists," 132.
25 "Newspacket," December 1959, 2.
26 NA, MCC, vol. 8, file 4, Kay Mathers to Madeleine Lavason, 7 March 1957.
27 Ibid. (emphasis in original).

Bibliography

MANUSCRIPT COLLECTIONS

ARCHIVES OF ONTARIO
M.O. Hammond
Hugh McKanday
Mary Bouchier Sanford
C.H.J. Snider
Sir John Willison
Frank Yeigh

CITY OF EDMONTON ARCHIVES
Edna Kells

CITY OF VANCOUVER ARCHIVES
Canadian Women's Press Club, Vancouver Branch
Helen Gregory MacGill
Alice Ashworth Townley

GLENBOW FOUNDATION, CALGARY
Dora Dibney
Elizabeth Bailey Price

HAMILTON PUBLIC LIBRARY, SPECIAL COLLECTIONS
Nora Frances Henderson

METROPOLITAN TORONTO LIBRARY, BALDWIN ROOM
Lawrence Burpee
Grace Fairbairn

Alice Harriet Parsons
Margaret Zieman

NATIONAL ARCHIVES OF CANADA
Kate Scott Aitken
Martha Louise Black
Canadian Authors' Association
Ethel Chadwick
Kathleen Blake Coleman
Dora Dibney
Dougall Family
Katherine Hughes
Elizabeth Long
Madge Macbeth
Kate Massiah
Media Club of Canada
Ottawa Press Club
Ida Margaret Clarke Thompson
Charlotte Elizabeth Whitton
John Stephen Willison

PROVINCIAL ARCHIVES OF ALBERTA
Canadian Women's Press Club, Edmonton Branch
Miriam Elston

PROVINCIAL ARCHIVES OF BRITISH COLUMBIA
Julia Henshaw
Nellie Letitia McClung

PROVINCIAL ARCHIVES OF MANITOBA
Canadian Women's Press Club, Winnipeg Branch
Dora Dibney
Florence Randal Livesay
Margaret McWilliams

PROVINCIAL ARCHIVES OF SASKATCHEWAN
Ruth Matheson Buck
Annie Elizabeth Mary Hewlett
Violet M. McNaughton

QUEEN'S UNIVERSITY ARCHIVES
W.W. Campbell
John Garvin

Lorne Pierce
E.W. Thomson

UNIVERSITY OF ALBERTA, BRUCE PEEL SPECIAL COLLECTIONS
Miriam Green Ellis

UNIVERSITY OF BRITISH COLUMBIA, SPECIAL COLLECTIONS
Isabel MacKay
Barry Mather collection, British Columbia Institute of Journalists
Blanche Holt Murison

UNIVERSITY OF SASKATCHEWAN, MURRAY MEMORIAL LIBRARY
Annie Elizabeth Mary Hewlett
Ida Janet Munro (Clarke) Thompson

UNIVERSITY OF TORONTO, FISHER RARE BOOKS
Printer and Publisher
Flora MacDonald Denison
Toronto *Star Weekly Magazine*

UNIVERSITY OF WATERLOO, SPECIAL COLLECTIONS
Martha Louise Black
Elaine M. Catley
Annie Elizabeth Mary Hewlett
E. Cora Hind
Elizabeth Long
Elizabeth Smith Shortt
Claire Wallace

CENSUS PUBLICATIONS

Canada. Dominion Bureau of Statistics. *Sixth Census of Canada, 1921.* Ottawa: King's Printer 1929.
– *Seventh Census of Canada, 1931.* Ottawa: King's Printer 1936.
– *Eighth Census of Canada, 1941.* Ottawa: King's Printer 1946.

NEWSPAPERS AND MAGAZINES

Newspapers

Calgary *Albertan*
Calgary *Herald*
Edmonton *Bulletin*

Edmonton Journal
London *Farmer's Advocate* (Winnipeg before 1925)
Montreal *Family Herald and Weekly Star*
Montreal Star
Ottawa Citizen
Ottawa *Free Press*
Ottawa Journal
Toronto *Globe* (*Globe and Mail* after 1936)
Toronto *Mail* (*Mail and Empire* after 1895)
Toronto Star
Toronto *Telegram*
Toronto *World*
Vancouver *News-Advertiser*
Vancouver *Province*
Vancouver Sun
Vancouver *Western Women's Weekly*
Vancouver *World*
Winnipeg Free Press (*Manitoba Free Press* before 1931)
Winnipeg *Free Press Prairie Farmer*
Winnipeg *Grain Growers' Guide*
Winnipeg *Tribune*

Magazines

Busy Man's Magazine
Canadian Courier
Canadian Home Journal
Canadian Magazine
Chatelaine
Maclean's
Saturday Night
Week
Western Home Monthly

SECONDARY SOURCES

Adams, Catherine. "An Annotated Edition of Sara Jeannette Duncan's Contributions to *The Week*." MA research paper, Carleton University 1980.
Adams, George H. "Wages or Salaries?" *Quill* 20, no. 2 (February 1932): 3, 4, 15.
Aitken, Kate. *Never a Day So Bright*. Toronto: Longmans Green [1956].
Aitken, Margaret. *Hey Ma! I Did It*, with Byrne Hope Sanders. Toronto: Clarke Irwin 1953.

Alden, Cynthia Westover. "Women in Journalism: The American Woman in Action – II." *Frank Leslie's Popular Monthly*, 18 December 1898, 208–21.

Allen, Eric W. "The Journalistic Type of Mind." *Journalism Bulletin* 1 (1924): 35–43.

Anderson, Margo. "The History of Women and the History of Statistics." *Journal of Women's History* 4, no. 1 (Spring 1992/3): 14–36.

Arnold, Gladys. *One Woman's War: A Canadian Reporter with the Free French.* Toronto: Lorimer 1987.

Bacchi, Carol Lee. *Liberation Deferred? The Ideas of the English-Canadian Suffragists, 1877–1918.* Toronto: University of Toronto Press 1983.

Backhouse, Constance B. "'To Open the Way for Others of My Sex': Clara Brett Martin's Career as Canada's First Woman Lawyer." *Canadian Journal of Women and the Law* 1, no. 1 (1985): 1–41.

Bainbridge, Cyril, ed. *One Hundred Years of Journalism: Social Aspects of the Press.* London: Macmillan 1984.

Baldasty, Gerald J. *The Commercialization of News in the Nineteenth Century.* Madison: University of Wisconsin Press 1992.

Banks, Elizabeth L. *Autobiography of a Newspaper Girl.* New York: Dodd 1902.

– *Campaigns of Curiosity: Journalistic Adventures of an American Girl in London.* London: Cassell 1894.

Bannerman, Jean. *Leading Ladies: Canada 1639–1967.* Dundas, Ont.: Carrswood 1977.

Barber, Marilyn. "The Servant Problem in Manitoba 1896–1930." In *First Days, Fighting Days: Women in Manitoba History*, ed. Mary Kinnear, 53–75. Regina: Canadian Plains Reseach Centre 1987.

Bayard, Mary Temple. "Eve Brodlique." *Canadian Magazine* (May–October 1896,: 515–18.

Bearden, Jim, and Linda Butler. *Shadd: "he Life and Times of Mary Shadd Cary.* Toronto: N.C. Press 1977.

Beasley, Maureen. *Eleanor Roosevelt and the Mᵾ ᷍: A Public Quest for Self-Fulfillment.* Urbana: University of Illinois Pre᷍ 1987.

– "Women in Journalism Education: The Formative Period, 1908–1930." *Journalism History* 13, no. 1 (Spring 1986): 10–18.

– "The Women's National Press Club: Case Study of Professional Aspirations." *Journalism History* 15, no. 4 (Winter 1988): 112–21.

Beasley, Maureen, and Sheila Gibbons. *Taking Their Place: A Documentary History of Women and Journalism.* Washington: American University Press 1993.

Beauchamp, Colette. *Judith Jasmin 1916–1972: De feu et de flamme.* Quebec: Boreal 1992.

Bennett, Arnold. *Journalism for Women: A Practical Guide.* New York: John Lane 1898.

Benson, Susan Porter. *Counter Cultures: Saleswomen, Managers, and Customers in*

American Department Stores 1890–1940. Urbana: University of Illinois Press 1986.

Berton, Pierre. "Hard Times in the Old West." *Canadian Heritage,* February/ March 1985, 11–14.

Beynon, Francis. *Aleta Dey.* London: C.W. Daniel 1919. Republished London: Virago 1988.

Bland, M. Susan. "Henrietta the Homemaker and 'Rosie the Riveter': Images of Women in Advertising in *Maclean's Magazine,* 1939–50." *Atlantis* 8, no. 2 (Spring 1983): 61–86.

Blore, Bette Noreen. "Women's Liberation as Portrayed through the Writing of Nellie McClung and Francis Beynon: An Agrarian Reform Perspective." MA research paper, Carleton University 1982.

Blum, Stella, ed. *Victorian Fashions and Costumes from Harper's Bazar: 1867–1898.* New York: Dover Publications 1974.

Boivin, Aurelien, and Kenneth Landy. "Françoise et Madeleine: Pionnières du journalism feminin au Québec." *Atlantis* 4 (1978): 63–74.

Bok, Edward. "Is the Newspaper Office the Place for a Girl?" *Ladies' Home Journal* February 1901, 18.

Boston, Ray. "W.T. Stead and Democracy by Journalism." In *Papers for the Millions: The New Journalism in Britain, 1850s to 1914,* ed. Joel Weiner, 91–106. New York: Greenwood 1988.

Boughner, Genevieve Jackson. *Women in Journalism.* New York: D. Appleton 1926.

Boultbee, Rosamund. *Pilgrimages and Personalities.* London: Hutchinson 1924.

Bowman, Charles. *Ottawa Editor.* Sydney, B.C.: Gray's Publishing 1966.

Boyce, George, et al., eds. *Newspaper History from the Seventeenth Century to the Present Day.* London: Constable 1978.

Brandenburg, George A.. "Research Shows Reader Prefercnce." *Editor and Publisher,* 16 January 1932, 30.

Brandt, Gail Cuthbert. "Postmodern Patchwork: Some Recent Trends in the Writing of Women's History in Canada." *Canadian Historical Review* 72, no. 4 (1991): 441–470.

Brann, W.C. "Women in Journalism." *Iconoclast* [c. 1890]. Reprinted in *Matrix* 17, no. 6 (August 1932): 13.

Brazelton, Ethel M. Colson. *Writing and Editing for Women.* New York: Funk and Wagnalls 1927.

Bridle, Augustus. "One of the Oddest of Editors," *Courier,* 23 September 1916, 1, 6, 21–2.

Brown, Charles H. *The Correspondents' War: Journalists in the Spanish-American War.* New York: Scribner's 1967.

Bruce, Charles. *News and the Southams.* Toronto: Macmillan 1968.

Buitenhuis, Peter. *The Great War of Words: British, American and Canadian*

Propaganda and Fiction, 1914–1933. Vancouver: University of British Columbia Press 1987.

Burkholder, Mabel. *"Kit" Kathleen Blake Coleman: Canada's First Female Journalist.* Hamilton: Hamilton Women's Press Club 1934.

Carter, Alixe. *Stop the Press! I've Made a Little Error, Notes on a Career 1932–1982.* Ottawa: Sunnybrae Books 1984.

Cash, Gwen. *I Like British Columbia.* Toronto: Macmillan 1939.

– *Off the Record: Personal Reminiscences of Canada's First Woman Reporter.* Langley, B.C.: Stagecoach 1977.

Caulfield, S.F.A. "New Employments for Girls." *Girls' Own Paper,* 5 March 1892, 363.

Chalmers, Floyd. *A Gentleman of the Press.* Toronto: Doubleday 1969.

Charlesworth, Hector. "The Canadian Girl." *Canadian Magazine* 1 (1897): 186–93.

– *Candid Chronicles: Leaves from the Note Book of a Canadian Journalist.* Toronto: Macmillan 1925

– *More Candid Chronicles.* Toronto: Macmillan 1928.

Chenier, Nancy Miller. "Agnes Maule Machar: Her Life, Social Concerns, and a Preliminary Bibliography of her Writing." MA research paper, Carleton University 1977.

Clarke, Patricia. *Pen Portraits: Women Writers and Journalists in Nineteenth-Century Australia.* Sydney: Pandora 1988:

Cleverdon, Catherine. *The Woman Suffrage Movement in Canada.* Toronto: University of Toronto Press [1950], 1970.

Coburn, Judi. "'I See and Am Silent': A Short History of Nursing." In *Women at Work: Ontario, 1850–1930,* ed. Janice Acton et al., 127–63. Toronto: Canadian Women's Educational Press 1974.

Cochrane, Jean. *Kate Aitken.* Don Mills: Fitzhenry & Whiteside 1979.

Coleman, Kathleen Blake. *To London for the Jubilee, by Kit.* Toronto: Morang 1897.

Connery, Thomas B. "A Third Way to Tell the Story: American Literary Journalism at the Turn of the Century." In *Literary Journalism in the Twentieth Century,* ed. Norman Sims, 3–20. New York and Oxford: Oxford University Press 1990.

Cook, Ramsay. "Francis Marion Beynon and the Crisis of Christian Reformism." In *The West and the Nation: Essays in Honour of W.L. Morton,* ed. Carl Berger and Ramsay Cook, 187–208. Toronto: McClelland and Stewart 1976.

Cott, Nancy. *The Grounding of Modern Feminism.* New Haven: Yale University Press 1987.

Covert, Catherine. "Journalism History and Women's Experience: A Problem in Conceptual Change." *Journalism History* 8 (1981): 2–60.

Craig, Susan, "Solidarity is a Sometimes Thing." *Content,* November/December 1987, 2.

Craik, William Arnot. *A History of Canadian Journalism.* Vol. 2. Toronto: Canadian Press Association 1908.

Cranston, J.A. *Ink on My Fingers.* Toronto: Ryerson Press 1953.

Crean, Susan. *Newsworthy: The Lives of Media Women.* Toronto: Stoddart 1985.

Creese, Gillian, and Veronica Strong-Boag, eds. *British Columbia Reconsidered: Essays on Women.* Vancouver: Press Gang 1992.

Currie, Margaret [Mrs Eldred Archibald]. *Margaret Currie: Her Book.* Toronto: Hunter Rose 1924.

Danylewycz, Marta, Beth Light, and Alison Prentice. "The Evolution of the Sexual Division of Labour in Teaching: A Nineteenth-Century Ontario and Quebec Case Study." *Histoire sociale/Social History* 16, no. 31 (May 1983): 81–109.

Davidoff, Leonore. *The Best Circles: Society, Etiquette, and the Season.* London: Croom Helm 1973.

– "Mastered for Life: Servant and Wife in Victorian and Edwardian England." *Journal of Social History* 7 (1973–74): 406–28.

Dempsey, Lotta. *No Life for a Lady.* Musson Books: Don Mills 1976.

Department of Labour of Canada. *Women at Work in Canada, a Fact Book on the Female Labour Force.* Rev. edn. Ottawa: Queen's Printer 1958.

Desbarats, Peter. *Guide to Canadian News Media.* Toronto: Harcourt Brace Jovanovich 1990.

Desmond, Robert W. *Tides of War: World News Reporting 1931–45.* Iowa City: University of Iowa Press 1984.

Dodd, Dianne. "Women in Advertising: The Role of Canadian Women in the Promotion of Domestic Electrical Technology in the Interwar Period." In *Despite the Odds: Essays on Canadian Women and Science,* ed. Marianne Gosztonyi Ainley, 134–151. Montreal: Vehicule Press 1990.

Donald, Robert. *The Imperial Press Conference in Canada.* London: Hodder and Stoughton [c. 1920].

Dorr, Rheta Childe. *A Woman of Fifty.* New York: Funk and Wagnalls 1924.

Dougall, Lily. *The Madonna of a Day: A Study.* London: Richard Bentley 1896.

Downie, Jill. *A Passionate Pen: The Life and Times of Faith Fenton.* Toronto: HarperCollins 1996.

Doyle, Richard. *Hurly-Burly: A Time at the Globe and Mail.* Toronto: Macmillan 1990.

Drobot, Eve. "Half Begun, Half Done." *Content,* (May 1978), 3, 5–7, 26–31.

Duncan, Sara Jeannette (Mrs Everard Cotes). *A Daughter of Today.* New York: D. Appleton 1894.

Edwards, Julia. *Women of the World: The Great Foreign Correspondents.* Boston: Houghton Mifflin 1988.

Eggleston, Wilfrid. *While I Still Remember: A Personal Record.* Toronto: Ryerson Press 1968.

Ellinthorpe, Blanche. "From Teaching to Writing." *Country Guide*, February 1953, 68, 76.

Ferguson, Ted. *Kit Coleman, Queen of Hearts*. Toronto: Doubleday 1978.

Fergusson, C. Bruce. *Alderman Abbie Lane of Halifax*. Windsor, NS: Lancelot Press 1976.

Fetherling, Douglas. *The Rise of the Canadian Newspaper*. Toronto: Oxford University Press 1990.

Filene, Peter. *Him/Her/Self: Sex Roles in Modern America*. Baltimore: Johns Hopkins University Press 1974.

Forbes, Ernest R. "Battles in Another War: Edith Archibald and the Halifax Feminist Movement." In *Challenging the Regional Stereotypes: Essays on the Twentieth Century in the Maritimes*, 67–89. Fredericton: Acadiensis Press 1989.

Fowler, Marian. *Redney: A Life of Sara Jeannette Duncan*. Toronto: Anansi 1983.

Freeman, Barbara. "'Every Stroke Upward': Women Journalists in Canada, 1880s–1900." *Canadian Women's Studies* 7, no. 3 (Fall 1986): 43–46.

– *Kit's Kingdom: The Journalism of Kathleen Blake Coleman*. Ottawa: Carleton University Press 1989.

– "Laced In and Let Down: Women's Fashion Features in Canadian Dailies – 1890s." Paper presented to the Canadian Historical Association, Victoria, 27 May 1990.

Fulford, Robert. *The Best Seat in the House*. Don Mills: Collins 1988.

Garvin, John. *Canadian Poets*. Toronto: McClelland and Stewart [1926].

– ed. *Lyrics and Sonnets*. Toronto: Nelson 1931.

Gerson, Carole. *A Purer Taste: The Writing and Reading of Fiction in Nineteenth-Century Canada*. Toronto: University of Toronto Press 1989.

Good, Howard. *Acquainted with the Night: The Image of Journalists in American Fiction, 1890–1930*. Metuchen, N.J.: Scarecrow 1986.

– *The Journalist as Autobiographer*. Metuchin, N.J.: Scarecrow 1993.

Goodbody, John. "The *Star*: Its Role in the Rise of the New Journalism." In *Papers for the Millions: The New Journalism 1850s to 1915*, ed. Joel Weiner, 143–63. New York: Greenwood 1988

Goodwyn, Rae. "The Early Journalism of Sara Jeannette Duncan: with a Chapter of Biography." MA thesis, University of Toronto 1964.

Gorham, Deborah. "Flora MacDonald Denison: Canadian Feminist." In *A Not Unreasonable Claim: Women and Reform in Canada 1880s–1920s*, ed. Linda Kealey, 47–70. Toronto: Canadian Women's Educational Press 1979.

– "Pen and Buckskin: Women Journalists Who Knew Wheat and Justice." *Content*, May 1977, 22–3.

– *Vera Brittain: A Feminist Life*. Oxford: Blackwell 1996.

– "Vera Brittain, Flora MacDonald Denison and the Great War: The

Failure of Non-Violence." In *Women and Peace: Theoretical, Historical, and Practical Perspectives,* ed. Ruth Roach Pierson, 79–106. London: Croom Helm 1987.

Gwyn, Sandra. *The Private Capital: Ambition and Love in the Age of Macdonald and Laurier.* Toronto: McClelland and Stewart 1984.

Hacker, Carlotta. *E. Cora Hind.* Don Mills, Ont.: Fitzhenry & Whiteside 1979.

Haig, Kennethe. *Brave Harvest: The Life Story of E. Cora Hind.* Toronto: Thomas Allen 1945.

Hale, Linda. "The Welcome Wagon: Canadian Presswomen and Western Settlement." Paper presented to the Canadian Historical Association, Victoria, 27 May 1990.

Hallett, Mary. "Nellie McClung and the Fight for the Ordination of Women in the United Church of Canada." *Atlantis* 4, no. 2 (Spring 1979): 2–16.

Hamel, Reginald. *Gaetane de Montreuil: Journaliste québécoise, 1869–1951.* Quebec: L'Aurore 1976.

Hamilton, C.F. "Canadian Journalism." *University Magazine,* February 1917, 17–40.

Harkness, Ross. *J.E. Atkinson of the Star.* Toronto: University of Toronto Press 1963.

Harrington, H.F., and T.T. Frankenburg. *Essentials in Journalism: A Manual in Newspaper Making for College Classes.* Boston: Atheneum Press 1912.

Harte, Walter Blackburn. "Canadian Journalists and Journalism." *New England Magazine,* December 1891, 411–41.

Harvey, Ruth. *Curtain Time.* Boston: Houghton Mifflin 1943.

Haymaker, Marion B. "Women's Opportunity in Journalism." *Publisher's Guide,* April 1913, 36.

Heilbrun, Carolyn. *Writing a Woman's Life.* New York: Norton 1988.

Hendley, W. Clark. "Dear Abby, Miss Lonelyhearts, and the Eighteenth Century: The Origins of the Newspapers Advice Column." *Journal of Popular Culture* 11, no. 2 (Fall 1977): 345–52.

Henry, Susan. "Changing Media History through Women's History." In *Women in Mass Communication: Challenging Gender Values,* ed. Pamela J. Creedon, 34–57. Newbury Park, Calif.: Sage Publications 1989.

– "Private Lives: An Added Dimension for Understanding Journalism History." *Journalism History* 6, no. 4 (1979–80): 98–102.

Hewlett, A.E.M. *A Too Short Yesterday.* Saskatoon: Western Producer 1970.

Hosmer, Mrs George E. "The Future of the Newspaper Woman." *National Printer-Journalist,* July 1916, 410–14.

Hutchison, Bruce. *The Far Side of the Street.* Toronto: Macmillan 1976.

Hyde, Grant Milner. *Journalistic Writing.* New York: D. Appleton 1922; 2nd edn., 1935.

Iacovetta, Franca, and Mariana Valverde, eds. *Gender Conflicts: New Essays in Women's History.* Toronto: University of Toronto Press 1992.

Jackel, Susan. "'First Days, Fighting Days': Prairie Presswomen and Suffrage Activism 1906–1916." In *First Days Fighting Days: Women in Manitoba History*, ed. Mary Kinnear, 53–75. Regina: Canadian Plains Research Centre 1987.

Jackman, Florence. "Chances for Women in Journalism." *Harper's Weekly*, 12 September 1903, 1492–3.

Jaher, Frederic Cople. "Style and Status: High Society in Late Nineteenth-Century New York." In *The Rich, the Well-Born, and the Powerful: Elites and Upper Classes in History*, ed. Jaher, 258–84. Urbana: University of Illinois Press 1973.

James, Jean. "What Journalism Schools Teach Women." *Ohio* 13, no. 8 (May 1931): 3–5.

Jameson, Sheilagh. "Give Your Other Vote to the Sister." *Alberta Historical Review* 15, no. 4 (1967): 10–16.

Jerrold, Mrs Clare. "That Woman's Column!" *Humanitarian*, n.s. 9, no. 3 (September 1896): 188.

Johnston, George. *The Weeklies: Biggest Circulation in Town*. Bolton: Canadian Weekly Newspapers Association 1972.

Keate, Stuart. *Paper Boy*. Toronto: Clarke Irwin 1980.

Keddell, Georgina. *The Newspapering Murrays*. Toronto: McClelland and Stewart 1967.

Kerr, Lois Reynolds, "Among Those Present." *Curtain Call* 10, no. 1 (October 1938).

– "Lois Kerr: Politics and the Canadian Theatre Yesterday." *Canadian Theatre Review* 27 (Summer 1980): 34–43.

– *Nellie McNabb*. Toronto: Samuel French 1937.

– *No Reporters Please*. Vancouver: New Play Centre 1971.

Kessler-Harris, Alice. *Women Have Always Worked: A Historical Overview*. Old Westbury, NY: Feminist Press 1981.

Kesterton, W.H. *A History of Journalism in Canada*. Toronto: McClelland and Stewart 1967.

Kinnear, Mary. *In Subordination: Professional Women, 1870–1970*. Montreal and Kingston: McGill-Queen's University Press 1995.

– ed. *First Days Fighting Days: Women in Manitoba History*. Regina: Canadian Plains Research Centre 1987.

Kochersberger, Robert C., Jr, ed. *More than a Muckraker: Ida Tarbell's Lifetime in Journalism*. Knoxville: University of Tennessee Press 1994.

Kroller, Eva-Marie. *Canadian Travellers in Europe 1851–1900*. Vancouver: University of British Columbia Press 1987.

Lamb, Bessie. "From 'Tickler' to 'Telegram': Notes on Early Vancouver Newspaper." *British Columbia Historical Quarterly* 9 (July 1945): 175–99.

Lancaster, William. *The Department Store: A Social History*. Leicester: Leicester University Press 1995.

Lang, Marjory. "Separate Entrances: The First Generation of Canadian Women Journalists." In *Re(dis)covering Our Foremothers: Nineteenth-Century Canadian Women Writers*, ed. Lorraine McMullen, 77–90. Ottawa: University of Ottawa Press 1988.

– "Women about Town: Chroniclers of the Canadian Social Scene at the Turn of the Century." *Journal of Newspaper and Periodical History* 6, no. 2 (1990): 3–30.

Lang, Marjory, and Linda Hale. "Women of the *World* and Other Dailies: The Lives and Times of Vancouver Newspaperwomen in the First Quarter of the Twentieth Century." *BC Studies* 85 (Spring 1990): 3–23.

Lee, Alan J. *The Origins of the Popular Press in England, 1855–1914*. London: Croom Helm 1976.

Lester, Tanya. *Women Rights/Writes: Some Historical Profiles of Western Canadian Writers*. Winnipeg: Lilith Pubications 1985.

Lewis, Norah. "Creating the Little Machine: Child-Rearing in British Columbia 1919–1939." *BC Studies* 56 (Winter 1982/3): 44–60.

Low, Frances. *Press Work for Women*. London: Upcott Gill 1904.

Lumsden, Linda. "'You're a Tough Guy, Mary – and a First-Rate Newspaperman': Gender and Women Journalists in the 1920s and 1930s." *Journalism and Mass Communication Quarterly* 72, no. 4 (Winter 1995): 913–21.

MacAree, J.V. *The Fourth Column*. Toronto: Musson 1934.

Macbeth, Madge. *Boulevard Career*. Toronto: Kingswood House 1957.

– [Knox, Gilbert]. *The Land of Afternoon*. Ottawa: Graphic 1924.

– *Over My Shoulder*. Toronto: Ryerson 1953.

McClung, Nellie. *In Times Like These*. Toronto: McLeod and Allen 1915.

– *The Stream Runs Fast: My Own Story*. Toronto: Thomas Allen 1965.

McCracken, Elizabeth. "Journalism for the College-Bred Girl." *Independent* 73 (1912): 435–6.

McDonald, R.A.J. *Making Vancouver: Class, Status, and Social Boundaries 1863–1913*. Vancouver: University of British Columbia Press 1996.

– "Vancouver's 'Four Hundred': The Quest for Wealth and Status in Canada's Urban West, 1886–1914." *Journal of Canadian Studies* 25 , no. 3 (Autumn 1990): 55–73.

MacEwan, Grant. *... And Mighty Women Too: Stories of Notable Western Canadian Women*. Saskatoon: Western Producer Prairie Books 1975.

MacGill, Elsie. *My Mother the Judge: A Biography of Judge Helen Gregory MacGill*. Toronto: Ryerson Press 1955.

MacGregor, D.A. "Adventures of Vancouver Newspapers, 1892–1926." *British Columbia Historical Quarterly* 10, no. 2 (April 1946): 89–142.

MacMurchy, Marjory. *The Canadian Girl at Work: A Book of Vocational Guidance*. Toronto: McClelland and Stewart 1919.

– *The Woman – Bless Her: Not as Amiable a Book as it Sounds*. Toronto: S.B. Gundy 1916.

MacPherson, Elsinore. "Careers of Canadian University Women." MA thesis, University of Toronto 1920.

Mahaffy, R.U. "The Tradition Makers: Colorful Moments in Canadian Journalism, Parts 2–6." *Canadian Journalist and Press Photographer*, January/ February 1960, 10–11, 14, 23.

Mander, Christine. *Emily Murphy, Rebel: First Woman Magistrate in the British Empire*. Toronto: Simon and Pierre 1985.

Marchildon, R.G. "Improving the Quality of Rural Life in Saskatchewan: Some Activities of the Women's Section of the Saskatchewan Grain Growers, 1913–1920." In *Building beyond the Homestead: Rural History on the Prairies*, ed. David C. Jones and Ian MacPherson, 88–109. Calgary: University of Calgary Press 1985.

March-Phillipps, Evelyn. "Women's Newspapers." *Fortnightly Review*, n.s. 56 (1894): 661–70.

Marvin, Gertrude L. "Newspaper Work for Women." In *Vocations for Trained Women*, ed. Alice Perkins, 227–40. Boston: Women's Educational and Industrial Union 1910.

Marzolf, Marion. *Civilizing Voices: American Press Criticism, 1880–1950*. White Plains, NY: Longmans 1991.

– *Up From the Footnote: A History of Women Journalists*. New York: Hastings House 1977.

Massey, Alice Vincent. *Occupations for Trained Women in Canada*. London: Dent 1920.

Melnyk, Steve. "Seventy-One Years Young." *Canadian Journalist and Press Photographer*, April/May 1959, 12, 40.

Meyer, Emma. "Society Reporting among the '400.' " *Editor and Publisher*, 12 December 1931, 11.

Miller, Orlo. *A Century of Western Ontario: The Story of London, "The Free Press," and Western Ontario, 1849–1949*. Westport, Conn.: Greenwood Press 1949.

Milliman, Loren H. "Writer Warns of Glaring Errors in Articles for Food Pages." *Editor and Publisher*, 28 November 1931, 42.

Mitchell, Catherine C. "The Place of Biography in the History of News Women." *American Journalism* 7, no. 1 (Winter 1990): 23–32.

Mitchell, Sally. "Careers for Girls: Writing Trash." *Victorian Periodicals Review* 25, no. 3 (Fall 1992): 109–13.

Mitchinson, Wendy. "The W.C.T.U.: 'For God, Home, and Native Land' : A Study of Nineteenth-Century Feminism." In *A Not Unreasonable Claim: Women and Reform in Canada, 1880s–1920s*, ed. Linda Kealey, 151–67. Toronto: Women's Press 1979.

– "Women's History." In *Canadian History: A Readers' Guide*. Vol. 2, ed. Douglas Owram, 202–27. Toronto: University of Toronto Press 1994.

Morgan, Henry, ed. *Types of Canadian Women and of Women Who Are or Have Been Connected with Canada*. Toronto: W. Briggs 1913.

National Council of Women of Canada. *National Council of Women of Canada Yearbook 1923*. Toronto: Bryant Press 1923.

– *Women of Canada: Their Life and Work*. 1900. Reprint, Ottawa: National Council of Women of Canada, 1975.

Nevitt, Terry. "Advertising and Editorial Integrity in the Nineteenth Century." In *The Press in English Society from the Seventeenth to the Nineteenth Centuries*, ed. Michael Harris and Alan J. Lee, 149–67. London and Toronto: Associated University Press 1986.

Newton, Janice. "The Alchemy of Politicization: Socialist Women and the Early Canadian Left." In *Gender Conflicts: New Essays in Women's History*, ed. Franca Iacovetta and M. Valverde, 118–48. Toronto: University of Toronto Press 1992.

Nugent, Andrea. "Canada's Silenced Communicators: A Report on Women in Journalism and Public Relations." *Atlantis* 7, no. 2 (Spring 1982): 123–35.

O'Hagan, Thomas. "Some Canadian Women Writers." *Catholic World*, September 1896, 779–85.

O'Neill, Patrick. "The Playwrights' Studio Group: An Interview with Two Women Playwrights of the 1930s." *Atlantis* 8, no. 1 (Fall 1982): 89–96.

Pazdro, Roberta J. "Agnes Deans Cameron: Against the Current." In *In Her Own Right: Selected Essays on Women's History in B.C.*, ed. Barbara Latham and Cathy Kess, 101–21. Victoria: Camosun College 1980.

Peacocke, Emilie. *Writing for Women*. London: A. and C. Black 1936.

Pedersen, Jeanne. "The Victorian Governess: Status Incongruence in Family and Society." In *Suffer and Be Still: Women in the Victorian Age*, ed. Martha Vicinus, 3–19. Bloomington: University of Indiana Press 1973.

Pelrine, Eleanor Wright. "Whatchamacallit and Why." *Content*, May 1978, 8–9.

Percival, W.P., ed. *Leading Canadian Poets*. Toronto: Ryerson 1948.

Perkins, Agnes. *Vocations for Trained Women*. Boston: Women's Educational and Industrial Union 1910.

Perry, John W. "Women Leaders of the American Press." *Editor and Publisher*, 23 April 1932, 18–19.

Pierson, Ruth Roach. "Experience, Difference, Dominance, and Voice in the Writing of Canadian Women's History." In *Writing Women's History: International Perspectives*, ed. Karen Offen et al., 79–106. London: Macmillan 1991.

– *They're Still Women After All: The Second World War and Canadian Womanhood*. Toronto: McClelland and Stewart 1986.

Poulton, Ron. *The Paper Tyrant: John Ross Robertson of the Toronto Telegram*. Toronto: Clarke Irwin 1971.

Prentice, Alison, et al. *Canadian Women: A History*. Toronto: Harcourt Brace Jovanovich Canada 1988.

Quilter, Harry. "A Question of Courage." *Fortnightly Review*, n.s. 57 (1895): 979–95.

Rasmussen, Linda, et al., eds. *A Harvest Yet to Reap: A History of Prairie Women.* Toronto: Women's Press 1976.

Read, Daphne, ed. *The Great War and Canadian Society: An Oral History.* Toronto: New Hogtown Press 1978.

Redditt, J.M. "She Loves a Murder and Kiddies Love Her." *Editor and Publisher,* 30 March 1946, 64.

Reinholt, Ferdina. "Women in Journalism." *Journalism Quarterly* 2 (1925): 38–41.

Rex, Kay. *No Daughter of Mine: The Women and History of the Canadian Women's Press Club 1904–1971.* Toronto: Cedar Cave Books 1995.

Richards, Sherry, and Virginia Young. *Women on the Deadline: A Collection of America's Best.* Ames: Iowa State University Press 1991.

Ridley, Amy E. "The Dual Struggle: Mary Agnes Fitzgibbon, Toronto Journalist 1899–1907." MA research paper, Carleton University 1938.

Roberts, Barbara. "Women against War, 1914–1918: Francis Beynon and Laura Hughes." In *Up and Doing: Canadian Women and Peace,* ed. Janice Williamson and Deborah Gorham, 48–65. Toronto: Women's Press 1989.

Roberts, Charles G.D., and Arthur L. Tunnell. *A Standard Dictionary of Canadian Biography.* Toronto: Trans-Canada Press 1938.

Roberts, Wayne. "'Rocking the Cradle for the World': The New Women and Maternal Feminism, Toronto 1877–1914." In *A Not Unreasonable Claim: Women and Reform in Canada, 1880s–1920s,* ed. Linda Kealey, 15–45. Toronto: Women's Press 1979.

Robertson, Heather. "The Last of the Terrible Men." In *Canadian Newspapers: The Inside Story,* ed. Walter Stewart, 127–37. Edmonton: Hurtig Publishers 1980.

Robertson, Nan. *The Girls in the Balcony: Women, Men and the New York Times.* New York: Random House 1992.

Robinson, Gertrude Joch. "The Future of Women in the Canadian Media." *McGill Journal of Education* 12, no. 1 (Spring 1977): 124–32.

Robinson, Judith. *As We Came By.* Toronto: J.M. Dent (Canada) 1951.

Rooke, Patricia. "Public Figure, Private Woman: Same-Sex Support Structures in the Life of Charlotte Whitton." *International Journal of Women's Studies* 6 (November/December 1983): 412–28.

Rooke, Patricia, and R.L. Schnell. "'An Idiot's Flowerbed': A Study of Charlotte Whitton's Feminist Thought, 1941–1950." In *Rethinking Canada: The Promise of Women's History,* ed. Veronica Strong-Boag and Anita Fellman, 208–25. Toronto: Copp Clark Pitman 1987.

– *No Bleeding Heart: Charlotte Whitton, A Feminist on the Right.* Vancouver: University of British Columbia Press 1987.

Ross, Ishbel. *Ladies of the Press: The Story of Women in Journalism by an Insider.* New York: Harper 1936.

Rowland, Robin. "Kit Watkins: The Journalist Who Opened the Way for Canadian Newspaper Women." *Content,* May 1978, 13–20.

Rutherford, Gillian. "Women of the Pen." *Horizon Canada*, February 1987, 2270–5.

Rutherford, Paul. *The Making of the Canadian Media*. Toronto: McGraw-Hill Ryerson 1978.

– *A Victorian Authority: The Daily Press in Late-Nineteenth-Century Canada*. Toronto: University of Toronto Press 1982.

Sanders, Byrne Hope. *Emily Murphy, Crusader*. Toronto: Macmillan 1945.

Scanlon, Jennifer. *Inarticulate Longings: The Ladies' Home Journal, Gender, and the Promises of Consumer Culture*. New York: Routledge 1995.

Schiller, Dan. *Objectivity and the News: The Public and the Rise of Commercial Journalism*. Philadelphia: University of Pennsylvania Press 1981.

Schlipp, Madelon Golden, and Sharon M. Murphy. *Great Women of the Press*. Carbondale: University of Illinois Press 1983.

Schudson, Michael. *Advertising, the Uneasy Persuasion: Its Dubious Impact on American Society*. New York: Basic Books 1984.

– *Discovering the News: A Social History of American Newspapers*. New York: Basic Books 1978.

Sebba, Anne. *Battling for News: The Rise of the Woman Reporter*. London: Hodder and Stoughton 1994.

Siggins, Maggie. *Bassett: John Bassett's Forty Years in Politics, Publishing, Business, and Sports*. Toronto: James Lorimer 1979.

Smith, Elizabeth. *A Woman with a Purpose: The Diaries of Elizabeth Smith, 1872–1884*, ed. Veronica Strong-Boag. Toronto: University of Toronto Press 1980.

Smith, I. Norman. *The Journal Men*. Toronto: McClelland and Stewart 1974.

Smith, Laura Alex. "Women's Work in the London and Provincial Press." *Newspaper Press Directory*, 1897: 14–15.

Sotiron, Minko. *From Politics to Profit: The Commercialization of Canadian Daily Newspapers, 1890–1920*. Kingston and Montreal: McGill-Queen's University Press 1997.

Steele, F.A. "Ladies' Papers." *Saturday Review*, 25 July 1903, 105–6.

Stevenson, O.J. "From Fort Garry, West." In *A People's Best*, 63–9. Toronto: Musson 1927.

Stewart, J.H. *Young Canada Goes to Work*. Toronto: Ryerson Press [1940s].

Strasser, Susan. *Never Done: A History of American Housework*. New York: Pantheon Books 1982.

Strong-Boag, Veronica. "Canadian Feminism in the 1920s: The Case of Nellie L. McClung." *Journal of Canadian Studies* 12, no. 4 (Summer 1977): 58–68.

– "'Ever a Crusader': Nellie McClung, First Wave Feminist." In *Rethinking Canada: The Promise of Women's History*, ed. Veronica Strong-Boag and Anita Fellman, 178–90. Toronto: Copp Clark Pitman 1987.

– "Feminism Constrained: Canada's Woman Doctors." In *A Not Unreasonable Claim: Women and Reform in Canada, 1880s–1920s*, ed. Linda Kealey, 109–29. Toronto: Women's Educational Press 1979.

- "Intruders in the Nursery: Childcare Professionals Reshape the Years One to Five, 1920–1940." In *Childhood and Family in Canadian History*, ed. Joy Parr, 160–78. Toronto: McClelland and Stewart 1982.
- "Keeping House in God's Country: Canadian Women at Work in the Home." In *On the Job: Confronting the Labour Process in Canada*, ed. Craig Heron and Robert Storey, 124–51. Kingston and Montreal: McGill Queen's University Press 1986.
- *The New Day Recalled: Lives of Girls and Women in Canada 1919–1939* Toronto: Copp Clark Pitman 1988.
- *The Parliament of Women: The National Council of Women of Canada.* Ottawa: National Museums of Canada 1976.
- "Setting the Stage: National Organization and the Women's Movement in the Late Nineteenth Century." In *The Neglected Majority: Essays in Canadian Women's History*, ed. Susan Mann Trofimenkoff and Alison Prentice, 87–103. Toronto: McClelland and Stewart 1977.
- Struthers, James. "'Lord Give Us Men': Women and Social Work in English Canada, 1918–1953." Canadian Historical Association Papers 1983. Reprinted in *The "Benevolent" State: The Growth of Welfare in Canada*, ed. Allan Moscovitch and Jim Albert, 126–43. Toronto: Garamont Press 1987.
- Stursberg, Peter. *Extra! When the Papers Had the Only News.* Sound Heritage Series no. 35. Victoria: Provincial Archives of British Columbia 1982.
- *Those Were the Days: The Days of Benny Nichols and the Lotus Eaters.* Toronto: Peter Martin 1969.
- Sutherland, Fraser. *The Monthly Epic: A History of Canadian Magazines, 1789–1989.* Markham: Fitzhenry & Whiteside 1989.
- Tausky, Thomas. *Sara Jeannette Duncan: Novelist of Empire.* Port Credit: P.D. Meaney Publishers 1980.
- ed. *Sara Jeannette Duncan: Selected Journalism.* Ottawa: Tecumseh Press 1978.
- Taylor, Alison. "Window on the World: A History of Women in CBC Radio Talks and Public Affairs." MA thesis, Carleton University 1985.
- Taylor, Georgina. "'Should I Drown Myself Now or Later?' The Isolation of Rural Women in Saskatchewan and Their Participation in the Home-makers' Clubs, the Farm Movement, and the Co-operative Commonwealth Federation." In *Women, Isolation, and Bonding: The Ecology of Gender*, ed. Kathleen Storrie, 79–100. Toronto: Methuen 1987.
- Thomas, Jo. "Sagas of Women Journalists," *Journal of Communications* 44, no. 1 (Winter 1991): 128–39.
- Trofimenkoff, Susan Mann. "Feminism, Nationalism, and the Clerical Defensive." In *Rethinking Canada: The Promise of Women's History*, ed. Veronica Strong-Boag and Anita Fellman, 123–36. Toronto: Copp Clark Pitman 1987.
- Usherwood, Stephen. "Flora Shaw on the Klondike, 1898." *History Today* 27, no. 7 (1977): 445–51.

Vipond, Mary. "The Image of Women in the Mass Circulation Magazines of the 1920s." In *The Neglected Majority: Essays in Canadian Women's History*, ed. Susan Mann Trofimenkoff and Alison Prentice, 116–24. Toronto: McClelland and Stewart 1977.

– *Listening In: The First Decade of Canadian Broadcasting 1922–1932*. Montreal and Kingston: McGill-Queen's University Press 1992.

Wachter, Phyllis E. "Ethel M. Arnold (1865–1930): New Woman Journalist." *Victorian Periodicals Review*, Fall 1987, 107–111.

Wadleigh, Helen R. "Why Go to a School of Journalism." *Publishers' Service*, 2 July 1931), 11.

Wagner, Lilya. *Women War Correspondents of World War II*. New York: Greenwood 1989.

Watt, Gertrude Balmer. *A Woman in the West*. Edmonton: News Publishing 1907.

Weaver, Emily P., et al, eds. *The Canadian Women's Annual and Social Service Directory*. Toronto: McClelland, Goodchild and Stewart 1915.

Weaver, E.W. *Vocations for Girls*. New York: A.S. Barnes 1912.

Weiss, Gillian. "As Women and as Citizens: Clubwomen in Vancouver 1910–1928." PH D thesis, University of British Columbia, 1983.

White, Julie. "It's Good, It's Bad: The Contradictions." In *Rethinking Canada: The Promise of Women's History*, ed. Veronica Strong-Boag and Anita Fellman, 226–45. Toronto: Copp Clark Pitman 1987.

White, Z.L. "A Decade of American Journalism," *Westminster Review* 128 (1887): 850–6.

Whitton, Charlotte. *Canadian Women in the War Effort*. Toronto: Macmillan 1942.

Willard, Frances E., and Mary A. Livermore, eds. *American Women*. New York: Mast, Crowell, and Kirkpatrick 1897. Republished Detroit: Gale Research 1973.

Willison, J.S. *Reminiscences Political and Personal*. Toronto: McClelland 1919.

Wilson, Bessie. "The Woman in Journalism." *National Printer-Journalist*, March 1916, 145–7.

Wolloch, Jeffrey. "Did Stinson Jarvis Hypnotize 'Kit of the Mail'?" *Ontario History* 67, no. 4 (1975): 241–6.

Woolf, Virginia. *A Room of One's Own*. London: Hogarth Press, 1929. New edn. 1974.

Wright, Cynthia. "'Feminine Trifles of Vast Importance': Writing Gender into the History of Consumption." In *Constructing Modern Canada: Readings in Post-Confederation History*, ed. Chad Gaffield, 288–310. Toronto: Copp Clark Longman 1994.

Wyandt, Frieda. "Don't High Hat the Tabloids." *Matrix* 16, no. 2 (December 1930): 11–12.

Young, Harvey R., and Mrs L.M. Spencer. "Women's Broadened Work – in Journalism – in Citizenship – Duties in the Home." *National Printer-Journalist*, May 1921), 236–8.

– "Women's Future in the Newspaper Field." *Publisher's Guide*, 30 June 1916, 20–6.

Index